Transforming Practice

TRANSFORMING
practice

Selections from the *Journal of Museum Education*, 1992–1999

Edited by Joanne S. Hirsch and Lois H. Silverman

Museum Education Roundtable

Printed in the United States of America

Library of Congress Catalogue Card Number 00–103418

ISBN 1–880437–01–05

This publication was made possible by a matching grant from the Institute of Museum and Library Services, Professional Services Program, Washington, D.C.

Managing Editors: Ann Hofstra Grogg and Ellen Cochran Hirzy

Designer: Polly Franchine, PrimaryDesign

Visit the section about this book on the Museum Education Roundtable Web site, www.erols.com/merorg/

 Museum Education Roundtable (MER) is a nonprofit organization dedicated to promoting the role of museums and other cultural institutions as primary resources for lifelong learning.

CONTENTS

Acknowledgments   9

Foreword
    Stephen E. Weil   11

Introduction
    Lois H. Silverman and Joanne S. Hirsch   14

_____
Part 1
Perspectives on Change   17

Introduction
Illuminating the Paradox of the Museum
    Carol B. Stapp   19

Museum Education in Europe: Societies in Transition
    David Anderson   24

Offering Safer Public Spaces
    Elaine Heumann Gurian   32

The Pursuit of Memory: Museums and the Denial of the Fulfilling
Sensory Experience
    Hooley McLaughlin   36

Listening Outside and Within
    Deborah Perry, Lisa C. Roberts, Kris Morrissey, and Lois H. Silverman   43

Discussion Questions   48

_____
Part 2
Responses in Practice   49

Introduction
Addressing External Change with an Eye to Internal Transformation: Strategy and
Practice
    Gretchen M. Jennings   50

_____

Strategies	55
Museum Education and the Genius of Improvisation Mary Ellen Munley	56
After the Elephant Roars: The Next Step in Diversification Namita Gupta Wiggers	61
Institution-Wide Change in Museums Will Phillips	71
The Future of Museums: Asking the Right Questions Bran Ferren	79
Educators on Exhibit Teams: A New Role, a New Era Lisa C. Roberts	89
Beyond the Turf Battles: Creating Effective Curator-Educator Partnerships Jeanette M. Toohey and Inez S. Wolins	98
Is There a Way to Make Controversial Exhibits That Work? Roberta Cooks	104
Crafting Community-Based Museum Experiences: Process, Pedagogy, and Performance Kathryn E. Wilson	110
Practice	119
One Museum Discovers the Web Larissa B. Fawkner	120
The Eye of the Beholder Janet A. Kamien	126
Toward Reconciliation: A Role for Museums in a Divided Society Sheela Speers, Sally Montgomery, and Deirdre Brown	133
Long-Term Museum Programs for Youth Stacey L. Shelnut	141
How Museums Can Shape Public Education: Chrysalis Charter School Paul Krapfel	149
A Laboratory for Museum Learning: New York City Museum School Sonnet Takahisa	155
Port Penn Interpretive Center: Trials and Transformations Michael Miller	162
Finding Public Purpose in a Public Place: The Missouri Historical Society A. T. Stephens and Eric Sandweiss	169
Discussion Questions	179

Part 3

Understanding: Theory, Research, and Evaluation 181

Introduction
Paradigms Shifted: Comprehending the Meaning from Without
  Kenneth Yellis 182

Theory 187

A Framework for Organizing a Cumulative Research Agenda in Informal Learning Contexts
  Leona Schauble, Gaea Leinhardt, and Laura Martin 188

Situated Motivation and Informal Learning
  Scott G. Paris 200

Constructivism in Museums: How Museums Create Meaningful Learning Environments
  Kodi R. Jeffery 212

Constructing Informed Practice
  Danielle Rice 222

Exhibitions as Educators; Or, The Mundane and Magnificent Art of Stringing Beads
  Signe Hanson 226

Making Meaning Together: Lessons from the Field of American History
  Lois H. Silverman 230

Why the "Public Understanding of Science" Field Is Beginning to Listen to the Audience
  Bruce V. Lewenstein 240

The Personal Past in Public Space
  David Carr 250

Research and Evaluation 256

Professionalism and Research in Museum Education
  Annie V. F. Storr 257

Questioning the Entrance Narrative
  Zahava D. Doering and Andrew J. Pekarik 261

Recalling the Museum Experience
  John H. Falk and Lynn D. Dierking 268

The Quandaries of Audience Research
  Minda Borun and Randi Korn 278

The Art Museum and the Elementary Art Specialist
  Denise Lauzier Stone 282

The Public Dimension Assessment: Reviewing the First 10 Years
    Elizabeth Merritt   289

Discussion Questions   296

Part 4
Linkages: Building Knowledge   297

Introduction
Transforming Practice through Change, Response, and Understanding
    Joanne S. Hirsch and Lois H. Silverman   298

A Discovery Room for Adults
    Wade H. Richards and Margaret Menninger   301

Borders and Encounters
    Marek Stokowski   312

Opening Up the Exploratorium
    Kathleen McLean   322

Strategies for Long-Term Community Partnerships
    Jim Zien   331

Contributors   341

ACKNOWLEDGMENTS

For more than 30 years, Museum Education Roundtable has stimulated professional development and discourse among a diverse audience of practitioners through the *Journal of Museum Education.* Inaugurated as *Roundtable Reports* in 1973, the journal was renamed in 1985 and has resulted in two anthologies: *Museum Education Anthology: Perspectives on Informal Learning, A Decade of Roundtable Reports,* which appeared in 1984, and *Patterns in Practice: Selections from the Journal of Museum Education,* published in 1992.

Drawing on nearly a decade of contributions to the journal, *Transforming Practice: Selections from the Journal of Museum Education, 1992–1999* continues MER's mission of helping museum professionals develop and sustain their effectiveness as educators, visitor advocates, and program and policy managers. We believe it also will be a useful resource for museum training programs. Together, the articles in this volume give the reader a historical perspective, documenting the maturation of the profession, the influence of theory and research, and the transformation of ideas and practice.

In preparing this publication, MER turned to its colleagues for vision, muscle, and collaboration. From the dedication of office manager Audrey Nash, to the advocacy for addressing needs of professionals in small or isolated museums voiced by Lisa Kightlinger and Paul Katz, to the unflagging sponsorship of members like Marcella Brenner and Caryl Marsh, we have many to thank. We called on professionals who volunteered their time and experience at all stages of this book. In 1999, at the annual meeting of American Association of Museums, MER conducted an evaluative session. We extend our appreciation to evaluator Randi Korn, principal of Randi Korn and Associates, Inc., for her dedicated friendship and guidance during this formative phase and to the more than 150 session participants who expressed their professional needs and interests in lively discussions and surveys. Experts representing a diversity of museums facilitated these discussions: Lisa Tremper Barnes, Minda Borun, Barbara Butler, David Carr, Michelle L. Craig, Elizabeth

Eder, Victoria Garvin, Alberta Sebolt George, Gretchen Jennings, Randi Korn, Robert Kret, Myriam Springuel, A. T. Stephens, Sonnet Takahisa, Ellen Willenbecher, Carol Wyrick, and Ken Yellis. Thanks to Laura Lewis and Ayumu Ota, members of MER's Technology Committee, for posting a report of the session on the MER Web site, www.erols.com/merorg.

Members of MER's Publications Committee, Special Projects Committee, and a panel of reviewers representing a range of experience and disciplines selected material for *Transforming Practice*. Special thanks go to committee members Selena Connealy, Jackie Eyl, Gretchen Jennings, Judith Landau, and Amy Bartow Melia; and reviewers David Anderson, Ronne Hartfield, Jo Hinkel, Mary Houts, Karen Luetjen, Kathleen McLean, Mimi Quintanilla, Peter Tirrell, and Carol Wyrick. Our deep appreciation goes to Mary Houts, who took on the task of organizing additional readings suggested by the authors. We are grateful to A. T. Stephens and David Kidd for their encouragement.

MER's long and productive association with three exemplary professionals—managing editors Ellen Cochran Hirzy and Ann Hofstra Grogg, and designer Polly Franchine—proved invaluable. We drew on the depth of their knowledge and skill at every juncture of the publication process.

This book is made possible through a grant from the Professional Services Program of the Institute of Museum and Library Services. We are deeply grateful for this support, which reflects IMLS's commitment to helping professional associations such as Museum Education Roundtable do an effective job of fostering the development of the field.

Last and especially, we acknowledge with gratitude the journal's writers and editors, along with the editors of previous anthologies, for their inspiration. We thank the authors who willingly agreed to allow their articles to be included and three former editors-in-chief of the journal who wrote essays for this volume. Together, their contributions reflect the richly textured thinking that is a hallmark of our profession.

FOREWORD
Stephen E. Weil

This is an exhilarating time for those of us who believe in the power of museums to make a positive and significant difference to the lives of individuals and communities. First, we have witnessed the metamorphosis in little more than a generation of this country's museums from institutions that were primarily turned inward and concerned chiefly with the preservation and study of their collections into institutions that are now turned predominantly outward and whose stated intent is to provide a service to the public. Now, just as that process of fundamental change seems to be nearing completion, a whole set of new—and perhaps equally unsettling—questions is quite suddenly being asked in its wake.

What these questions concern is boundaries. Under scrutiny are both those disciplinary boundaries by which one type of museum (art, history, natural history) has traditionally marked itself off from another, and, more significantly, those institutional boundaries by which the museum field as a whole has—with some degree of aloofness—marked itself off from organizations of other kinds.

That these questions were not asked earlier is perhaps understandable. So long as museums were fundamentally focused on their collections, many of the boundaries now in question were useful in clarifying what made the museum so distinctive an institution. It was only after the museum's change of direction—its reorientation toward a public service role—that questions began to be raised about the continuing utility of these boundaries, about why museums still thought it necessary to differentiate themselves so sharply from other like-intended entities. No sooner had these questions begun to surface, though, than some of those boundaries very palpably began to dissolve.

Concerning disciplinary boundaries, how might we conceive of a museum without such boundaries? The museum field already has two well-established models from which a great deal could be learned: the regional museum and the children's museum. As an example of the former, consider the Anchorage Museum of History and Art. By its recent decision to add a substantial natural history presence to what already was a bi-disciplinary institution, it will considerably enhance its ability to address the subject matter specified in its mission: "Alaska and the circumpolar North." Arguably, by adopting this approach the Anchorage Museum can deal with the complex interplay of material culture and the Arctic's natural environment in a far more integrated manner than any discipline-specific museum might ever be able to do.

Children's museums are triply important. They are today the fastest growing segment of the museum field, they have the capacity to deal with human experience in far more holistic ways than traditional disciplinary museums, and their potential impact on future museum practice may be far greater than their still relatively modest numbers might suggest. As time goes by, and as ever greater numbers of visitors to adult museums base their expectations of those museums on their earlier experiences in children's museums, it should come as no surprise if these visitors ultimately expect—even demand—that adult museums provide them with some equivalent to the stimulating, interactive, visitor-centered, and cross-disciplinary experiences that they enjoyed when they were younger.

With regard to institutional boundaries, nothing could enhance the impact of museums more powerfully than to begin to remove those impediments that still inhibit them from working productively with other organizations. In terms of potential collaborators, the two most obvious candidates—too well known to require further elaboration here—are schools and libraries. Indeed, several articles in this volume describe some of the extraordinary ways in which museums have already started to work with local education systems. More recently, the Institute of Museum and Library Services has initiated a formal program directly aimed at forming partnerships between libraries and museums.

Beyond schools and libraries, though, organizations of every kind—not-for-profit, for-profit, and governmental—offer museums rich possibilities for collaboration. There is scarcely any kind of an organization within a community with which a potentially beneficial partnership might not at least be explored. In *A Common Wealth*, his 1997 Report to the UK's Department of National Heritage, the Victoria and Albert Museum's David Anderson (also represented in this volume) spelled out the many and surprisingly varied advantages that such partnerships can provide. "Partnerships," he said, "allow museums to extend the boundaries of what is possible: to share risks, acquire resources, reach new audiences, obtain complementary skills, improve the quality of service, achieve projects that would otherwise have been impossible, acquire validation from an external source, and win community and political support."

As the selections included in *Transforming Practice* make clear, in the museum's redirection from an inwardly to an outwardly focused institution the roles played by educators have been anything but passive. Sometimes instigators, almost always participants, educators have been prime movers throughout the process. The challenge they face now is whether they can play a similar leadership role as their institutions move through this next level of change. To do so, a double set of skills—one for inside the museum, the other for outside—may well be required. Inside, to convince museums to relinquish their long-held sense of singularity will be no small matter. There will be resistances to overcome, new ideas to be nourished. And yet, if museums are to realize their full potential, it can only be by ending their isolation and by linking themselves to a larger constellation of service providers whose mission-in-common is to enrich the quality of individual and communal lives. What will be required for leadership inside—together with persuasive zeal and passionate conviction—is a clear understanding of the many ways in which a museum might do its work better by doing it in collaboration with others.

Leadership *outside* the museum will require still other skills. Successful partnering requires a high degree both of insight and creativity—the ability to analyze the nature, needs, and strengths of potential collaborators and the imagination to envision what possible "fits" with those collaborators might truly be mutually beneficial. And sustaining partnerships once established requires still further skills that center on tact, empathy, and patience.

What these selections from the *Journal of Museum Education* also make abundantly clear is the richness of ideas, the dedication to excellence, and the extraordinary depth and variety of talents to be found among this generation of museum educators. Those qualities should equip them to provide the leadership that the field will so sorely need in this coming time of continuing, profound, and fascinating change for museums. As they embark on that venture, *Transforming Practice* should prove an indispensable guide.

INTRODUCTION

Lois H. Silverman and Joanne S. Hirsch

During the almost eight-year time span of *Journal of Museum Education* articles culled for this volume, we have witnessed profound events across the globe—from the spread of democratic values to the rise of technology and rapid worldwide communication, from the aging of the population to the outbreak of violence by children. Indeed, our world is transforming.

Museums, too, are transforming. In reviewing and selecting exemplary works from the journal, four specific changes stand out. First, this decade has seen a sweeping interest in, and response by museums to, societal change. Museum professionals have shown a renewed sense of social responsibility in considering the varied roles museums can play in communities and cultures. Second, the past 10 years have yielded an ever-broadening range of strategies and practice for engaging the public. Third, the museum field has enjoyed a deepening sophistication of the theoretical underpinnings and body of knowledge available about museum practice. And fourth, there is a growing recognition that every institution and every professional shares the critical responsibility of contributing to this knowledge. In these ways, museum practice is transforming. In the process of doing so, museum practice has sometimes helped to transform individuals, groups, and societies.

What about you? How has your practice been transforming? How have you been transforming practice?

Perspectives on Change

What moves you? When was the last time you recognized some influence, force, or need that you just couldn't ignore—that caused you to rethink what you do or how you do it, or simply propelled you to act, maybe without thinking? Yesterday, last week? Perhaps it was the feedback of visitors, asking for more, for different, for new. Maybe it was the tension in your community, misunderstandings you've witnessed, and a great idea you had for helping out. Maybe it was your board or your boss, mandating a particular program, of which you suddenly found yourself in charge. How many life-changing transformations begin with a need, a force, a challenge—and more important, the act of a single individual in response? No one is an island: enduring change requires the support, acceptance, and action of many. Yet amid important museum talk of teamwork, partnerships, and collaborations, it's easy to lose sight of the fact that change can, and often does, begin with one.

Responses in Practice

How do you respond? What do you do in the face of that need that moves you? If museum practitioners in the year 3000 found this book in a time capsule, they'd surely be struck by the creativity and tenacity of their 1990s counterparts. Changes in political, social, and economic factors both inside and outside the museum have given rise to compelling strategies and programs. From advocating for diversity to utilizing new technologies, from testing educational theories to mounting exhibitions on volatile topics, responses in museum practice over the past 10 years have slowly and subtly transformed the nature of museums and the face of museum education. Long-standing ideas have been refined; new approaches have been developed. The articles in this volume reveal a decade of courage. What risks have you taken on behalf of your museum, your community, yourself?

Understanding: Theory, Research, and Evaluation

How do you know? What support or inspiration tells you that your particular response might work? What theories, beliefs, or information support your action; how does your action in turn confirm or disconfirm your theories, beliefs, or information? Museum professionals have become sophisticated learners—increasingly skilled at reflecting on what we do, explaining why we do it and how it works. Our learning, be it in the form of theory development, research on museum visitors, or evaluation of exhibits and programs, is forging new paths in theory as well as practice. Our understanding transforms our practice; our practice transforms our understanding.

Linkages: Building Knowledge

Whom will you tell, and how? Through magazine and journal articles, conference presentations, conversations, classes, chat rooms, books, and countless other means, your questions and answers help transform the profession. Together, we share the responsibility for building a body of knowledge—describing our tested theories, our model programs, our lessons learned, our techniques for evaluation. The voices and styles of expression will be as different as we are—bold, sarcastic, poetic, analytic; spoken, written, drawn, acted, felt—as this book shows. How have you interwoven forces of change, responses, and understanding in your museum practice? Your story helps create the fabric and the future of museum education.

Transforming Practice

Like the two previous *Journal of Museum Education* anthologies, the goal of *Transforming Practice* is to present a sampling of rich and exemplary *JME* writing in one accessible resource. Inspired by the ideas and the diverse writing styles in these articles, we intend this book as a professional development tool, as well as a resource for museum training programs, small museums, practitioner groups, staffs, and friends to inspire conversation, critique, debate, and perhaps most important, your own writing. To this end, three of the four parts feature an introductory essay by a former editor of the *Journal of Museum Education*. Each part has "sparks," or ideas excerpted from within each piece that alone might ignite debate; "reflections" written in 1999 by some of the authors looking back upon their work; and discussion questions for your consideration. The last part presents four case studies, articles that highlight and illustrate the fascinating interplay among change, response, and understanding and reflect an inspiring sample of communication styles. "Further Reading" sections are included throughout, some with new entries added.

We hope you find this book useful and motivating for your own transforming practice.

Part 1

PERSPECTIVES
ON CHANGE

Introduction

ILLUMINATING THE PARADOX OF
THE MUSEUM

Carol B. Stapp

A paradox characterizes the museum's perceived image and its actual position as an institution. From neoclassical building to undisturbed parkland, the museum radiates the aura of a refuge from daily life, a place that is set apart from the world. As a public venue for private contemplation or exploration, the museum seems at a distance from the press of current affairs. But its presumed insulation fails to do justice to the reality of the its relationship with forces beyond its walls.

In a "From the Editor-in-Chief" column five years ago, I elaborated on the nature of this relationship:

> Museums exist within the broad context of large-scale national and international developments. Their status and viability cannot be separated from the world events that shape popular attitudes and resource allocations. Thus, a major quandary for the museum arises from the seeming intractability of meeting its public service commitment in an era of limited fiscal and ideological support. The museum—no less than various elements of its professional corps—finds itself justifiably uncertain and perplexed about how best to proceed in the face of the complexities of our times. Yet if understood correctly, the very economic and political circumstances that might seem to threaten the museum may simply call for a reassertion of its mission.[1]

And during the 1990s, several highly respected analysts from outside the field drew attention to changes looming on the horizon that inevitably influence the museum at its very core. Two commentators, in particular, delineated the profound nature of the realignments that challenge an institution like the museum. According to Robert B. Reich:

> We are living through a transformation that will rearrange the politics and economics of the coming century. . . . All that will remain rooted within national borders are the people that comprise a nation. Each nation's primary assets will be its citizens' skills and insights. Each nation's primary political task will be to cope with the centrifugal forces of the global economy which tear at ties binding citizens together—bestowing ever greater wealth on the most skilled and insightful, while consigning the less skilled to a declining standard of living.[2]

In like vein, Peter F. Drucker declared:

> No century in recorded history has experienced so many social transforma-
> tions and such radical ones as the twentieth century. . . . In the developed free-
> market countries, . . . work and work force, society and polity, are all . . . quali-
> tatively and quantitatively different not only from what they were in the first
> years of this century but also from what has existed at any other time in his-
> tory: in their configurations, in their processes, in their problems, and in their
> structures.[3]

More recently, a number of impassioned observers have echoed this
focus on the remarkable tensions of an era of seismic upheaval. Leroy S.
Rouner emphasizes that the marvel of America's multicultural democratic
society is now being tested in the extreme both internally and externally.
What previously functioned as a "binding ingredient"—"that transcendent
loyalty to the values and purposes of American civilization that makes a community of an individualistic and culturally diverse people"—currently pro-
vokes questioning, given radical pluralism at home, and breeds cynicism, given
"the arrogance of power" abroad.[4] Cohesiveness can no longer be assumed.

The exponential growth in the number of the elderly also carries mon-
umental implications for American institutions. Douglas J. Besharov and Keith
W. Smith set forth a series of revelatory "new thoughts about old age":

> Until the Industrial Revolution, people over 65 represented no more than 2 or
> 3 percent of the population. Today, in the developed world, 14 percent of people
> are 65 or over. In 30 years that percentage will have nearly doubled to 25 per-
> cent. . . . Worldwide, by 2050, the over-65 population will triple, from about
> 400 million today to 1.3 billion.[5]

Thus Reich warns that nations might be torn asunder by the gulf
between the haves and the have-nots, especially as exacerbated by the global
economy; Rouner points to the danger of national dissolution stemming from
cultural divisiveness. And while Drucker underscores the unprecedented characteristics of life in the 20th century, Besharov and Smith call attention to
what will be an unprecedented aspect of living in the 21st century. We in
museums must regard all these messages as fundamentally significant, for
failure to heed important changes in the economic, political, and human
dimensions of our era, nationally and internationally, can imperil our institutions. Simply put, the changes of our era may counteract the propensity of
institutions to self-perpetuate.

The rationale and the justification for the museum's place on Planet
Earth derive from what lies at the very heart of the museum: its obligation to
the public, with the ethical and the practical equally in play. As institutions,
museums have sought a role of stewardship that will not permit their with-

drawing into ignorance and indifference. Their nonprofit status springs from an educational mission that demands that public needs and interests be met. Thus, an awareness of and a willingness to act upon the major issues and trends in the world-at-large are essential if museums are to serve the public, visitors and nonvisitors alike. For pragmatic as well as moral reasons, sweeping shifts in the assets, work, relations, and age of the general population must be taken into account for museums to fulfill their commitment to society.

The range and speed of the new and different—whether concrete or conceptual—understandably challenge the museum's reasoned response, especially when linked to its charge of providing opportunities for engagement with meaningful experiences and ideas. If museums fully comprehend their responsibilities as "agents of social and political change," as David Anderson claims in one of the following articles, then they must not only accept but also welcome the fact that "cultures, not objects, are our real concern." Moreover, the museum's offerings should run the gamut of experiences for a spectrum of visitors. Because they are "one of the few safe, neutral congregant spaces in our communities," says Elaine Heumann Gurian, museums are ideally situated to foster civility by "capitaliz[ing] on human interaction." Yet Hooley McLaughlin reminds us not to overlook the museum's "capacity . . . to lift us out of our ordinary lives," a capacity that stems from its history as a place "designed to evoke the imagination at the level of the primitive passions."

Current practitioners—in the United Kingdom, the United States, and Canada—thus concur both when they express deeply held convictions about the reason for the museum and when they manifest, as Deborah Perry, Lisa Roberts, Kris Morrissey, and Lois H. Silverman put it, a growing eagerness to listen to "voices from both within and outside museum walls. . . . [to] hear about things visitors expect to see, hear, and do; . . . about how visitors learn. . . . [to] hear about changing expectations, roles, and responsibilities as the climate, complexion, and structure of communities change." Sensitivity to the potential for "discomfort and miscommunication" gives rise to forums for addressing "questions of diversity and equity [that represent] long-term endeavors" in regard to both museum staff and audiences. These have, concludes Gretchen Jennings, another *JME* editor in the 1990s, profound implications "in the way we think about the communities with which we wish to work; and in the way we think about ourselves and our institutions in relation to these communities."[6]

A sense of professional camaraderie clearly infuses such receptivity to what is happening outside museum walls. Most tellingly, the realms of business and government are being studied as influencing, rather than viewed as impinging on, what museums do for the public, since business is rapidly evolving to capture customers and government is swiftly proceeding to assess results. For business, the increased commodification of services leads to selling "an experience [which] occurs when a company intentionally uses services as the stage, and goods as props, to engage individual customers in a way that creates a memorable event," as at the Hard Rock Café.[7] This building of profit making on a model reminiscent of the museum requires serious examination, especially when the museum—to receive any funding from *any* government agency—will soon become increasingly subject to exacting measurements of effectiveness. The Government Performance and Results Act, a 1993 federal law, by "focus[ing] not just on outputs such as the number of participants in a program, but also outcomes—how the program actually affected participants," raises expectations for museum accountability.[8] Business and government thereby confront the museum with an intersecting concern: making certain that an undertaking is successful from the perspective of the customer or participant. This shared respect for the quality of the experience functions as a bridge, with the museum centered between two seemingly disparate entities.

The significance for the museum of pressures from all quarters—economic, social, political—can always best be measured in light of the museum's obligations to society. Especially in these times of extraordinary transformation, the basic principles of this mandate absolutely hold fast. Moreover, the museum's mission has the potential to guide the profession as it moves into the future. By opening our collective minds during this period on the millennial cusp, the museum can thrive most reliably through embracing with renewed dedication its essential purpose as a public institution immersed in the world.

Notes

1. Carol B. Stapp, "Quandary Transformed," *Journal of Museum Education* 20, no. 1 (Winter 1995): 24.

2. Robert B. Reich, *The Work of Nations: Preparing Ourselves for 21st-Century Capitalism* (New York: Vintage, 1992), p. 3.

3. Peter F. Drucker, "The Age of Social Transformation," *Atlantic Monthly*, November 1994, p. 53.

4. Leroy S. Rouner, "Civil Religion, Cultural Diversity, and American Civilization," *Phi Beta Kappa Key Reporter* 64, no. 3 (Spring 1999): 3, 6.

5. Douglas J. Besharov and Keith W. Smith, "Getting Old Ain't What It Used to Be," *Washington Post*, August 1, 1999, p. B3.

6. Gretchen Jennings, introduction to "A Safer Place: Seeking Ways to Deal with Difference," *Journal of Museum Education* 20, no. 3 (Fall 1995): 13.

7. B. Joseph Pine II and James H. Gilmore, "Welcome to the Experience Economy," *Harvard Business Review* 76, no. 4 (July–August 1998): 98.

8. Susan A. Timberlake, "The Effect of the Government Performance and Results Act on Museums," *Visitor Studies Today* 2, no. 2 (Summer 1999): 8.

Museum Education in Europe: Societies in Transition

David Anderson

There is a tradition in European museums, once strong and now growing strong again, that museums should be agents of social and political change. Most institutions and museum staff accept that they should provide a service (however limited) to their public (however narrowly defined). This passive relationship with society, while safe, is inadequate. It is our responsibility to provide the museums that our societies need, not necessarily always the museums that our publics want. The decision to develop a more proactive cultural role raises challenging questions.

I should make it clear at once that when I say that museums should be agents of social and political change, I use the word "political" to mean pertaining to public affairs and the structure of power within society. I am, most emphatically, not suggesting that museums should take sides in party politics or present one point of view on political issues. Rather, I propose, a museum's responsibility is first, to ensure that important contemporary issues relevant to the institution are raised and discussed within an ethical framework and, second, to identify social and cultural needs in society and take positive steps to address them.

Every society has its myths—and deadly delusions—by which we must live. The collapse in the last few years of Marxism, one of the materialist ideologies of the 19th century, may be the defining moment in the intellectual as well as the political development of our own age. The peoples of Eastern Europe, while mostly now enjoying the benefits of a democracy, have also suffered from the erosion of guaranteed basic provision by the state of the essentials of life. They are struggling to cope with escalating social problems, including organized crime, religious and ethnic conflict, mass unemployment, and hatred of foreigners, all of which have increased in the wake of revolution.

Arguably, it is the misfortune of Eastern Europe that this revolution occurred at a time when that other great materialist, dehumanizing ideology—the belief that we are all secular individualists pursuing economic objectives through the market—is once more dominating the political discourse in many Western European countries. In the 1980s in Britain, our then prime minister, Margaret Thatcher, famously declared that "there is no such thing as society," and her government then and since has gone some small way toward the fulfillment of that objective.

We in the West are also experiencing many of the symptoms of social disintegration that are blighting some Eastern European countries. Hegemonic cultural assumptions are misplaced, yet we often act as if we believe "West is best" and that it is only our colleagues in Eastern Europe and not ourselves who have anything to learn from the other. In fact, we have much to gain from the experience of our colleagues in Eastern Europe who have deliberately struggled to maintain and extend essential human and civil values.

What we in the West are observing in Eastern Europe is, in part, our own present and future, for in reality the countries of Eastern and Western Europe have much in common. For the first time, they are coming to terms with a shared European identity that is cultural as well as economic, an identity in which complex histories of ethnic and linguistic diversity, regionalism, population movements, and changing political boundaries, temporarily suppressed during the balance of terror of the postwar period, are playing an important

---

The new Labour government has made education, access, social inclusion, and support for the creative industries its main goals for the museum sector. This is a policy that was inconceivable five years ago.

---

part. We now need urgently to create a new political and social framework to help us bring order to the process and reconstruct our societies.

These are not marginal issues for museums. As publicly funded institutions, as providers of services to our communities, and as interpreters of cultures, we are having to adjust to changed realities. The adjustment has, of course, been most painful in the East. But one positive consequence of uncertainty in the West and hardship in the East is that we have been forced to confront our old assumptions and to reaffirm the values, as professionals and as individuals, we hold to be fundamental. This, I believe, is one of the reasons why there is now a renewed commitment to the development of the social and political role of museums on the part of some individuals and institutions.

The proposal that museums should have an active social and political role is not, of course, new; it was the reason for the foundation of so many of our museums in the 19th century. My own institution, the Victoria and Albert Museum, provides an excellent example. Established by Henry Cole, its first

---

director, and Prince Albert after the popular success of the Great Exhibition in 1851, the South Kensington Museum (as it was then known) was part of a new government department with a mission of extraordinary clarity and vision. Its aims were to spread art "among all classes of the community," to raise standards of art and design education, and to improve the quality of industrial design. By addressing in turn consumers, producers, and the producers and consumers of the future, the government hoped to achieve both social improvement and international commercial success. The new museum in South Kensington, a museum for ordinary people that was also a truly national center for learning, was part of a great educational experiment. For the first (and last) time in their history, museums in Britain moved to the center of public policy, with the full support of government, new money, and the talents of some of the country's most able administrators. In the decades that followed, the V&A—in collaboration with art schools, schools of design, and innumerable regional museums—developed a model for public education and training, known as "the South Kensington system," that was widely imitated in Britain and abroad.

But was the initiative effective? Contemporaries certainly believed so. A report for the French government in 1862 concluded that "the upward movement is visible, above all, among the English. The whole world has been struck by the progress made since the Great Exhibition in designs for stuffs, in the distribution of colours, also in carving and sculpture, and generally in articles of furniture."[1] By the 1880s the role that the South Kensington Museum had played in this revival in the decorative arts in Britain was universally recognized. Oscar Wilde, in a lecture delivered during his tour of the United States in 1882, praised "the South Kensington Museum in London, whereon we build greater hopes for the future than on any other thing. There I go every Saturday night, to see the handicraftsman, the woodcutter, the glass blower and the worker in metals."[2]

Such faith in the power of museums, local and regional as well as national, as instruments of political action and social improvement was characteristic of mid-Victorian Britain. Yet a century later this conviction was long dead. At the V&A, the closing in 1979 of the Circulation Department, the department responsible for the development of exhibitions for loan to colleges and museums throughout the country, marked the symbolic end of a last relic of the great experiment. Henry Cole had said, "Unless museums and galleries are made subservient to the purpose of education, they dwindle into very sleepy affairs,"[3] and William Morris, a key figure in the development of the V&A, celebrated the fact that, "Here [at the V&A] things are only wanted for educational purposes and not as commodities."[4]

It is only in recent years, following the appointment of Elizabeth Esteve-Coll as director, that the strong educational traditions of the institution, kept alive by many individual curators as well as educators, have once more come to the fore. The South Asian Arts Education Initiative is one of the fruits of the new Education Strategy approved by the trustees in 1990.[5]

Why did so many museums lose their sense of social purpose, once central to their work? There are many reasons: few museums had such clear strategic objectives as the V&A; the staff who were recruited were mainly object specialists rather than educators; the disciplines most relevant to museums' social objectives (such as educational psychology and anthropology) were underdeveloped until recently; the development of state-funded compulsory education in many countries made other instruments of public education seem redundant; modernism eroded the industrial and educational rationale for museums in society; the growth of alternative mass leisure facilities reduced the popular appeal of museums; and not least, in many countries of Western Europe, governments lost faith in the capacity of museums to achieve the social and commercial objectives those governments desired.

Why, then, is there now a discernible movement in European (and American?) museums to restore this dimension of our work? In part, this is a consequence of changes to the external social and political environment within which we operate. The failures of the formal government-run education system are increasingly apparent, and governments are keen to find effective and inexpensive alternatives to the weakened educational bureaucracies. Museums, supported by recent research by leading educators and educational psychologists such as Howard Gardner and Rosalind Driver, are now seen to provide a credible alternative. Also, modernism, if not dead, has been decidedly humbled, opening up once again a creative dialogue between past and present in scholarship and education. In addition, reductions in public funding have forced museums to appeal to the public above the heads of politicians and to build their own political constituencies. Above all, the decline in public confidence in the political process has created a vacuum that public institutions cannot ignore and are forced in some way to address.

The history of the V&A represents the benign (if paternalistic) face of state intervention for social and political purposes. But in this century, in Eastern Europe, museums did not lose their overt political significance as in the West; instead they often became the agents of social control and propaganda on behalf of the state. The dangers (both professional and personal) of this development are explored with moving insight in *The Keeper of Antiquities* by Yury Dombrovsky.[6] The book is a fictionalized account of the experiences of the author as a curator at the National Museum in Alma-Ata in Kazakhstan in the late 1930s, a time when Stalinism tightened its grip on every aspect of public life in the Soviet Union. As Nadezhda Mandelstam, wife of the poet Osip Mandelstam, wrote many years later:

> Dombrovsky [is] the author of a book about our life which was written, as they used to say in the old days, with his heart's blood. . . . It is a book which gets to the very core of our wretched existence. Anybody who reads it cannot fail to understand why the camps were bound to become the main instrument by which "stability" was maintained in our county.[7]

The recent emergence of democratically elected governments in Eastern Europe, to join those of Western Europe, should ensure that such dreadful and unethical control as was exercised by the communists over museums is a thing of the past. In this respect, there is no comparison between the horrors of life during the worst excesses of the Soviet era and life today in any country in Europe except Yugoslavia and some regions of the former Soviet Union (although the list is growing). However, we cannot assume because of this that our museums are not still, in various subtle and even unconscious ways, agents of dominant ideologies and values. Faced with increasing financial pressures, and lacking a coherent rationale to justify their existence that all staff can agree upon, museums in Europe may be sorely tempted to avoid raising awkward and unpopular issues.

Ernest Gellner, professor of anthropology at the University of Cambridge, has pointed out that:

> in industrial or industrializing societies, with unstable occupational structures and semantic rather than physical work, a standardized, shared, education-linked culture becomes enormously important and can only be maintained by a formal education system which in turn needs political protection. This engenders that marriage of state and culture, whose exclusive legitimacy is the central moral intuition of nationalism.[8]

Gellner's analysis of education could apply with equal force to museums. Museums generally embody an official culture or, at best, a selection of licensed politically correct cultures. They rarely encourage mass popular culture and often deliberately oppose independent cultural activities. What may seem from an official perspective social improvement may, from another, be cultural oppression.

Yet government intervention or passive acquiescence by museums to majority opinion is justified by the authority of the democratic process, however flawed. What sources of authority can museums use to justify the implementation of an alternative, independent social agenda? There are, in fact, many such sources. Some are well established, such as the concept of impartial public service on behalf of the state (as opposed to the government). Others—

such as accepted codes of professional ethics and the authority of the subject and collections of the museum—are not dependent upon legitimacy conferred by the state. But for those of us working in museum education, museum codes of ethics and institutional collection policies are often disappointingly silent on the positive responsibilities of museums to society (as opposed to the avoidance of curatorial misdemeanors). If professional sources of authority fail to meet society's needs (and there are plenty of failures in recent European experience), then it falls to particular museums or to the individuals who work in these institutions to follow their consciences, if they have the courage, in the face of opposition that may range in severity from the opposition of colleagues to the risk of their own livelihoods and even, in the past, life and liberty. There are basic human values of tolerance, respect, justice, and care for individuals and communities that manifest themselves in small, everyday incidents as well as in significant social structures. We are not just entitled to defend these but also duty bound actively to promote them. How they translate into policies and programs depends on the mission of the institution and the social conditions that pertain.

It must be acknowledged that, if one wished to implement an agenda of social and cultural change, museums and galleries are not the obvious place to start. When revolutions happen it is the television station, not the museum, that is seized first. But once the revolution is secure, the museum is then certain to be turned over as well. It must also be admitted that museums may be better able to initiate social and cultural change from above—as at the V&A in the 19th century—than to operate as cultural dissidents. The permanence and institutionalization of museums and their collections—and their inevitable separation from their host cultures, which is potentially both their strength and their weakness—leaves them ill equipped for an autonomous role. But this consequence does not invalidate their contribution; nor does it mean that they cannot also work effectively within their communities.

It is probably no coincidence, in view of the fact that most of the projects described in this issue of the journal and the next operate across the boundaries between dominant and minority cultures, that many came into being because of the personal commitments of individuals, with official support that ranged from enthusiastic endorsement to neutral acquiescence. Museums have their own internal political (in the broadest sense) environments that must be negotiated before any initiative is developed. The rise to the top of the profession since the 1960s of some museum leaders who are themselves committed to the social role of their institutions has often been a key factor in the growth of programs of social action.

"At different times," said Neil Postman at the Triennial Conference of the International Council of Museums in 1989,

> cultures need to know, remember, contemplate and revere different ideas in the interest of [human] survival and sanity. . . . I feel I am saying nothing outrageous, by observing that there are scores of museums, worldwide, whose truths are, at least for the moment, mistimed. . . . I should like you to imagine the following: that the year is 1933; that you have been given unlimited funds to create a museum in Berlin; and that it has not occurred to you that you might be shot or otherwise punished for what you will do. What kind of a museum would you create? What ideas would you sanctify? What part of the human past, present or imagined future would you wish to emphasize and what part would you want to ignore?[9]

Although few of us then knew it, in 1989 Europe was about to embark on the changes that would make that year as significant a date in the lives of the peoples of Europe as 1933 had been. We have learned that any year may become a 1933 or a 1989, and that the consequences may depend on what we did or did not do in 1918, or 1968, or any other year. Our societies need us, like other cultural institutions, to challenge historical myths and to explore the roots of racism. They need us to validate alternative histories and to encourage critiques of fashionable, politically correct interpretations. They also depend upon us to act as the memory of their cultures and as their conscience.

Cultures, not objects, are our real concern. It is the cultural space around and between objects that gives them their meaning and makes it impossible for museums to avoid a social and political role. To ignore or deny this role, despite all the difficult problems it entails for us, would be to evade a fundamental public responsibility.

Journal of Museum Education 19, no. 1 (Winter 1994): 3–6.

Notes

I am grateful to the U.K. Museums and Galleries Commission for a travel grant to attend the regional conference of the International Council of Museums Committee for Education and Cultural Action (Europe) held in Brussels in June 1993, for purposes of research.

1. Quoted in Barbara Morris, *Inspiration for Design: The Influence of the Victoria and Albert Museum* (London: Victoria and Albert Museum, 1986), pp. 107–8.

2. Quoted in ibid., p. 83.

3. Quoted in ibid., p. 19.

4. Quoted in ibid., p. 96.

5. Shireen Akbar, "Social Change and Museum Education," *Journal of Museum Education* 19, no. 1 (Winter 1994): 6–10.

6. Yury Dombrovsky, *The Keeper of Antiquities* (Manchester: Caveanet Press, 1988).

7. Nadezhda Mandelstam, *Hope against Hope: A Memoir* (London: Collins and Harvill Press, 1971), p. 387.

8. Ernest Gellner, "What Do We Need Now?" *Times Literary Supplement*, July 16, 1993, p. 3.

9. Neil Postman, "Extension of the Museum Concept," in *Museums: Generators of Culture*, International Council of Museums, 15th General Conference, August 27–September 6, 1989 (The Hague: ICOM, 1991), p. 42.

Further Reading

Anderson, David. *A Common Wealth: Museums and Learning in the United Kingdom.* London: Department of National Heritage, 1997.

REFLECTIONS

While many fundamental issues of the social role of museums in their communities and of the impact of political change on museum activities remain unchanged, the political environment itself has shifted in some European countries, to a quite remarkable extent. The United Kingdom is one country whose cultural and educational policies have been transformed beyond all recognition over the last few years. The new Labour government has made education, access, social inclusion, and support for the creative industries its main goals for the museum sector. This is a policy that was inconceivable five years ago and has come as a significant shock to many traditional museums. Educators and other staff who have the expertise to help their institutions achieve the new government goals are no longer a low-status group.

At the European level, the European Community has become active in cultural policy across the continent. The project "Museums, Key Workers, and Life-Long Learning" (of which the Victoria and Albert Museum's program for young people in the inner city is part) is just one of many EC efforts that enable museum staff to work across national and cultural boundaries. It explores the role of "key workers"—such as artists working in the community, older adult volunteers, youth workers, and even police and taxi drivers—as agents in helping museums reach excluded groups in their communities. Through initiatives such as this, museums across Europe have the chance to learn from each other's good practice and try to find shared principles and methodologies despite national political, educational, and cultural systems.

—*David Anderson*

Offering Safer Public Spaces

Elaine Heumann Gurian

Let us presuppose that people like being, and even need to be, in the presence of others. They do not have to know or interact directly with other people; just being in the proximity of others provides comfort and someone to watch. Let us further postulate that in order to find a certain amount of human contact, people will travel to places where they know other people will be. Being with others is an antidote to loneliness. This "traveling to be with others" activity can be called "congregant behavior." If we agree that everyone, or nearly everyone, needs some amount of congregant behavior in their lives, then let us consider what this need has to do with museums and what opportunities it offers us as museum professionals.

People go to some crowded events for the pleasurable experiences they hope to find there. Think about the many group activities you have voluntarily participated in. At some, the group's actions were coordinated and synchronous; pep rallies, political rallies, athletic events, musical performances, movies, and religious rituals or observances are a few examples. At other events, you expected the people you encountered to be mostly peaceable strangers whose actions were uncoordinated and independent; occasions like visiting museums, shopping malls, markets, carnivals, and fairs fall into this category. In either case—the coordinated or the uncoordinated—the expectation that others would be present contributed to your feeling of pleasurable anticipation.

Yet while some congregant behavior is mild-mannered and peaceable, some can be more dramatic and more volatile than the individual might wish. People in crowds can egg each other on. Inherent in group activity is the risk that it might deteriorate into violence, riots, or stampedes. A surge of thoughtless behavior can be contagious and overtake the good sense and inhibitions of the individual.

It is the safe, peaceable crowd behavior that interests me. John Falk and Lynn Dierking's research about museums has shown that people spend about 50 percent of their museum visiting time engaged in some kind of social activity—engaging with the people with whom they came to the museum, watching strangers, and interacting with staff.[1] In a study called "Bowling Alone," we learn that more people than ever go bowling, but fewer bowl as members of teams, a sign that we choose individualism to the detriment of camaraderie.[2] In current literature that focuses on re-creating a civil society, there is renewed respect for the value of group responsibility.

Continuing with the bowling example, what if we were to redefine the meaning of a group or a gathering to include all those who go to the bowling alley at a particular time, even though they are not on the same team? Then the bowling alley manager could begin to plan activities for transient and even unintentional groups. He or she could enhance the feeling of group cohesion by setting up teams for an evening, giving out team clothing, providing name tags, and periodically changing bowling partners. Then the activity of bowling would promote the formation of group responsibility. As another example, think about square dancing. Four couples are needed to create intricate patterns. If the couples start out as strangers, they soon become responsible acquaintances, if not friends. Square dancing does not work without group cooperation. This cooperation is not necessarily based on the dancers' personal knowledge of one another.

The internal climate of a . . . museum—its organizational culture—can help create a safer space for the public.

American society today still has a sense of responsibility toward the collective whole and toward individual strangers. Consider the etiquette that governs standing in line. We hold places for people we do not know, and we allow someone to step in front of us if we feel that the need is legitimate. We wait patiently, believing in the inherent fairness of the system and the responsibility of line members to discipline strangers who disobey the agreed-upon but unspoken rules. A review of line etiquette reassures us that we still voluntarily form and function as a group when we need to.

What does all of this have to do with museums? If we believe that congregant behavior is a human need, then one of the things that all museums offer is an opportunity for people to be with and see other people. Why not make that a virtue? Why not introduce programs that capitalize on human interaction?

For example, we sometimes use exhibition signage strategies such as talk-back boards that allow the visitor to be the expert and teacher, but we rarely make it possible for visitors to speak directly with one another. We could create online conversations and Internet chat rooms for this purpose. We could also install a "soap box" location in the museum that invites visitors to command the attention of others. We could experiment with programs such as parades, interactive theater, and group discussions in which every visitor can play a part. How often do we begin docent-led groups by asking the unrelated individuals in the group to introduce themselves? How often do we start public programs by taking a show of hands so that we can learn about our audience and they can learn about each other? Why don't we focus on creating programs that enhance the way museum visitors affect other visitors? Our attitude extends to museum amenities. We rarely place cafés in the heart of museums because we are trying to protect our collections. Why don't we situate them to encourage conversation about objects? We could promote object watching as well as people watching. We could provide tables where strangers can share a meal as they do in private clubs.

We can aspire to make museums one of the few safe, neutral congregant spaces in our communities. If we do our work well, we could help all members of society—no matter what ethnic, racial, or economic group they belong to— feel welcome in museums. To create such safe environments, we must look at the most subtle aspects of our presentations. Do the guards think all people are equally welcome? Does the signage contain words that assume a certain education level or specialized knowledge? Is there any way for the non-English speaker to decode the message? Is the staff sufficiently representative so the public senses that everyone is not only welcome but potentially understood? Do we sensitize our staff to the many acceptable, though culturally specific, ways of acting when in a public space? Is the location of the museum seen as someone's turf? If so, is there anything we can do to help others come in safety? Is the museum accessible by public transportation? Does it have evident security? Is information about neighborhood amenities such as restaurants and other attractions visible and available in the lobby? Do we invite the museum's neighbors in to see our work and be seen by our visitors? Can we help visitors leave the museum building feeling less frightened about the foreignness of the neighborhood?

Some museums now see themselves as forums that foster balanced conversations on issues of the day. They create an atmosphere and a structure that invite colloquy. They are not lecture halls, but umbrellas for debate and the airing of ideas. Sometimes these exchanges are broadcast to a wider audience and sometimes they are not. Sometimes the debate is part of an exhibition and sometimes it is spoken. Whatever the format, these programs stem from the belief that serving as a "town hall" is an appropriate role for a museum.

The internal climate of a public enterprise such as a museum—its organizational culture—can help create a safer space for the public. Our visitors probably intuit this internal set of beliefs and behaviors. Stated simply, if staff members care for each other, visitors believe that the staff will care for them. Safety and equity begin at home. If the internal administrative process is not transparent and evenhanded, if respect for the value of each employee is not expected, if the internal discourse is allowed to be abusive, then no matter what we do with our program, the public will remain cynical and on edge. The opposite is also true: if our program is a little ragged but our spirit is enthusiastic, if we are really happy to see our visitors, the public will forgive us and get on with the business of learning while exuding a palpable sense of well-being.

There is a growing feeling that in order for civility to predominate, we as citizens must balance individualism with group adherence and independence with compliance. We must celebrate diligence and discipline as we celebrate spontaneity and individual creativity. We must not allow repression, but neither can we condone chaos. We must adhere to a core expectation for orderliness in our families, our cities, and our society. Collectively, we cannot survive with only anarchy.

Museums will have to change a great deal if they are to be truly welcoming to all. Yet we have a core purpose that is inherently important to our survival. It is not, as you might automatically think, that we have collections, access to the "real thing." Instead, it is our role as institutions of memory. As members of a society, we must be rooted in our collective past as well as willing to face our collective future. Museums can capitalize on their significant place in the community. They can enhance and celebrate the congregant behavior that happens within their walls. As they provide a safe space that welcomes everyone to their buildings and their programs, they can also contribute to preserving and building a sense of safety and community.

Journal of Museum Education 20, no. 3 (Fall 1995): 14–16.

Notes

1. John H. Falk and Lynn D. Dierking, *The Museum Experience* (Washington, D.C.: Whalesback Books, 1992).

2. Robert D. Putnam, "Bowling Alone: America's Declining Social Capital," *Journal of Democracy,* January 1995, pp. 65–78.

The Pursuit of Memory:
Museums and the Denial of the Fulfilling Sensory Experience

Hooley McLaughlin

As I step back and review our work at the Ontario Science Centre, I am struck by how difficult it is for museums to touch the hearts of the women, men, and children who come to visit every day. The facade is there. The children play happily on the rocket chair and briefly experience the heat and humidity of the miniaturized living rainforest, while their parents look on and smile approval. In the art gallery downtown, I watch as people shuffle from painting to painting, engrossed in meaningful murmurings with one another. And in the local museum that specializes in natural history, archeology, and anthropology, there are delighted expressions as a small family comes into a room filled with Egyptian antiquities or hovers excitedly over a display case of raw emeralds.

But for the most part, the public visitors are co-conspirators with the museum community; they have limited expectations based on the thin product we have entrained them on. They know, as we know, that our wares must be taken with a strong dose of educational material. In our science center, the rocket chairs are only occasional offerings in a sea of interactive gadgets and written material designed to lure them back to the classroom. And our visitors know that museums are devoted to the preservation of history, so the rare artifacts are encased under plexiglass and the paintings are shown in dim light.

What sadness I feel when I think of what we are missing. What I see happening in the museums of the world is a pale reflection of what might be. We could be evoking the strongest of emotional experiences. We could be stimulating the sense of memory to its highest level.

Museums are in the memory business. Many have collections that represent the work of centuries; on display, there are artifacts from civilizations that go back to before recorded history. And then there are the bones and the fossils—traces of the memories of living systems from long ago, preserved in the memory bank of the earth. There are the collected works of artists who have acted as our eyes through history. A painting by Renoir can provide a window into the expression of an era and at the same time an intimate look into a small coterie of friends and acquaintances. Even science centers specialize in preserving memories—memories of discoveries by men and women who have unraveled the mysteries of the universe and whose exciting epiphanies can be re-enacted through play and physical activity.

Memories are not only preserved in museums. They are also made. A visitor can come away renewed and changed for life. The exotic reaches of learning are made into reality in a museum. No longer the subject of books, a dinosaur skeleton becomes real. The electrical nature of the body is learned literally as the hair of a little girl stands straight up during the Van de Graaf generator demonstration at our science center. A person's self-identity can be defined as a result of a museum visit. Some people will become secret experts in Egyptology, or ecology, or textiles, based to a large extent on excursions made to a local museum.

I am reminded of the character Enoch Emery in Flannery O'Connor's novel *Wise Blood*. Enoch becomes enthralled by the story's antagonist, Hazel Motes, who is an unhappy man, filled with a desire to find meaning in his life, and who resorts to religion and violence. A curious episode in the story is Enoch's interest in a local museum, a chamber of grotesques: preserved fetuses, artifacts collected by travelers into the Amazon basin, and other such things. A shrunken body, a kind of idol from some place obscure and curi-

---

Why do we practice our craft in isolation from the people around us?

---

ously antithetical to Enoch's professed interest in Hazel's Christian-styled belief system, becomes the object of his deepest desires. He eventually steals the hideous object for Hazel, and it becomes a Christ figure for the characters in the novel, their "new Jesus."

I believe that the museum has always had the capacity to stimulate our imagination and to help define us, to lift us out of our ordinary lives. While I am not proposing that the experiences of Enoch Emery and Hazel Motes are typical, it is true nevertheless that in the actions of the more impressionable, deluded souls in our society we see ourselves to some degree. Personal self-definitions abound. There are owl people, or osprey people; there are rock hounds; there are amateur radio enthusiasts. Children become dinosaur experts. It is not just the facts they absorb; they center their lives around a self-definition that incorporates the collected cultural knowledge that is on display in museums.

But do museums actively participate in this passionate act of identity, or do they ignore it, or even try to suppress its development? Museums see themselves in the business of creating historical and cultural memory, not personal memory. The collection of travelers' curiosities that Enoch Emery showed Hazel Motes in a little, out-of-the-way museum is not unlike most of the great treasures housed around the world. The history is written from the point of view of the collector. The juxtaposition of primitive tools from the Amazon along with the stone axes of Borneo creates a history of the world, one that is laden with the educational message of our European collectors. Placed carefully into cases and presented with the historical coolness of the scholar, the history of human endeavor is being written in the museum, and we are to walk carefully through this textbook of desiccated artifacts. We are to accept the presentation as factual, not arbitrary and not biased. But that is where the museum experience begins to unravel and to become either dull or unpredictable. We in the museum business are constantly trying to hold our audience members in. While preserving memories and while re-creating history, we are also, sometimes unwittingly, touching on the deepest levels of human identity. Yet we are shaken by any demonstration of wildness under the polite facade that we have grown to expect from our visitors.

The wildness, or passion, of the museum experience seems almost incomprehensible to us today. When do we ever ask our visitors if they have had a "passionate" experience at the museum, for example? A colleague of mine, Agnes Gomes, until recently a student in museum studies, decided that her investigations into virtual reality experiences in museums required asking questions that approached that level of discussion. The co-conspiracy of publicly maintained politeness was well in place. Many of the visitors, she tells me, were not disposed to answering questions that alluded to their personal esthetic experiences, and all were a little surprised. Yet, is not this denial of the emotional experience itself a little surprising? Museums have a history as places that were designed to evoke the imagination at the level of the primitive passions, capitalizing on the breathlessness of the anticipation of the sensational, the shiver of the unveiling of the grotesque, the flush of the aroused libido.

A few years ago I saw a museum of curiosities for myself, preserved without modernizations, in the Arctic and Antarctic Institute in Leningrad, now St. Petersburg. The curious thing was the desire of those in charge to keep it unchanged, as a reminder of their heritage. It was not open to the public since this would be inappropriate for a place that was trying to develop a level of cultural understanding based on modern theories of anthropology and Arctic exploration technology. But the preserved hands of people from remote places in Africa, the strange idols of the Siberian north, the penis bones from large carnivores of the world, and the prerequisite two-headed babies floating in formaldehyde were a testament to the history of the institute. This curious back closet was also an indication that we in the museum business still do understand, albeit mostly secretly, that the curiosity of people is what stimulated the beginnings of our science, our great collections. It is still what stimulates our visitors to arrive at our doors today.

Further into the back closet I found that the collections of history are often felt very deeply by the museum staff. Artifacts of the northern tribes of Siberia figure largely in the collection of the Arctic and Antarctic Institute. But these artifacts come from more remote regions still. In western Siberia, in Salekhard, a town on the Arctic Circle at the foot of the Yamal Peninsula at the mouth of the Ob River, I visited a museum that was very close to the memories of the past. And they had not forgotten the wildness and the passion that underlies these memories. They could not forget because, in 1990, the history was still unfolding around them. The people of the north were still living in skin tents as they followed the reindeer migrations. Perhaps, though, the most striking images in the museum in Salekhard were associated with their displays on the Gulag camps. The Gulag was a system instituted under Stalin; millions of people, arrested as political threats to the government, were transported to places like Salekhard to work on projects such as the construction of railroads. Tens of millions may have died in the process; the numbers will never be completely accurate. Lyudmila Lipatova, director of the Salekhard Museum, was one of the first people in the Soviet Union to record the historical events of the Gulag camps. Even though the camps had officially ended in the mid-1950s, it was not until the late 1980s that Lyudmila dared to mount a display.

Lyudmila had lived her life under the regime that could create the atrocities of a Gulag railroad. Her memories as a young girl in Sverdlovsk, a town in the Ural Mountains, included the sight of shallow graves, in the nearby woods, of people labeled as enemies of the state. Upon arrest and conviction of treason, they had ceased to be human. Lyudmila's display in Salekhard was a tribute to her desire to rehabilitate the millions of dead who had left the world as something less than human. Her display was a passionate memory, one that was not filtered to a level of politeness and one that was unabashedly biased or, at least, that admitted to its bias. We all produce biased works, of course, but very often we have convinced ourselves otherwise.

For an exhibition that was to be held in Toronto on the northern Siberian experience (*Siberia: The Spirit of Survival*, 1991–92), we arranged for Lyudmila Lipatova and her associates to send over pieces of a real barracks from one of the dormitories of the old Gulag, a place where people would sleep after a terrible day of slave work on the railroad. It is estimated that in each of the 32 sleeping camps that existed near Salekhard in the late 1940s and early 1950s, 10 to 20 people died each night during the cold winters from hypothermia, overwork, and starvation. What we were going to receive in Toronto was to be a physical piece of real history. We were delighted when we heard that the artifact, a complete bunk area, contained a poem gouged into the wood of the bunk written by one of the prisoners. However, I was not prepared for the results of what passion can bring to a museum experience. When the bunk section arrived, the poem was there, all right, but it appeared to have been written over in ballpoint pen. It was destroyed, in my eyes; the memory had been obliterated. Yes, Lyudmila admitted, bewildered by my anger, she and her assistant had written over the poem, but only to make it more legible.

During the restless night I spent after that episode, I had a revelation. My Russian colleagues saw the emotional value of the memory. The wooden bunk from the Gulag was a palimpsest, a manuscript that could be written over again and again, a memory talisman whose true value lay in the passion that was a reality in the hearts of those who lived it. My desire to have a perfect untouched specimen was typical of a museum curator. I wanted to drive out the association between the curator and the object. I wanted to be the aloof anthropologist.

So, we presented the ruined bunk to the public with the story of how the museum curators from Siberia felt so strongly that the poem should be understood that they had written over the words in ballpoint pen. We presented the artifact as a part of the ongoing living history of Siberia. But more than that we presented the passion of the remote Siberian museum of Salekhard, a passion that I rarely see in Toronto, or in any other major center in North America or Europe for that matter.

Since the Siberia exhibition, I have seen a number of examples of this curious desire we have, museum staff and public visitor alike, to eschew any connection to the actual human experience—the pain and the ecstasy that museums are proposing they are the repositories of. While developing *A Question of Truth*, an exhibition that explores the nature of prejudice in Western science, we worked with many community people. One of the subjects examined in the exhibition is the forced transport of people from Africa to the Americas during the slave trade. We intended to make this an emotional experience by creating an accurate replica of the coffin-sized sleeping quarters each person occupied in the hold of a slave ship, a terrible space that would house a person for 23 hours of every day. Upwards of one-third to one-half of all people transported under these conditions died during the six-week voyage. We designed the exhibit to allow the visitor to lie inside and experience the claustrophobic and inhuman space. We never built the exhibit. We did end up with a powerful "confinement box" that worked as a metaphor of the experience, but we never approached the horror of the actual slave decks. Our desire to come close to the emotional memory resulted in volatile opinions on all sides. Both within the institution and among our public, people were calling on us to stop the move to such a radical, "real," emotional experience. I finally held a public meeting; after much heated discussion, I announced that we would not be creating the slave ship experience at our science center.

Memory requires emotional associations. Emotions are an intrinsic part of our personal histories: as caring people who nurture children and create communities; as geniuses, each of us, in our discoveries of the world around us; and as lovers, people who have caressed and who have known ecstasy. In a movie I saw recently, *O Amor Naturel*, a Dutch filmmaker asks elderly people in Rio de Janeiro to read the erotic poems of the deceased poet Carlos Drummond de Andrade. Rather than be offended, the old men and women tell her how moved they are by the poems and by being asked to read them, and they tell her about their own memories of lovers in the past. Their memories are made of these things that we cannot mention in our society. I would maintain that all memory is touched with passion—the passion of loving; the passion of death; the passion of conquest and discovery; the passion of the discovery of beauty; the passion of knowledge; and the passion of living through a life. Many or most of these passions, defined by episodes that fill our minds every day, are banished from our daily conversations with one another, and they are increasingly not to be found in public institutions such as museums, art galleries, and science centers.

What I am suggesting is this: we have forgotten the roots of our business. Museums, be they traditional museums with historical collections or be they collections of experiences that we find in interactive science centers, are a part of the living pulse of a civilization. In the past, they have been closely associated with the human desire for the exotic, for the sensational. In our modern zeal for level-headed historical analysis, museums now strive for careful educational programming of the visitor. But this formalized "educational experience," defined as it is by a denial of the unruly libido and the embarrassing passion for the taboo, is increasingly responsible for lowering the intrinsic excitement that it is possible to achieve in a museum. The museum community, in turn, is forgetting that the educational and historical message is still one step removed from the human sensual experience that it is trying to represent. Let us not forget that the wildness that is in the human spirit will be the real basis for a meaningful visitor experience.

Journal of Museum Education 23, no. 3 (1998): 10–12.

Further Reading

Barrett, Andrea. *Ship Fever*. New York: W.W. Norton, 1996.

Bradford, Phillips Verner, and Harvey Blume. *Ota Benga: The Pygmy in the Zoo*. New York: St. Martin's Press, 1992.

Gould, Stephen Jay. *The Flamingo's Smile: Reflections in Natural History*. New York: W.W. Norton, 1987.

McLaughlin, Hooley. *The Ends of Our Exploring: Ethical and Scientific Journeys to Remote Places*. Toronto, Ontario: Malcolm Lester Books, 1999.

O'Connor, Flannery. *Wise Blood*. New York: Noonday Press, Farrar, Straus, and Giroux, 1949.

Wiesenthal, Simon. *The Sunflower: On the Possibilities and Limits of Forgiveness*. New York: Schocken Press, 1976.

REFLECTIONS

When I first wrote this article, I feared objections. Instead, many of my colleagues told me they, too, worry that we are ignoring the humanity of our visitors. I found these reactions comforting, but what am I to make of them? If we care, why do we practice our craft in isolation from the people around us? While in Calcutta recently, I was offered food by a young mother feeding her starving children in a foul refuse heap outside the gates of the Indian Museum. The smell of human excrement and the vision of running sores and wasted flesh made it impossible for me to accept; I was too nauseated to speak. But what love and generosity spoke to me from that young woman's face! Where do I really belong, I asked myself, inside or outside? Inside the museum, I was a member of a world congress that debated the merits of computers versus hands-on exhibits. We never discussed the disease and poverty that assaulted us on the pavement outside. Leaving the museum, I walked the streets until far into the night, wondering at the passionate display of lives lived all around me.

—*Hooley McLaughlin*

Listening Outside and Within

Deborah Perry, Lisa C. Roberts, Kris Morrissey, and Lois H. Silverman

Last summer [1996], the Visitor Studies Association held its ninth annual conference in Colorado. Nestled in the heart of the Rocky Mountains, we "listened outside." We listened to the sounds of the birds, the rain, the nearby river. We listened to the mountains, and we listened to each other. One exciting aspect of the evolving museum field is that museums, too, are listening. And as they listen, they are noticing a change in the voices from both within and outside museum walls. From within, they hear about things visitors expect to see, hear, and do; they hear about how visitors learn. From outside, they hear about changing expectations, roles, and responsibilities as the climate, complexion, and structure of communities change.

Museums Listening

From within, visitors are saying that they perceive museums as places of relaxation and leisure. People often come with their families and other social groups, and they often come first and foremost for social reasons. Although visitors say they come to museums to learn things, more often than not the social agenda takes precedence. Quality family time, a date, something to do with out-of-town guests, a place to hang out with friends: these are some of the primary reasons people choose to go to a museum.

While visitors may have a primary social agenda, they also want and expect to learn something new, have their curiosity piqued, see something they've never seen before, or in some cases revisit an old favorite. However, this learning occurs not only through traditional methods, but through social mediation, dialogue, and joint construction of meanings. By listening to visitors, museum professionals have realized that they are not—and should not be—in the business of teaching. Instead, they are in the business of creating environments that facilitate the construction of appropriate meanings, that engage people in the stuff of science, art, and history.

From outside, the very role of the museum as a social institution is being redefined. Museums are more than ever agents of public service, and they are becoming forums for public debate, dialogue, and controversy. Once defined primarily in terms of their collections, museums are now collections-based only as far as their collections serve people—through research, education, stewardship, and more. This shift means that the institution's role must be defined as much by how it serves people as by how it preserves objects.

The Public Dimension of Museums

Museum professionals are responding to these voices from within and outside with an increased emphasis on the public dimension. Statements such as "the public understanding of [fill in the blank]" are becoming popular and important components of museum mission statements and exhibition philosophies. Educators, evaluators, and visitor service personnel are increasingly being asked to consult on a range of museum operations, from exhibition development to marketing. Education now permeates all aspects of what goes on behind the scenes in museums. The American Association of Museums' report *Excellence and Equity: Education and the Public Dimension of Museums* (1992) places education and the public dimension squarely at the core of museums' missions, cutting across departments and divisions. It changes how museums view themselves. It changes what they do.

As museums become more visitor- and audience-centered, what are the implications for assessment? What does it mean to be successful? How do museums know when they have achieved their educational missions? And what does this focus on visitors mean for the future of visitor studies? As four museum professionals, we have been discussing and arguing these very questions for many years. Rather than advocating a particular methodology or proposing specific research topics, we believe that the answers to these questions depend on how museums address three issues: continued discussion and articulation of what it means to be a museum in today's society, ongoing support for research and evaluation so that museums can continue listening to their audiences and communities, and training and research that focuses on the public dimension.

Sketch for the Future

First, the museum field needs a clear articulation of what it means to be a museum today. As museums' public dimension comes to the fore, their focus shifts. While it is essential that individual museums hold on to their unique identities, mutually shaping (rather than mutually exclusive) visions and philosophies need to be spelled out. Public and private forums should be held to discuss not only what museums could be but what museums should be. The relationships between and among museums and their communities should be discussed and debated. And as the public dimension becomes increasingly central to museums' philosophies, who is in a better position than educators to take the lead in defining what it means to be public institutions in the broadest sense? For only when museums have a clear notion of who and what they are and should be, especially in relation to their communities and society, will they be able to assess the many different ways they are and are not effective.

Second, ongoing research and evaluation must be conducted throughout museums as a way for museum professionals to continue listening within and outside. Research and evaluation require engaging in dialogue rather than monologue. They involve listening to, valuing, and responding to what visitors and communities have to say. They involve a change in perspective and assumptions as well as actions. Listening to audiences and communities is an informal process as well as a formal one. It happens in an elevator, overhearing a family conversation; it happens when we pay attention to what docents, security personnel, and store managers have to say.

As the relationships between museums and communities begin to change, the questions museum professionals ask also change. They begin to study the relationship between museums and communities. They start investigating what happens between visitors within the context of a museum.

What does it mean to be successful? . . . Public and private forums should be held to discuss not only what museums could be but what museums should be.

Questions about the impact of museums on visitors are replaced with questions about the relationship between museums and visitors and the ways in which they shape each other. As a result of listening, museum professionals recognize a more complex, two-way relationship in which museum and visitors both contribute. Instead of asking, "Did visitors learn what we wanted them to?" the question becomes, "In what ways are both the museum's and the visitors' agendas met (and not met) with this exhibition?"

Educators in particular have the opportunity to advocate increased research and evaluation. Although ensuring adequate funding is an obvious first step, the job of supporting, promoting, and advocating research goes beyond money. It includes informal and formal conversations with visitors. It means active dissemination of research and evaluation reports; it means acting on and incorporating the results of formal and informal studies.

The third issue affecting how we think about visitors, museums, and effectiveness is the training of museum professionals—not just educators and evaluators, but everyone. As museums redefine who they are and what they are all about, training should be developed with an eye to the broad notion of the public dimension. Museums need ex-hibit designers who understand learning theory, educators who are sensitive to marketing and public relations, administrators who are knowledgeable about visitor interests and perceptions.

Visitor studies and other areas have contributed a wealth of information and knowledge about museums, their audiences, and their communities. Museums need to capitalize on this knowledge by promoting and advocating graduate training and research programs with an eye to the public dimension of museums. Master's and Ph.D. degrees with this focus will enhance the continuing professionalization of the museum field by establishing a community of scholars, researchers, and reflective practitioners. These academic programs will consolidate what is already known, generate new theory and philosophy, provide training in research and evaluation, and ultimately improve museum practice.

These are exciting times for museums. As our institutions continue to change, they offer museum professionals opportunities to look at their audiences and communities in new and different ways. Past assumptions about decision making, authority, departmental boundaries, communication patterns, and what it means to be effective are reflected upon and challenged. And ultimately there are opportunities to be flexible and creative as we continue listening outside and within.

Journal of Museum Education **21, no. 3 (1996): 26–27.**

Further Reading

Gurian, Elaine Heumann. "What Is the Object of This Exercise? A Meandering Exploration of the Many Meanings of Objects in Museums." *Daedalus* 128, no. 3 (Summer 1999): 163–83.

Weil, Stephen E. "From Being about Something to Being for Somebody: The Ongoing Transformation of the American Museum." *Daedalus* 128, no. 3 (Summer 1999): 229–58.

REFLECTIONS

In our original article, we asked the presumptuous question, "What does it mean to be successful?" Do we know the answer yet? Thankfully, we do not. To answer the question would mean that the dialogue is over, the listening completed.

We suggested three issues: continued discussion about what it means to be a museum today; ongoing support for visitor research and evaluation; and training and graduate education focused on the public dimension of museums. Today topics of conference presentations and journal articles suggest that these issues are being discussed at all levels and positions in many museums. New programs in museum studies are being offered, and courses have a broader focus (although there is still no Ph.D. program in the United States). Evaluation is becoming the rule rather than the exception.

We wrote in 1996 that "these are exciting times." Today we would emphasize the excitement and the opportunities, but also the difficulties and the complexities, the need for vigilance, resilience, patience, and optimism. We are more accepting of uncertainty and ambiguity as the foundations of growth, as museums—along with communities, families, and other institutions—struggle to determine what is meaningful.

What is success? May we all be debating, discussing, and contemplating this and other questions well into this millennium. Let the dialogue continue!

—*Deborah Perry, Lisa C. Roberts, Kris Morrissey, and Lois H. Silverman*

PERSPECTIVES ON CHANGE— WHAT MOVES YOU?

Use these questions and the essays in this section to stimulate discussion. You may want to consider your own museum, or you may draw on your experience in other museums or other settings.

1/ How do you define a successful museum? Do you think this definition will change in the future? Why? Why not?

2/ What impact does your museum have on your community? What impact does your community have on your museum?

3/ What forces or influences do you anticipate will have the greatest impact on museums in the next decade? Why?

4/ You are part of a task force charged with creating an ideal museum that addresses the needs of society and the notion of a museum as an agent of social change. Write the mission statement for this museum.

5/ As a contemporary practitioner, in what area or on what topics do you need more information in order to respond to the rapid and complex changes influencing the museum profession?

6/ If you were to contribute an article to this section on "Perspectives on Change," what would you write? What changes that are not considered in these articles would you explore?

Part 2

RESPONSES IN PRACTICE

ADDRESSING EXTERNAL CHANGE WITH AN EYE TO INTERNAL TRANSFORMATION: STRATEGY AND PRACTICE

Gretchen M. Jennings

Museums are among the public institutions that felt the effects of broad societal change in the 1990s. Their responses to these social forces have had an impact on their internal policies and structures, producing change from the outside in. Beyond reacting to external influences, many museums have also taken the initiative to rethink their role, organizational structure, and place in the community, changing from the inside out. The articles in Part 2 reveal a variety of museums engaged in developing strategies and practice that address external change with an eye to internal transformation. These articles tend to fall into two major categories: those that deal with strategies and long-term plans, and those that discuss specific practices and programs. It is instructive to note that, while they were written over 10 years, and by authors working in a variety of museum settings, common themes emerge quite clearly.

Strategies and Long-Term Plans

Will Phillips sets the stage for institutional change through a series of recommendations that find confirmation in the views of other authors in this first section. Together, the points for emphasis can be summarized in three broad statements.

Museums should assess their roles in light of economic, demographic, and technological changes in the world at large and in their own communities. A number of authors in Part 2 call attention to the ways changing economic and demographic forces are affecting museum audiences. As Mary Ellen Munley points out, a key concern of museum educators has been access—physical, cultural, and intellectual. Ironically, just as museums have begun to acknowledge and address a more audience-driven philosophy in their mission statements and in their policies, the definition of who that audience might be has changed. Museums have always attracted, and will continue to attract in large numbers, the white, middle-class, and well-educated visitor. Our nation's population, however, is becoming increasingly diverse in many dimensions—in race, ethnicity, language, and age. Addressing these diverse audiences involves fundamental shifts in museum policy, staffing, and programming.

Namita Gupta Wiggers makes a strong case for diversity training at all levels, from boards of trustees to volunteers. In promoting the folkloric approach to programs and exhibitions, Kathryn E. Wilson advocates the cultural understanding that Wiggers believes is required for pluralism in museums.

The technological changes cited in articles written in the early 1990s are proceeding at a dizzying pace. Bran Ferren provides sound advice for museums struggling to stay abreast of the rising tide: seek ways to use electronic media to their fullest potential while retaining what is unique and essential to the museum experience; do not forget the human element and the basic needs of the museum audience; and beware of expensive and complicated electronic solutions for which there is no corresponding problem.

Museums should strive for institutional self-awareness, creating processes to identify what is done well and what should be changed. Internal transformation is often slow and painful for museums. A number of authors highlight the ups and downs involved in shifting to a team approach to exhibition development. In her case study of the creation and touring of an exhibition about AIDS, Roberta Cooks delineates the complex and sensitive strategies involved in internal change and the consequences of the team approach. This project, which involved expanding the circle of those in the planning process to include a wide range of advisers and community voices, had many obstacles to overcome—reluctant board members, staff fears and misconceptions about the topic, and the objections, even anger, of specific audiences. In the process of creating and/or hosting this controversial exhibition, the museums involved devised approaches to exhibit development, staff training, and communication with constituents (both friendly and suspicious) that affected subsequent policies and practice.

As Cooks demonstrates, the team approach to exhibition development provides an instructive model for institutional change. To achieve success with this approach, Jeanette M. Toohey and Inez S. Wolins stress the importance of internal communication, of acknowledging differing roles and perspectives, and of a willingness to work through difficult situations toward a common goal. Lisa C. Roberts believes that a move to the team approach can have a radical impact, for it signals a shift not only in how staff members work together but in how museums understand the visitor experience. Visitors are perceived not as passive receptors but as active participants in the interpretive process.

The guiding principle for museums' response to change should be their educational mission. Both Munley and Roberts see museum educators as catalysts for change. Often without the administrative clout to order change from above, museum educators continue nonetheless to foster and initiate change from within as they participate actively on exhibition teams, develop innovative programming that addresses wider audiences, and use their understanding of learning theory and interpretation to direct the use of technology in ways that enhance rather than distract from the visitor experience.

Specific Practices and Programs

The articles in the second section provide many practical examples of the strategies outlined in the first. The programs and exhibitions described here bear witness to three overarching themes.

Museums need firmness in their commitment to educational goals and flexibility in responding to social change. When commitment to mission undergirds the approach to societal change, museum programs are both focused and flexible. Larissa B. Fawkner provides a lively example of a very small museum's efforts to address technological change, create its own Web presence, and provide a Web-based project for a financially strapped school system. This project provides a model for the kinds of productive collaborations small museums can initiate by linking with larger and more generously funded institutions. It also exemplifies the much-touted "virtual" interlocking and heightened communication that the World Wide Web is intended to create.

In another example, Stacey L. Shelnut underscores the need for programs that create a sustained relationship between museums and young people, long a neglected museum constituency. Shelnut's descriptions of efforts to address the needs of adolescents by working directly with them, rather than through schools, are especially relevant in light of the increase in school violence in the late 1990s. Museums may be uniquely equipped to address some of the needs that schools are not meeting, becoming, as she describes, "safe and productive places in which young people can gain a better understanding of the world, each other, and themselves."

Museums must view the visitor as an active and essential participant in their educational mission. Michael Miller, Janet A. Kamien, and A. T. Stephens and Eric Sandweiss provide a variety of examples of the efforts that museums, both small and large, are making to include their audiences in the planning of exhibitions and programs. Miller recounts a small museum's successes and failures in communicating with its local community. Kamien outlines the steps involved in including a wide range of stakeholders and advisers in the creation of a children's exhibition about death and loss. Stephens and Sandweiss describe the Missouri Historical Society's intensive efforts to ensure that its new exhibition spaces reflect and address the changes, tensions, and aspirations of the diverse communities that make up its constituency.

The creation of museum schools, as described by Sonnet Takahisa and Paul Krapfel, represent another avenue for the application of current understanding of the visitor experience. In this approach museums apply to the school curriculum what they know to be valuable and unique about their approaches to learning. These experiments provide an important opportunity to study in a more rigorous way the differences and the connections between what has come to be known as formal and informal learning. Such studies should enhance both school and museum practice and further our understanding of the visitor experience.

Museums need renewed commitment to their role and responsibility in addressing diverse audiences. In general, the articles in the second section confirm that there is still much to be done to achieve the principles of excellence and equity espoused by the field. In an example of a notable success, Sheela Speers, Sally Montgomery, and Deirdre Brown expand the notion of diversity to include religious and cultural differences. Through collaborative programs and sustained effort, the museums in Northern Ireland that they represent have played an important role in addressing and healing devastating divisions within their society. A clue to the sustained success of these programs, as the authors report in an update, may lie in the fact that the staff of each of the collaborating museums is representative of each group. Thus when the museum staff model effective communication between Protestants and Catholics, the collaboration is authentic and the lesson is not lost on the students and teachers who make up the audience.

In our country, where racial divisions are still severe and where museum staff remain for the most part white, programs that model racial awareness and cultural communication may have less impact. Until our boards, administration, staff, and volunteers mirror our own society more clearly, many programs designed to attract more diverse audiences are probably destined to fall short of the mark.

Responses to Change

All the articles in Part 2 show us that change can, and probably should, come from a variety of directions and in many guises. The demands of our wider audiences and the challenges presented by the computer age are movements that museums simply cannot ignore. Well-conceived responses to societal change, grounded both in experience and theory, leave their mark on the museum professionals and institutions that create and sustain them. Long-term programs create the time and the structures for change. Articulated goals and strategies that are attuned to society provide continuity and grounding. Thus does change come from the outside in.

At the same time, museums are being transformed through the implementation of a variety of internal initiatives: changes in approaches to exhibition development, in defining new learning communities, and in restructuring and reconceiving the entire way a museum responds to its public. The impact of all of this rethinking and reorganizing will be known only as we move further into the 21st century. In the meantime, the strategies and practices featured in this part give us direction and insight—much to ponder and much to do.

Strategies

Museum Education and the Genius of Improvisation

Mary Ellen Munley

To understand the development of museum education over the last 25 years, one must consider and understand the creative genius for responsive improvisation demonstrated by those who have worked to strengthen the educational relevance of museums in this country. Since I am current chair of the American Association of Museums' Education Committee (EdCom), Viki Sand asked me to place the *Statement on Professional Standards for Museum Education* and the EdCom action plan, *Goals 25*, into a historical context. As I began the task, my thoughts turned to Mary Catherine Bateson's remarkable book, *Composing a Life*, which suggests ways to understand change and accomplishment when the development path is not a traditional one. I concur with the reviewer who compliments Bateson for offering "a powerful, convincing argument that diversity, adversity, disorder and disappointment are hardly impediments to success."[1]

Bateson says, "Each of us has worked by improvisation, discovering the shape of our creation along the way, rather than pursuing a vision already defined . . . solving problems for the first time . . . [finding it] no longer possible to follow the paths of previous generations." She compares composing a life to improvisational jazz. Listen to what she says about jazz, and see if you find it as true of the practice of museum education as I do.

> Practicing improvisation [is] clearly not a contradiction. Jazz exemplifies artistic activity that is at once individual and communal, performance that is both repetitive and innovative, each participant sometimes providing background support and sometimes flying free.[2]

Bateson's book is about life—particularly the lives of women—as the improvisatory art of combining familiar and unfamiliar components in response to new situations, following an underlying knowledge and an evolving set of principles and values. Bateson likens combining available ingredients in preparing a meal to the times in her career that she "picked up the pieces" and moved on to another opportunity. I think of the times I gather together an eclectic collection of knowledge and approaches to put together a public program or cull equally eclectic files and notes to prepare a speech, an article, or a workshop. Others might remember creating a new agenda on the spot in response to feedback during an advisory group meeting or redesigning a program in the gallery because something just wasn't working. Is it a last resort? A signal of not being in charge of life or work?

Bateson thinks not: "Improvisation can be either a last resort or an established way of evoking creativity."[3] Creative response to changing times is precisely what this participant-observer believes characterizes developments in museum education in the last 25 years. Museum education is an elaborate improvisation. Museum educators and their leaders noticed problems, turned them into challenges, and improvised responses. As such, museum education has been fluid, and not always predictable. It has been carefully crafted—most often by female hands and minds—into a rich and complex tapestry of activity and accomplishment.

In the last 25 years, various people—Elaine Heumann Gurian, Bonnie Pitman, Mary Alexander, Carolyn Blackmon, Rex Ellis, and Patty Williams, to name a few—have worked much like a jazz band, composing solo and combo pieces in an act of creation as, over time and joined by others, they created the definition of museums as educational institutions for our time and, in turn, the

---

Museum educators are known for their experimentation and risk taking—for improvisation. Their work requires them to be responsive to audiences and context.

---

changing role of the museum educator.

The AAM's Education Committee began at the 1973 annual meeting. It was the first standing professional committee in the history of the association. Today there are 12 standing professional committees and a greater acknowledgment of the importance of equitable access and the varieties of professional expertise that contribute to a high-quality museum. This committee is only one visible instance of educators' pioneering efforts. In their own museums educators have often been the ones to address particular problems for the first time. Consistent with "practicing improvisation," they have been responsible for many "firsts" in museums: outreach programs, neighborhood museums, reasonable accommodations for people with disabilities, teaching exhibits, and discovery rooms are a few examples. The central issue educators have persistently addressed in professional organizations and in museums is access.

Museum educators are known for their experimentation and risk taking—for improvisation. Their work requires them to be responsive to audiences and context, and museum programs are noted for their creativity and originality. Yet as any student of improvisation knows, the music is not only new and original, it also follows an underlying grammar and esthetic. So, too, for museum education. Museum educators introduce variations on the "museum as educator theme" that range from storefront museums and community advisory boards, to labels written with language suitable to a lay audience and, now, museum schools. Is this series of innovations just one fad after another? A failure to understand the essence of museum education? I think not.

For all the variety and variation—for all the improvisation—there emerges a set of underlying convictions that provides continuity to this work. These are the themes museum educators, and those who support museum education, have been sounding as they improvise the particulars of strategic goals and of priorities and programs. I offer the following as an attempt to identify the fundamental principles that guide the practice of museum education.

1. Museums are public institutions, open to all who have interest.

2. Museums are about education for all those interested in learning. And it is the responsibility of the museum to communicate its messages in ways that are interesting and understandable to members of a highly diverse constituency.

3. Museums are about lifelong learning, and they can strengthen basic skills, basic knowledge, basic comprehension, and basic understanding. In short, museums can, and do, play an important role in the process of transmitting culture and giving meaning to life.

4. Features that differentiate museums from other community educational institutions include voluntary participation and the presentation of authentic material.

5. Education is a museum-wide responsibility and endeavor. It takes many forms of expertise, including that of the public, to make a great museum.

While the publication of the AAM's *Museums for a New Century* in 1984 clearly stated the central role of education in the life of a museum, it provided no prescriptions. Joel Bloom, then president of the AAM and an impassioned champion of museum education, called attention to this problem shortly after publication of the report. Few people had concrete ideas about how to make education central, and there were no sanctions—or incentives—for museums to examine and strengthen their educational goals and programs. To address this challenge, Bloom formed the task force that would publish *Excellence and Equity: Education and the Public Dimension of Museums* in 1992.[4]

As important as the task force's policy statement about museums and learning was, it had the undesired effect of muddying the waters about the role of the museum educator. If, as *Museums for a New Century* and *Excellence and Equity* state, education is the responsibility of the entire museum, what, then, is the role of the museum educator? *Excellence and Equity* was forthright in saying that the educational responsibility was not sufficiently met through school programs and an assortment of public programs alone. The public, educational responsibility of the museum means that museums must address such matters as increasing the diversity of its audience; improving the accessibility of the museum to all people; reinforcing its duty to present accurate information and multiple perspectives; affirming its obligation to communicate effectively with its intended audience; and taking steps to open its decision making not only to all professionals within the institution but to a variety of community representatives as well. Obviously, the museum educator is no longer the only person in the museum responsible for education. Yet, clearly, the museum educator is still an important player and leader.

In 1990, in an effort to reinforce the notion that responsibility for education was shared throughout the museum and to articulate the responsibilities, competencies, and talents a museum educator is expected to bring to the museum staff, EdCom—under the leadership of its then national chair, Patterson Williams—published the *Statement on Professional Standards for Museum Education.*[5]

The publication of *Excellence and Equity* in 1992 posed yet another challenge. Were museum educators prepared to fulfill their new responsibilities for research about museum learning, community organization, exhibit development, evaluation, and much more? Museum educators needed to keep pace with the changes their own colleagues were so instrumental in bringing about. There was no obvious place to look for a coordinated, concerted effort to define the practice of museum education and to provide museum educators and, indeed, all museum professionals interested in education with the knowledge and tools needed to perform at the highest levels in this ever-changing world of museums. *Goals 25* is a conscious effort to transform the AAM Education Committee so that it, and its members, improvise once again.[6] EdCom is working to create a new governing structure, expand its membership by inviting others to join museum educators on the committee, establish close ties with other institutions of learning in this country, and assure that the policies and research needed to support the work of museums as educational institutions are in place. In fact, *Goals 25* is the EdCom response to principle 10 of *Excellence and Equity:* "Commit leadership and financial resources—in individual museums, *professional organizations,* and training organizations and universities—to strengthen the public dimension of museums."[7]

Each generation of leaders must listen carefully enough to stay on theme and still provide the improvisations that are right for a specific place and time. As we approach the 25th anniversary of the establishment of

EdCom, the *Statement on Professional Standards for Museum Education* and *Goals 25* are responses to rapidly changing conditions. They are EdCom's most recent improvisations.

Journal of Museum Education 21, no. 1 (Winter 1996): 18–20.

Notes

1. Mary Catherine Bateson, *Composing a Life* (New York: Penguin Books, 1991), pp. 1, 2; review from *Waterbury Sunday Republican,* quoted on book jacket.

2. Bateson, *Composing a Life*, pp. 2, 3.

3. Ibid., p. 4.

4. American Association of Museums, *Museums for a New Century* (Washington, D.C.: AAM, 1984); American Association of Museums, *Excellence and Equity: Education and the Public Dimension of Museums* (Washington, D.C.: AAM, 1992).

5. AAM Education Committee, *Statement on Professional Standards for Museum Education* (1990), reprinted in *Journal of Museum Education* 21, no. 1 (Winter 1996): 20–22.

6. AAM Education Committee, *Goals 25: An EdCom Action Plan* (1995), reprinted in ibid., pp. 22–23.

7. AAM, *Excellence and Equity,* p. 24, italics added.

After the Elephant Roars: The Next Step in Diversification

Namita Gupta Wiggers

An Indian legend tells of six blind men who encountered an elephant. The first, stumbling against the animal's side, declared the elephant to be a wall. The second, feeling the pointed tusk, determined it to be a spear. The rest of the men, upon discovering the knee, trunk, ear, and tail, successively identified the animal as a tree, a snake, a fan, and a rope. Each man, thoroughly convinced that his was the correct definition, refused to accept any other assessment. Only a collective and cooperative vision could reveal the elephant's true identity.

Contemporary society is the elephant, and museums are using a wide variety of efforts to describe the beast. We are a nation attempting to define the "New Man: *homo multiculturans.*"[1] This evolving creature has had several stages of development, from the melting pot to cultural pluralism. The current form is often described as a "salad" of five cultures: African American, Native American, Hispanic (Latino) American, Asian American, and Anglo-Saxon Euro-centered. The United States is a complex nation of incredible diversity, where people come both to escape and to cherish their native histories and cultures. It is a nation composed for the most part of people from other places. With the struggle to define the United States as a place, it is experiencing the growing pains of self-definition.

Where Museums Are Today

Museums are participants in the effort to define our collective culture. In examining where they stand in their evolution from exclusive to inclusive institutions, James Boyer's eight-step process is useful (table 1).[2] When applied to children, Boyer's theory holds that the higher the stage of ethnic awareness, the greater the potential for academic achievement. It follows that the higher the stage for museums, the greater the ability to reflect society throughout the institution. Museums as a collective entity have reached level three: diversity is tolerated at all levels and mandated by law. Individually, the level they have attained ranges from four to eight, with most struggling to move from recognition of the needs of a pluralistic society (level four) to acceptance of those needs (level five). Ethnically specific institutions have often reached higher levels of development than mainstream institutions because of the nature and specificity of their focus. The Chinatown History Museum is an excellent example of an institution that has successfully reached the celebration stage.[3]

Most museums would see a reflection of themselves in Boyer's description of the recognition level: acknowledging or taking formal notice of ethnic diversity and admitting diversity as being of some particular status meriting special notice.[4] Internal and external pressures hold museums accountable for their effort—or their lack of effort—to become more diverse and representative of society as a whole. Museums are actively "noticing" all segments of the American population through the presentation of a variety of viewpoints in exhibitions and programs and through the composition of their boards, staff, and volunteer groups. What is difficult and tricky to determine, however, is whether these efforts are forced—guided by "doing the right thing"—or sincere efforts to be inclusive.

"Doing the right thing" poses complex and highly sensitive questions. Museums compete with one another to obtain funding, increase audience support, and capture the media spotlight, all of which are difficult to achieve if the

---

To move from recognition to celebration [of diversity], museums must put mechanisms in place to recruit, retain, and manage diversity.

---

museum is not addressing multiculturalism. It is easy to learn the appropriate jargon. But how many museum trustees, staff, and volunteers can back up the jargon with personal conviction? Thinking discriminately but acting equally is the misguided notion under which institutions "do the right thing." The public can spot this thin veneer of acquiescence, however, and our perceived lack of sincerity may be part of the reason the audiences to whom we reach out do not return. (Robert Merton's Prejudice Discrimination Model offers one way of evaluating prejudicial attitudes; see table 2.)[5] Personal philosophies that do not support diversity or inclusion cannot help but influence institutional policy, operations, and image.

The Euro-American nature of museum collections, created in an earlier era, makes it difficult for museums to address issues of pluralism. Museums rely on educational programs and changing exhibitions, rather than on their collections, to build new audiences and reach society as a whole. Professionals in all departments do not sufficiently acknowledge the gaps in their own knowledge regarding unfamiliar audiences and cultural groups. As a result, programs trivialize culture by reducing it to the most accessible common

Table 1

Stages of Ethnic Development

8 Celebration

Embracing of ethnic literacy at the institutional level, signaling festive freedom for active participation in the larger society at a level void of apprehension and negative environmental response, which inhibit sharing

7 Appreciation

Acceptability of ethnic profile as a legitimate element

6 Respect

View that diversity is of significant worth within any given environment

5 Acceptance

Communication of positive notions of "institutionalization" of diversity

4 Recognition

Acknowledgment or taking formal notice of ethnic diversity, admitting diversity as being of some particular status meriting special notice

3 Tolerance

Implication of the existence of some entity that is not officially sanctioned, not readily deemed an ongoing part of the endorsed setting or format; suggests that that "something" is an allowable deviation from standard services or expectations

2 Existence

Assumption that an individual's profile is part of American humanity

1 Nonexistence

Absence of cultural, racial, linguistic elements

Source: James B. Boyer, *Curriculum Materials for Ethnic Diversity* (Kansas City, Kans.: Center for Black Leadership, Development, and Research, University of Kansas, 1990).

denominators, such as food, clothing, or music.[6] The continuity provided by a permanent collection or installation is lost when programming and changing exhibitions provide sporadic opportunities to involve new audiences and educate museum trustees, staff, and volunteers.

The real issue at the heart of the cultural debate is differing values and norms. When attempts at diversity are reduced to the presentation of a variety of viewpoints with no opportunity to address differing values, the result is little more than exposure; there is no permanent change. Change cannot and will not occur quickly or easily. One of the mistakes of school integration, for example, was the overnight move from separate but equal to multiracial institutions without adequate discussion, preparation, or sharing of experiences. Students, teachers, administrators, and parents were suddenly faced with peers from vastly different backgrounds. Unless we as a society address the need to create institutional mechanisms to prepare for change, we will continue to encounter preexisting prejudices and biases. Until museum professionals— and thereby institutions—come to terms with their own cultural baggage and learn to open lines of communication and apply newfound knowledge to personal and professional situations, multicultural efforts will fail repeatedly to address society's pluralistic needs. To move from recognition to celebration, museums must put mechanisms in place to recruit, retain, and manage diversity.

Where Do We Go from Here?

The most effective way to recruit, retain, and manage diversity is to institute training sessions for trustees, staff, and volunteers. Training for trustees would assure institutional policy change, broaden funding sources, strengthen community relations, and fully represent the interests of the museum to the public and of the public to the museum.[7] Measures at the staff level would create a fuller understanding of audience identity and interests and stimulate the development of substantive programs that do much more than pay lip-service to diversity. For volunteers and docents, learning how to adapt teaching techniques used in other multicultural settings to the museum will foster more effective communication with diverse audiences.

Pathways for Change

Museum professionals can look outside their own field for successful approaches to managing diversity. One example is the program instituted at Exxon Chemical Company in Baytown, Texas. During a recent organizational restructuring, rumors began circulating that minorities and women were unhappy with their treatment and their apparently limited advancement opportunities. Exit interviews, however, did not reveal these concerns to management. As a technology organization, the company relies heavily for its effectiveness on creativity, innovation, and multiple approaches to problem solving. It would have suffered from a loss of diversity in its work force. In an effort to ameliorate the situation, Donald C. Hylton, senior staff scientist in the Converting Technology Polymers Group, and his colleagues surveyed the attitudes of all 300 employees toward their work situations. The employees' answers to the open-ended questions revealed their honest feelings. Management was convinced that sensitivity, or awareness of the impact of the system on people, needed to be addressed.

Independent consultants were brought in to conduct a workshop involv-

Table 2

Prejudice Discrimination Model

	NONDISCRIMINATORY	DISCRIMINATORY
UNPREJUDICED	Think equality Practice equality (All-weather liberal)	Think equality Practice discrimination (Reluctant liberal)
PREJUDICED	Think discriminately Practice equality (Timid bigot)	Think discriminately Practice discrimination (Active bigot)

Source: Robert Merton, "Discrimination and the American Creed, " in *Discrimination and the National Welfare,* ed. Robert M. McIver (Port Washington, N.Y.: Kennikat Press, 1969).

ing the entire work force that was designed to increase awareness that people were frustrated, hurt, and affected personally and professionally by alienation and exclusion. Realizing that simply revealing information was insufficient to promote change, the company decided to design a program that applied the knowledge gained through the survey and workshop to the specific needs of the work site.

Using representatives from all levels of the work force, consultant Tom Kochman and his associates helped the company examine how cultural differences are played out. Employees wanted to emphasize that differences are not bad, just different, and that a system that accepts, values, and encourages differences is more effective than the limiting "corporate" system. Focus groups that included representatives from a variety of ethnic groups developed a set of characteristics for the diverse populations represented on the site. Because these characteristics were introduced from the perspectives of ethnic group members, they can be used to break down stereotypes. Managers were then asked to describe the characteristics they deemed appropriate for higher-level positions. The company is now considering how to merge the varying characteristics and styles to create a truly inclusive environment.

Hylton describes the process as having three steps:

Step 1: *Awareness.* Participants share personal and professional experiences to reveal how certain actions may affect or cause miscommunication among diverse populations.

Step 2: *Understanding and Appreciating Our Differences.* Participants move from awareness to understanding, learning how to apply their new-found knowledge to change behaviors or patterns.

Step 3: *Inclusion.* This part of the process, now being designed, will lead to increased diversity at higher management levels. Hylton describes the ultimate goal as synergy, or a strength in diversity.[8]

Another successful program aimed at increasing awareness of cultural diversity is under way in the Alief Independent School District in Alief, Texas. Ken Bower, director of employee relations, has developed a series of workshops for teachers and school system administrators that guide participants through cultural self-analysis and behavior modification. While the population of the district 20 years ago included only a handful of African-American students, it now contains roughly equal proportions of Asian, Hispanic, African-American, and Anglo-American students.

Participants in Bower's workshops can begin with "Gaining a Better Understanding of Yourself by Dealing with Prejudice, Stereotyping, Discrimination, and Racism," a three-hour course available for advanced academic credit to school system employees. The workshop involves a nonaccusatory self-examination process. A powerful activity in which participants "label" themselves reveals the stereotypes we assign to ourselves and others. Participants then examine how misunderstandings may occur when individuals from different backgrounds interact. They explore approaches to learning about new cultures and methods of changing discriminatory behavior.

For some participants, Bower notes, the first workshop is enough to stimulate introspection and independent personal growth. Others require more guidance. The second workshop in the series, "The Learning Styles of Asian, Hispanic, and African-American Students," provides theoretical approaches to problems experienced by students from minority cultures, strategies for serving as a cultural resource for the school staff, and guidelines for teaching in a multicultural setting.[9]

Dealing with cultural issues in a workshop setting requires sensitive leadership. Individuals who have planned and conducted diversity workshops have varying opinions as to the most appropriate ethnic background for workshop leaders. Using a person of the same cultural background to introduce the concepts of cultural pluralism to a homogeneous group may not create the sense of defensiveness or guilt that could arise if the same session was conducted by a person of color. At one of Ken Bower's workshops, the audience was primarily Anglo American, with the exception of three women: a Hispanic, an African American, and myself (Asian American). The message was delivered by an instructor whose cultural experiences were similar to those of the homogeneous audience. The session planted a "seed of change" in a quiet but powerful manner.

Judy Dawson, training administrator for the Public Utilities Department, City of Houston, offers another point of view based on her ethnicity and personal experience and her attendance at many similar workshops. She notes that each individual brings his or her own experiences to the table. Those who have not experienced discrimination cannot effectively discuss, understand, or educate others about the issues.[10] An approach that blends both perspectives could be to introduce the issue using a person of the same cultural background as most of the participants and then follow up with a session led by a person of a different ethnicity. This technique would broaden the perspectives of the participants and help to ensure that the sessions do not begin with misdirected anger, guilt, or defensiveness.

Workshop planners and participants agree that every diversity workshop or program should have the following elements:

•session leaders who maintain sensitivity, control, and open communication

  •experiential learning activities

  •activities that address a variety of learning styles

  •activities that break down stereotypes and discriminatory attitudes and provide skills and knowledge to change behavior

  •a nonaccusatory and cathartic atmosphere.

A Diversity Action Plan for Museums

Karen Davis of the American Association of Museums notes that "the economic and social challenges of the 1990s will result in museums having less revenue, a higher demand for their programs, and more diverse staff and audiences. Efficient use of human resources, including a sensitivity to cultural, regional, and gender-based differences, is an essential component to effectively dealing with these challenges."[11]

Our nation's educational system helps to break down cultural barriers. Yet when we all reach for the same thing, such as jobs, the barriers go back up. Open communication is the key to keeping the barriers down in the professional environment.[12] In the museum field, many barriers make people feel excluded from the system. Many professionals say that their frustration stems in part from their position as people of color within a predominantly homogeneous and nonethnically oriented field. Some feel pigeonholed and trapped. While ethnicity provides a conduit to the community, it creates a barrier when used as a label. Professionals have, on occasion, been excluded from participating in programs or events that are not ethnically specific. Others find themselves speaking for all ethnic minorities, many of which they know little about, simply by virtue of being the only minority on staff.[13]

There is a way to begin breaking down the barriers in the museum field. Building on the experiences of individuals in the business and public education arenas, a four-step diversity training and awareness program can be established as a standard part of trustee, staff, and volunteer training. The blind men could not define or fully understand what the elephant looked like without working as a team. Similarly, implementation of diversity training must take place at all levels: board, professional and support staff, and volunteer group composition; exhibition development; and collection policy formulation. Systematic, institution-wide change will support greater diversity in programming, community service, and fund raising.

Step 1: Awareness

Assess feelings and perceptions about the cultural policies of the institution through awareness sessions involving all trustees, staff, and volunteers in an open, frank, and inclusive manner. Because of sensitivity to the power structure and to cultural conflict, it might be advisable to first conduct separate sessions for trustees, professional and support staff, and volunteers and then hold sessions involving all three. The session leader could be an individual—preferably a senior-level professional—who is capable of discussing cultural issues in a nonaccusatory but investigative manner. This person would then present the results of the assessment to the trustees, director, staff, and volunteers in separate, confidential sessions.[14]

Step 2: Understanding and Appreciating Our Differences

Build on knowledge gained in step 1 to develop methods for behavior modification and institutional change. Establish committees or focus groups involving trustees, staff, and volunteers to analyze the information and develop methods for changing behaviors. Representation from the top of the museum hierarchy to the bottom will promote consideration of ethnic, economic, geographic, and educational differences.

Step 3: Inclusion

Apply and utilize the information gathered to encourage diversity in all areas of the institution. The museum should draw upon its cultural strengths and help ensure that social and cultural reciprocity is reflected in all museum policies.

Step 4: Maintaining Change

Issues of cultural diversity in the composition of boards, staffs, and volunteer groups should be included in the museum's long-range planning to ensure implementation of change over time. Goals for retaining and managing diversity should be established, and mechanisms should be created for achieving the goals. These mechanisms should include regular and frequent sessions involving trustees, professional and support staff, and volunteers to ensure progress and keep the lines of communication open. Human resources personnel or department managers could receive training in dealing with cultural issues.

The sourcebook and audiocassette series created in conjunction with the American Association of Museums workshop, "Current Issues in Museums: Recruiting and Retaining a Diverse Staff," address the question of maintaining change. Two points in particular should be addressed: (1) providing the skills and knowledge needed to develop effective human resource management skills for a diverse work force, and (2) recognizing that all staffs are diverse in age, geographic origin, education, and other characteristics, regardless of the ethnic composition of community.

Where Do We Want to Be?

The American Association of Museums report, *Excellence and Equity: Education and the Public Dimension of Museums,* emphasizes that museums must play a role in "fostering the ability to live productively in a pluralistic society and to contribute to the resolution of the challenges we face as global citizens.¹⁵ The "elephant," or society, continues to change. The six blind men missed the most rewarding and critical stage of collaborative learning: the sharing of information. The *process* by which museums are defining the elephant is more critical than the elephant's appearance. If museums are to remain fresh, current, and relevant, they must focus less on obtaining quantitative proof of change and more on establishing mechanisms to retain, manage, use, and share the power of diversity.

Journal of Museum Education 18, no. 2 (Spring/Summer 1993): 5–9.

Notes

1. Bonnie Marranca and Gautam Dasgupta, eds., *Interculturalism and Performance: Writings from the Performing Arts Journal* (New York: PAJ Publications, 1991), p. 10.

2. James B. Boyer, *Curriculum Materials for Ethnic Diversity* (Kansas City, Kans.: Center for Black Leadership, Development, and Research, University of Kansas, 1990), pp. 34–52.

3. See Fay Chew Matsuda, "Memories of New York Chinatown," *Journal of Museum Education* 18, no. 2 (Spring/Summer 1993): 16–17.

4. Boyer, *Curriculum Materials for Ethnic Diversity,* p. 44.

5. Robert Merton, "Discrimination and the American Creed," in *Discrimination and the*

National Welfare, ed. Robert M. McIver (Port Washington, N.Y.: Kennikat Press, 1969), pp. 99–126.

6. Kevin Meyers, interview with sociologist James Davison Hunter, "Weekend Edition/Sunday," National Public Radio, December 6, 1992.

7. Pamela Mays McDonald, "Cleaning House for Company," *Journal of Museum Education* 18, no. 2 (Spring/Summer 1993): 13–15.

8. Donald C. Hylton (senior staff scientist, Converting Technology Polymers Group, Exxon Chemical Company, Baytown, Texas), interview with author, February 4, 1993.

9. Ken Bower (director, employee relations, Alief Independent School District, Alief, Texas), interview with author, February 4, 1993.

10. Judy L. Dawson (training administrator, Public Utilities Department, City of Houston), interview with author), January 13, 1993.

11. Karen Davis (assistant director of education, American Association of Museums), interview with author, February 2, 1993.

12. Dawson, interview with author.

13. These frustrations take their toll: of the 15 participants in the 1992 Smithsonian Museum Leadership Program, at least two were no longer in the field by February 1993. Although one left to pursue graduate studies, the other had experienced the difficult circumstances described here.

14. Debbie Albuquerque (director of human resources, Fine Arts Museums of San Francisco), discussion with author, February 16, 1993.

15. American Association of Museums, *Excellence and Equity: Education and the Public Dimension of Museums* (Washington, D.C.: AAM, 1992), p. 6.

Further Reading

American Association of Museums. *Museums for a New Century.* Washington, D.C.: AAM, 1984.

Barnhart, Terry. "Museums as Agents for Inclusion." In *Sourcebook 1992,* pp. 305–14. Washington, D.C.: American Association of Museums, 1992.

Kadoyama, Margaret. "Translating the Vision: The Next Step with Diverse Populations." In *Sourcebook 1992,* pp. 265–71. Washington, D.C.: American Association of Museums, 1992.

Jenness, Aylette. "The Kids Bridge Exhibit." In *Sourcebook 1992,* pp. 311–14. Washington, D.C.: American Association of Museums, 1992.

Museum Education Roundtable. *Patterns in Practice: Selections from the Journal of Museum Education.* Washington, D.C.: Museum Education Roundtable, 1992.

Nichols, Susan K., Mary Alexander, and Ken Yellis, eds. *Museum Education Anthology: Perspectives on Informal Learning—A Decade of Roundtable Reports.* Washington, D.C.: Museum Education Roundtable, 1984.

Tomhave, Roger D. "Value Bases Underlying Conceptions of Multicultural Education: An Analysis of Selected Literature in Art Education." *Studies in Art Education: A Journal of Issues and Research* 34, no. 1 (1992): 48–60.

Institution-Wide Change in Museums

Will Phillips

Change agents have been a part of human society since prehistoric times; they have been called prophets, wizards, shamans, and seers. But these labels and the roles they embody fell into disuse and disrepute with the age of science and the Industrial Revolution. In turn, during the 1950s the organizations created during the Industrial Revolution were challenged to change in ways that stretched their own internal capabilities. New models and new tools for change were needed, and so the modern wizard was born—the organizational consultant. I use this term to describe the outsider who views an organization holistically and works to bring it to a new state of health that allows it to thrive in the current and future world. This article will briefly outline some tools of the organizational consultant that seem appropriate for museums to consider at this point in their history. Reading about them, of course, is only the first step. You must learn how to put them into practice in your museum.

Tool 1: Understanding the External Forces of Change

The forces that began challenging the organizations in the 1950s have accelerated and boomed in the 1990s, and they are now shaping our future in dramatic ways. They are the forces that broke up of some of the largest and most significant organizations of this century—IBM, General Motors, Sears, and the Soviet Union—and they threaten museums of all sizes. They include globalized competition, demographic shifts, electronic technology, audience fragmentation, and the democratization of museum support. I will highlight these for their special impact on museums. For more information read *The Popcorn Report* and *Megatrends 2000*.[1]

Globalized Competition

The economy of the world's richest seven nations is on the skids, and there is no clear prospect of recovery. To a large extent this decline is due to a new brutally competitive world economic order that is emerging with the demise of the cold war. The forces that are propelling this new order will persist for years and promise to make life tougher for almost everyone. To the extent you raise the standard of living of developing countries, you must have a corresponding drop in the living standard in the West.[2] As a result, the inflation-adjusted income in the United States has been declining since the 1970s.

Demographic Shifts

The demographic profiles of your audiences and your donors have changed. For example, many large communities in the southwestern states now have a majority of Spanish-speaking residents. Even Green Bay, Wisconsin, has a significant and growing Southeast Asian population, and New York City's Puerto Rican population is an increasing force. These new populations have yet to find proportionate representation on the staff or boards or in the programs of the museums in their respective areas. We talk about diversity; we have not yet done it.

Are you up to date on demographic changes? If not, demographic changes are creeping up on you. Most community planning boards have specific local data on these trends. Get it. Understand it. Share it. And finally, use it in building your staff, board, and audience.

Electronic Technology

Recent advances in electronic technology are having and will have a dramatic impact on how we handle information and how we do our work. Some current capabilities include:
- instant access to data
- simultaneous availability of data
- expert systems that enable generalists to become experts
- replacement of photography with digital images.

Organizations that are not exploring and using technology in these ways will move more and more slowly at higher and higher operating costs.

Audience Fragmentation

More choices are competing for the discretionary time and dollars of potential museum visitors and donors. Many leisure time options are doing a better job than museums of targeting and serving growing populations. If a museum remains passive in this environment, it will be passed up. The challenge is to create new ways to carry out your basic mission and still compete with video, sports, Disney, and 500-channel interactive television.

The Democratization of Museum Support

Museums were founded and financially supported by the aristocracies of their nations. But the aristocracies of our society are no longer willing and able to be the exclusive supporters of museums. Museums have been very slow to adapt to this change and serve new audiences. After an interim stage when aristocratic persuasion led to public monies being assigned to museums for the "public good," the public has begun to seriously question the value of the "good" supposedly delivered by museums.

Most museum professionals will find little new information in the above summary of trends. But they need to be addressed. These are the questions to ask:

•Have staff leaders in your museum discussed these external trends and agreed on the critical few that are most likely to affect your museum?

•Have these top trends been clearly stated and communicated to all staff and board?

•Is there an ongoing effort to better understand the specific local manifestation of the trends?

•Have you assigned someone to investigate how other museums are addressing these trends? Do you have data on what has or has not worked for them?

•Have you explored the impact the top trends will have on your museum if they continue at their present rate? What if the trends accelerate?

•Do you have plans in place and actions under way to respond to the trends in a way that truly addresses the causes rather than simply providing

---

The successful museum of the future is likely to need speed over sheer size, flexibility over job clarity, and integration over specialization.

---

symptomatic relief? Are you making sufficient progress to keep up with each critical trend?

When a museum can answer each of the above questions positively, it is thinking strategically and managing for the future. By addressing and responding to these questions a museum can convert anxiety to action. Then it can mobilize the necessary energy and creativity to succeed. When the answers are "unsure" or "no," the museum has failed to take full responsibility and is building its future on the hope that the external trends will change and become more supportive.

Tool 2: Understanding the Internal Barriers to Change

Forces naturally grow inside any institution that reduce its ability to respond positively to change. These internal forces gain momentum so slowly that they are not readily noticed. They even take on a life of their own and become revered as ends in themselves. Some of the major internal barriers are described below. Assess the strength of these internal forces in your museum by having staff rate them on a scale of 1 to 10.

Mental Aging of the Board, Director, and Key Staff

Mental aging is characterized by a shift from accepting risks in order to grow to avoiding risks in order to preserve the status quo. There are two remedies for mental aging. The first one is a whack on the side of the head to wake up the leadership. This usually happens when the crisis really hits. Before the real crisis, however, there are usually many smaller crises that trigger short-term financial solutions, but they rarely get to the root causes of the crisis.

The second remedy is a proactive whack on the side of the head by a skilled organizational consultant (or *in*sultant). It takes more courage to be proactive, but the benefit is that the museum is in control of the change process instead of change being in control of the museum.

Plateau Market Share

When the tried-and-true mechanisms for attracting audience, volunteers, and donors reach a point of diminishing returns, the museum's market share plateaus. At this plateau there is a feeling of accomplishment ("We've done it; let's relax.") or a feeling of hopelessness ("What more can we do to attract them?"). Museums have great difficulty understanding their potential new markets and are often unwilling to learn about them. This irresolution represents a lack of respect for the diversity and differences in an expanded market.

Museums can open up huge new audience and donor markets if they are willing to do the hard work of understanding demographic shifts and learning about these potential new markets aggressively and respectfully. Then they must make changes to better serve the needs of their expanded markets.

Silosclerosis

As a museum matures, its functional structure begins to harden in place and the walls between functional departments grow. Curators vs. educators vs. administrators vs. developers—each staff person develops allegiance to his or her functional specialties and professional associations and journals rather than to the institution or the field as a whole. It's as if each department is willing to have the museum weaken as long as its own function remains strong.

These barriers between specialties can create a climate of disrespect, dramatically increase the time it takes to complete complex projects, and add enormous cost to the bottom line. They breed waste, rework, duplication, and poor coordination between departments. Radical redesign of the organizational structure may be needed to break down the walls that form between the silos of individual departments. Cross-functional teams are powerful ways to reduce the costs of these silos and deliver on your museum's mission.

Tool 3: A Model for Creating Change

Change seems to occur in a three-step process. Since the change itself only occurs in the last step, it is easy to neglect the first two steps, but each is a necessary part of the process.

1. *awareness* of the reasons why a change is necessary
2. *acceptance* of the awareness and the need for change
3. *action* to make the change.

Awareness

People are most willing to change when they are aware of the reason for the change. When everyone is busy at work and someone runs in and announces a desired change, few will change unless the reason is clear to them.

Unfortunately, many museums seek to change by announcing the solution without clarifying and agreeing on the problem. By aborting step 1, museum administrators fail to inform and involve the staff and volunteers. One of the most powerful ways of making change happen is to clarify and define the threats facing your museum in a way that encourages participation.

Acceptance

In some situations no change occurs even though the threat has been clarified and the tiger is at the door. Skeptics say, "It's only a paper tiger; don't let it scare you." The natural human reaction at this point is to jump up and down and accuse the skeptics of being blind, stupid, or negative. Of course, such accusations do not lead to change.

When the tiger or threat has been clearly identified and is still not accepted, resistance is usually the reason. Those who are resistant usually harbor a personal fear of change. There may be some hidden issues that are not yet on the table.

An initial attempt to surface this hidden resistance will always fail, unless each individual feels it is safe to put his or her agenda on the table. Once these agendas begin to be revealed, they must be totally respected. Laughing, discounting, and joking will scare these revelations away. Respecting what is revealed might sound like, "Ah, now I see why you are so concerned about making a change. The way you explain it, it makes sense to avoid the change. Thank you for sharing that with me."

Once the dialogue has gone through several cycles of surfacing and respecting, the resistance will no longer be hidden. Then it is possible to explore the resistance with those who are resisting. This process of exploration almost invariably leads to a solution that better integrates the organization's need for change with the individual's need for safety.

Here are some ideas for building acceptance of the tiger's reality:

1. Learn about resistance and how to bring it to the surface and respect it. The principles for dealing with resistance to change while building acceptance are:

•Surface the resistance.

•Respect the resistance.

•Explore the resistance so you better understand it.

•Explore ways of responding to the desired change and respecting the real fears of the resister.

2. Start talking regularly and openly in staff meetings about changes in the world that are having an impact on your museum. Avoiding such discussions encourages denial.

Action

Only when the individual or organization is fully aware and accepting of the reasons for change can action begin. Once awareness and acceptance have occurred, action is fairly easy and straightforward. Without awareness and acceptance, a great deal of effort is often spent trying to sell, push, or force the action. In spite of the effort put into the details of implementing the change, no real change occurs.

In trying to achieve change, we must keep our goals in sight and be flexible with our methods. Once a director or senior staff person decides that a change is needed, he or she often jumps to push for action immediately without building awareness or acceptance. If met with any resistance or reluctance to change, the initiator pushes harder for change, thereby increasing resistance to it. When this happens, the initiator has lost the fight because he or she has not laid the foundation for change by building awareness and acceptance. To allow for these first two steps, it is necessary to back off from the push for change to build a foundation of awareness and acceptance.

An experiment illustrates the point. Hungry chickens were placed on one side of a fence and their food on the other. The chickens tried to go directly through the fence to get to their food and failed. In subsequent experiments, the fence was shortened so that they could easily run around the end of the fence and reach the food. Although the fence got as short as three feet, the chickens could not back off far enough to see the possibility of an end run to achieve the goal. Similarly, those wishing their organization would change sometimes behave like hungry chickens.

Change is paradoxical. A direct effort to cause change will often fail; an indirect effort will often succeed.

Tool 4: Creating a Climate for Organizational Learning

All significant learning changes the learner. In today's fast-changing museum environment, it is no longer adequate to have a director or a few key staff members who can change. What is needed is an entire institution that can learn and change collectively. The director, staff, board, and volunteers will have to redesign the museum together. Your institutional learning quotient will determine how well and how fast this is accomplished. If the internal learning environment is weak, it will limit change and block attempts to connect with new and diverse audiences. The primary condition for such internal learning is a psychological environment that fosters learning between and among people.

Four elements are needed in a learning environment:

1. *Open, honest, and proactive communication.* Museum staff and volunteers tend to favor courtesy and pleasantries, often avoiding issues until they explode or go underground.

2. *Mutual respect of one another's experience.* Respect requires accepting the other person's view as truth and then working to understand how it could be truth rather than disagreeing, discounting, or explaining it away. Many museums focus on respecting the diversity of their potential audiences but fail to build internal respect among, for example, the curator and educator and security guard. Until museums learn to respect the diversity within their staff and volunteer corps, they will have an especially difficult challenge grappling with the diversity in their communities.

3. *Willingness to explore and experiment with new ideas and methods.* To create a climate for organizational learning, it is particularly important to consider new ways of structuring and operating the museum.

4. *Taking responsibility for what is happening instead of blaming or becoming a victim.* It is helpful to describe outside forces as "opporthreats." These events or trends are in themselves neither opportunities nor threats; it is the museum's response that determines what they become. This view encourages the museum to take responsibility for the outcome instead of being a passive victim.

Education, Tradition, Learning, and Change

Educators have an interest in learning, but there are two very different aspects of learning that must not be confused. The first is learning about the past. This traditional kind of learning dominates classroom education. It is based on memorizing correct answers that authorities have given.

The second type of learning is learning how to change in order to be successful in the future. This nontraditional type of learning requires significant creative input and risk. It involves reframing the questions and letting go of the past in order to move into the future. Good museums do this when they present objects and leave learners free to interpret their own meaning and discover their own answers.

Museum educators often find themselves in the position of leading internal change. They must become comfortable with this role by learning as much about change as about tradition. The tools presented in this article were selected to help educators help their museums start learning about themselves as institutions. Only then can they successfully change and adapt to the new forces that are challenging museums.

Journal of Museum Education 18, no. 3 (Fall 1993): 18–21.

Notes

1. Faith Popcorn, *The Popcorn Report* (New York: Harper and Co., 1992); John Naisbitt and Patricia Auburdene, *Megatrends 2000* (New York: Morrow, 1990).

2. Christopher Farrell and Michael J. Manvel, "What's Wrong?" *Business Week*, August 2, 1993, p. 54.

Further Reading

Ashkenas, Ronald N., ed. *Boundaryless Organization: Breaking the Chains of Organizational Structure.* San Francisco: Jossey-Bass, 1995.

Bennis, Warren G. , Kenneth D. Benne, and Robert Chin. *The Planning of Change.* 4th ed. New York: Holt, Rinehart and Winston, 1985.

Newsletter on Institutional Transformation (NoIT). Quarterly newsletter published by Qm². Available at: www.qm2.org/noitindx.html.

Peck, M. Scott. *The Road Less Traveled.* New York: Simon and Schuster, 1978.

Stone, Douglas, Bruce Patton, and Sheila Heen. *Difficult Conversations: How to Discuss What Matters Most.* New York: Viking, 1999.

REFLECTIONS

A major barrier to internal change is the hierarchical structure. The successful museum of the future is likely to need speed over sheer size, flexibility over job clarity, and integration over specialization. To achieve these characteristics museums must learn how to abandon traditional organizational structures, which were fine for managing 19th-century steel mills and assembly lines. Museums are just learning how to replace structure with process and changing their internal culture to achieve this.

—*Will Phillips*

The Future of Museums: Asking the Right Questions

Bran Ferren

When the subject of the future of museums comes up—which it often does—and the word "technology" rears its ugly head, the word "interactive" is usually close behind. So today I would like to give you a demonstration of the most sophisticated and advanced interactive technology developed to date. It combines sensor systems such as vision, haptics, and speech recognition (with limited multilingual capability), with a coordinating neural-net processor, multiple effectors, and, unlike most other systems, it can do commonsense reasoning. It truly is the state of the art in interactive technology, and nothing else on the horizon even comes close.

It's me.

It is important that you realize that I am the state-of-the-art interactive technology because I am the same interactive technology that makes up your audience, your supporters, and your critics. Appreciating that human beings are, and always have been, the state of the art in interactivity is the first giant step necessary for evaluating the potential role of electronic technology in our institutions and in our lives. There is a set of fairly fundamental values that affect people's perceptions of things, and it is important to understand how we "interactive systems" find joy or enlightenment or a number of other personal states.

I remember my first interactive consulting experience. They said, "We have a big challenge for you; we're doing a 'Future Choice Theater.'"

"A Future Choice Theater?" I said. "Terrific! But what is it?"

"It's a place where you go and pressing topics of our time are presented to you. At various moments during the presentation, you will be asked to push buttons attached to your seat. These selections will affect the outcome of the film and, metaphorically, the outcome of our civilization."

I said, "Very nice. What would you like me to do? Help conceptualize how this might work, write the script, create a philosophy for branching story syntax?"

"No, we have all of that under control. We would like you to figure out how to hook up all the little push-buttons—*cheaply*!"

I said, "Okay" (it's a living). I thought about it carefully that night and proposed that what they should do is install all the push-buttons but not connect any of them. As the show is in progress, ask a question every so often, flash some numbers on the screen, and run a different ending each consecutive show. They accused me of having a bad attitude. I explained to them that, actually, it was probably the most cost-effective way to get what they wanted, because in the scenario they had proposed, no one in the audience would know the difference. If audience members got the answers they wanted, it would be because they were enlightened, sophisticated, and equally insightful. If they got some selection other than the one they had personally picked, it would be because the degenerates "they let into the theater" clearly just didn't get it.

That is an example of the broad class of Technical Interactivity (as contrasted with Human Interactivity) that I call Dumb Interactivity—by far the most often executed type of interactive system. It can be found in most institutions that I have seen employing electronic interactive systems technology thus far. The "don't-connect-the-buttons" issue is pretty fundamental. If no one can tell if the technology is really working (or worse still, they know and don't care), you might want to rethink your hypothesis.

Perhaps it's an artifact of the environment in which I was brought up, but I firmly believe that "the Story" is everything. I eat, breathe, and live for stories. Stories provide much of the context that makes our lives interesting. A big part of your job is contextualizing the objects in your collections for your visitors. Storytelling is the most powerful technology at our disposal for accomplishing this. For example, an otherwise ordinary little gray rock takes on new meaning when you are told (and believe) that it is actually a part of the planet Mars and, by the way, it looks an awful lot like it contains the first real signs of life from afar. There are literally dozens of overlapping stories here. There is the story of the search for life elsewhere in our visible universe, the history of this particular lump and how it came to be discovered, the history of the person who first peered at it through a microscope and realized that what he was seeing could have once been alive, and there is your story. And it is about your sense of why all of these things add up to make you take this little gray lump somewhat more seriously than others in your backyard.

There's something about technology (and us) that I feel compelled to caution you about. Beware of solutions for which there are no corresponding problems. Do you remember high-definition television, HDTV? It was going to change our lives. Any of you who watch television and think the problem with television is the number of horizontal scanning lines, rather than the lines of dialogue spoken by the actors, are watching a television that is different from mine. Have you ever watched television and said, "That is a great show, but if it only had another 427 scanning lines, it would really really change my life"? I doubt it.

Please remember that the one thing all of the computer technology you've seen to date has in common is it is all junk. It is all bad, it is all awful, it is all embarrassing. I think it is important you understand that you are dealing with primitive technology. I think it is also important for you to appreciate that you don't have a choice. It is as good as it gets at the moment, and we need to learn how to use it to our advantage. But if, for even one moment, you look at any of this and think it's really good, you are missing the point. The computer technology of the future will learn to adapt to *our* needs, not require us to do the opposite. What we have to do is struggle through together, figure out what these things are good for, but keep our eye on developing a palpable vision of the future. Ask what's the highest and most valuable role your institution can serve for the people of our world, and then ask what's the best way to get there. Once you have a vision, get the technology and technologists to apply or invent the solution.

This "asking-the-right-questions" thing is pretty important to me. In my career as a consultant, I saw an awful lot of really dedicated, smart people

---

Technology will not replace museums or teachers. It will revitalize them.

---

go down in flames because they provided excellent answers to the wrong questions—and then acted on them. So far this year, I've received three calls from major institutions asking, "Can you help us computerize?" And I say, "Why are you computerizing?" To date, there isn't a good answer. The fact that everybody else is doing it isn't necessarily a great reason for you to do it. Probably the best answer to the "why-do-it" question I can imagine is that we're all a little scared—scared that something potentially profound is going on, that we don't understand, and that has implications we just can't quantify. And, my God, what about the World Wide Web! Over a hundred million people all communicating! But communicating what? And why are they doing this? And is this good for us, or is it competition?

We are all in the business of adding value to people's lives. We live with a fiction that people have spare time and disposable income. I don't; do any of you? If you can't effectively compete for people's time and money, odds are, in the long term, you will cease to exist (because someone else will compete effectively). So how can we look into the future to determine what technologies will be the enablers that allow us to deliver value? The World Wide Web—

broadband, interactive communication that will evolve in a very short period of time—I suspect is, in fact, the most important and profound technological invention of our history since language and storytelling—the equivalent of fire, period. I think we are at the threshold of an extraordinary moment in our history. The evolution of societies, or of species, is not linear. It happens in leaps. Technology often plays a key role in these evolutionary surges. Take the telephone and telegraph, for example. The fact is, the telephone didn't seem terribly important to people back then. Why couldn't the smart folks of that time appreciate its potential? Being the first on your block with a telephone was not necessarily all that exciting. *One* phone is like one tube of epoxy: it has some novelty value, but it's not particularly useful. You had to wait until the person you wanted to call also got a phone for yours to become useful. The phone companies also had to train the populace to use this new invention properly. This was not obvious. The typical scenario: your nice new phone would ring, you would pick it up, hear nothing, and then hang up. The protocol of automatically saying "Hello" when you answer a telephone had not yet been established. There is nothing intrinsically obvious about a telephone that makes you say "Hello" when you answer it.

Any time a technology was invented that enabled a person to communicate more richly or conveniently with another, or tell stories to one or more people in a more compelling manner, it had major impact on society. The Net, and what it will evolve into, is clearly the most powerful and important storytelling technology ever developed. It has the potential to interconnect the peoples of our planet in a rich storytelling environment that transcends the limits of time, space, and language.

Are these network technologies going to change society in simple, measurable ways? For example, will they replace books? I don't think networked computers, per se, will replace books. I think books are joyful objects. They are a very mature technology. They are high-resolution, random access, portable. You can cut and paste; you may get yelled at by your librarian, but you can do it. Books are a pretty great technology. Periodicals, on the other hand, will probably be outlawed in this country within 20 years. I would argue that most of the media and messages and stories intended to be read once and then disposed of will migrate to electronic form. What we will need is electronic paper. We will need something that looks like magazine paper, has the same contrast, is tactically pleasant, and yet is a networked device and lets you function in that way. That is 10 years away.

Ultimately, say within 50 to 100 years, you are probably going to find bio-electronic implants a pretty effective (and routine) way of communicating ideas to people—better than TV, better than movies, better than books. There are a whole range of technologies in common use today that, 25 or 50 years ago, people would have rejected as complete fantasy. We just get used to these things very quickly.

Truth is, I'm really as clueless as the rest of them about where this is all going to end up. But so were Gutenberg, Bell, Marconi, and the hundreds of other inventors who helped shape our world. Evangelizing about this is like talking to the Wright Brothers about the advantage of the mileage program and why it would be a sensible strategy for their future business—commercial aviation. When you're struggling to get a tomato soup can to work as a carburetor on a chilly winter day in Kitty Hawk, it's just plain hard to look that far into the future.

Just what do museums do, and how could technology help? I am looking in from outside your community. Let me tell you what I think the great museums do. The first thing they do is manage their brand. If it's the Smithsonian, if it's the Exploratorium, the brand image is well managed. This is of the highest priority. Done well, we are given a sense that these are institutions of quality, with depth and insight, a strong point of view, taste, a great collection, or what have you. But they manage that brand consciously and effectively.

I got the best lesson of my life in brand management two years ago in Death Valley. I was there in August and it was 127 degrees in the shade. I went searching for the two essential fluids necessary for my life in the desert: water and gasoline. It turns out they are sold in the same place. At a little gas station in Stove Pipe Wells I fueled up and bought water. I bought a brand that will remain nameless (Evian), and I paid five times as much per fluid measure for the water as I did for gasoline. That struck me as interesting. Why would I, and probably most of you out there, pay this astonishing amount of money for something you know is worth pennies? It is because we have been convinced by great brand management that it's worth it—not only worth it but that you shouldn't complain about it. If the price of gasoline goes up 10 cents a gallon, you are all in a panic and the increase is on the evening news. If the price of water goes up 10 cents a gallon, nobody even notices. I guess it's because we don't really need gasoline.

So what else do museums do? They establish context for the artifacts in their possession. This context, usually presented in a story-based form, engages the visitors who made the pilgrimage because they bought into the brand. The contextualization process lets them know why what they are going to experience is important. I mean "context" in two different senses of the word. First, human commonsense-based context. If you drove here today along the same road I did, you probably passed a million trees. Your memory of these trees was likely similar to mine—"Gee, lots of trees." Few, if any, stood out in your memory or seemed particularly noteworthy. However, if one of those trees were upside down—imagine a big pine tree standing on its point with the roots in the air (and no visible means of support)—odds are you might remember it for the rest of your life. All that happened, technically, was a 180-degree geometric rotation of one out of a million objects, but because the context changed to something beyond your experience, it became significant and memorable. Try hanging a famous painting upside down in your gallery and see if you get the same effect.

Establishing context is an essential part of making people believe they are getting a valuable museum experience. Sometimes it's been done for you—like Dorothy's ruby slippers. Other objects require more exposition. If I present to you an old piece of wood and say, "This is an old rotting piece of wood," you will say, "Yes, please get it off my desk." If, however, I can present the case with some degree of authority that the wood is, in fact, a piece of the True Cross, it will take on a whole new meaning. So does a little gray rock if you can get people to believe that it came from Mars and contains signs of life.

The ability to effectively establish and understand context—both human context and historical context—is what any great institution does well. Displaying and conserving artifacts and maintaining a quality collection must be taken seriously. That's a given. I would argue that developing your brand image and maintaining a trusting relationship with your audience are also a critical part of what you do. Whether it is a museum shop selling something to remember you by, printed material that visitors take home, a presence on the Web, an ad, or anything similar, the idea is to bring people back. And, to bring them back, you have to create and establish a relationship with them. That is pretty fundamental. And if you can't find an effective way of doing that, in the long run you will fail, because people forget about you. They may go once and say, "Gee, it was okay." But if you ask, "Do you want to go back?" they say, "No." Why do people come back? I would say it is about content (the collection plus its context) and trust. It's about trusting that you will continue to give them something important each and every visit.

So I think what great institutions do is create content. Some of it may be artifactual, some of it may be contextual, but people go there because they are taking away something valuable. That experience, the message, and a bunch of other things are constantly changing, as is what your audience thinks is important. We are going to have to start dealing with the notion of what digital artifacts are like, how to display them, and, as a society, how to assign value to them. Works of art are now being created entirely in the digital domain. The last nine animated films that Walt Disney made were 100 percent digital. The people and shareholders of Disney would argue that the bits that make up *Aladdin* or *The Lion King* are pretty valuable bits. But this notion of the migration into a digital world, where valuable works of art and objects will need to be displayed that have never, and will never, exist in physical reality, is right around the corner. Are we ready to meet this challenge?

Another great thing about museums is that they provide an opportunity for pilgrimage. They provide a communal experience. You leave your home; you go somewhere. Once you are there, you experience new things with other people. But the definition of community is changing. The Internet is changing how a community can be defined. The idea of distributed and virtual communities is something that never existed before. But it's real, and it is involving millions of people, literally, as we speak. We are just starting to understand MUDDS and chat rooms and all of these things, which are very primitive now because the available bandwidth is so low. When it goes up (and it will rise dramatically as technologies like cable modems hit), almost all ideas that people care about will be shareable in these new communities. How will that affect the sense of community and the role of the institution?

Any institution that survives for the long haul must periodically reinvent itself. This could be necessary every few years or after decades. But it's always necessary. The first part of this process is to pay attention. You must understand the dynamics of who and what you are. Understanding why people come to our museums and support them is essential if you are going to get the right answer about what technology can do for you (or how it could hurt you). If you think what you do is just manage a collection, then all the technology you need could consist of a card file, an air conditioner, and a checkbook. Who needs the Web? If, on the other hand, you think your job is to change people's lives by exposing them to the treasure of your collection, then the Web is probably essential to your future. And if, like the rest of us, you don't really understand it, you need to get with the program.

I want to talk about some real technology-enabled opportunities that could have direct value to your business—the technological low-hanging fruit, as it were. From the most basic operational point of view, there is a huge opportunity in just getting money efficiently extracted from people and then delivering the people into your museum. You would never have your guests stand outside in the heat for 45 minutes before coming into your home; yet I've seen museums do it without seemingly giving it second thought. There have to be better ways of taking money from people, or selling them tickets. There have to be better ways of preparing them for the experience and magic that lie within. The World Wide Web and other interactive technologies can provide great ways to accomplish this.

I think you need to start thinking about employing database management to better understand the history and interests of people visiting you, rather than just who they might be. If you know what they saw last time they were there and what they have seen at other institutions, you begin to have the information necessary to customize and personalize the experience for them. You learn about their interests and what they are getting from the experience. There are technologies now that, for the addition of a few pennies to the cost of producing a ticket, can let you know where everybody in a building is at a time, what they did, what they didn't do, and literally dozens of other valuable things. This is possible now.

You could customize catalogs. They could be electronic tour guides that you carry around with you or materials printed on demand. You just have to define what you want it to do, get some hardware and software, and train your staff in how to use it.

Anyone in this room who doesn't have a chill run up and down his or her spine when the word "software" is mentioned isn't paying attention. Software is a disaster. You have to admit to yourself that you don't understand what it is and how it works, and that it is going to be fundamental to your success. If you believe computers are here to stay, software becomes part of your business. When you are building your collection, you probably wouldn't farm out the acquisitions job. You are not going to be able to farm out software either. Hardware is the cheapest part of a computer. It changes all the time. Software and understanding how it works, and understanding the impact of these technologies, must be brought into our institutions. I don't see it happening except from a maintenance perspective, but from a creative and artistic perspective, it is critical.

Your biggest and most extraordinary opportunities are, I think, in creating experiences that are a hybrid of what cyberspace and the physical world of museums have to offer. Imagine a world where the museum experience can start in a person's home or office, continue into their pocket computing environment, continue into the museum and its archives, and then back home again. And you will know, all along the way, who these "visitors" are and how to best create a unique and enriching experience for them. Soon we will have the ability to extend the museum experience to every place that a person wants it, to capture more of a person's time and attention, and to contextualize dynamically. We will be able to individualize the visit in a way that has never been possible before, to take artifacts and assign greater meaning to them by knowing about the interests and experience of each guest. This is an extraordinary opportunity. It can make transformational experiences out of things that, if done in a traditional presentation form, no one would look at twice.

Telepresence and VR (virtual reality): you can bet on it. This technology isn't ready yet, but when we get it right it will be the next best thing to being there. Ideas and experiences lost to history, waiting to happen, or those still trapped within the confines of our imagination will become available for our guests to experience firsthand. They will change everything.

Next generation interactivity: if you are doing multimedia and you see computer terminals, you are missing the boat. If you have a multimedia installation and it doesn't know that your guest is really there, you're missing the point. What if it were you? Someone asks you a question. You start to answer, but the asker walks away. Would you just keep on babbling into thin air? How many of you have multimedia installations that do this? Fix this; it's not hard. Learn from the most advanced interactive technology we have: us.

The quality of your people—or rather your ability to attract, grow, and retain top talent—is ultimately what will determine your long-term success. And it will predict your ability to affect society and remain relevant and vital. When it comes to talent, you can't afford anything but the very best. And the old maxim is as relevant as ever: It's hard to find good people! (and to keep them)—people who have the ability to tell stories in a compelling and entertaining way. That is more important than anything else—except for one thing. *A Great Idea!* We've all seen our colleagues design major, expensive well-executed projects that failed. It doesn't matter how much money you have or how hard you work, if you don't start with a good idea, you are in big trouble.

What keeps me going these days is one word—a word I think means more to me than almost anything else, and that word is "education." I don't think you can take any critical problem in our society at the moment that doesn't, in some way, have its roots in education—or, rather, the lack of it. The fact is if you go to an inner-city school, the most sophisticated technology you will see is the metal detector that frisks kids for weapons when they go into the building. That is fundamentally unacceptable. By utilizing the skills of our storytellers to contextualize the treasures of our museums, I know we can fix this. The art and technology of storytelling combined with empowering interactive tools like the Web will give us the ability to touch people's hearts and to open their minds. What you provide are the things that are real. History and the best products of our human imagination and spirit are housed in our museums. Let's work together to use these treasures to enrich our world. Technology will not replace museums or teachers. It will revitalize them. Anyone who thinks computers are about to replace teachers doesn't know what a teacher does. What this technology can do is provide the equivalent of power steering for educators and museum professionals. It can dramatically extend the reach of our professionals and their capacity to serve more people more effectively. In this manner, technology becomes a creativity amplifier.

These sorts of tools, I think, will play a profoundly important role in the future. But to make them work, we have to ask the right questions, we have to pay attention, and we have to realize that we really do have the power to change the world.

Journal of Museum Education 22, no. 1 (1997): 3–7.

Educators on Exhibit Teams: A New Role, a New Era

Lisa C. Roberts

In the early 1980s, for the first time in any systematic fashion, educators began to be invited to sit at the exhibit development table. This noteworthy occurrence marked the beginning of an approach to exhibit development that took into account curatorial, design, and now educational perspectives. "The team approach to exhibit design"—it rang of democracy, fellowship, and collaboration. During the next decade, museums throughout the country would jump on the exhibit team bandwagon, part of a growing national conscientiousness about museums' public dimension.

It has not all been smooth sailing, however. Exhibit teams have been dogged by problems that range from establishing priorities to achieving consensus. And no wonder. The inclusion of educators on exhibit teams has introduced new interests, criteria, and influence into the process of exhibit making. Change on this scale can hardly happen overnight. Role definition has been especially problematic because on the surface it has appeared so straightforward: curators are responsible for an exhibit's content, designers are responsible for its look, and educators are responsible for the visitors—as well as for other potential audiences, and pedagogical soundness, and communication, and supplementary programming to enhance the exhibit.

Well, it *seemed* straightforward, anyway. At the very least, it is safe to say that educators are in some sense responsible for assuring that an exhibit is intelligible to viewers. Exactly what that means—to make an exhibit "intelligible"—is the subject of this article. Educators' role in the exhibit development process has never been clear-cut. It is relatively new, after all, and it is still evolving. Broadened notions of learning, growing knowledge about visitors, new complexities in interpretation, and expanded responsibilities—all continue to influence the role educators are expected to play.

Just as this role has been subject to change and refinement, so are these attempts to define it. This article is meant to be not prescriptive, but descriptive. I hope to begin to lay out some common guidelines for understanding precisely what educators are responsible for on exhibit development teams. I will also consider the consequences of that responsibility for the exhibits visitors now encounter: How have exhibits changed as a result of educators' involvement? And what are the implications of these changes for the museum as an institution?

An Evolving Role

The Children's Museum in Boston and Field Museum of Natural History in Chicago are widely credited with originating the models that led to what we now call the team approach to exhibit design. Realizing that this approach was the wave of the future, Field Museum presented a series of workshops between 1982 and 1987 on the team approach; they were attended by some 300 educators, curators, and designers from 105 museums throughout the country. These workshops mark one of the first concerted efforts to define team members' roles in the exhibit development process. Over the course of five years and as many workshops, definitions for the three perspectives emerged:

> Curator: The curator provides the scholarly expertise based on knowledge of the collection. As subject matter specialist, the curator is responsible for establishing the overall concept of the exhibit.
>
> Designer: The designer is responsible for the visual appearance and coherence of the exhibit. The designer's expertise assures that the exhibit material is set out in an appealing, understandable, and attractive manner.
>
> Educator: The educator establishes the link between the content of the exhibit and the museum audience. The educator is a communication specialist who understands the ways people learn, the needs that museum audiences have, and the relationship between the museum's program and the activities of other educational institutions, including schools. The educator plans evaluation activities that will examine the exhibit's success in meeting its intended objectives and communicating with visitors.[1]

Such clear-cut definitions did not always translate so neatly into the realities of the job. In actual practice, exhibit teams might comprise any number of staff representing these or other museum occupations, and some museums developed their own nomenclatures to describe the roles of team members. Teams have had to tinker with process-related issues like defining task stages and determining team leadership. But the essence of the team idea was that the three types of expertise outlined above—subject matter, design, and communication—needed in some way to be represented.

As newcomers to exhibit development, educators have found that their role on the team has remained the murkiest. It has not always been clear just what they are expected to do; and in some cases their responsibilities seemed to overlap those of other team members. Herein, then, is the beginning of a primer for educators serving on exhibit teams.

Areas of Responsibility and Expertise

At this point in time, it is safe to say that educators' responsibilities embrace at least seven general areas:

Audience Advocacy

As advocates for museum audiences, educators must represent the interests of the variety of visitors an exhibit will potentially serve. Youth, families, seniors, disabled people, schoolchildren, and multicultural groups are common visitor types. Each has characteristic needs and interests that it is the responsibility of the educator to know and represent. Information about some of these groups is readily available in visitor studies literature. More specialized resources may be found elsewhere. In the case of school groups, for example, educators need to be familiar with state goals for learning and school curriculums that an exhibit might support. For people with disabilities, educators must be able to speak to the accessibility requirements of the Americans with Disabilities Act.

When knowledge about target audiences is lacking, or when exhibit developers have specific questions about visitors' interest or knowledge levels

---

How have exhibits changed as a result of educators' involvement? And what are the implications of these changes for the museum as an institution?

---

in some subject, it is incumbent on the educator to conduct front-end studies to find out this information. This responsibility leads directly to the next.

Evaluation

In the ideal world, there is an evaluator at the exhibit development table who is responsible for conducting visitor studies that will improve an exhibit's effectiveness. Indeed, many museums are beginning to employ professional evaluators to fill this need. Until they become a permanent presence, however, the responsibility must fall to educators.

Two types of evaluation studies are central to the development process. Front-end studies occur at the beginning and are designed to investigate visitors' knowledge, assumptions, attitudes, or expectations about some topic. Formative studies occur during the course of exhibit development and consist of prototyping exhibit elements to assess their effectiveness with visitors before going into final production.

Evaluation can be as quick and dirty or as thorough and costly as one makes it. While one need not be a professional evaluator to conduct evaluation studies, the achievement of accurate, usable results does require knowledge about some basic principles of study design and sample selection.

Learning Theory

It has long been held that educators should have expertise in how people learn. It has also been said that educators should be conversant in philosophy of education, developmental psychology, communication theory, cognition research, and perception studies. Exactly how informed educators need to be about these fields is arguable. Not all of this knowledge translates well into the informal learning setting of a museum. Yet these disciplines do constitute a base of knowledge from which educators can draw when determining the best way to present exhibit messages.

At the very least, educators must have a good grasp of those elements that contribute to effective learning experiences in museums (intrinsic motivation, reinforcement, and so on). Educators should also be abreast of current visitor research. A great many studies that deal with various aspects of the visitor experience are now available. Familiarity with this research, or at least knowledge of where to find it, can help take much of the guesswork out of decisions related to communicating effectively.

Finally, educators must be able to speak to that most basic of questions, What is learning? While the word "learning" continues to connote information transfer and cognitive engagement, in museums it has come to refer broadly to a whole range of experiences that describe different ways of connecting people to the collections. Learning in museums includes emotional, social, contemplative, recreational, and attitudinal aspects, all of which have been documented by researchers seeking to characterize the nature of the visitor experience. An understanding of these aspects is essential to developing exhibits that reach learners in ways meaningful to them.

Communication

Effective communication is key to producing visitor-friendly exhibits. What is an exhibit about? What are the three most important messages? Are they comprehensible? Are they interesting? Communication is hardly limited to the words on the wall, and yet words are the primary means through which exhibit messages are conveyed.

While the task of writing exhibit copy may not fall to the educator, the responsibility of assuring its comprehensibility does. Good writing is both an art and a science: an art, because it still takes a voice to make a narrative come alive; and a science, because it follows principles of good narrative construction. Educators must be sensitive to a whole range of factors embedded in a text to which visitors might respond. Prior knowledge and assumptions, personal relevance, and age appropriateness all relate importantly to how messages are crafted.

To the extent that the medium is the message, educators may also be called upon to help conceptualize how messages are conveyed. Particularly with the growing use of interactives, the effectiveness of a message is linked to the manner in which it is presented. To this end, educators must be able to draw on teaching skills—the one area of expertise with which they have always been associated. Good teaching is, at bottom, about good communication, and educators need to be able to recognize how effective teaching methods can be adapted to the communication needs of exhibits.

Finally, as experts in communication, educators must recognize when exhibit messages might more appropriately be conveyed by other means. First-person interpretation, written handouts, and program curriculums all present alternative options for conveying information. Familiarity with supplementary media will help educators advise on the shaping of exhibit messages.

Interpretation

Interpretation is the single most basic purpose of an exhibit. Whether implicit or explicit, interpretation is embedded in the very act of display—in how a thing looks, in what surrounds it, in what is said or not said about it. As such, interpretation is the business of every member of the team.

As content specialist, the curator has traditionally been responsible for shaping an interpretation. With the advent of exhibit teams, educators may now have a hand in determining interpretive messages. This responsibility goes beyond how well exhibits communicate to what they communicate. Does this musket represent the bravery of American frontiersmen or the conquest of native peoples? To the extent that educators serve as audience advocates, it is their responsibility to present to the team views about the meanings of collections that will resonate with museum audiences.

Furthermore, it is the educators' responsibility to assure that visitors understand something about the decisions behind an interpretation. Why is this an important or valued story? Whose story is it? Too often museums present an anonymous, authoritative view that bears no relation to the interests or meanings important to visitors. Interpretation is in part an act of negotiation—between the values and knowledges upheld by museums and those that are brought in by visitors.[2]

Subject Matter

Although it is generally the responsibility of the curator to provide subject matter expertise, educators will function more effectively on the team if they hold some knowledge about the subject under development. Not only will they be better equipped to participate in exhibit discussions, but they will be able to speak to alternative, visitor-centered approaches from a more informed position. Exactly how knowledgeable educators need to be is hard to say and probably depends on the particular situation. But the more familiar with a subject they are, the more weight their views will carry.

Flexibility and Respect

As the preceding discussions make clear, some of the responsibilities delegated to educators overlap those that fall to designers and curators. Many designers, for example, describe their role less in terms of esthetics than in terms of service to visitors. For them, good design is as much a matter of function as it is of looks. Likewise, curators now find themselves sharing their interpretive role with educators who are versed in visitors' perspectives. However clearly articulated team members' roles and responsibilities, there will always be shades of gray. Educators, along with every other team member, need to be cognizant of this fact and exercise flexibility and respect as they are required.

The Educative Museum

So educators have finally made it on to exhibit teams. What effect have they had on the face of exhibits and museums? Have they had an effect?

There is no question that exhibits produced in the last 15 years have been increasingly sensitive to the viewing public. Legibility has improved, evaluation techniques and advisory groups are being more widely employed, and exhibit content better reflects visitors' knowledge and interest levels. In some museums, these changes are the direct result of educators' involvement. In others, they reflect a growing sensitivity among staff as a whole toward museums' public dimension.

How these changes have improved visitors' experience varies widely. While overall visitor satisfaction seems to be on the upswing, many exhibit teams still need practice in making exhibits that are truly visitor centered. And the challenge remains of balancing the needs of the visitor against the interests of the scholar. As more space has been given over to interpretation, less is made available for objects; and in some minds, the collections—for which many museums were even founded—are being given short shrift. How this balancing act will play out in the future remains to be seen.

Outwardly, then, educators—or at least, educational perspectives—have had a considerable impact on the way exhibits are made. The significance of this impact, however, goes beyond the physical facade. Educational interests strike at the heart of what it means to be a museum. Long-standing assumptions about the purposes of museum collections, the meanings they hold, and the authors of those meanings have been upended by educators' insistence on a more broadly shared authority over collections and what they represent.

These changes mark the occurrence in museums of a much wider epistemological shift, one that has touched nearly everyone in the business of knowledge. This shift has seen traditional views in which knowledge is objective and absolute overturned by the notion that knowledge is socially constructed, shaped by the interests and values of the knower. Museum educators, with their concern for audience, diversity, and multiple meanings, have been at the forefront of this shift in museums.

This shift in definitions of knowledge and knowledge derivation first took place in the the practices of academicians—many of whom surely counted curators among their numbers. Historians, for example, became increasingly conscious of the extent to which their questions and approaches to the past are shaped by the character of the historical moment in which they work. Similarly, anthropologists began paying closer attention to the cultural biases in their studies and the racist undercurrents often embedded in their depictions of other cultures. Fields like art and literary criticism tested their own boundaries by demonstrating how social forces ultimately shape definitions of art, beauty, and quality. The development of psychoanalytic theory turned attention within, to the repressions and desires of individual human consciousness as the ultimate shaper of thought and perception.

History, culture, society, personality—while each variable represents a distinct set of influences, all are united by one thing: they describe conditions that shape what we think we know. Whatever the object, whatever the analytical method, knowledge exists in reference to a wider context of interests and values. To speak of a historical event or an artistic masterpiece, in other words, is also to speak of criteria of taste and value by which they are judged to be important. Knowledge, then, may be understood to be linked inextricably to the context of its production, for it is the prevailing interests, values, social mores, and beliefs that prescribe the standards of quality and criteria of truth according to which it is defined.

As practicing scientists and historians, curators cannot have been untouched by these developments. With but a few exceptions, however, they have failed to consider the implications for exhibits. Educators are the ones who have sounded the cry for more inclusive exhibits that take into account how others might view the collections. While educators can hardly lay claim to the new scholarship and interpretations that have come out of making exhibits more inclusive, they can be credited with taking an activist role in insisting that such interpretations be considered.

It is here that the real significance of the inclusion of educators on exhibit teams becomes clear. When educators represent the views of exhibit audiences, when they argue for more diverse messages, they are bucking traditional ways of knowing and treating objects. As such they have been the catalysts in museums for the wider shift to a more context-based definition of knowledge. Their concerns raise questions—about the authority of curators and the primacy of their knowledge—that not only break with traditional, absolutist views of knowledge, but that touch on the very purposes of collections display. What do objects mean? Who are they for? Museums have throughout history struggled with questions such as these. Educators have now brought the discussion to a new level of meaning.

Final Thoughts: Equipping Educators to Do the Job

At present, museum educators can enter the field with any of a range of backgrounds and expertise. Until professional training requirements are established, this trend will likely continue. While this diversity can be a strength, it has inhibited efforts to establish museum education as a bona fide profession. And now that educators are being called upon to participate more actively in museum affairs such as exhibit development, it is important that they be able to rise to these new challenges and effectively manage the area they have worked so hard to make their own.

Educators have made a strong case for their expertise in informal learning, visitors' perspectives, communication, and more. Having established this niche, they must now do what it takes to assure that they are effective at their jobs. This means making available information, resources, and training opportunities as they are needed. Few museum educators, for example, really have a good grasp of learning theory. Fewer still know the ABCs of evaluation research. Short of truly professionalizing the field through the establishment of certification requirements, a standard body of literature, and so on, museum educators must begin to build professional development opportunities into the job. Just because they've made it onto the team does not mean they've been fully accepted. Part of that acceptance is going to come with their demonstration that they are skilled professionals whose contribution to the team is not just valuable, but integral.

Journal of Museum Education 19, no. 3 (Fall 1994): 6–9.

Notes

1. Mary Ellen Munley, *Catalysts for Change: The Kellogg Projects in Museum Education* (Washington, Chicago, and San Francisco: Kellogg Projects in Museum Education, 1986), p. 31.

2. For more on this idea, see Danielle Rice, "On the Ethics of Museum Education," *Museum News* 65, no. 5 (1987): 13–19; Rice, "The Cross-Cultural Mediator," *Museum News* 72, no. 1 (1993): 38–41.

REFLECTIONS

"Educators on Exhibit Teams: A New Role, A New Era": it sounds so groundbreaking. Of course, historically speaking, it is. And yet five years later, five more years in the trenches, it also seems so evident. That educators should play a key role in exhibit making, the primary means by which museums communicate and teach, is by now widely embraced, at least in concept if not in actual practice. The idea that education is at the core of the museum mission has taken strong hold, and the field of visitor studies continues to grow.

At the same time, other forces have sharpened the competitive edge. New and increasingly sophisticated forms of entertainment are shaping public taste and influencing the way exhibits are made. Marketing considerations factor ever more closely into the way exhibits are developed and even named. And attempts to push the envelope in the way museum education is defined have been slow to succeed. It should be no surprise that philosophical questions would take a backseat to more basic and pressing operational needs.

Yet the fact is, educators are probably better positioned in museums than ever before. Tomorrow, of course, may bring another story. For that reason, museum educators would do well to take steps to ensure the long-term value and necessity of their work. That means honing their skills, continuing efforts to professionalize the field, and acting as relentless self-promoters. These acts are not well defined, but they are vital to the future. Along with all the other areas of activity outlined in the original article, they will help guarantee that what was once a new era will become an abiding era.

—Lisa C. Roberts

Beyond the Turf Battles: Creating Effective Curator-Educator Partnerships

Jeanette M. Toohey and Inez S. Wolins

Professional roles in museums define divisions of labor that are codified by job description, professional practice, or institutional culture. Within museums, professional roles are usually assigned a set of tasks or products for which staff members are responsible. For example, registrars are responsible for the documentation and movement of collections and loan objects, conservators are responsible for the care and restoration of objects, and designers create expressive environments for the presentation of objects. Turf battles arise when staff members from different departments lack shared goals or values or lose sight of complementary skills or expertise and when divisions of labor create barriers to cooperation.

The most notorious turf battles arise between curators and educators when both claim the interpretation and presentation of collections as major aspects of their job responsibilities. Traditionally, curators and educators have been primary stakeholders in the development of different products that museums offer in service to the public. Art museum curators, for example, are the primary stakeholders for products such as exhibitions, reinstallation of collections, the presentation of study collections, and research publications. Educators are often the primary stakeholders in docent education, teacher and school services, outreach, and public programming. If these products are envisioned as two sides of the same coin, conflicts about content and the most appropriate methods of presentation are easy to predict. Rather than being a liability, however, shared interests can provide partnership opportunities that enrich the quality of the services museums offer their audiences and allow growth and cross-fertilization among professionals within the same institution.

Several assumptions can be made about effective partnerships. First, they require communication, mutual trust, and respect. Second, once a curator and an educator enter into a partnership, something about their work or their methods of working will change. Third, the partners believe that the result of their work will be better than it would have been had they not worked together. Fourth, effective partnerships provide opportunities for museums to reflect upon issues of structural change.

This article offers guiding principles and practical strategies for creating effective curator-educator partnerships. They were born of a specific partnership in the exhibition arena that heeded calls from the field for new models of working together in order to situate the public dimension uppermost in our minds and in our work. Exhibitions are the central hub that connects all museum work and the most visible public expression of work that often occurs behind the scenes—from registration to conservation, to research, to interpretation and programming, to design and gallery preparation.

Clearly, exhibitions are the most important public products that museums create. As the American Association of Museums task force report *Excellence and Equity: Education and the Public Dimension of Museums* asserts, "Museums can no longer confine themselves simply to preservation, scholarship, and exhibitions. . . .They must recognize that what we are calling the public dimension of museums leads them to perform the public service of education—a term we use in its broadest sense to include exploration, study, observation, critical thinking, contemplation, and dialogue." The partnership model presented in this article extends the dialogue in the realm of the team approach to exhibition planning and its usefulness in art museum settings.

Guiding Principles and Practical Strategies

1. Communicate what you believe your territory to be and agree on the "givens" of the project and working relationship. Turf battles emerge from fuzzy territories and boundaries. This guideline may mean that the curator "claims" the role of the object-content protector (concerned with *what* is communicated) and the educator "claims" the audience advocate role (*how* the message is best communicated). It is important to distinguish roles, whatever they may be, early on in the product development process. A clear delineation of roles facilitates the friendly and effective resolution of conflicts that will inevitably arise in the course of working together.

2. Acknowledge your starting place. Describe your background. A curator may have taught at the college or university level, and an educator may have worked in the public school system. Both believe they know something about education, but they come to the project with different starting places about styles and processes of teaching and learning in the museum context.

3. State the assumptions you bring to your work, and challenge each other's assumptions when they conflict. Examples of assumptions are abundant in museums. A curator may assume that an exhibition celebrates the completion of a catalog and illustrates the ideas that can be found in the catalog. The assumption is that the catalog is the primary form of scholarship and that the exhibition is secondary to it. An educator might assume that visitors do not move in a linear fashion within an exhibition gallery, so they might not read every label and text panel. And, while an educator may want a lot of light in the gallery to facilitate viewing and reading, a curator knows the need for limited light levels to conserve a work on paper.

4. *Work at listening to each other.* Each partner should strive to know the other's "bottom line" on the project they are creating together. Each should learn what's important to the other—the thinkers, ideas, and literature that guide the other's work and problem-solving approaches. When a curator asserts that a certain set of concepts must be communicated through the exhibition and when an educator asserts that learning requires active involvement either intellectually or physically, partners are articulating their "bottom lines."

5. *Recognize the validity of the kinds and levels of education and experience that each brings to the joint venture.* To do this, each partner may need to stretch, learn, and grow in new ways. Partners will probably have different backgrounds—distinct types of academic training, numbers of years in the field, ranking within the institution, and, if one partner has held different posi-

---

The shared responsibility for audiences is nonnegotiable.

---

tions in the same museum, number of years of on-the-job experience. Remember, partnerships assume equality, so each partner will need to resist the temptation to hold his or her background as superior. Each needs to think of the partnership as a fertile ground for mentoring relationships and apprenticeships.

6. *Come prepared with the materials needed to begin a substantive dialogue.* For an exhibition partnership, the curator might need to provide a checklist and a summary of important concepts. The educator might need to provide an outline or a calendar of the kinds of programs that are typically offered.

7. *Build a climate for expression by creating or taking advantage of structures and vehicles for communication.* One way to accomplish this is to establish "sacred" time, a regularly scheduled time partners set aside to meet and exchange and explore ideas, along with ground rules for the time spent together—no telephone calls, no postponements, no interruptions, a strict time limit. "Sacred" time may necessitate overcoming institutional barriers, such as bureaucratic divisions or architectural separations. Interoffice memos, voice

mail messages, and face-to-face interactions are different styles of communication. So are eating lunch and taking coffee breaks together. Some styles are formal, some informal. Learn which modes of communication work best for each of you.

8. Be a change agent. Take responsibility for modeling the working relationship once it is established so other staff members can be inspired by it. Partners can learn something from observing and discussing other partnerships in the same institution, helping others to understand what works and what doesn't.

9. Provide opportunities for the extended staff to "own" a piece of the product. For example, solicit troubleshooting feedback and a new pair of eyes on a particularly stale problem, then empower the staff member to solve the problem. Those outside the team are sometimes perceived as subordinates. Helping others to own a piece of the product broadens communication across the museum. In traditional divisions of labor, there are few opportunities to discuss substantive issues of mutual concern because departments work autonomously. Partnerships help the institution see the importance and validity of teamwork. For example, if the decision to create partnerships comes from the top down, it may impose values not shared by the rest of the staff. Conversely, if it's a bottom-up decision, change can be seen as threatening. Change often implies that the "old" way of working is not right, valued, or wanted any longer.

10. Identify yourselves as a team, and announce it so often that everyone thinks of you as a team. Your partnership reminds the institution that decision making is shared and that contributions are jointly made. The personal visibility and credibility of each partner are heightened when given the opportunity to grow in new professional ways and when acknowledged for shared contributions.

11. Allow additional time for each aspect of the project. The time it takes to complete each aspect of a task increases exponentially with the addition of one or more people. Negotiating this time is crucial. During times of frenzy, one partner may need to remind the other that the end goal is in sight. Partners can provide a sense of calm and balance for one another. Create a timetable that allocates fairly the major activities and products of the partnership. It will not only help you move toward the timely completion of tasks at hand but also remind the institution of the time it takes to achieve change.

12. Celebrate milestones together. The first time one partner finds that he or she is protecting the other's point of view, or turf, is a milestone. With it, the partners are beginning to change the ways they work. When recognized and shared, these significant events confirm that the partnership is successful,

Implications for Museum Management and Structural Change

In some museums, collaboration occurs naturally in the course of daily work. Yet, few institutions have codified processes for creating curator-educator partnerships. To facilitate partnerships across many product areas, a museum might restructure its education department so that it is parallel to the structure of its curatorial departments (i.e., by historical period, geographical area, or medium). Many education departments are currently organized by audience function (i.e., head of school programs, head of adult education, etc.). This division of labor inhibits true partnerships because the curator is assigned to think about ideas and objects in a single collection area, and the educator is assigned to an audience or program in many collection areas. While "content" is almost always the primary concern for collection curators, it is often secondary to educators, whose first allegiance is to audience. Bureaucratic divisions may explain why communication between the curatorial and education departments is limited or, worse yet, nonexistent.

For museums to achieve their full potential as educational institutions, they must strive for parity between education and curatorial departments in the sizes of staffs and budgets. Museums need the leadership that enables new models to be developed, monitored, sustained, and evaluated so staff members can implement projects that bring creative vision and greater focus to the museum's public service mission.

In *Rethinking the Museum* (1990), Stephen E. Weil asked the provocative question: Do our museums make a real difference in, and do they have a positive impact on, the lives of other people? He stated that if the answer is no and if museums are only the servants of collections and not of other human beings, then our work has been largely wasted. If, on the other hand, we contribute to the life of our communities, we will have lived up to our biggest challenge: providing experiences that empower our visitors to look at and think about their place in the world in new ways.

We believe that the museum's public is every museum staff member's concern. Commitment to the public must be a "given" when one enters the museum field, regardless of job title. The shared responsibility for audiences is nonnegotiable. Staff partnerships have the potential to establish common ground, common goals, and shared vision for the benefit of all audiences.

Journal of Museum Education 18, no. 1 (Winter 1993): 4–6.

Responses in Practice

REFLECTIONS

While most museums have adopted long-range plans and written job descriptions to guide what we do and why we do it, there are probably fewer codified processes to inform how we work together. It is widely accepted and generally believed that exhibitions provide the arena for teamwork and that inclusive exhibition development processes enhance their quality. Since no institutional policies were in place regarding how people work together, we forged an exhibition development alliance. This alliance led to the creation of a new model for teamwork and sharing our experiences in workshops, presentations, and the article we published in the *Journal of Museum Education*. We continue to urge museum staff members to pioneer and share the best practices for working together regardless of job titles, areas of responsibility, and institutional cultures.

—*Jeanette M. Toohey and Inez S. Wolins*

Is There a Way to Make Controversial Exhibits That Work?

Roberta Cooks

Our world is changing, faster than most of us can grasp. Every night we can watch an instant television replay of world history in the making. Scientists have given us the power to clone sheep and destroy whole cities. Artists use canvas and cameras to make sense of a constant stream of violence and sex.

With so many changes in our society, museums can't always take the safe road in what they present to the public. Our world today is filled with emotional minefields of controversy. Some of us who work in museums relish the idea of looking at the social implications of science, history, and art. Others cringe and want to hide under their desks. But I'm not sure that museums, as public institutions, can avoid hosting controversial exhibits and displaying controversial subjects unless we want to close the doors and give up. Since I don't hear any doors slamming, consider this: Is there a foolproof recipe to make controversial exhibits that work?

The answer to that question is no—not in a public space like a museum, where every person who comes in the door has his or her own ideas on what is right and wrong, true and false. Here's a list of guidelines, however, that helped in developing and touring a potentially controversial exhibit called *What about AIDS?* which was circulated by the Association of Science-Technology Centers (ASTC) beginning in 1993:

- Believe in what you're doing.
- Prepare your museum.
- Reach out to your community.
- Host a preview and invite your potential enemies.
- Learn from the stories of people who have already hosted the exhibit.

How did this list play out in *What about AIDS?*

Believe in What You're Doing

What about AIDS? is a 3,000-square-foot traveling exhibit that was developed at the Franklin Institute Science Museum with members of the National Health Exhibit Consortium. It was funded by the Centers for Disease Control and Prevention. When the original idea for this exhibit was first discussed in the late 1980s, AIDS was starting to kill many young people, an important part of our target audience. The general public had many misconceptions about AIDS, and we felt that by educating our visitors we could have a real effect on preventing the spread of AIDS. We believed in what we were doing.

Although each of us thought it was important to tackle this sensitive and controversial topic, no single exhibit developer in the consortium was sure how to frame a science museum exhibit on AIDS. By working together we felt we could support each other, figure out how to approach the subject, and still be true to our science museums' missions. Our collective concept was to explore the science of HIV and AIDS and weave in stories to link the exhibit to people's lives. We felt it was important to include information on how to protect yourself from HIV, but we were very careful not to tell people how to behave. This was an approach we felt we could live with and explain to our administration and board of trustees.

Prepare Your Museum

Support from other National Health Exhibit Consortium members was

---

With so many changes in our society, museums can't always take the safe road in what they present to the public.

---

very important to the lead exhibit developers when we began to work on the project at the Franklin Institute. Quickly we found that although other Franklin Institute staff believed it was a good idea, in theory, to create an exhibit about AIDS, they were terrified that it was going to be developed and tested on Franklin Institute exhibit floors. Staff at every level had their own prejudices and fears about AIDS. Some were worried that people living with HIV would come into the museum bathrooms and infect other people. Others were worried about how visitors and potential funders would react. How would the public view our museum for creating an exhibit about a virus that is passed on by dirty needles and sex?

So what did we do? We brought in American Red Cross representatives, who gave training classes to everyone—guards, exhibit technicians, educators, public relations staff—on the science of AIDS, public health policies, misconceptions about AIDS, and how to talk to people about HIV and AIDS. We formed a committee of education, design, public relations, programs, development, exhibits, and floor staff. We worked out many knotty problems together, and along the way we decided this process would be great for every new exhibit we developed.

We also worked with the education committee of the board of trustees. The board was extremely concerned about this exhibit. We met with this predominantly Catholic committee and found that members had one main question: How were we going to emphasize abstinence? In that first meeting I wasn't sure how to reply. We certainly felt that abstinence was the best choice for teenagers, but we also knew that many teens are sexually active and need accurate information on how to protect themselves. We were committed to having this information prominent in the exhibit. At the next meeting I brought a brochure called *101 Ways To Make Love Without Doing It*, a long list of safe and romantic things for couples to do, like eating ice cream together, bicycling, and watching the moon. The committee loved it—and so did I. I suggested enlarging the brochure to make an exhibit panel. Committee members thought it was a great idea. Out of this simple connection came a strong partnership. The education committee committed itself to the exhibit and sold the idea to the rest of the board of trustees. We learned that there are ways to listen and work with people of different minds without compromising our own ideas.

Reach Out to Your Community

As we developed the exhibit we worked with science advisers, public health officials, AIDS activists, teachers, and child development experts to make sure the exhibit text was complete, accurate, and easy for families to understand. One concern was whether the subject matter was suitable for younger children, a big part of our core audience. We were committed to giving detailed information about how to protect yourself from HIV, but some of the committee felt uncomfortable having this information seen by six- and seven-year-olds.

Two ideas came out of these discussions. First, we decided to put signs up in the "Protect Yourself" area of the exhibit to let parents know it contained information here that might not be suitable for younger kids. Second, we realized that young kids do need to learn about AIDS. They might know someone in their family or neighborhood who has HIV. They might also pick up dirty needles on the street. But we needed to approach younger kids differently using different language and addressing their concerns. So we created a kid's area in the exhibit, and it became one of the most powerful and busy areas of *What about AIDS?*

Our work with AIDS organizations and local public health workers led to some extra benefits. From Action AIDS and the National AIDS Library we got exhibit photographs and access to people living with HIV and AIDS whose stories we included. The public health organization decided to become a partner and gave us a paid AIDS educator to be in the exhibit for the whole time that *What about AIDS?* was on the floor.

Host a Preview and Invite Potential Enemies

Because this exhibit was so terrifying to our museum's administration, the public relations staff insisted on a three-month preview period during which visitors would evaluate the exhibit and we would make changes before the real exhibit opening. This approach is almost unheard of in the science museum community. Usually the public relations staff are pushing us to finish the exhibit a month before the opening date so they can take pictures and invite the press.

This idea, inspired by fear, was a stroke of genius that saved our museum's skin. We invited general visitors who filled out evaluation sheets and gave us their critiques. We also invited religious school officials and, on another day, we brought in all the local AIDS organizations. The representatives from the Archdiocese of Philadelphia loved the personal stories and felt empathy for the people living with HIV, but they hated a photograph of color condoms that covered one wall. We decided not to change the condom wall. The archdiocese did not endorse the exhibit, but it did not speak against it to its congregations. We concluded that silence, in this instance, was a blessing for *What about AIDS?*

The biggest surprise to us was the response of the AIDS activists. We had been working closely with a person from Action AIDS who felt that the exhibit was sending out the right message about HIV and AIDS. But when other AIDS activists came to see the exhibit, some felt that their story wasn't being told in a strong enough way. We told them that we appreciated their comments and were willing to make some changes in the exhibit. In this case our sincerity wasn't believed, and they wrote scathing letters about our insensitivity to the alternative press. Happily, when we finished the changes and invited them back, they were pleased. A few months later they showed us their support by being the main audience at our exhibit opening.

Our experience dealing with strong feelings around this exhibit made us realize that we needed a place where visitors could safely express their views. We tried many kinds of exhibit talk-backs. The most successful was a table with index cards that visitors wrote on and put into the slot of a wooden box. Museum staff emptied the box periodically and placed some of the cards in a book for all visitors to read. We also covered a wall with visitors' positive and negative comments to let people know this was an exhibit that welcomed many different points of view.

Learn from Others' Stories

After our trial-by-fire experience developing *What about AIDS?* we decided that this was not an exhibit to send to other museums cold. If our experience was any indication of the controversies that could arise, museums needed plenty of time to prepare for the show. The National Health Exhibit Consortium created three copies of the exhibit to be circulated by ASTC. Together we decided to have a workshop every year for the nine museums getting the show. During the workshop museum professionals would see the exhibit and listen to the experiences of a variety of museum staff—exhibit, education, programs, public relations, and development. There was also plenty of time to talk and ask questions. A woman from the National AIDS Library attended each workshop and offered her incredible resources, experience, and support to each museum on the tour.

Perhaps the most important part of the workshops was the sharing of stories and enthusiasm. At that point, those of us who had gone through the development and exhibit opening at the Franklin Institute were feeling pretty proud of ourselves. We let people know that we had worked hard and had overcome many difficulties to make *What about AIDS?* a success. We were confident that other people could make it work too.

What Happened to the Exhibit on Tour?

One lesson we learned from the tour is that the same exhibit can get very different reactions in different places. Here are three examples of how *What about AIDS?* was received:

•At the Miami Museum of Science preview, many people, particularly senior citizens and religious leaders, told staff they were comfortable with the exhibit but they were very worried about what visitors would think. When the exhibit opened the reaction from old and young was enthusiastic. A sponsor gave money for special teen outreach programs and funds to keep the exhibit in Miami for an extra three months.

•Before the exhibit opening at the Cranbrook Institute of Science, Bloomfield Hills, Michigan, Blue Cross decided to sponsor the exhibit and paid the admission fee for members who showed their Blue Cross cards. At the same time, the local schools announced that each district had separate guidelines for AIDS education. Each principal would have to approve the exhibit, and parents would have to sign special permission slips. The museum was worried that no schools would send their students, but it turned out that many schools did approve the exhibit and got parental permission to send their classes.

•Local school board officials in Charlotte, North Carolina, were invited to a preview of the exhibit at the North Carolina Museum of Life and Science,

Discovery Place. They said they liked it. But the next day, one official who was up for reelection objected to a video condom display and decided that schools should not be allowed to send students to see the show. In a panic, the museum director called ASTC and the AIDS Library, both of which suggested calling the media. The local newspaper ran the story on the front page. There was so much protest from the community over the official's comment that every middle school and high school class was required to see the exhibit and take a minicourse on how the immune system works.

Was It Worth It?

More than 40 museums have hosted *What about AIDS?* and their reports show that they all felt it was a lot of work, but worthwhile. Why? Although no one likes to deal with stress and hard work as a daily diet, it is invigorating to do something you really believe in. We saw people using an exhibit to deal with tough issues in their lives. The work we did brought museum departments together and made us develop new ways of working on all exhibits. We reached out to our community in ways we hadn't before. And we found new strength in ourselves—new ways to compromise and deal with anger without losing our own point of view.

Journal of Museum Education 23, no. 3 (1998): 18–20.

Crafting Community-Based Museum Experiences: Process, Pedagogy, and Performance

Kathryn E. Wilson

Communities are increasingly on the minds of museum professionals.[1] Likewise since the 1960s, folklorists who work with communities have an ever-increasing role to play in the creation of public culture in museums, festivals, and heritage preservation.[2] I am one such folklorist, currently at the Balch Institute for Ethnic Studies, a multicultural museum and library in Philadelphia devoted to exploring the American ethnic experience. Like many other folklorists who work in museums, I present diverse cultural traditions and community histories to a wider public. In this role I have been involved in exhibition planning and have served as an advocate for the inclusion of community involvement at all stages of project development. In the capacity of public programming coordinator, I have designed public education programs exploring the history and experience of local ethnic communities and involving community members in presentations. I also direct outreach and field research efforts undertaken with new immigrant communities in the greater Philadelphia area.

Reflecting on how folkloristics inform my work in the museum context, I discuss in this essay areas in which museums can collaborate with local communities to shape how groups are represented in museum programming and increase community involvement in the museum as a whole. In particular, I outline three overlapping areas of application for folklore theory and method in museum contexts: a process for incorporating community perspectives into multiple areas of museum work, a pedagogy for promoting learning in informal settings, and a social frame (performance) that instigates discussion and reflection. While these ideas have been very helpful to me in my work, they are not without tensions, so I will reflect on the unique challenges that such approaches present as well.

Folklore as Process: Ethnography and Reciprocity

The primary contribution folklore can make to the production of museum experience is that of methods for community collaboration and outreach. Folklore as a field is primarily concerned with the exploration of "vernacular" or "folk" culture, or the cultural patterns that emerge from the localized practice of everyday life in communities, ethnic groups, or geographic regions. Working with a research methodology known as ethnography, through interview and participant observation, folklorists try to understand a community on its own terms through these patterns of everyday life. In conducting their research, folklorists work through informal social networks. They attend community events, visit families, and converse with individuals. They taste new foods and try new dance steps. They watch and listen carefully for expressions or interactions in a community that seem heightened or more important to the participants because they are artful, meaningful, or contested, such as rituals and festivals, performances (stories, jokes, music, dances), gestures, and greetings. Most important, they try to establish rapport and trust and generate their scholarly interpretation in dialogue with members of the community. This act of interpretation is fundamentally multivocal as the ethnographer moves back and forth between the vernacular perspectives of her field consultants and her own, negotiating meanings and content at every turn. It requires that the researcher examine her own culturally and socially shaped position and reflect back on herself in relation to her field con-

---

Mechanisms for community input must be an integral part of the project design, from initial planning to final evaluation.

---

sultants, to understand how her own assumptions and identity shape the interpretation of field encounters. This back-and-forth approach is known as "reflexivity," and it is an important value for contemporary folklorists.[3]

Thus ethnography is collaborative and reciprocal in nature. The implications for museum outreach are clear. To incorporate community residents, histories, and cultures in museum representations means not only inviting the community in as an audience for programs, as much of museum programming currently does under the rubric of "outreach." It also entails going out to a community to learn more before planning, with the community's input, new programs that can represent their experiences and meet their social or cultural needs. In many cases, this process necessitates hiring fieldworkers with ethnographic training (and in some cases language skills or cultural knowledge) who can investigate a community in depth and establish relationships with key contacts. These outreach workers should act as liaisons to the community and work in conjunction with a full-time permanent staff member who can provide long-term institutional continuity. They should be integrally involved in planning, meeting regularly with the museum and education staff to provide information and guidance on the preparation of exhibition and educational materials.

This kind of community collaboration often entails working outside normal museum procedures. Mechanisms for community input must be an integral part of the project design from initial planning to final evaluation. Community advisory committees can be organized to advise curators and educators on an ongoing basis. These committees should not just be brought in to "rubber-stamp" completed work but rather should have input into and the opportunity to review all representations produced by the museum to ensure accuracy and the community's comfort level. Often project timelines must be adjusted to allow more time and space for discussion and review when communities are consulted. For example, when the Balch undertook a project with Asian Indian Americans in 1997, conversations with the advisory committee continued for almost a year before any field research began. These conversations gave community representatives space to share and reflect and helped both the staff and the community map out what themes an exhibition might explore. This process does not mean that the museum cedes control completely to the community. Rather, museum professionals must honestly demystify the process and negotiate with community representatives the content, format, and scope of presentations within the given conventions of museum representation and the institution's resources.

These interactions require sensitivity to the power dynamics between an institution and a community, particularly when dealing with marginalized groups or organizations with fewer resources. Likewise, assumptions of community homogeneity must be avoided, as a community may have many inner divisions of class, sexuality, age, gender, religion, and political ideology. Such divisions complicate outreach logistics and the politics of community representation. For example, gender has presented challenges in a current Balch project under way with Arab Americans in Philadelphia. Many of the men in the largely conservative Muslim Palestinian community are uncomfortable with the idea of their female relatives attending mixed-gender events in a downtown public space. One woman who was otherwise very active in the community was prohibited by her husband from serving on the community advisory committee for the project. She is still involved in a behind-the-scenes way, as we seek her advice informally in her own home. Even now it is uncertain how much of these women's experience we will be able to show in the final exhibition and programming without alienating some of our friends in the community. We will design additional programs that can reach this community in a way that makes cultural sense to them: the exhibition will travel to a community center in the neighborhood where women may attend, and we will host at least one program event for women only. While these measures may not fully incorporate these women into the project (just as they will not represent more controversial aspects of the community), they will involve them in the project and allow them to be a part of the museum's activities and representations.

Working in nonstandard channels is one of many important ways to embody folklorists' ethical sense of reciprocity—a way of "returning the favor" when people offer their time, arts, ideas, and lives. Recognizing that communities make an invaluable contribution to the museum's reputation and resources, a museum must help meet any community needs it can satisfy. Exhibitions can be designed to be remounted in neighborhood sites, and educational programs can be offered at community centers or schools, reaching many who would never come to the museum. In-kind services, such as free admission or tours to youth and senior groups, use of museum space for events, donations of equipment to organizations, technical assistance for projects or artists, and publicity for a community organization's efforts, are just a few of the ways that museums can give back to a community with which it has collaborated. It is essential that museums see themselves in an ongoing relationship with communities and continue to involve community people in long-term planning after a specific exhibition or program project has been completed.[4]

Folklore as Pedagogy: Learning in Informal Settings

Collaborations with communities also represent unique opportunities to address current concerns in the field of museum education, particularly about interactive learning.[5] In vernacular settings, individuals learn in the context of a community and its values, through interactions with others. They grow up watching performances and learn through hands-on practice with the opportunity to ask questions. Commentary on skill or meaning takes the form of conversation, storytelling, or humor. When I was a child, for instance, my mother taught me to bake, demonstrating the tricks her mother had taught her and letting me try my hand with her guidance. This learning took place primarily during special family occasions, when she also shared reminiscences of my grandmother. If my efforts ended badly, my father teased me and boasted of his own mother's skill in the kitchen. Thus I learned not only baking skills but also the rich cultural and familial contexts of these recipes and the meanings they had for others (especially women) in my family. These inherently pedagogical aspects of everyday life can be adapted to education programs that create spaces for self-representation and allow community members to teach interactively. Drawing on visitors' vernacular understandings, they can also mediate among different understandings of history, culture, or identity, promoting dialogue among cultural worldviews.

Vernacular culture can instigate informal learning processes in programs that feature folk "experts" and abundant space for conversation and hands-on activities. When drawing on community people as presenters (particularly nonprofessionals), staff must adequately prepare them for their presentation, since they may or may not be comfortable with the milieu of the museum. Dialogue between the museum programmer and presenter must cover the content and the context of the event, making expectations clear. Failure to do so risks leaving some participants alienated, embarrassed, or just plain confused about what they are doing.[6] Museum staff must acknowledge their own expertise and need for control even as they acknowledge folk expertise and attempt to offer control to the presenter or visitor. Reflexively recognizing their own role allows educators to craft explanatory elements that can be incorporated into natural pauses or breaks in a performance or demonstration. Mini-interviews with presenters during demonstrations or after performances are a good way for educators to interject into and frame the proceedings while still allowing ample space for a community presenter's voice and self-representation.[7]

This framing is key since even the most accurate or straightforward presentation of an ethnic or folk cultural form can collapse into problematic misunderstanding when visitors try to make sense of a presentation in terms of their own cultural resources, which may include stereotypes or bias. The need to connect with visitor's cultural worldviews while also broadening them raises questions of authority and heightens tensions between the poles of education and representation in community-based programs. Who has the right to speak, particularly when the educational program is aimed at presenting cultural knowledge that is often misunderstood or marginalized (such as that of ethnic minority or new immigrant groups)?

Museum programs need to present information in identifiable communicative forms while also understanding and engaging the more latent or naturalized assumptions that visitors (who are also part of folk cultures) bring with them as part of their everyday way of seeing and interpreting the world.[8] This lesson was brought home in a recent Balch program exploring *bhangra*, a South Asian diasporic music (incorporating elements of rap, reggae, house, and Punjabi folk) through which second-generation youth articulate intergenerational conflict, protesting traditional Indian customs (such as arranged marriage) and American racism. A screening of the film *The Bhangra Wrap* was attended by a diverse audience including a contingent of African

Americans, some of whom resisted validating this South Asian cultural form because it appropriates elements of their own vernacular culture. The conversation following the film had ground to a standstill when one older African American man asked the provocative question, "Am I the only person who thinks this is a bad imitation of rap?" This question stimulated the audience into an additional half-hour of discussion on issues of race and cultural ownership. These visitors were making sense of *bhangra* within their own esthetic and cultural understandings. What they could see was that *bhangra* was like rap (that likeness had drawn them to the event in the first place), but in ways that were crucial to their understanding of the art form, it was not like rap at all. They sought to conserve their own knowledge and validate their own vernacular culture, informed by the complex dynamics of race in America. Importantly, the museum programmer allowed space for this conversation to happen in a way that several vernacular perspectives were simultaneously validated and challenged in relation to one another.

Folklore as Performance: Social Frames for Representation and Reflection

Performances such as drama, narrative, and music can stimulate dialogue by moving visitors to think, feel, and experience in new ways. According to folklorist Richard Bauman, performance is a heightened mode of communication that binds performer and audience together.[9] Most performances contain formal features that signal to the audience that a performance is happening, shaping their expectations for meaning and artfulness. In theater, for example, the presence of a stage, curtain, and scenery create this expectation, known as a "performance frame." In vernacular contexts this performance frame is created more informally. For example, one might begin telling a story with the phrase, "once upon a time," a verbal cue that "frames" the performance by communicating to listeners that the speaker is taking responsibility for communicating something esthetically and socially meaningful—a story. A performance also emerges from a specific social context and often reflects back on that context (like the social setting in which the story is being told, for example). Thus a performance sets up a "reflexive arena," in which individuals enter an ongoing stream of cultural discourse that is actively interpretive, addressing social issues or expressing coded feelings.[10]

Creating a reflexive arena in the museum context can have rich educational results when a multilayered discourse is allowed to emerge across genres within a given program presentation. Utilizing this approach in the public programs accompanying the Balch Institute's 1999 exhibition on the Indian immigrant experience allowed for some intriguing emergences of discourse and display. For example, one program featured South Asian performance artist Mohan Sikka, whose work centers on personal memories "retold as bio-mythography." The formal performance pieces (which incorporated story-telling and the enactment of multiple personas from the artist's life) were followed by a discussion segment in which Sikka was briefly interviewed and then conversed with audience members. This segment marked a shift from formal dramatic performance into other communicative genres, such as interview, anecdote, and conversation, in which Sikka told interrelated personal stories and visitors made explicit connections with their own cultural narratives. The discussion segment constituted another performative frame, a social space in which audience, performer, and museum educator interactively discussed changing life course after immigration, coming out as a gay man, disappointing one's parents, and whether an ethnic artist's work must address his or her ethnicity. The discussion itself became a kind of commentary on the nature of identity, questioning the very identity politics on which the program series and exhibition was predicated. Audience evaluations of the program suggest that Sikka's narratives clearly reached audience members within and across cultural boundaries. One young South Asian women identified with his questioning of family expectations, commenting, "Like Mohan I was not permitted to have distractions such as career choices deviating from engineering, business, medicine. . . . It was nice for me to see someone going beyond . . . family expectations so publicly." One visitor learned "a greater understanding of Indian friends and the struggles they experience, of how my culture is similar to others," while another emphasized the universality of Sikka's narrative, taking away "a sense of the sensitivity we all share in divulging to our parents an insight that will disappoint them." These remarks illustrate that visitors identified with the anecdotes related in the discussion segment as well as with the formal performance. The broad appeal of the family story genre resonated with the audience members' experiences while stimulating them to think beyond their own cultural worldview to the unique nature of the South Asian immigrant experience.

Recognizing that performance is a reflexive arena allows educators to draw on some of a presentation's metacommunicative messages—that is, the informal ways in which participants describe, evaluate, and interpret the nature of communicative events. The program setting itself becomes a multivocal, performative frame in which stories and jokes are related, meanings communicated, and social relationships negotiated and (re)created. The aim of this kind of educational program is to evolve from a didactic presentation to the creation of a richly layered visual, verbal, and material context—an experience in which performative behaviors can emerge not only from official presenters but from visitors as well. Family folklore and oral history represent some promising areas for such exploration.[11]

Just as performances encourage reflexivity from visitors and presenters, they can also encourage museum professionals to thoughtfully examine their own positions in relation to various communities, histories, cultures, and identities. Who is creating representations of communities being produced by the museum? To what end? As museums become more entrepreneurial in the multicultural marketplace, co-optation and commodification of ethnic and other folk communities by dominant cultural institutions are still a real danger. Working in reflexive dialogue and actively conversing with communities may help mitigate against the way in which "official" representations of difference in the public culture tend to reinforce dominant social relationships or hierarchies.[12] Collaborating and empowering communities mean including them at all levels of the museum structure, not just as subjects for ethnographic inquiry. They can play ongoing and valuable roles as volunteers, docents, or board members, to name a few possibilities.

Community collaborations will likely entail a shift in the structure and expectations of museum programs that may be out of the control of staff members at a time when nonprofit boards and administrators are interested in increasing visitor volume and earned income. Sincere, long-term collaboration with communities may seem initially threatening to those whose professional identity is invested in interpretive or financial control over a museum's programs. Obviously the impact of folkloristic thinking remains to be seen when an educator's mandate is to shepherd 150 schoolchildren through the museum. What is clear is that going outside the museum walls, inviting newcomers in, and opening up to the interpretive power of vernacular discourses can transform museums and communities so that both may flourish.

Journal of Museum Education 24, no. 3 (Fall 1999): 3–6.

Notes

1. Ivan Karp, Christine Mullen Kreamer, and Steven D. Lavine, eds., *Museums and Communities: The Politics of Public Culture* (Washington, D.C.: Smithsonian Institution Press, 1992).

2. Patricia Hall and Charlie Seemann, eds., *Folklife and Museums: Selected Readings* (Nashville, Tenn.: American Association for State and Local History, 1987); Robert Baron and Nicholas Spitzer, eds., *Public Folklore* (Washington, D.C.: Smithsonian Institution Press, 1992); Burt Feintuch, ed., *The Conservation of Culture* (Lexington: University of Kentucky Press, 1989).

3. Elaine Lawless, " 'I was afraid someone like you . . . an outsider . . . would misunderstand': Negotiating Interpretive Differences Between Ethnographers and Subjects," *Journal of American Folklore* 105, no. 471 (1992): 302–14.

4. Robert Baron, "Folklife and the American Museum," in *Folklife and Museums*, ed. Hall

and Seemann, pp. 12–26; John Kuo Wei Tchen, "Creating a Dialogic Museum: The Chinatown History Museum Experiment," in *Museums and Communities*, ed. Karp, Kreamer, and Lavine, pp. 285–327.

5. Constance Perin, "The Communicative Circle: Museums as Communities," in *Museums and Communities*, ed. Karp, Kreamer, and Lavine, pp. 182–221; Susan Sternberg, "The Art of Participation," in *Museum Education: History, Theory and Practice*, ed. Nancy Berry and Susan Meyer (Reston, Va.: National Art Education Association, 1989), pp. 154–71; Lisa Roberts, *From Knowledge to Narrative: Educators and the Changing Museum* (Washington, D.C.: Smithsonian Institution Press, 1997).

6. Richard Bauman and Patricia Sawin, "The Politics of Participation in Folklife Festivals," in *Exhibiting Cultures: The Poetics and Politics of Museum Display*, ed. Ivan Karp and Steven D. Lavine (Washington, D.C.: Smithsonian Institution Press, 1991), pp. 288–314.

7. Charlie Seemann, "Presenting the Live Folk Artist in the Museum," in *Folklife and Museums*, ed. Hall and Seemann, pp. 59–66; Nicholas Spitzer, "Cultural Conversation: Metaphors and Methods in Public Folklore," in *Public Folklore*, ed. Baron and Spitzer, pp. 77–104.

8. See Barre Toelken, *The Dynamics of Folklore* (Boston: Houghton Mifflin, 1979), for a discussion of folklore and cultural worldview.

9. Richard Bauman, *Verbal Art as Performance* (Prospect Heights, Ill.: Waveland Press, 1977).

10. Richard Bauman and Charles Briggs, "Poetics and Performance as Cultural Perspectives on Language and Social Life," *Annual Review of Anthropology* 19 (1990): 59–88; Charles Briggs, *Competence in Performance: The Creativity of Tradition in Mexicano Verbal Art* (Philadelphia: University of Pennsylvania Press, 1988); Lila Abu-Lughod, *Veiled Sentiments: Honor and Poetry in a Bedouin Society* (Berkeley: University of California Press, 1986).

11. Steven Zeitlin, Amy Kotlin, and Holly Cutter Baker, eds., *A Celebration of American Family Folklore* (New York: Pantheon, 1982).

12. Shalom Staub, "Folklore and Authenticity: A Myopic Marriage in Public Sector Folklore," in *Conservation of Culture*, ed. Feintuch, pp. 166–79.

Further Reading

Schensul, Jean J., and Margaret D.LeCompte. *The Ethnographer's Toolkit*. Walnut Creek, Calif.: AltaMira Press, 1999.

Practice

One Museum Discovers the Web

Larissa B. Fawkner

It was by a circuitous route of surfing radio waves that the idea to bring the Internet to our museum came about. The Discovery Creek Children's Museum of Washington, D.C., had been operating for just a year when I was invited to preview a science radio show for children. When the show's director told me what his annual operating budget was, I was stunned. I had him repeat the figures to make sure I had understood him correctly. His show had been on the air for a year, and he had a $2 million budget. My museum had been open for a year, and we were rationing the pennies from our piggy bank. It seemed obvious that one of the main reasons the radio show could secure that kind of funding was that it could reach the masses. Reaching the masses might not be a problem for our neighbor, the Smithsonian Institution, but Discovery Creek is off the beaten path in a historic one-room schoolhouse, with about 1,200 square feet of internal space and an education staff of three. Nevertheless, with unyielding energy and a schedule packed with school and weekend programs that took advantage of our 12-acre woodland site, we had managed to see 10,000 visitors during our first year. I felt that by going online, we could reach even more children. This possibility sparked the fire that would bring the World Wide Web to the museum and, I believed, the museum to the world.

I told anyone who would listen about my plan to create a "virtual" Discovery Creek. Of course, there were some minor obstacles: I'd never been online before, had no idea what the World Wide Web was, and didn't have access to a computer. I learned about the Web by visiting a trendy techno-cappuccino shop in Boston, where one could get doubly wired by drinking coffee and renting computer time to surf the Web. I also researched online education projects by subscribing to *MultiMedia Schools*, a magazine about education and multimedia technology.

Although I was all fired up and ready to go, there was some hesitation at first on the museum's side. The board of directors had legitimate concerns about incorporating the Internet into the museum's educational programming—issues relating not only to children and access to unwanted information, but philosophical questions about the museum's mission to help children learn about stewardship of the environment by hiking our nature trails and seeing, hearing, and touching the *real* world, not some technological reproduction. So while my idea of a virtual museum may have not been the direction our new museum wanted to pursue, I still felt it was possible to bring technology into our programming without compromising children's direct experience with nature. We all agreed to experiment with using the Internet.

We planned our first experiment for the Salamander and Snake Sense summer nature camp, in which children identify and distinguish reptiles and amphibians by observing their physical characteristics and adaptations. At a series of hands-on animal stations, they compare the habits and diets of a live salamander and lizard, touch a snake's scales, and learn about turtles and tortoises. Then they hike down our nature trails and search for real reptiles and amphibians that live in the woodland habitat next to the museum.

One of our educators had heard about an online virtual frog dissection site for high school and college biology students, developed by the University of Virginia (http://curry.edschool.virginia.edu/go/frog/). The site seemed

---

We've started to build a foundation locally by using the World Wide Web as a resource that empowers children, teachers, and even our staff to learn about and find their role in the global community.

---

to be a perfect addition to our summer program. It was scientifically accurate, involved no loss of animal life, and let kids be "scientists" as they constructed and dissected a virtual frog, organ by organ. After establishing Internet access through a temporary account with America Online, we set up the virtual frog station. It was extremely popular with the students. I knew there were other useful environmental science–related activities on the Web. I thought that our small education staff—who served as both educators and content specialists and never had enough hours in the day—could use the Internet to research and develop education programs.

The prospects were promising, but we needed Internet access through a provider that could meet the needs of a small museum with limited resources. I called WETA/CapAccess, a new local community network that uses public television and radio, as well as telecommunication and technology, to connect people and information across the metropolitan Washington, D.C., region. The director of online services agreed to give the museum free, unlimited access to the World Wide Web and develop the museum's first home page,

One Museum Discovers the Web

www.discoverycreek.org. This partnership enabled us to launch our second experiment: incorporating the Journey North project into our programming. Funded in part by the Annenberg/CPB Math and Science Project, Journey North, www.learner.org/jnorth, enables students throughout North America to track wildlife migration and spring's journey across the continent. It seemed a natural fit because our goal is to provide hands-on experiences for students studying the environmental sciences, and Journey North offered many opportunities for students to practice observing nature and collecting scientific data. For example, students could monitor the migration of the monarch butterfly, the humpback whale, and the Canadian goose and predict the arrival of spring through animal sightings in their hometown. Then they could report and exchange information among classrooms via the Internet.

Since humpback whales don't migrate down the Potomac, I wanted to select an environmental factor that urban students of Washington could see. Tracking the emergence of spring by observing tulip growth, a Journey North offering, seemed to be an ideal addition to the museum's existing Green Thumbs school program, a botany class that focuses on the anatomy and life cycle of flowers. So I set out to create a horticulture project that would enhance Green Thumbs and complement the elementary science curriculum of the D.C. public schools. I called the program Tracking Tulips.

Why would a museum of our size put so much effort into the local schools? Unlike many larger museums, which emphasize exhibits and visitation by the general public, Discovery Creek is program based, and most of our visitors are school groups. Our programs take an interdisciplinary approach to environmental science. With advanced teacher training, we can offer teachers activities and curriculum materials that they can use to integrate nature with social studies, literature, math, geography, and technology back in the classroom. When the students visit the museum, our educators can concentrate on hands-on outdoor environmental science. Although this approach is more labor intensive up front, the students generally arrive at the museum better prepared to learn and with a strong foundation of knowledge.

While the Tracking Tulips program had much promise, I knew it would not be easy to carry out. The District of Columbia was in financial difficulty. Most schools didn't have the basic materials and background knowledge they needed to participate—tulip bulbs, planters, soil thermometers, gardening knowledge, dedicated phone lines, multimedia hardware, software, an Internet provider, and more. They had just started wiring the elementary schools for access, so few teachers had ever experienced the Internet. I wrote proposals to get the tulips and related materials donated, and WETA/CapAccess came to the rescue with the technology. With its technical support, the 10 schools participating in the project received wiring, software, and free Internet access.

The hardest part was yet to come: training the teachers to implement the horticulture program and use the computer technology. We literally started from the ground up, showing them how to plant a tulip bulb, how to use a computer mouse, and how to search the World Wide Web for information. While the training was well attended, the success of the program depended on each teacher's willingness to change the curriculum and incorporate Internet resources into daily lesson plans. It takes time, motivation, and an openness to risk to try a different approach to teaching and accept a new, more participatory way of student learning.

By the end of the 10-month Internet experiment, we could boast of several very successful class projects. Others, however, never fully bloomed. A formal evaluation is in progress. Informally, success is evident in the number of teachers who called to tell me they had moved beyond my basic training and were busy in their classrooms involving students in new activities, such as measuring air temperatures, exchanging that information via electronic mail with students across the country, and using the daily temperatures reported from other regions in the morning's geography lesson. However, teachers need more assistance in using the World Wide Web to find information and related resources, so I continue to work in partnership with WETA/CapAccess to train D.C. teachers. In addition, multimedia hardware must be readily available in the schools. Internet technology can't be effective if a school has only one computer with Internet access and it is tucked in a corner of the library several floors away from the classroom.

Considering our initial philosophical questions, the museum has pronounced the Internet experiment a success. We have decided to continue incorporating existing online educational sites into our hands-on environmental programming, move ahead with developing our home page, and establish partnerships with organizations that have parallel missions and multimedia expertise. For example, this fall we are considering the Globe program, www.globe.gov. In this international Internet project, student scientists study the atmosphere, climate, hydrology, biology, and geology near their schools and collect environmental data such as air temperature, precipitation, clouds, surface water temperature, and soil moisture. They use a global positioning system satellite receiver to determine their school's location, record data outside, and then send the results over the Internet to a processing center to compare their data with data obtained from satellite images of earth. Students can also compare findings from other Globe class sites around the world. The information collected from all of the sites will be used in real scientists' research to create maps of the earth's environment. Access to the Globe program will be provided through the museum's partnership with WETA/CapAccess.

Since the museum doesn't yet have the resources to develop fully interactive computer activities on its own home page, we have formed a partnership with Conservation International (CI). CI supports the study of wildlife, indigenous cultures and complex environmental problems, and scientific, economic, policy, and community solutions facing rainforests and other fragile biosystems. Working with CI staff, Discovery Creek will develop a page on the CI Web site, www.conservation.org, that will give children the opportunity to discover global ecosystems. The page will contain interactive lessons, educational games, and virtual reality eco-expeditions. For example, children may take a virtual walk on the Macaw Trail, a bridge suspended in the rainforest canopy. There, more than 100 feet above the forest floor, they may learn how monkeys in the rainforest help make chocolate or how using a rainforest tagua nut to make jewelry can save an endangered elephant.

While Discovery Creek may not have yet reached the world, we've started to build a foundation locally by using the World Wide Web as a resource that empowers children, teachers, and even our staff to learn about and find their role in the global community. We don't expect the virtual experience of the Internet to replace us as environmental educators, but instead we continue to look for innovative ways it can support what we do. Although we might think of ourselves as teachers embracing this new form of technology, in the field of museum education, we're the Internet pioneers as well as the students. So set a shiny red apple on the keyboard and get ready to surf.

Journal of Museum Education 22, no. 1 (Winter 1997): 12–14.

REFLECTIONS

Soon after this article was published, Discovery Creek Children's Museum experienced a lag in updating its internal technology to catch up with that of the project. Like other small museums, we had too few personnel to maintain a Web site.

More recently, we worked with a design company (funding permitting) on a three-phase project to establish a Web site that parallels our museum's physical site. We thought of the Web site as if we were opening another museum, complete with staffing implications, programming philosophy and goals, and funding initiatives. It would incorporate critical thinking activities encouraging children to examine and investigate the natural world surrounding them.

Here's where the problems emerged. Some board members doubted that Discovery Creek could be accurately represented in cyberspace. After all, we are a museum that prides itself on "low technology." How could you simulate the experience of being outdoors—touching the bark of a 400-year-old tree, climbing into the secret crevice in the "bear tree," or picking just the right stone to step on as you cross the creek? How could these experiences be replicated on a Web site? Should they be?

These were all questions that we asked ourselves as we thought this project through. We now view the Web site activities as a means to encourage outdoor investigation and play. As we develop the activities, we will aim to stimulate children's excitement about getting outside and to give at least some experience of the outdoors to those who do not have access to the forest.

—*Jacqueline Eyl, Director of Education, Discovery Creek Children's Museum.*

The Eye of the Beholder

Janet A. Kamien

It has been almost 15 years since *Endings: An Exhibit about Death and Loss* appeared at the Boston Children's Museum, and it seems that I've been talking about it ever since, though far more controversial exhibits have shown up since then. That means either that I'm a sucker for writing when asked or that the environment at the Children's Museum remains an exemplar for the kind of experimentation and risk taking that controversial topics demand. Or, maybe the later explosions have simply highlighted the issues we must grapple with when considering provocative subject matter. In any case, in this article, I'll try to outline the four potential problem stages in doing such exhibits—involving staff, sponsors and funders, outside stakeholders, and finally visitors—and then describe how each of these played out in the single example of *Endings*.

Initial Debate

Generally, internal misgiving is the first hurdle a controversial project must jump. Many ideas don't make it. It's easy to see why. Every institution has to find funding, please a board, serve up work in an equitable way among staff, and worry about the gate. Few institutions have mission statements that outrightly encourage the kind of experimentation that difficult subject matter demands. It's only when there exists some unanimity of belief about the importance of a topic, and some passion on the part of its internal promoters, that an overtly provocative project can get under way. The societal importance of AIDS education can override internal fears. The necessity of conservation messages to the core ideology of an institution can create an environment in which the pointed tackling of oil spills and industrial waste is possible. If this kind of internal agreement is not present at the outset of a project, it's probably not worth starting in the first place.

The more insidious problem is the possible dilution of the message during the development process. We may all agree that AIDS education is imperative for teenagers, but how graphic are we going to be about the means of its transmission? Are we going to make sure that our teaching device actually works for the intended audience? These issues are, of course, where the rubber meets the road, and our best and bravest intentions may fail us. Clarity of purpose and real evaluation of results are the only defense. And this defense must be used in the most politic of ways. Polarization can be death.

Sponsors and Funders

When administrators sound the death knell on a topic or an approach to a topic, it's often funders that they have in mind. How will it look to our car company corporate sponsor if we make a big deal about automobile emissions in our new transportation exhibit? What will the conservative board member say about a sex education exhibit? How will the city feel about our political history exhibit? What will state funders do if they see our name in the headlines because of a provocative piece of art or an ethnic hot button somehow pushed? There's a lot to protect, and it's a dirty job, but somebody has to do it. And people—mostly directors—have lost their jobs over such things.

The irony is that the sponsor or funder of an exhibition is sometimes the very element that creates controversy. Can an exhibit funded by an extermination company be telling us the truth about insects? How is it possible that a women's sporting event can be funded by a cigarette manufacturer? And when

---

We stood firm and finally found a small state-level funder who was not only unafraid but excited by our straightforward approach. This had taken about five years.

---

federal funding is involved, things can get even more complicated. The Mapplethorpe and *Enola Gay* exhibits would not have aroused half the controversy they did had they been privately funded and displayed. It was the very idea that citizens' tax dollars were being used that allowed so much pressure to come to bear.

Outside Stakeholders

Without provocation and publicity, none of the issues mentioned above are likely to amount to anything, but with provocation and publicity, the mildest exhibits can find themselves in difficult straits. Perhaps the institution has overlooked potential stakeholders. This problem may result from "ivory towerism," lack of homework, or just plain denial, or the controversy may arise from a source so unlikely that prediction is impossible. (I once heard about a big natural history museum doing the definitive human evolution exhibit and prepared for the creationists at the gate, only to discover that an anti-apartheid group had arrived to picket because a skull in the exhibit had its origins in South Africa.) When institutions don't know what's coming, they can't engage potential stakeholders before the fact, and they can't prepare their staff, their visitors, or themselves for the controversy that may follow. They are blindsided.

Potential publicity may be even harder to handle, but the same rules apply. Homework to uncover possible problems can clarify the institution's reasons for attacking the issue in the first place, so staff can be prepared to address the press with unity, logic, and a collective cool head.

There is, of course, also the theory that all publicity is good publicity. While probably true, it's only in retrospect that this adage can be appreciated, and not when the director is on the phone with a city council member who's just read the morning paper.

The Visitor

Oftentimes the formless fears of picketers, bad press, and rampaging funders are not invoked to reject or dilute an exhibit. It sounds too paranoid. Rather, staff too often call up a Dickensian version of "The Visitor"—who will presumably be offended—to buttress a particular point of view and is not present to agree or disagree. There are two things to note. The first is that visitors are far and away the easiest group to take the temperature of, as the exhibit developer can simply go out onto the floor and ask them. Naturally, asking questions is best done throughout the process by an accomplished interviewer with sophisticated instruments. But, at the outset of a project, there is no reason on earth not to ask 25 or so visitors what their take would be on the institution's doing an exhibit about AIDS prevention, human evolution, nuclear waste disposal, or live whales. It's amazing what one can learn. Of course it's also useful to talk to colleagues who have attempted such topics before, and, if the exhibit topic goes on to the development stage, to bring together an advisory committee representing various points of view to address issues as they arise.

The second thing to note is that an interesting and well-made exhibit that has taken into consideration the possibility of opposing points of view (even if it doesn't subscribe to them) is unlikely to be the butt of a debilitating controversy. Visitors are not stupid, and they have, after all, selected your museum and this exhibit to see though they had many, many other choices.

The Example of Endings

Endings: An Exhibit about Death and Loss was first proposed many years before its implementation by a natural history developer who was dying of cancer. Through her museum teaching experience and now her very personal experience, she had come to believe that the difficult subject of death was very much worth exploring for both children—who were extremely interested in it—and for adults, who had the hard job of trying to explain something to kids that was also difficult for them. This gifted teacher died before the exhibit could be funded, but the idea stuck, partly in memory of her and her passion to do the exhibit but also because it rang true to the rest of us: we believed we were an organization whose job it was to create communication about subjects that were important to children and parents. So internally, the first hurdle had been jumped without much ado. However, the interesting issues of dilution were still before us.

These issues arose first in our board. One member in particular was dead set against the exhibit and did everything in her power to first prevent it and, when that failed, to dilute it. Her suggestion was to incorporate the subject matter into other exhibits. The Japanese Home would celebrate O-Bon every August, the natural history exhibit would contain labels among the mounted specimens that addressed the confusion many younger kids express about the "realness" of "stuffed" animals. This is the point at which the exhibit might have vanished had not equally passionate voices both on the board and on the staff come to its rescue.

Funding this exhibit was not easy either. The topic was often picked out from our wish list for discussion on trips to agencies and foundations, but rarely seriously considered. When we were finally invited to submit it to a federal agency, the proposal never went to review after the agency staff read it. They called in a panic explaining they hadn't realized that our proposal about death and grieving was actually about death and grieving! They suggested we resubmit a version that took a more "anthropological" view—death among the Victorians, or tribal peoples in Amazonia for instance. We stood firm and finally found a small state-level funder who was not only unafraid but excited by our straightforward approach. This had taken about five years.

In the meantime, we were out on the floor talking to the public. I would go to the pet store and collect dead goldfish or set up a table when one of our turtles or guinea pigs died and simply talk to children and adults. This is what I learned: First, everyone, almost without exception, wanted to engage over this subject—asking questions, telling stories, showing their children, touching something that is dead. Second, no adult, almost without exception, wanted to be surprised by the subject matter, and I soon learned to announce that "I have some live animals here and some dead animals here." (Visitors of all ages flocked to the table. However, if I neglected this introduction, many adults were upset to discover after arrival that some of the animals were dead.) And finally, three-year-olds do not perceive that a goldfish is dead unless it is floating belly up in a fishbowl. (I think they think that if you take it off the paper towel and put it in water, it will be alive again.) This kind of experimentation and conversation convinced me that the exhibit was not only doable but important. It also gave me a well of experience with real visitors to draw on later both to develop the exhibit and to counter dilution attempts.

The advisory committee we formed was also an important part of the equation. The most useful members were those from the psychological community who had an even bigger well of experience in talking to real people around issues of death and grieving. Their assurances that one could straightforwardly broach the topic without in any way "uncorking" or damaging participants were a great source of strength. Other advisers included members of the educational, religious, and support group communities.

As development continued, almost everyone engaged in fearful behavior. It became clear to us that if every object that made someone uncomfortable were removed, there would be no exhibit left. What's most interesting is that the same object was rarely cited by more than one individual. Objects brought up for discussion included bottles of embalming fluid (fluid replaced with colored water), a time-lapse film from *Nova* of a decomposing mouse, a video that talked about death on TV (this was curtained off with a parental discretion sign), a dead frog, a casket (finally displayed opened, upright, and plexed over). You get the picture. Dismay (and a need for dilution) was in the eye of each individual beholder.

Of course, when we finally opened the exhibit, it felt like a whole experience and all the talk about this object or that object ceased. We did do two important things not previously mentioned. Remembering the early tryouts, we made the entrance distinct and set back, so that entering the exhibit would be a choice, and we put four different talk-back areas in the exhibit so that everyone had a chance to state an opinion. These were heavily used, and some visitors did want to tell us that they thought the exhibit was inappropriate in some way, but they mostly wrote to thank us or tell us a story of their own. There was one exception—a very small, but quite vocal contingent of people of fundamentalist Christian belief. They wrote nastily to tell us to read our Bibles to see that there was no such thing as death! (I think they were also upset by the exhibit's "secular humanist" stance: all major religions and afterlife beliefs—including that there was no afterlife—were represented in the exhibit.) We were blindsided by them. The rabbi-minister-priest contingent on the advisory council had never foreseen this objection, and neither had we.

Fortunately, the media were also blindsided. Not knowing exactly how to do public relations for this exhibit, we simply didn't. An AP editor came to the opening, however, and asked to write a blurb. We agreed. Six or eight paragraphs suddenly appeared in more than 70 newspapers all over the country. Local TV then showed up en masse, as did *Today* and *Nightline*. Except for

Nightline, most reporters did the kind of human interest story we were used to having. *Nightline* smelled a controversy and went for the jugular. The show sent a particularly nasty stringer to interview me and rattle me into admitting the exhibit was somehow dangerous for kids. (This made me angry but, fortunately, not stupid.) *Nightline* staff went to the psychological community in Boston (the very community most supportive of the exhibit!) to find someone to debate me on national TV. *Nightline* reporters interviewed visitors on-site—all of whom told them how much they enjoyed the exhibit! One grandfather even said he'd made a special trip with his grandkids as a way to broach the subject of his own nearing death. *Nightline* never found the fundamentalists. Thank God!

In the end, all publicity was good publicity, and while this exhibit was never a blockbuster, it did reasonably well for us. I like to think we followed the rules. We were clear and committed as an organization. We did our homework and stuck to the things we learned. We produced a good exhibit that offered room for many kinds of ideas and points of view. When the media came, we remained clear and kept our heads. But it was a risky business, and it wasn't easy. And some of it was just plain luck. Had *Nightline* located the fundamentalists, who knows if I'd be writing this now?

Journal of Museum Education 23, no. 3 (1998): 15–17.

Further Reading

Gyllenhall, E., Jeff Hayward, and Janet Kamien. "Voices of Doom." *Visitor Studies: Theory, Research and Practice* 8, no. 2 (1996).

Henderson, Amy, and Adrienne L. Kaeppler, eds. *Exhibiting Dilemmas*. Washington, D.C.: Smithsonian Institution Press, 1997.

Kamien, Janet. "Sensitive Issues for Children." *Hand to Hand* 4, nos.1 and 2 (Winter/Spring 1990).

REFLECTIONS

A very special blend of circumstances is necessary to take on a controversial subject. It may be easier to pull off the risky stuff in smaller institutions. There are simply fewer conflicting points of view floating around, and it's sometimes easier to bring a smaller group of people together into some kind of unity of effort. Yet it's not a confluence of circumstances that can necessarily be created through sheer willpower or passion. It's probably especially important for younger professionals to know that, so they won't feel defeated if things don't work out. We need to be able to keep our passions alive for the moment the chance arises.

—Janet A. Kamien

Toward Reconciliation: A Role for Museums in a Divided Society

Sheela Speers, Sally Montgomery, and Deirdre Brown

Schooling in Northern Ireland mirrors and to some extent reinforces the division in our society: Catholic and Protestant children are, for the most part, educated separately up to the age of 18 (16 if they opt to leave full-time education at the minimum legal age). There is, in effect, a dual system of public education. Both state "controlled" (largely Protestant) and Catholic "maintained" schools are government funded, enter pupils for the same public examinations, and are subject to performance appraisal by the Department of Education Inspectorate. The dual system is not discriminating—both "controlled" and "maintained" schools offer excellent educational opportunities and achieve high standards—but it is most certainly divisive. At best, separate schooling contributes to the development of feelings of social and cultural exclusivity, and at worst, when compounded by a multitude of alienating factors, it can significantly contribute to the development of a ghetto mentality. This effect is most pronounced in areas such as west Belfast, where social and economic deprivation, including catastrophic levels of unemployment suffered by both communities, intensifies inbred political and religious antagonisms.

In this divided society, museums offer an avenue for reconciliation. Northern Ireland's three major museums—the Ulster Museum, the Ulster Folk and Transport Museum, and the Ulster-American Folk Park—are national institutions, financed by the government through the Department of Education, Northern Ireland. Their education departments are closely involved in the development of services and resources to support new government initiatives designed to enhance educational opportunities and promote better community relations.

The Ulster Museum's Science Discovery Bus

The government's Making Belfast Work initiative hopes to improve educational opportunities and employment prospects in the most severely deprived areas of Belfast. Funding from this initiative has enabled the Ulster Museum in Belfast to convert a coach to provide a flexible, mobile, hands-on science education facility. The Science Discovery Bus uses the museum's resources to enrich science and technology programs in the schools and to raise the level of science awareness in parts of the city, both Catholic and Protestant, where children are exposed, daily, to the worst effects of "the Troubles."

The inside of the bus is a surprise, as the one-way glass gives no hint of the conversion. The smart cupboards, work tops, and seats, although highly functional, give a feeling of space and sophistication that the children react to with delight. "It's like going into a spaceship, Miss," was the enthusiastic response of one of Belfast's inner-city schoolchildren.

Once inside the bus, the children engage in a wide variety of activities. They carry out experiments and investigate natural history specimens, from dainty butterflies to a multitude of rocks and impressive fossils. They use computers to study the weather and microscopes to explore the fascinating landscape of their fingerprints. With objects of different colors, textures, shapes, and smells, children are encouraged to use all their senses. On some days the bus is full of excited five-year-olds clutching unfamiliar objects and shouting excitedly, "Miss, Miss, look!"

For older children, schools choose one of five themes that are directly

---

The Science Discovery Bus uses the museum's resources . . . to raise the level of science awareness in parts of the city, both Catholic and Protestant, where children are exposed, daily, to the worst effects of "the Troubles."

---

related to the Northern Ireland Science Curriculum. Each theme is explored through eight activities that combine the use of science equipment and museum specimens. As the children work through a circus of experiments and practical activities, they become scientists. In their enthusiasm to finish a task so that they can move on to the next one, they forget the artificial barriers of physics, chemistry, geology, and biology. They are unaware of time, and, for most, the two hours disappear too quickly. "Although it was the final week of term and concentration was at a low ebb, the pupils enjoyed themselves so much they didn't realize they were working," said one teacher. With so much excitement and interest, the most serious discipline problem to date has been the eating of chocolate brazil nuts in the "Rain Forest" display.

The themes draw upon museum resources to relate aspects of science to everyday life. Butterflies camouflaged to blend into their environment are as much a part of the light display as reflection and refraction.

"Materials" explores the properties of metals through electricity, magnetism, and ductility. Soft drink cans are used alongside bauxite specimens to

---

emphasize the importance of recycling. Children are amazed when they see bauxite. They cannot believe that this dark red dust can be the raw material of aluminum.

Beautiful tropical butterflies and extraordinary-looking beetles demonstrate the fascinating and varied wildlife of the "Rain Forest," whose riches also include strange fruit and spices. Many of these exotics, which we take for granted, are new to the children. They eagerly look forward to the tasting session. Occasionally this activity is interrupted by the crashing of weights, as the balsa wood breaks in their flexibility experiments.

"Earth in Space" and "Ourselves" are also popular displays. The children investigate these topics with an enthusiasm that inspires their teachers, who find themselves refreshed and delighted at their students' approaches. "A busy, worthwhile and enjoyable session and a great stimulus, not a single child was less than enthusiastic": this response by one teacher reflects the comments of many.

Last year the Science Discovery Bus provided science education programs for about 10,000 children and their teachers, and there is a waiting list for repeat visits. Currently, however, the staff are planning to extend the service to include children with special needs and parental support groups attached to the schools the bus visits. Parents will be able to preview the Science Discovery Bus experience, thus enhancing their own understanding of science and their capacity to help and encourage their children's educational development.

The Science Discovery Bus is one small element in the Making Belfast Work initiative, which funds major city regeneration projects and job-creation schemes. We cannot predict long-term outcomes, but we already know that the bus experience encourages children to feel valued. "The visit was like a little bit of the museum brought specially for us and we were allowed to touch!" was one response.

The Ulster Folk and Transport Museum's Educational Residential Centre

It is not unusual for children in Northern Ireland to grow to adulthood without meeting, much less forming friendships with, anyone from the "other" community. Separate schooling significantly reduces the opportunity to share the common experiences of childhood and adolescence and to develop understanding and respect for different points of view. Some parents have "voted with their feet." In the 1970s the All Children Together movement began to work for the establishment of integrated schools in which Catholic and Protestant children would be educated together and staff would be recruited from both communities. There are presently 21 integrated schools educating around 3,500 children, representing between 1 and 2 percent of the school-age population. Once operational, integrated schools are fully publicly funded. The movement for integrated schools is growing, but in the foreseeable future the vast majority of children will continue to be educated separately.

The introduction of a new curriculum for all schools in Northern Ireland, however, has provided an opportunity to incorporate a number of compulsory cross-curricular elements. Among them are Cultural Heritage and Education for Mutual Understanding. The aim of Cultural Heritage is to enable pupils "to know about, understand, and evaluate the shared, diverse, and distinctive aspects of their cultural heritage." Education for Mutual Understanding (EMU) aims "to enable pupils as an integral part of their education to learn to respect and value themselves and others and to appreciate the interdependence of people within society." As part of EMU, many schools have initiated cross-community contact programs. The Ulster Folk and Transport Museum is a popular venue for EMU activities.

The Ulster Folk Museum, amalgamated with the Belfast Transport Museum in 1967, was established by act of Parliament in 1958 to illustrate the way of life and the traditions of the people of Northern Ireland. From the beginning the museum, representing a common heritage of material culture and oral tradition, was seen as a symbol of unity in a divided but not as yet violent society. Following the outbreak of intercommunal violence in 1969, a small number of schools began to use the museum as the venue for cross-community work. This action, while valuable and enriching for those involved, was small-scale and unlikely to make much impact upon society. An opportunity to make a more meaningful contribution came in the late 1980s when the Department of Education made the decision to allocate significant resources to cross-community projects and when Education for Mutual Understanding and Cultural Heritage were designated as cross-curricular themes in the Northern Ireland Schools Curriculum. The increase in funding enabled the museum to build residential accommodations and greatly to expand its cross-community programs, and the curricular changes encouraged schools to make use of both.

The Educational Residential Centre at the Ulster Folk and Transport Museum consists of two self-contained blocks inside the facades of terraced houses in the reconstructed urban area of the museum. These provide accommodation for 64 children and 12 teachers. The first block opened in April 1990, the second in September 1991. Additional buildings, which will include space for drama and recreation, are almost complete. After a slow start, the residential center is now catering for about 8,000 "bed nights" a year. The majority of school visitors are in cross-community groups. Weekend users are almost entirely youth groups, many of them cross-community. The center has also been used by Co-operation North, a program that promotes contracts between schools and community groups in Northern Ireland and the Republic of Ireland.

Planning the program for each visit is the responsibility of the EMU officer (a post funded by the Department of Education, Northern Ireland), who also supervises the programs of schools making daily visits. While each program is tailored to the wishes of the teachers, who may want to relate activities to particular areas of the curriculum, most schools opt for a combination of practical crafts, farming, traditional games, and the study of transport. Many have 19th-century lessons in the schoolhouse and participate in courtroom drama in the courthouse. In the evening there is a choice of cultural activities, such as storytelling or traditional dancing. Most cross-community groups also choose to make patchwork wall hangings as a memento of their visit. Many groups bring period costumes to wear during these activities, which add to the fun and make nice photographs for their local newspapers.

The location of the residential center in the heart of the open-air museum, which is closed to the public in the evenings, adds an exciting dimension to the experience. Residents have the freedom of a 160-acre estate that includes some wooded parkland and re-creations of the rural landscapes of Ulster around the year 1900. The sheer size of the open spaces is in itself a source of wonder to children from inner-city schools. While museum staff provide most of the residential program, teachers are expected to take full responsibility for their pupils during their stay. They are also expected to ensure that during EMU visits genuine interaction takes place between the children of the two schools. Since the residential experience is usually planned as the culmination of a program of one-day visits, both children and teachers are usually already on good terms with each other when the residential visit begins.

While our evaluation of the residential program confirms that we are providing an enjoyable experience, the question remains: Will it make any difference? An attempt to answer this question is provided by a teacher from one of the most troubled areas of Belfast who has made regular use of our one-day and residential EMU programs. Her comments are particularly poignant because some time after she began to work with us, her son lost both his legs in a terrorist explosion.

> Here we have city children in the country learning together. As well as that, all the things that are here belong to both traditions and we have an opportunity for sharing.

> I told the children I am not a Catholic teacher or a Protestant teacher, I am just a teacher and you are all my pupils.

The problems are not going to be solved until people accept one another as people, until we can get away from labeling, in every situation. If you can accept a person as a friend, then the labels Catholic and Protestant are unimportant, the friendships can grow, the labels can be forgotten and we can move forward as one community, not two communities.

The teacher from the school linked with her on the program echoed these words.

We do not believe that things are going to change overnight, but it is just possible that what we are doing may have one small impact on the troubled society in which we live.

A second educational residential center will shortly be opened at the Ulster-American Folk Park at Omagh, County Tyrone. This development emphasizes the value placed on museums in this region as agents of social change, regeneration, and reconciliation.

The Timescapes Project

Another initiative involving museums throughout Northern Ireland provides additional evidence of the variety of ways museums can contribute to reconciliation through education.

Funded by the Community Relations Branch of the Department of Education, Northern Ireland, a team of museum educators and professional officers from the Northern Ireland Centre for Learning Resources is currently working on the development of a CD-ROM/CD-I resource to support the teaching of history and the cross-curricular themes of Cultural Heritage and Education for Mutual Understanding. Drawing upon the collections of the museums and the archives in the Northern Ireland Public Record Office, the Timescapes disc will enable users to investigate aspects of the social and cultural lives of the people of this region from the earliest times to the 20th century. Nine Timescapes explore the ways of life of successive waves of settlers—the rich cultural mix from which today's inhabitants of Northern Ireland are descended—Mesolithic hunter-gatherers, Neolithic farmers, Celtic metalworkers, Viking town-builders, Anglo-Norman colonists, English and Scots planters. Later Timescapes will include information about the reverse process— emigration to Britain, Europe, North America, and Australia during the last 300 years.

Users will be able to explore each Timescape in depth or follow a single theme through the ages, such as domestic life, ideas, beliefs and customs, transport, language, art, and music. Investigations will offer users the opportunity to examine objects and documents—the evidence of the past. Alternatively they will be able to read descriptions and interpretations of this evidence or listen to voices discussing key issues arising from the evidence available for each period.

Timescapes is about the everyday life and shared experiences of the people of this island, from its first settlement, nearly 10,000 years ago, down to recent times. It will offer users the opportunity to study our past without the politics and to focus on the common ground of human experience rather than the political and religious events that divided our society and are constantly invoked to justify and perpetuate the gulf fixed between Protestant and Catholic, Orange and Green.

Timescapes will be available to schools and colleges, to adult open-learning centers, and to visitors in museum galleries. It has been planned as an educational resource that, in terms of technology and content, will present a novel view of our heritage. The medium is likely to attract the attention and interest of the target audiences. Whether the message alters perceptions of the past or modifies present attitudes remains to be seen.

Journal of Museum Education 19, no. 1 (Winter 1994): 10–13.

REFLECTIONS

The intervening years in Ireland have reinforced the need for museums to act as a neutral territory for cross-community groups to learn and share their heritage. The Science Discovery Bus is approaching its 10th year of operation and has increased its service to community groups. The success of this service led to funding from the Millennium Commission for the Ulster Museum to build the first interactive science center in Ireland, which will open in spring 2001. Following the success of the Ulster Folk and Transport Museum, a second residential center has been established at the Ulster American Folk Park in Omagh, in partnership with the local education authority. Timescapes is still used throughout the education sector and is now available in CD-I and CD-ROM formats.

It remains essential for museums to act as facilitators for communities to explore a shared heritage. During its 1998 exhibition, the Ulster Museum employed a community history officer, funded by the European Community's Special Support Program for Peace and Reconciliation for Northern Ireland and administered by the Community Relations Council. This staff member talked to the communities about the history of that period and how it affected both

Protestant and Catholic groups and then showed community groups around the exhibition. The museum again acted as neutral ground for cross-community groups. The funding for this initiative has been extended for three years to cover the period from 1912 to the present.

—Sally Montgomery

(Editors' Note: Since this article was published, the Ulster Museum, the Ulster Folk and Transport Museum, and the Ulster-American Folk Park have merged into the National Museum and Galleries of Northern Ireland.)

Long-Term Museum Programs for Youth

Stacey L. Shelnut

The yellow buses parked outside a museum are a familiar sight, but they reflect more the past of museum education than the future. Programs that bring young people back to the museum, on their own, day after day—not just once a year—represent a new era for the way young people and museums interact and therefore a turning point in museum programming as a whole. Programs for youth characterized by long-term involvement (several months to several years) and highly personal relationships among museum staff, youth, and members of the community are unfolding as museum professionals respond to the challenges of *Museums for a New Century* and *Excellence and Equity*.[1] Both reports called on museums to find new ways to reach broader audiences, particularly communities they had long neglected, exploited, or misrepresented. These estranged communities are traditionally depicted as various ethnic groups, special needs audiences, the poor, or women, but young people could be considered within this dynamic. Until recently, museums approached children and adolescents through middlemen (or "middlewomen")—through school curriculums, teachers, and parents—content to be separate from youth and the needs young people have identified.

How often do museums approach children directly as independent learners? Do museums recognize and respond to young people as having their own interests, values, and learning agendas or goals? What does it mean for a museum to look at children and adolescents as audiences in their own right—existing outside of school and family groups?

At the Brooklyn Children's Museum, visitation by children and adolescents unaccompanied by adults has been welcomed and encouraged for more than a decade. Museum staff have worked with community representatives to develop a comprehensive, multifaceted program for neighborhood youth, ages 7 through 18, focusing on self-exploration and discovery. Program developers study the ideas and interests of young people to create activities based on children's curiosity, developmental needs, and continuous growth.

This program, now called Museum Team, is divided into four sequential tiers. The base tier, Kids' Crew, supports the casual visitation of children, ages

7 through 14. The other tiers, designed to accommodate a higher level of participation and youth ages 10 through 18, are volunteer-in-training, teen volunteer, and internship programs. Participants have the opportunity to advance from one tier to the next based on their age and evolving knowledge of the galleries, level of program involvement, and leadership ability.

Currently more than 1,000 young people are registered in Kids' Crew. Two hundred of them visit the museum regularly and participate in thematic-based programming geared for repeat visitation. In addition, at least 25 young people are advancing through the other three tiers at any one time. Most will participate fully in the program for three years, but some for as long as eight.

Time and the personal relationships that can only develop over the long term are the key factors to the success of Museum Team. Program developers and other museum staff have the opportunity to know participants extremely well and to plan educational experiences and activities that meet affective and cognitive needs. Using the vast resources of the museum—collection, staff, facility—the program fosters a stronger self-image among the young participants and encourages a desire to learn and achieve success. As educators know, learning can occur within a 90-minute school visit or short family outing, but

---

Programs that bring young people back to the museum, on their own, day after day . . . represent a new era for the way young people and museums interact.

---

growth takes time and commitment. Young people, particularly those in urban settings, need institutions willing to support their development in the long-term.

The different stories that make up Museum Team are prime examples of the different types of activities engaging children and adolescents at various museums throughout the country.

Needs and Networks

Scenario: In the heart of Mississippi, Malesha, age 16, and Afealliah, age 17, put their heads together to create their own plan for the future of the Brooklyn Children's Museum. Surrounding them are young representatives from 14 other children's museums and science centers in the United States, doing the same thing. Over a five-day period, these young people receive training in conflict resolution, leadership, and science skills.

Long-term programs have been extremely effective in creating greater access to museums for adolescents. Many museums have teen docent, volunteer, and internship programs, and the number of discussions and forums on programming for adolescents has increased substantially. Adolescents—12- to 18-year-olds—have long been the "untouchables" of museum audiences. Impeded by complicated junior high and high school schedules, as well as by the challenges of this age group, museum educators often did little more than adapt programs originally designed for children or adults. Adolescents received accelerated versions of children's programs stripped of the participatory or interactive elements deemed "too juvenile." Or they were subjected to adult programs that even adults found flat.

To be successful, programs for adolescents must be targeted to their distinct interests and needs. National initiatives and innovative research have made it clear that adolescents are looking for opportunities to grow and test new ideas, and, again, these opportunities take time. In early adolescence young people become increasingly aware of adult values and abilities and try to adopt them to gain entrance into the "adult world." As Erik Erikson established, young people are seeking an identity, searching to establish who they are and how they fit into society.[2] As many of us remember, this is a confusing and painful period. But it is also a time of great creativity. Adolescents have an intense desire to learn and an openness to new ideas and challenges. Within the context of a long-term program, adolescents can find the security they need to voice their thoughts and fears while achieving and learning.

In supportive and structured museum environments, young people have learned new skills and channeled their energies in imaginative ways. At the Exploratorium in San Francisco, explainers, ages 14 to 21, are the visitors' only intimate access to the exhibits, and most of these young people develop an awareness of science and people beyond their years. The Chicago Botanic Garden's College First program links high school students with staff mentors and gives them life skills and college prep training. Adolescents at the Roger Williams Park Zoo in Providence, Rhode Island, are trained as environmental educators and conduct programs for children from different community groups.

The recent success of the national program YouthALIVE! (Youth Achievement through Learning Involvement, Volunteering and Employment) has proven the ability of museums to generate strong adolescent audiences. Beginning in 1991 the Lila Wallace–Reader's Digest Fund made leadership awards to nine children's museums and science-technology centers that had a long history of innovative youth programs and aggressive study in this area. The recipients were the Austin Children's Museum in Texas, the Brooklyn Children's Museum, the Children's Museum in Boston, the Children's Museum of Indianapolis, Discovery Place, Inc., in Charlotte, North Carolina, the Exploratorium in San Francisco, the Museum of Science in Miami, the New York Hall of Science in Queens, and SciTech in Aurora, Illinois.

Over a period of four years, 36 additional children's museum and science-technology centers received grants to develop or expand programs that increase employment opportunities and exposure to science and technology for young people, 10 to 17 years old, especially young women and adolescents within "underserved" communities. Administered by the Association of Science-Technology Centers, this network of 45 institutions shares resources, actively participates in peer counseling, provides technical assistance to new institutions entering the field, supports scholarship and national evaluation efforts, and plays a major role in youth advocacy on both the local and national levels. Program staff from each organization in the YouthALIVE! network meet twice a year to share successes and challenges in their youth program efforts. Through a series of discussions, workshops, and network meetings, participants look at specific factors they have identified as integral to youth programs—community partnerships, cultural diversity, and institutional integration—and strategic program ideas. As described in the above scenario, YouthALIVE! has also made a particular effort to bring young people together. This past summer the program held a Youth Summit in Louisiana and Mississippi in which young people from all over the United States participated.

YouthALIVE! has provided an incentive for museum educators in all types of museums to research the feasibility of developing long-term programs for youth in their institutions. While children's museums and science-technology centers have taken the initiative, many traditional museums are now following their lead.

Social Responsibility

Scenario: A teen actress portraying a young battered woman describes how she loves her husband and does not want to leave him. In the audience Latoya, age nine and a frequent visitor to the museum, counters with the dire possible results if the wife stays. She knows they are acting, but she also knows the issue is real. After the performance, the young actors and audience members discuss possible solutions to situations of physical abuse within a family.

The limited time frame and structure of school programs can serve to insulate museums from the problems young people face, but those museums that deal directly with young people cannot remain insulated. Compelled to address these problems, museums with long-term youth programs have begun to work closely with public housing systems, alternative high schools, youth advocacy organizations, and career training programs.

The Washington State Capital Museum in Olympia is working with young adults in the state's juvenile rehabilitation system. Two years ago, while studying and evaluating the museum's visitorship, Susan Warner, curator of education, was alarmed to learn that the juvenile crime and violence statistics in Washington's smaller cities rivaled that of major cities across the country. In response, she started a program in which incarcerated adolescents worked with professional artists and craftsworkers over extended periods of time. Through art and projects related to the historic conservation mission of the museum, these adolescents gain opportunities to achieve success and express themselves in a productive manner. Working closely with Washington's Juvenile Rehabilitation Administration and local school districts, the museum has expanded this program to sites throughout the state, including two maximum security facilities. More than 200 young people are involved in a variety of projects. The work they produce is exhibited, and educational programs are developed around the exhibits.

The Washington State Capital Museum's program has been extremely effective in giving young people a chance to find alternative methods of communication and develop options for themselves. It has also educated communities about young people who are too easy to forget.

In Boston a program at the Children's Museum created a space in which young people, ages 10 through 18, could find information on contemporary issues such as violence, racism, sexuality, drugs, and AIDS and create exhibitions dealing with similar issues, or just talk. Young people want to deal with such topics directly. They also want to interact with their peers in formal and informal settings. This program helped meet both needs. The program also facilitated workshops led by youth on AIDS prevention, violence prevention, self-esteem, and other pressing issues. Those who participated appreciated the supportive environment in which to explore and express their concerns and feelings.

Responsible Education

Scenario: On a computer outside the director's office, during a break between his job assignment and a science program, Hasan, age 11, checks his e-mail. He is looking for a letter from his pen pal, 1,000 miles away, in a similar program. Wearing a tie-dyed T-shirt he made at the museum almost a year ago in a pattern and design workshop, Hasan goes virtually unnoticed by staff members. His presence is expected, appreciated, and valued. Hasan hopes to become an intern like his older brother and sister.

For a positive and productive learning environment, young participants need to feel wanted and valued by staff on all levels. Programs formed in isolation within a particular department or program area may achieve moderate success but, without strong institution-wide commitment, may fail to achieve long-term goals. In addition, young people need to have a sense of ownership in their programs and educational development. They need to participate in decision making, even at the highest levels. Some museums have formed Youth Advisory Councils. Science Central, opening in Fort Wayne, Indiana, in 1996, currently has young people represented on its board of directors. But this level of youth involvement may be difficult for some museums to accommodate.

It is naive to think that young people do not realize the flaws within the formal educational system. The popularity of informal learning systems indicates that young people are looking for alternative learning experiences wherever they can find them. They are learning science from television's Bill Nye ("The Science Guy"), politics and history from the rap group Public Enemy, and cultural and scientific awareness from community-based projects and organizations like Global Kids.

Their increased familiarity with informal educational systems makes today's young people eager for just the learning environment museums can offer. At the same time, long-term youth programs allow museums to reach a familiar audience in a direct, new way. But those museums that have undertaken these youth programs know that the commitment is serious and the involvement extensive. Museum staff members become not only role models for participants but significant figures in these young people's lives. For participants in the Brooklyn Children's Museum's Museum Team, some of whom have been in the program for as long as eight years, the museum is "a home away from home." The interpersonal interactions, value systems, and accepted rules of behavior they encounter in the museum offer them clues about what can be expected from society as a whole and patterns on which they fashion their lives.[3] This is a major responsibility.

The best long-term youth programs outline clearly what is expected of both youth and staff. They display consistency while understanding the need for flexibility. They recognize the varying life experiences and backgrounds of young people by providing multiple points of entry, responding to "multiple intelligences,"[4] and respecting multicultural differences. A staff reflective of the communities served attracts adolescents to the museum, encourages them to feel connected, and affirms the authenticity of their museum experience. Ivan Karp has observed: "Museums assert that they can compensate for the failures of other cultural institutions, such as schools, to perform the work of social reproduction. These assertions define the museum as one of the central institutions of civil society; they also make museums answerable for how well they educate and represent the citizens who compose society."[5]

Through long-term youth programs, it is possible for museums to expand their role in society and support families and schools in comprehensive ways, offering young people an array of educational opportunities and tools by which to make meaning of life.

The museums that are forming long-term partnerships with youth are creating relationships from which there is no turning back. These museums are becoming environments—safe and productive places—in which young people can gain a better understanding of the world, each other, and themselves. Through these museums, young people are growing into productive, well-integrated adults. In turn, these young people inspire the staff and invigorate the museum.

Museums were founded as the keepers of history and the exhibitors of culture. Objects have been the constants, while people come and go. For those museums now stretching to extend the care long bestowed on objects to their audiences, especially to young audiences, the results are nothing less than transforming.

Journal of Museum Education 19, no. 3 (Fall 1994): 10–13.

Notes

1. Commission on Museums for a New Century, *Museums for a New Century* (Washington, D.C.: American Association of Museums, 1984); American Association of Museums, *Excellence and Equity: Education and the Public Dimension of Museums* (Washington, D.C.: AAM, 1992).

2. Erik Erikson, *Childhood and Society* (New York and London: W. W. Norton and Co., 1950), pp. 261–63.

3. Edna Shapiro and Barbara Biber, "The Education of Young Children: A Developmental-Interaction Approach," *Teachers College Record* 74, no. 1 (September 1972): 55–78.

4. Howard Gardner, *Frames of Mind: The Theory of Multiple Intelligences* (New York: Basic Books, 1983).

5. Ivan Karp, "Museums and Communities: The Politics of Public Culture," in *Museums and Communities: The Politics of Public Culture*, ed. Ivan Karp, Christine Mullen Kreamer, and Steven D. Lavine (Washington, D.C.: Smithsonian Institution Press, 1992), pp. 9–10.

Further Reading

Cowan, Brenda, and Stacey Shelnut. *School's Out. . . Kids In: Developing an Education-Based After-School Program.* Brooklyn: Brooklyn Children's Museum, 1997.

REFLECTIONS

Soon after writing "Long-Term Museum Programs for Youth," I realized that my vantage point—that of a children's museum—made it easy for me to point fingers and propose high levels of engagement with youth. Youth museums, founded with audience-centered purposes, are not entangled by their collections, like history or art museums. In fact, most children's museums, particularly those founded in the last 20 years, don't even have collections. It occurred to me that if I truly wanted to expand and deepen youth experiences in a broad range of museums, I would have to abandon my comfort zone and practice what I preached in a more traditional museum setting. And for me, that meant an art museum. Now that I work in an art museum, I find it extremely challenging to initiate programs that empower youth and expand the thinking and operations of the museum. Art museums suffer from long-standing images of exclusivity, and they are still struggling to define themselves in visitor-friendly ways. Though my work is challenging, I will continue to create programs that engage youth in long-term museum programming. Inspiration comes from all the young people who have had their lives changed positively from their involvement with museums.

—*Stacey L. Shelnut*

How Museums Can Shape Public Education: Chrysalis Charter School

Paul Krapfel

More than half the states in the country now have legislation allowing an organization such as a museum to create and operate a chartered public school in almost any form the museum wants. This article is a fervent though sober invitation to museum educators to consider this possibility. The process and the possibilities will be illustrated with examples from Chrysalis Charter School.

Carter House Natural Science Museum in Redding, California, started Chrysalis Charter School in August 1996, in collaboration with Enterprise School District. This public school focuses on nature study and systems thinking. The 94 students (ages 5 to 14) spend 25 percent of their school time in the field learning to see and understand the natural patterns around them.

My wife Alysia and I, who were part of the museum's education team, began dreaming of a museum school for several reasons. We loved creating hands-on interactions by which students could construct a sense of the natural world. But we were also growing frustrated with the limitations of the one-hour, one-time-only nature of many museum programs. We wanted deeper involvement in our students' intellectual development. Our vision received funding from the Howard Hughes Medical Institute. For five years, we developed and field-tested hands-on biology investigations using playground species.

Most kids responded richly to our week-long, 10-hour field tests. Their responses got us imagining what could happen if this 10-hour experience could expand into 8 years. There was something about the open-ended complexity of nature that matched the human spirit. We wanted a school founded on that match.

The other thing that came out of our field-testing was a growing certainty that most of the problems in education were problems with schools as organizations. The problems did not lie with the teachers. The solutions did not lie in enriched curricula or systemic reforms that skirted around basic organizational issues. We began imagining a new kind of school organized around the student-teacher interaction rather than command and control hierarchies including prescribed curricula and standardized salary schedules. A member of our museum's board, a former school principal, suggested creating a charter school. We were dubious at first. "We can't start a public school. We're just a small museum." But we could.

Now that we have, we see many attributes that make museums strong candidates for operating chartered public schools:

•Most museums have classroom facilities. Charter schools are not eligible for building funds, so one of the biggest barriers is the cost of creating facilities. Museums with existing educational facilities are already past this major impediment.

•Museums have business offices experienced at handling complex, publicly accountable finances. A school must maintain public trust by responsibly handling the cash flow. Museums have this experience.

•Museums have good relationships with their local schools, teachers, and families that help them build credibility and political support for a museum school.

•Most important, museums have staff passionate about education, often with a focus different from the traditional offering. "Constructivism," "inquiry-based," and "integrated" are heart and soul to museum educators, not just jargon.

Why should these passionate educators want public schools at their museums? For one reason, a charter school increases inspiration to the museum's educational mission. Charter schools represent a more engulfing, more immediate, and more prolonged immersion with children than most museums' educational programs currently represent. Staff can see the seeds that sprout from constructivist experiences years later in their students. One rarely has this opportunity with museum visitors. The day-to-day interactions keep educators fresh and on their toes. Developing traditional museum programs tends to focus large amounts of talent and resources on developing hour-long, materials-rich, repeatable programs. As these programs become polished, a psychological separation can grow so that a child's question has less chance of leading the educator away from the script. Daily classroom teaching requires the creative juices to flow in a different way. Spontaneous improvisation occurs each day, creating powerful opportunities to experiment, innovate, and develop new educational offerings. A charter school can be a fast-track educational laboratory for the museum.

For example, my class was studying a 25-acre chaparral site that had burned one month earlier. It was apparent to me that the angle of slope influenced the power of the fire. But how could I give my students a hands-on experience with this concept? After a few days of thought, I came up with an experiment. I fan-folded several pieces of paper. I laid a piece on the actual burned slope and lit it from the direction the original fire had come. Students timed how long it took the flame to reach the other end of the 11-inch-long paper. On the gentle slope at the base of the hill, it took 12 seconds. On the steep midslope, it took 5 seconds. Beyond the crest when the fire had to burn down the slope, it took 1 minute and 23 seconds to burn down the paper. The experiment then evolved into a classroom investigation of how fire works that I tried with two younger groups of students. This investigation is now forming the scientific foundation for a class on how to build a campfire.

A second reason for creating a museum-based public school is to serve the local community. A charter school is a full-fledged public school open to all families who think the particular focus or educational philosophy of that school is appropriate for their children. A charter school is not a magnet school. Discrimination based on ability (or race, income, behavior, religion, and so forth) is not allowed. But what is allowed is the freedom to offer a very different kind of education. The museum serves the community by increasing

---

Spontaneous improvisation occurs each day, creating powerful opportunities to experiment, innovate, and develop new educational offerings. A charter school can be a fast-track educational laboratory for the museum.

---

the chances for students to find an educational approach that fits their learning style. As a result, the entire school system will be more responsive to the unique abilities of each student.

A third reason for a museum school is to explore a powerful hybrid between formal and informal learning. We in museums are familiar with questioning strategies that help learners reflect on their learning from a different point of view. We recognize and respect the power and outcome of constructed understanding, so we patiently respect the nonlinear, unpredictable path it can take. On the other hand, we must be honest that informal learning (as modeled most of the time in museums) could be much more powerful if it possessed two attributes of formal learning.

The first is an interacting mentor. The presence of a mentor can help a learner work through a difficult concept that the learner, if left alone, might abandon. More important, a mentor helps convert a very private learning process into a social conversation. Talking about an investigation often leads to insights. The second attribute lacking in museums is long-term engagement with the learner. Our interactives are usually presented as first-time encounters. Random paths through exhibits make it challenging to introduce simpler concepts and then use them to build more complex concepts. A long-term relationship with a learner develops a network of friendship, confidence, and interconnections that can be used to guide the learning into deeper territory.

A hybrid between formal and informal education promises enormous synergy. This hybrid can take many forms. Currently, it takes the form of museums providing "enrichment" through interactive explorations for students or interactive in-service programs for teachers. These efforts help nudge the educational system toward teaching for understanding. I say "nudge" because such an approach accepts and works with the large inertia that standards, frameworks, limited staff development days, pay scales, state-approved textbooks, testing, and so on create in the educational system. This inertia limits the synergy possible between informal and formal learning.

Other hybrids are possible, hybrids that alter fundamental institutional forces such as the relationship between teacher and student, the goals and motivations for learning, the structure of classes, and the flow of money so that thousands (rather than hundreds) of dollars can flow into classroom equipment each year. In most schools, children enter kindergarten eager to learn and graduate from eighth grade playing the game. The heart of informal learning is the faith that the human mind has evolved to delight in finding patterns and meaning within the world. If a school is founded and organized around this premise, how will schooling look different? This is what we try to explore at Chrysalis.

For example, school starts with kids coming into the classroom as teachers get ready for school. We say good morning. Some kids go out to play, and others hang around and share. By the time school "starts," we have already made personal contact with every student. In another school I'm familiar with, the kids stay outside until after the bell rings. Then they get in line, the teacher opens the door, and the class walks into the classroom. In that setting, there is no time to greet each child individually. The teacher's first contact with students is en masse, and the students' first contact with the teacher is as the teacher treats the students en masse. What difference does that make? There are hundreds of similar examples in which a museum's informal learning approach can alter the procedures and feel of a classroom. And all of these hundreds of ways, with their silent lessons, are untouched, uninfluenced if museums are restricted to providing curricular enrichment.

To emphasize this important point, I reluctantly refer to an article I read about another museum school. The museum had an exhibit on Greek pottery, but the school curriculum (which the museum did not have the power to influence) called for the students to study colonial American history. So the teachers were trying to use ancient Greek pottery to explore ideas in colonial history. I admire the teachers for their mind-stretching effort, but the curricular constraint they were forced to work within insults students and teachers alike.

Let me pass through this central point again with a counterexample. A central focus of Chrysalis is teaching kids systems thinking. There is agreement that average American education does not develop systems thinking. There is disagreement on how it should be taught. Systems thinking is creeping into frameworks and standards, but it doesn't fit nicely into any subject so it is usually included in science. Making systems thinking central to our schools probably could happen only within the freedom of a charter school, especially since our work is experimental. Each week, our fourth- through sixth-grade students practice analogies, cause-and-effect chains, and graphing relationships. Our junior-high students practice seeing objects as expressions of underlying flows of materials. How will these students think after six years of this practice? We don't know, but we are delighted with the way they think after two years.

A chartered museum public school offers a powerful opportunity for exploring the synergy between formal and informal learning. Museum educators have a deep awe for the process and individuality of learning. A school with this sort of freedom will look very different from the current norm in public education and model a provocative alternative.

Fortunately, support for charter schools is increasing. The federal government's support is helping more states adopt charter school legislation and providing more funding to help charter schools with start-up costs. The Web site developed by the U.S. Department of Education and the California State University Institute for Education Reform, www.uscharterschools.org, is a good place to link to the circumstances and resources specific to your state. The Institute for Education Reform's Web site is another good resource: www.csus.edu/ier/charter/charter.html. Both sites have links to other resources. While you are surfing, you can also check out Chrysalis's home page: www.enterprise.k12.ca.us/chrysalis.

Starting a chartered museum public school is hard work. But to teach there and watch students rise to the challenges and inspirations is, oh, so much fun.

Journal of Museum Education 23, no. 2 (1998): 11–13.

REFLECTIONS

Thirty-seven states now have charter school laws. The federal government is providing more money to assist start-up efforts. The public is more aware of charter schools and looks with favor on any organization creating a charter school. So pursuing the vision painted in this article is easier now than when I wrote it. On the other hand, a push for national standards could interfere with the implementation of an innovative curriculum, and, here in California at least, the teachers' union and school board associations are successfully passing legislation to restrict the spread of charter schools.

The vision that inspired Chrysalis Charter School is just starting to come into focus in this, our fourth year. California charter law allows a school five years to "make its case" for renewal. This is good. I would advise museums to start small, use existing facilities, and not make grandiose promises. Stay small and humble until the work grows a firm foundation.

—*Paul Krapfel*

A Laboratory for Museum Learning:
New York City Museum School

Sonnet Takahisa

Museum schools are a hot topic. A host of local and national initiatives are encouraging new kinds of long-term collaborations between museums and schools. As exciting as these opportunities are, this work is not for everyone; creating a school requires skills and resources that are not in a traditional museum portfolio. Museum schools represent a paradigm shift that requires new organizational structures, new role definitions for museum personnel and teachers, and new relationships among students, parents, and museum organizations. A museum school implies a consistent, long-term commitment that, unlike other "projects," cannot simply be abandoned upon the completion of funding.

Six years ago, a group of museum administrators collaborated with one of New York City's more progressive superintendents to answer a call for smaller, community-based schools that would better serve the needs of adolescents. We proposed a school in which students would use museum resources to meet city and state curricular mandates in all subject areas. Convinced that the richness of the museum environment would stimulate curiosity and provide opportunities for engaged learning and the construction of knowledge, we recruited staff, parents, and students and opened as a fully accredited school in September 1994.

The New York City Museum School (NYCMS) is "linkage" in the extreme, an intense collaboration that requires museum and school professionals to share responsibility and equal accountability for the students' total education. Every day, we must face the students with the conviction that we are providing them with an excellent, well-rounded, rigorous education. Our students are not subjects; we cannot "experiment" with their education, because there is no second chance.

Now in its fourth year, the New York City Museum School is codifying a particular model for educating adolescents that stimulates excitement about learning by actively involving the youngsters in exploring, discovering, and creating knowledge. Positioned on the cutting edge of both museum and school reform, NYCMS provides a "learning laboratory" for museum professionals and for educators by offering collaborative opportunities to develop museum learning modules and to observe and document how people—students and instructors—learn in different environments.

Our ongoing research has important implications for museum and school reform, for research in teaching and learning, and for the public dimension of museums. For believers in both museum-school and museum-museum collaborations, we have identified strategies for defining common issues and concerns. We can share our adventures in developing performance-based standards and assessment strategies with practitioners and policy makers in school, arts, and educational reform initiatives. And we are amassing a great deal of information about how people learn in museums to be used by administrators and educators interested in the visitor experience.

However, it is the business of imagining and constructing an ideal educational environment for real students and teachers that integrates the above concerns and drives our day-to-day work. We have defined a "museum learning" pedagogy that raises the standards for our teaching and learning practices and holds us accountable to the traditions of academic excellence and equal access that are so fundamental to both museums and schools in a democratic society.

Background

NYCMS was conceived and designed collaboratively by representatives from Community School District 2 of the New York City Public Schools, the Brooklyn Museum of Art, the American Museum of Natural History, the Children's Museum of Manhattan, and the Jewish Museum. We currently serve more than 200 students in grades 6 through 10. By fall 2000, we will reach the full capacity of 420 students in grades 6 through 12. The school's home base, which is shared with two other schools, is the O. Henry Learning Center in the Chelsea section of Manhattan.

New York City Board of Education resources committed to the school include tax levy dollars based on per-pupil allotment and state and federal reimbursable dollars for furniture, books, computer supplies, and personnel. District 2 commits a significant portion of its annual budget to staff development. The school and its museum partners also receive support from the New York Networks for School Renewal and the Center for Arts Education, two Annenberg School Reform Projects.

Each of the founding museum partners has committed significant staff and space, including new classrooms and laboratories, dedicated museum educators, and teaching interns. The museums provide identification cards that enable students to enter as "staff," bring guests for special programs, and receive discounts in museum shops. Most important, the museums provide the objects and resources to be studied. The National Endowment for the Arts, the New York State Council on the Arts, and the Institute of Museum and Library Services have funded the museums to support their efforts in establishing the school. Each museum also receives support from private foundations.

The students are selected through the district's middle school options program and the city-wide high school choice process. The student population is diverse: African American (24.9 percent), Asian (8.4 percent), Caucasian (36.0 percent), Latino (21.8 percent), Native American (0.4 percent), and mixed (8.4 percent) backgrounds. While 31 percent of our students qualify for the federal lunch program, 8 percent come from private or parochial schools. Academically, our students have demonstrated a broad range of academic achievement (10th to 99th percentile), with 7 percent categorized as special education/resource room students.

Professionals from two worlds have come together on the faculty to establish the school and design its unique curriculum. The codirectors bring complementary experience in museums, arts education, classroom teaching,

---

The students do not consider themselves privileged; this way of learning is part of what they think of as "school." Perhaps this is truly what is meant by "school reform."

---

and interdisciplinary curriculum development. The teaching staff includes 21 licensed subject specialists and professionally trained museum educators who share full teaching responsibility working in rotating teams.

Student Program

NYCMS embodies the idea of an integrated curriculum while maintaining the rigors of discipline-based education. Representing an academic tradition of excellence, intellectual rigor, and high standards, the wide range of collections offered by partner museums provides opportunities for interdisciplinary learning and a renewed spirit of inquiry. In their day-to-day work in the museums, students deepen their abilities to perceive and comprehend natural and human-made objects. The objects stimulate curiosity about historic and contemporary people, places, and natural phenomena.

The structure of the school gives museums and classrooms parallel status as learning environments and reflects the time required for collaborative planning, ongoing reflection, and revision. Each middle school class works on four interdisciplinary modules a year. The students study at one museum for eight weeks: six weeks of individual and collaborative research, a week of formal presentations, and a week of reflection. They spend up to three days each week at their assigned museums and the remainder at the home base to establish a sense of continuity and community among the student body and to learn aspects of subject area studies more appropriate for the classroom.

For example, in the classroom the sixth-grade social studies teacher focuses on the topographical features of ancient Egypt and their impact on civilization; at the Brooklyn Museum of Art the same teacher and students join the museum educator to study Egyptian art and gather evidence about the natural environment from a survey of the materials used or the iconography of images. Similarly, seventh-graders comprehend the complexities of evolution through classroom lessons on DNA and then, in the newly renovated prehistoric mammal and dinosaur halls at the American Museum of Natural History, analyze fossils and bones to determine the evolution of a species. At the Children's Museum of Manhattan, eighth-graders studying geometry create computer animation programs, plotting shapes and moving them around coordinate axes. For their presentations they add color and music to produce one-minute videos. Eighth-graders studying patterns of American immigration read historical novels in their language arts class and then listen to selections from the Jewish Museum's collection of radio broadcasts.

Museum collaboration for ninth-grade students currently focuses on the humanities. A museum studies teacher works with the global studies and world literature teachers to ensure that students meet all city and state learning standards. Seminars on Museum Learning and Expository Writing are required; other seminars include one held in conjunction with the Margaret Mead Film Festival at the American Museum of Natural History, a research seminar on a collection of 19th-century puzzles at the Brooklyn Museum, and an exhibition planning seminar at the Children's Museum. Eventually, high school course work at museums will include mathematics and the sciences.

Museum Learning

NYCMS models the pattern of learning practiced by museum professionals—learning that is intellectually rigorous, uses authentic and primary resources, and requires scholarly training, an innate sense of curiosity, and the ability to synthesize and evaluate information from a variety of sources. A museum professional uses many skills to accomplish these tasks, and then must be able to exhibit or present what has been learned and accept feedback and criticism from colleagues and the public. NYCMS seeks to apply this process of museum learning to all aspects of the mandated city and state curriculums.

The school's sequential museum learning curriculum for sixth to eighth grades develops students' abilities to construct knowledge from individual objects, from objects in the context of collections and installations, and from different institutional contexts. It features content specific to each institution; a critical thinking or reflective component; and a museum studies component that includes examining objects, exhibitions, and institutions.

Based on collaborations among museum educators, classroom teachers, and students, we have begun to identify the particular skills and behaviors necessary for success and to establish some routines of study for students at each grade level. Our "laboratory" is focused on understanding the ways that we can integrate the specifics of the museum learning curriculum with the challenges posed by city and state curricular mandates and the rigorous expectations of other high school and college admissions officers.

The elements of "museum learning" in our curriculum are as follows:

Sustained looking: Careful observation over long periods of time allows the viewer to notice more and more. Objects don't always reveal themselves in glimpses. Learners experience the rewards of slowing down and focusing on fewer objects. Sustained looking enables learners to amass evidence that can be used to support a thesis.

Articulating observations: Verbal, written, and sketched descriptions of what is actually seen in an object, a series of objects, or an exhibition promotes careful observation. By sharing observations, learners see objects through others' eyes and recognize aspects they may not have noticed.

Making connections: Learners connect what they see in an object with previously acquired academic or personal knowledge and with other objects. Learners must be aware of the differences between objective and subjective observations. They need to draw reasonable conclusions about objects and find evidence in the object that supports their ideas.

Generating questions: Curiosity and the ability to formulate high-order thinking questions about objects are hallmarks of a museum learner; an inquiring mind is a prerequisite for learning. Over time, learners distinguish the questions that can be answered by looking at an object from those that require further research.

Undertaking research: Learners seek "answers" from a variety of sources: labels, field notes, catalogue entries, other objects, texts, the media, personal interviews, and computer searches. Information is evaluated and synthesized to create a supportable thesis that, in turn, must be tested against the original object observations. Learners look for evidence that strengthens their theses while constantly wondering: "How does this new information fit?" and "What do I still want to know?"

Preparing presentations: Learners use a range of formats, including three-dimensional exhibitions, visual displays, written essays, public talks or performances, and multimedia demonstrations to communicate ideas and evidence that support their theses. The act of "teaching" newly acquired information requires that learners assume a sense of ownership of what has been learned and provides a mechanism for celebrating effort and marking progress. Ideas must be communicated well; in their "presentations," learners must meet established standards of excellence.

Promoting reflection and criticism: Feedback from peers and experts offers learners new information and questions. Learners must listen and be able to respond to and/or incorporate appropriate and thoughtful challenges. They are held accountable for their ideas and their work, must be able to honestly assess their work, and must acknowledge what additional work may still need to be done (i.e., what new questions have arisen).

A New Way of Thinking about School

The many administrators, funders, teachers, museum educators, parents, and students who have been part of NYCMS have had a unique opportunity to imagine an ideal learning environment—one that is stimulating, scholarly, and creative. We have learned from museum colleagues about a model for passionate learning and struggled to integrate that model with the demands of a rigorous and broad-based academic curriculum.

Our collaboration has generated new responsibilities for partners from two very different worlds. Museum staff see the same students over extended periods—longer days, whole semesters, and even over many years; they are concerned about the students' academic, social, and emotional development as well as their intellectual progress. Teachers work in gallery environments that are designed to provoke curiosity, contemplation, and conversation, and they must balance student excitement with the demands of discipline-based skills, content, and assessments.

The faculty members of NYCMS are in a fortuitous position. We take part in many different conversations, and we learn from them because the nature of our work crosses disciplines and institutional boundaries. Policy makers in education, museum educators, arts educators, science educators, academics, teachers, and parents share the goal of "raising standards" and developing strategies to ensure that all students benefit from excellent teaching and learning practices.

Established as a "laboratory," the NYCMS community includes research practitioners trained in school reform, collaborative learning and performance -based assessments, natural history and science education, the visual arts and arts education, experiential learning and children's museums, religious and cultural studies, and child development and parenting. As "researchers" we have defined the museum learning curriculum and are developing standards of achievement and assessment. We continue to document the strategies that best encourage learning, and we hope that schools and museums will translate our research into improved educational opportunities for all learners.

As "practitioners" we have spent extended time in museums with real students and discovered that museums do stimulate curiosity. We have helped students become engaged in the learning that happens in a museum and watched them realize the value of interacting with primary sources, of having direct access to objects, of seeing how others imagine the world. The students do not consider themselves privileged; this way of learning is part of what they think of as "school." Perhaps this is truly what is meant by "school reform."

_____ *Journal of Museum Education* 23, no. 2 (1998): 5–8.

Port Penn Interpretive Center: Trials and Transformations

Michael Miller

The recent history of the Port Penn Interpretive Center, Port Penn, Delaware, saw the transformation of a private, community-based museum into a public interpretive center of the state's Division of Parks and Recreation. Originally a project of the Port Penn Area Historical Society, the museum fulfilled a unique mission and served diverse constituents. The mission was to educate visitors on Port Penn's local history and folkways; the constituents included the founding organization, regional scholars serving as advisers, and the museum's audiences. As a result of the transfer, the division became the museum's steward. As with many museums, the steward and the constituents did not always share similar visions for the museum's operations. The application of folkloristic methods, such as identifying, translating, and communicating cultural meanings, helped resolve many conflicts and define the new visions necessary for the museum's success. Effective use of these methods proved essential to creating appropriate interpretations for the Port Penn Interpretive Center.

Port Penn's tale revolves around the museum's role as a community-sanctioned cultural icon. It served many functions: landscape marker for the town, symbol of local history and culture, repository of artifacts and records, social space for visiting, touchstone of identity. Created in an unincorporated Delaware River town just 20 miles from urban Wilmington, the icon held a high cultural value for rural life. After the museum's transfer to the Division of Parks and Recreation, the challenge was to preserve these functions while presenting professional interpretations of the village's history and culture. The project's potential, and its potential pitfalls, both derived from the many layers of cultural issues attached to the simple document that conveyed the facility to the state.

Following the transfer, conflicts arose over the style and content of displays, the use of the museum's space, and perceptions of the division's ability to serve as the museum's steward. The conflict over the displays involved the visual impact of the first exhibits installed by the Division of Parks and

Recreation. The community's displays, nearly 20 years old, had virtually filled the museum space with dense assemblages of objects. Organized along the functional themes of agriculture, education, commerce, and recreation, the displays were a community-created artwork and a repository of community memories. The division's new presentation included similar themes yet visually emphasized the room's almost cubical space. Large artifacts and cases, placed in the center of the room and along the walls, drew out the room's linear dimensions. This configuration felt almost empty to community members. And since it was empty, where was the rest of their stuff? Resolving these fundamental conflicts became essential to the project's survival.

By exploring the cultural dimensions embedded in the museum's transfer, we can see how the use of folkloristic methods helped guide the process to a successful outcome. Several factors were involved: the museum's original purpose and role in the community, the constituents' expectations and values, the methods used to identify and communicate their common goals, and the actions taken to implement those goals. Since each factor involves the expression and negotiation of cultural meaning, each influenced the project's outcomes. Museums can employ folkloristic methodology to sort through multi-

---

Accomplishing this common vision required the negotiation of several levels of cultural meaning between the steward and its constituents.

---

ple layers and nuances of meaning to find appropriate actions that satisfy myriad cultural priorities.

The shared vision created with these methods includes preserving the museum's original mission, enhancing the interpretation of the town's history through the acquisition of other important cultural sites, using a folk esthetic in displays, and professionalizing the museum's management to ensure effective operations. Accomplishing this common vision required the negotiation of several levels of cultural meaning between the steward and its constituents. This small project is a microcosm of the complex issues embedded within museums' function as forums of negotiated cultural values.[1]

In 1975, Port Penn, Delaware, was like many other small communities in the United States—excited about the Bicentennial celebration the following year. Many regional scholars had long been interested in the village's architecture, economic history, and folkways, reinforcing the community's sense of identity and pride. Talk in the town's social circles included sponsoring parades, listing buildings on the National Register of Historic Places, commissioning a shad skiff sailboat replica from the Philadelphia Maritime Museum, and hosting dinners, socials, and fund raisers. Someone joked that the newly formed Port Penn Area Historical Society could turn the old schoolhouse, then a bait and tackle shop, into a museum. The historical society did just that.

The Port Penn Museum opened in 1976 replete with displays, artifacts, photographs, and a curator, Bob Beck. Beck grew up in Port Penn and worked in the area for the state's Division of Fish and Wildlife for many years. With the help of many community members, he collected artifacts, created displays, and staffed the museum. The historical society now had more than 100 members, the village had been designated a National Historic District, and the museum had quickly grown to symbolize the town and serve as its front porch to the rest of the state.

In 1992, Beck said, "I wanted to educate people to the early way of life in Port Penn. . . . We had something to tell and show people. You can't replace what the area stood for." Society member Bill Sidwell, who helped create the displays, related, "Somebody stopped by and said, 'Do you mind if I take a look?' He looked at that place and says, 'You people got something here. I'm from Texas. We got nothing. It's all been stolen, sold off, and everything. You folks have got something here.'"[2]

The folklorists and scholars interested in Port Penn saw the locally inspired, locally designed, and locally operated museum as one of the only genuine folk cultural sites in the region. These supporters aided the museum's development and operations. Architectural historian Bernie Herman of the University of Delaware documented the town's buildings and wrote the National Historic District nomination. National Park Service archeologist David Orr donated hunting decoys and helped interpret the museum's collection of boats. Folklorist Bob Bethke of the University of Delaware, along with a generation of students, documented the town's folkways. Folklorist Kim Burdick wrote grants and served as the museum's advocate. Yet, as its members grew older through the 1980s, the historical society decided the museum's survival depended on transferring the facility to a state agency.

Through years of efforts by individuals and organizations like the Delaware Folklife Project, Inc., the museum finally found a steward. When the Division of Parks and Recreation started a folklife program to interpret Delaware's cultures, the museum seemed an excellent opportunity to give the program a firm foundation. The schoolhouse building and its collection were conveyed to the division on November 2, 1990.

Community members supporting the transfer hoped the agency would maintain and professionalize the museum's function of educating visitors about area history, culture, natural areas, and landscapes. Those opposing the transfer feared that the museum would be lost in a large agency with competing priorities. Each view had some truth to it.

Following the transfer and a name change to the Port Penn Interpretive Center, the facility remained otherwise unaltered for nearly three years. Division personnel learned about the displays, local history, and cultural meanings the community wanted to share with visitors. Park interpreters staffed the site, presented programs, and maintained the building. Yet the frame structure, built in 1886, needed substantial rehabilitation to remain in public use. The building renovation, which required dismantling the displays and storing the artifacts, led many community members to believe their worst fears would be realized. The museum and its displays were the cultural symbol of the town and its identity. Was it still their cultural space? Would they lose their symbol, their work? These concerns, central to their hopes of finding a true steward for the site, contributed to tensions surrounding the museum's renovation.

Aware of the need to maintain an effective partnership, division staff conducted a series of meetings to identify the ideas and themes most important to the community. Participants included historical society members, regional scholars, and staff. Each agreed on the general themes for the exhibits, specifically the town, the people, the land, and the marsh. Displays presenting these themes were installed in 1994. Unexpectedly, community members were dissatisfied, even upset, with the installation. Relations became strained at times as the interpretive center, like all such spaces, became contested space.

The exhibition staff was baffled by the community's reaction. How was this possible given that everyone had agreed on the themes? The primary difficulty arose from the visual configuration of the displays presenting those themes. From what had been a dense assemblage of items accumulated and arranged over many years, museum professionals produced an uncluttered presentation emphasizing the schoolhouse's space. The original presentation reflected a folk esthetic, while the new one reflected a conventional style of contemporary gallery design. The problem was that the community found the new style incompatible with the center's meaning as a community icon. Port Penn resident Thelma Bendler said, "The only thing I hear about that is there is not enough in the museum. A lot of people say the museum is much too empty. They liked it with that older look."[3]

The loss of the museum's original displays, a highly emotional loss to the community, inhibited subsequent dialogue. Bob Beck's death in 1993 left the community without a single voice, further hindering communication. Addressing these problems required the maintaining of dialogue, clarifying issues, identifying possible solutions, and, most important, implementing actions the constituents found meaningful. All the issues that arise in the complex negotiations of large institutions existed in this one-room schoolhouse museum near the banks of the Delaware River.

The community's main priority was preserving the center's function as a cultural icon. The regional scholars interested in Port Penn saw the museum as a landscape marker created to express a distinct community identity and view of the past. Recognizing the site as an emotionally charged identifier gave them a greater appreciation of its meaning and significance. These constituents, especially Bernie Herman and David Orr, tried to preserve this function throughout the transfer process and kept it as the reference point to assess the division's actions as steward. After helping to identify the basic themes for the displays, these constituents were also deeply concerned with the initial presentation.

The group of scholars expected displays and programs to reflect local values and esthetics. Having seen many such villages absorbed into urban areas long ago, the scholars were concerned that Port Penn could become a generic site. David Orr said, "The material becomes very important to present. These things are important as a collective memory, as a cultural identity. To make the linkage, all history is local. Port Penn is symbolically a mirror to the past, an avenue to the future."[4]

As a steward ultimately responsible for the site, the Division of Parks and Recreation's priority was to maintain the museum while efficiently managing its limited resources. Port Penn was a small site among a dozen parks throughout the state, each with its own needs. The acquisition of sites, rehabilitation of the building, staffing, and program development represented a significant investment of capital and personnel resources. Despite the unexpected reaction, the agency had to turn to its main mission of operating and maintaining its many facilities across the state.

The series of actions taken to resolve the dilemmas in Port Penn included refining the project's mission and objectives, installing more appropriate displays, and maintaining communication between the museum's steward and its constituents. While the entire project may not be completed for several years, significant progress has been achieved on almost every critical dimension. The division took two incremental actions to address the immediate issues of the use of the museum's space and the organization of the artifact collection.

As a first step, we reconfigured the display by realigning the existing cases and pedestals to allow greater use of the space and added new presentations reflecting the community's esthetic. The current hybrid configuration is not the final display that will ultimately occupy the space, yet it provides a great deal of reassurance to the community that the agency not only could hear and understand local concerns, but could respond with meaningful actions. The additional investment of staff time and funding for the changes was a small fraction of the cost of the building rehabilitation and initial installation, yet it has proven critical in maintaining a positive relationship between the center's steward and constituents.

The second action was the first complete inventory and organization of the artifact collection. At the time of the transfer, the museum's list indicated a collection of about 600 pieces. A physical count revealed more than 2,000 objects, including a substantial range of photographic and archival records. The division quickly identified the most fragile items, about a quarter of the total, and placed them in a heat- and humidity-controlled repository. A collection management method was still needed to allow more effective use of the collection for interpretive tasks. Once a new system was implemented, exhibit and program development proceeded more efficiently.

Having seen the immediate issues addressed, constituents naturally turned back to the big picture. What was the division up to, and why? How would it complete the project? What was the community's role? A third and major step, reforming the planning process, helped to articulate those goals and develop a method to implement them.

The division led a master planning process to define the long-term goals of the museum's constituents. The process involved a series of facilitated meetings with staff, the community, historical society members, and scholars. The resulting master plan document reviews the roles of the division and historical society, details mutual goals, and outlines actions the division will take to realize those goals. In addition to fostering communication, the process gave the division's interpretive staff a broader view of the project's dimensions.

Unlike most park master plans, where a distinct piece of land is designed for recreational uses for general audiences, this plan had to incorporate a cultural project in the midst of a living town. Within the division, the folklife program led an interpretive planning process to ensure that staff understood the project's cultural dimensions and to develop plans reflecting the community's esthetic priorities. This planning process also involved a series of meetings and required a review of basic concepts in history, culture, folklife, and museum education. Once the division's interpretive staff understood the project, it was easier for them to identify suitable display esthetics.

The master plan indicates the community's desire for the rehabilitation of the state's existing properties and the presentation of interpretive stories in the local folk esthetic. A cultural historical approach, incorporating economic, social, and folk history and their meanings, allows the cohesive interpretation of several key but separate sites within the village. Once they comprehended the overall plan, the community had a better understanding and acceptance of the division's actions. Many in the community are now working with agency staff to acquire the financial resources needed to implement the plan.

The staff interpretive plan incorporates each of the state-owned sites, indicates methods to include the built environment, economic history, and folkways, and prescribes folk display esthetics reinforcing these interpretations. With this alignment between steward and constituents, the project now has a significant chance of success. Making that chance a reality is the challenge remaining for the project's steward.

In summary, the Port Penn project can be seen as a microcosm of museums and their cultural relationships. As the museum field matures to better represent American history and culture, museum professionals are compelled to work with local sites, their communities, and their cultural values in a manner meaningful to them. Cultural stewards and constituents need the ability to focus on the contributions each one brings with an appreciation of the constraints each must face. Folkloristic methods that focus on cultural forms, their functions, and their meanings can help broker such complex and contested projects. If the Port Penn project is ultimately successful, it could serve as a model for other cultural projects well into the future.

Journal of Museum Education 24, no. 3 (Fall 1999): 11–14.

Notes

1. Steven D. Lavine and Ivan Karp, "Introduction: Museums and Multiculturalism," in *Exhibiting Cultures: The Poetics and Politics of Museum Display*, ed. Ivan Karp and Steven D. Lavine (Washington, D.C.: Smithsonian Institution Press, 1991), pp. 1–9.

2. Bob Beck, interview by Greg Jenkins, Delaware Folklife Program, 1992, Delaware Division of Parks and Recreation, no. DFP92–T013; Bill and Julia Sidwell, interview by Michael Miller, Delaware Folklife Program, 1997, Delaware Division of Parks and Recreation, no. DFP97–T005.

3. Thelma Bendler, interview by Lee Jennings, Delaware Folklife Program, 1996, Delaware Division of Parks and Recreation, no. DFP96–T001.

4. David Orr, interview by Michael Miller, Delaware Folklife Program, 1998, Delaware Division of Parks and Recreation, no. DFP98–T003.

Finding Public Purpose in a Public Place:
The Missouri Historical Society

A. T. Stephens and Eric Sandweiss

> *The extraordinary attractions of the park, even in its present state, will well reward the visitor. Its dense woods, its majestic trees, wide spreading lawns, offer an enticing spectacle to all who seek a reasonable share of recreation.*

—Report of the Commissioners of Forest Park, St. Louis, 1875

When the commissioners of St. Louis's Forest Park dedicated its 1,300 acres for public use in 1875, they continued a century-old tradition of relating the city's landscape to the interests of its people. From the late 1700s, when French and Spanish colonial administrators marked off the surrounding countryside into hundreds of "common-field" lots—narrow strips of land owned, in spite of their name, individually by the village's inhabitants—and a single shared pasture, or "town common," the notion of balancing public and private good in the young city was most evident in the disposition of its changing landscape. This article focuses on a search for a different sort of "common ground" in St. Louis, carried out by a longtime tenant of Forest Park—the Missouri Historical Society.

By 1872, when the Missouri legislature authorized the purchase of the woods, fields, and swamps that would become Forest Park, St. Louis was a vastly different place from the colonial outpost where administrators had doled out common-field lots a century earlier. Soon to take its place as the nation's fourth-largest city, St. Louis was already touted as "the Future Great City of the World" by local boosters. An industrial and financial center perched at the edge of the western frontier, the city drew tens of thousands of immigrants each year from the East Coast and from across Europe. What the city lacked, for all its promise, was some of the social cohesion that had characterized the colonial village. This perceived sense of fragmentation, and its potential for political repercussions, motivated civic leaders to set aside a new common ground four miles west of the city's crowded commercial waterfront. Forest Park was at once a promotional scheme for upper-class residential development, a resort for the masses, and an act of genuine public philanthropy. Within a decade, private carriages and public streetcars were bringing nearly 3 million visitors a year to enjoy the park's miniature lakes, cascades, handsome drives, and shady walks. Forest Park had indeed become a "spectacle to all."

As one of the nation's largest urban parks, Forest Park has from its inception demonstrated the remarkable variety of ways in which a public place can serve its community. Just as St. Louisans by 1875 no longer needed a town common, so have citizens in succeeding generations continually reassessed the value of their shared spaces. The evolution of Forest Park and the master plans drawn up in response to changing needs also leads, not incidentally, to the case of the Missouri Historical Society.

The park was redesigned most dramatically, and not without controversy, for the city's greatest civic prize, the 1904 Louisiana Purchase Exposition. With $15 million in private subscriptions, corporate donations, and pledges from the states of the Louisiana Purchase—an amount equal to what the United States paid Napoleon for the Louisiana Territory—park planners built 43 international exhibition buildings, 45 pavilions for the Plateau of States, and a "Ten Million Dollar Pike" of concessions and popular exhibits.

As embedded as the World's Fair became in St. Louisans' enduring civic mythology, its lasting impact on Forest Park was limited. The fair's dramatic landscape of lagoons and waterways was maintained, but only the Palace of Fine Arts (today the Saint Louis Art Museum) remained from among the exposition's hundreds of buildings. As officials grappled with the problem of restoring the park's public buildings and rolling fields, they seized an opportunity to explore its social uses as well. Their evolving rationale for park space emphasized active recreation over the old model of passive leisure and esthetic enjoyment. Incoming commissioner Dwight Davis, writing in 1915, emphasized that the city's parks should "perform the maximum social service to the community," adding that "to the element of natural beauty has been added the conception of social utility, that the primary purpose of the park system has become the raising of men and women rather than grass and trees."[1]

In keeping with Davis's focus on "social service," exposition officials dedicated the fair's $600,000 surplus to the construction of "an enduring monument to Thomas Jefferson" that might stand in the park long after the fair was forgotten. The Jefferson Memorial, dedicated in 1913, was intended as "something more than architecture and art," as "a living institution in the memory of Jefferson."[2] The classically styled, granite and limestone building was designated as the repository for the archives and relics of the exposition and also as "the home of the Missouri Historical Society—a safe and abiding place for the rare and invaluable records of a section whose early beginning will become more and more interesting as it grows in wealth and population and culture."[3] Through this mingling of impulses toward monumentality, public service, and public memory, the Missouri Historical Society came to occupy ground that was consciously devoted to the public welfare.

A Changing Public Mission

Established in 1866, the Missouri Historical Society had a history not unlike that of Forest Park. While never a public institution, the society was conceived by its founders as the repository of a shared public memory. As in other historical museums of the time, that conception was betrayed by an exceptionally narrow perspective on the past, born of the trustees' own shared but endangered sense of noblesse oblige in a fast-changing city. The move from offices downtown to the Jefferson Memorial—a public site funded with private and public dollars—represented an early, if unwitting, union of traditional institutional goals with a broadened sense of public responsibility.

In its first six decades in Forest Park, however, the Missouri Historical Society continued on a path that was typical for institutions of its kind. In its archival and artifact collections, exhibitions, and public programs, the society presented values and perspectives of an entitled portion of the community in

---

Rather than thinking of our future programs as being defined and divided by medium . . . we are better prepared to think of them in terms of their underlying message or their contribution to our sense of purpose as a community institution.

---

a manner that suggested that this was the entire community. By the 1970s, the changing climate in museology and the expanding matrix of social history had begun to affect the Missouri Historical Society just as it did many other museums and historic sites. A broadened audience for educational programming and increased attention to matters of race, class, and gender characterized this period of development. Each helped pave the way, in turn, for a more fundamental shift in the society's relation to its public—its admission into the St. Louis Zoo-Museum District (ZMD), a small group of cultural institutions funded in part by a property tax assessment in St. Louis City and County. Inclusion in the ZMD, approved in 1987 by a majority of area voters, was both a reflection of the progress the society had already made in appealing to a wider cross-section of the community and a material spur to the continuation of that progress.

Today, with our success materially dependent on public support, we struggle to reconceive, more consciously than ever before, the institution's relationship to the community it serves. While that effort is manifest in a variety of public and civic initiatives, it is taking shape most visibly on the shared ground of Forest Park in a 129,000-square-foot addition to the Jefferson Memorial that is scheduled to open early in 2000. By the 1980s, with a growing commitment to programs, collections, and exhibitions that were more reflective of the public's interests, we felt increasingly limited by our building. The Jefferson Memorial's 12,000 square feet of exhibition space were an obstacle to highlighting significant parts of the collections that represented the city's many communities. In the mid-1990s, we launched a capital campaign to expand the museum. Mindful of our setting within the park, we conceived of the new structure not just as a container of objects but as something akin to Jane Jacobs's concept of a successful public space as "a stage setting for people" and a continuation and enhancement of the park that surrounds us. The "new" Missouri History Museum, if our ambition and wishes come true, will tell stories. It will be a revelatory place where visitors can, to borrow from one-time St. Louisan T. S. Eliot writing in "Little Gidding," "arrive where we started / And know the place for the first time." The staff is committed to making the building an unparalleled setting for examining the diverse perspectives, common values, and shared legacies that have brought us to the opening of the 21st century in metropolitan St. Louis.

Missouri Historical Society president Robert Archibald set the tone for our conception of the building as a common ground for St. Louisans to explore the evolution of their shared or separate communities. "Out of individual and collective memory," he wrote, "identity evolves for people and their communities, which makes them distinct from others. The Missouri Historical Society is specific to this place—the St. Louis area—and is only relevant here. This is because history is never generic, it is always about people, a place, and the passage of time." Archibald went further in positing a set of underlying social challenges "that persist through time and that must inform future decision making in order to create a community that is more just, more civil, more humane, and that provides adequate economic opportunity and spiritual sustenance for [the community's] members in a manner that is sustainable."[4] This notion sounds wonderful, dauntingly ambitious for those of us working in a museum-configured universe. But what would St. Louisans make of our mission? And, of greater significance, how could we truly represent the questions, dreams, and stories of the people who will come to the museum and who live here?

Seeking St. Louis

Within the institution, we began the process of translating vision to reality through a project that we have come to call "Core"—short for the core exhibits, collectively called *Seeking St. Louis*, that will fill three of the four major galleries in the new addition. Nearly 4,000 objects—close to one-tenth of the society's holdings—will be on display, many for the first time. In the four years since project planning began, some 85 of 140 staff members have been engaged in *Seeking St. Louis*. The program divisions—Collections and Conservation, Education and Community Programs, Exhibits and Special Projects, Publications, and Research—have contributed curators, archivists, librarians, museum educators, program facilitators, exhibit designers, historians, conservators, and other related specialists to the task.

But *Seeking St. Louis*, as the society's principal exhibition over the next decade, will be more than an organizational challenge. It is also an important statement of our conception of the institution's role in relation to its public audience. Beyond seeing the project itself as a kind of public service—that is, as a response to people's often-expressed desire for a comprehensive history of the region that simultaneously showcases our extensive collections—we resolved to take a frankly advocative role in our selection and interpretation of the stories that make up this history. We expected our own viewpoints to color our analysis of people and events, as the viewpoints of the museum staff and trustees of a century ago had affected their work. We hoped those viewpoints, unlike theirs, would be more frankly critical of the ways in which the region's history had been shaped and more positive about the possibility for significant social change. The initial tasks, then, became first to articulate a more inclusive conception of the community and then to develop a clear rationale, internally and externally, for our stance in relation to that community.

We developed our rationale through a more explicit working-out of the goals that accompanied our building campaign. Archibald challenged staff to design an exhibition that responded to four broad propositions:

•In a world of finite resources, each generation has an obligation to temper its own needs with a commitment to the welfare of those who will follow.

•Individual liberties afforded by a free society require a corresponding commitment to shared civic responsibilities.

•A successful society gives its members the freedom to pursue meaning in diverse, personal ways.

•History is a process of discussion and change rather than an accumulation of static facts.

While each of these values is itself situated within a long and familiar tradition of Western social and cultural development, we knew that the task of elucidating them through artifacts—and particularly through our existing collections—would not be easy. The tension between our abstract beliefs and our material resources required flexibility from two directions. It meant aggressively adding to the collections and to the stories that we tell, and it meant putting the core values into terms that made them more directly responsive to, and suggestive of, the material evidence that visitors ultimately search for in museums.

The task of keeping the project true to its initial aims and achievable in a short span of time became even more complex as we sought to include the outside feedback that we had long thought necessary. After we had developed our ideas into an articulated but still malleable state, we initiated ongoing relationships with a variety of new audiences and formed community-based focus groups to solicit advice and ideas. One group drew broadly from people with a commitment to cultural life in St. Louis. Another consisted of African American St. Louisans, most of whom had an interest in history but were unfamiliar with the museum. A third group helped us focus on the needs of those visitors with learning or physical disabilities. In another, the staff of a public elementary school gave us the opportunity to develop kid-focused activities in cooperation with their students. At several steps along the way, scholars and museum professionals reviewed our work and offered us valuable feedback from their areas of expertise.

Lessons for the Future

Because of its size, historical scope, and interpretive ambition, the Core project has challenged the Missouri Historical Society in ways that other museum professionals will surely recognize from their own work on projects of a similar scale. Our responses to these opportunities, while not always perfect, have helped us model ideas for expanding the notion of institutional collaboration and public responsibility beyond one project and into the fabric of all our programs. What we have learned so far has clear implications for our future definition of our role as a "public" institution.

Procedural Lessons

The same democratizing impulse that has characterized our changing relationship to the community has, with relative success, been applied internally on this project. The task of applying the skills and resources of every division of the institution to the Core exhibition was vexing but necessary. In the recent past, exhibition planning had settled into a fairly focused structure: a director of interpretation was responsible for defining exhibit subject and interpretation, supervising research and artifact selection, and writing labels; an exhibits staff was in charge of design and installation. This arrangement seemed neither desirable nor feasible in light of our task. Instead, we asked how the exhibition might look if we placed curatorial, educational, and design concerns on a par with historical interpretation as the driving force behind the exhibition's conception.

Working from the outside in, by identifying stories, themes, and exhibit techniques that seemed important enough to merit further research, and from the inside out, by locating artifacts in the collections that seemed most intriguing or worthy of display, interdisciplinary project teams created a range of suggestions for further exploration. Their work was guided by the director of research and the director of exhibitions. These teams developed a combined interpretive and experiential outline of the exhibition that drew from the initial work and focused its subsequent development.

As the project progressed, the character and selection of the exhibits evolved. So, too, did the work necessary to move each stage to completion. Teams shifted; the decisions of one sector or another gained or diminished in importance; new relationships were forged, and a few were strained. While a more focused or hierarchical structure might have minimized these shifts, it clearly would have foundered given the scale of the experience we were planning.

By the summer of 1999, the exhibition is reaching what promises to be a trying, but rewarding, stage. Staff are focusing on the fine points of artifact conservation and mounting, label editing, design specifications, and fabrication. Now, as at each step over the past few years, the process of creating *Seeking St. Louis* proceeds partly in response to a clearly articulated set of advance goals and partly in hasty reaction to day-to-day crises. The flexibility and the shared sense of responsibility that were built into the process from its earliest days continue to stand us in good stead as we enter this concluding stage. Further, they seem to have generated the feeling among staff that all our internal projects must proceed from a shared effort that draws on the talents and capabilities of a variety of individuals. Rather than thinking of our future programs as being defined and divided by medium, as we have in the past, we are better prepared to think of them in terms of their underlying message or their contribution to our sense of purpose as a community institution.

Interpretive Lessons

Related to a sense of purpose is the second and equal challenge: developing an exhibition that satisfies broad public expectations for a general explanation of the region's history while focusing attention on persistent social challenges that ultimately outweigh, in our estimation, the importance of the particular stories contained within that history.

Since the ideas for the exhibition were first discussed, we have tried to stretch in both these directions. The core values are restated throughout the exhibition as simple questions or challenges facing St. Louisans over time: How do we provide for ourselves? How do we get along with one another?

How do we find meaning in our lives? How do we remember? The stories that we tell (primarily, though not exclusively, through material evidence) are weighted toward demonstrating those challenges at work, often leading us to borrow or acquire artifacts that were not part of our extensive collections. While the exhibition will, we hope, answer our visitors' commonly expressed desire for an "explanation" of St. Louis history, the traditional chronological narrative shares experiential weight with thematic sections that emphasize the continuity and persistence of social challenges across time. These sections are entered not through summaries of key events or dates, but through more intimate "story places," re-creations of specific sites in which specific individuals, from the legendary explorer William Clark to a 1940s armaments worker named Margaret Kuhnert, responded to a moment of challenge. An entire gallery, called "A Place in Time," is devoted not to historical storytelling but to the broader questions of how, precisely, one defines this place and how historical awareness can engage us to reshape it for the future.

The procedural and interpretive lessons of *Seeking St. Louis* are little different from the lessons now being learned at many museums that have embarked on a similar revival of mission and relevance in the marketplace. In our case, the concrete task of expanding our facilities on the cherished ground of Forest Park has forced us to focus on realizing many of the claims, and furthering the initiatives, that were set in motion long ago. As a tenant of this region's greatest public space, and as one of the beneficiaries of a generous tax levy, we can afford nothing less than to continue challenging ourselves to provide a significant public service to our neighbors and fellow citizens. For all of its cost, space, and years of staff effort, *Seeking St. Louis* is really no more than a point of debarkation. Our aim is not only to "offer an enticing spectacle to all," but to be, in Bob Archibald's words, "always about people, a place, and the passage of time." The "new" Missouri History Museum is our offering to an expanding constituency that is already seeking ways to rekindle a sense of common purpose, to provoke a new search for the common ground that will bring St. Louisans together in the future—in their shared park and in the streets and neighborhoods beyond.

Journal of Museum Education 24, nos. 1 and 2 (1999): 26–30.

Notes

1. *Annual Report*, Division of Parks and Recreation of the Department of Public Welfare, City of St. Louis, 1915, p. 3.

2. David R. Francis, *The Universal Exposition of 1904* (St. Louis: Louisiana Purchase Exposition Company, 1913), p. 678.

3. John T. Scharf, *History of St. Louis City and County* (Philadelphia: Louis H. Everts & Co., 1883), p. 751.

4. Robert Archibald, *Annual Report*, (St. Louis: Missouri Historical Society, 1994), p. 4.

Further Reading

The following citations are listed chronologically to provide a progression of thought on the role of museums in public discourse and the many ways individual organizations have met the challenge of addressing their communities' needs.

Karp, Ivan, and Steven D. Lavine, eds. *Exhibiting Cultures: The Poetics and Politics of Museum Display*. Washington, D.C.: Smithsonian Institution Press, 1991.

Karp, Ivan, Christine Mullen Kreamer, and Steven D. Lavine, eds. *Museums and Communities: The Politics of Public Culture*. Washington, D.C.: Smithsonian Institution Press, 1992.

Karp, Ivan, and Steven Lavine. "Communities and Museums: Partners in Crisis." *Museum News* 72, no. 3 (May/June 1993): 44–45, 69, 79–84.

Anderson, David. "Museum Education in Europe: Societies in Transition." *Journal of Museum Education* 19, no. 1 (Winter 1994): 3–6.

Ames, Kenneth. "Anonymous Heroes: Background History and Social Responsibility." *Museum News* 73, no. 3 (September/October 1994): 32–35, 59.

Bunch, Lonnie. "Fighting the Good Fight: Museums in an Age of Uncertainty." *Museum News* 74, no. 2 (March/April 1995): 32–35, 58–62.

Museums in the Life of a City: Strategies for Community Partnerships. Washington, D.C.: American Association of Museums, 1995.

Booth, Kathy, ed. *Culture Builds Communities: A Guide to Partnership Building and Putting Culture to Work on Social Issues*. Washington, D.C.: Partners for Livable Communities, 1995.

Carr, David. "The Personal Past in Public Space." *Journal of Museum Education* 20, no. 2 (Spring/Summer 1995): 3–5.

Zien, Jim. "Strategies for Long-Term Community Partnerships." *Journal of Museum Education* 20, no. 2 (Spring/Summer 1995): 17–21.

Museums in the Social and Economic Life of a City. Summary of a conference sponsored by the American Association of Museums, Partners for Livable Places, and the Philadelphia Initiative for Cultural Pluralism. Washington, D.C.: American Association of Museums, 1996.

Fischer, Daryl K., ed. *Museums, Trustees, and Communities: Building Reciprocal Relationships*. Washington, D.C.: American Association of Museums and Museum Trustees Association, 1997.

Rosenzweig, Roy, and David Thelen. *The Presence of the Past: Popular Uses of History in American Life*. New York: Columbia University Press, 1998.

Glassberg, David. "Presenting History to the Public: The Study of Memory and the Uses of the Past." *Cultural Resource Management* 21, no. 11 (1998): 4–8. Available at: http://tps.cr.nps.gov/crm/issueindex.cfm.

Lila Wallace–Reader's Digest Fund. *Opening the Door to the Entire Community: How Museums Are Using Permanent Collections to Engage Audiences.* New York: Lila Wallace–Reader's Digest Fund, 1998. Available at: www.wallacefunds.org/lilaframesetpub.htm

Tucker, Marcia. "Museums Experiment with New Exhibition Strategies." *New York Times,* January 10, 1999, 40.

Archibald, Robert. *A Place to Remember: Using History to Build Community.* Nashville, Tenn.: American Association for State and Local History/AltaMira Press, 1999.

Ellis, Rex. "Issues of Inclusion and Access." *Virginia Association of Museums Quarterly,* Spring 1999, 3–5.

Carr, David. "The Need for the Museum." *Museum News* 78, no. 2 (March/April 1999): 31–35, 56–57.

Lila Wallace–Reader's Digest Fund. *Engaging the Entire Community: A New Role for Permanent Collections.* New York: Lila Wallace–Reader's Digest Fund, 1999. Available at: www.wallacefunds.org/lilaframesetpub.htm

RESPONSES IN PRACTICE—
HOW DO YOU RESPOND?

Use these questions and the essays in this section to stimulate discussion. You may want to consider your own museum, or you may draw on your experience in other museums or other settings.

1/ What current policies, strategies, and programs were inconceivable at your museum a decade ago? What has changed? What drove the changes? How are such changes echoed in other sectors of society?

2/ What museum programs or strategies that you know of best represent a new era for museums? Why?

3/ Museums increasingly address controversial and sensitive topics in their exhibits and programming. How effective are these efforts? Why? Why not?

4/ If you could be mentored in a particular museum strategy or practice, what would it be? Who would you want to learn from? Why?

5/ Does the board or staff in your museum look any different from the way it did 10 years ago? Discuss the motivating factors or barriers to such change.

6/ Which articles in this section do you find most useful? Why? Outline an article that you would contribute. How would you ensure its usefulness to readers?

Part 3

UNDERSTANDING: THEORY, RESEARCH, AND EVALUATION

PARADIGMS SHIFTED: COMPREHENDING THE MEANING FROM WITHOUT

Kenneth Yellis

When I lived in Washington, D.C., a fellow member of the museum education mafia would call me up every so often and the conversation would go something like this: "I want you in this group I'm forming to discuss the philosophy of museum education." Typically, I would respond, "Sure, but I think what we really need to be talking about is the theory of museum education." "What," she would reply, "is the difference?"

Well "theory," says my 1989 *Webster's Ninth New Collegiate Dictionary*, is "an analysis of a set of facts in their relation to one another . . . the general or abstract principles of a body of fact, a science, or an art." On the other hand, the definition of "philosophy" my colleague had in mind, I suspect, was "a search for general understanding of values and reality by chiefly speculative rather than observational means."

My dictionary goes on to note the popular sense of the word "theory" as "conjecture," which is how most people use it. "My theory is that he's lying" was a perennial favorite in D.C. then and remains so now. While the popular definition is diverting, it is worth our while to pause for a moment on the formal meaning of theory in the context of Part 3. The significance lies in the matter of verifiability—that is, the relationship between theory and research, what distinguishes theory from guesswork, hunches, intuition, wishful thinking. Research is what allows us to test, controvert, and adjust theory, our formulation of apparent relationships of observed phenomena.

Research without theory would be mere data, lacking the structure that would make it information susceptible of translation into action, or even intelligibility. Theory without research, on the other hand, is mere metaphor. In the museum world for much of the 20th century, our metaphors, because they were tacit and never subjected to analysis, much less testing, were dangerous, shaping our behavior and our spiritual stance toward our work—often without our even recognizing it. In organization theory, it would obviously make a big difference if the metaphor for bureaucracy were machine or octopus or fogbank. One could say the same about how museum people view the public—as machine, octopus, fogbank, or whatever. The point is not that the metaphor is negative but that it is tacit, that it is not examined, tested, or even recognized. As a result it may or may not be useful, accurate, healthy, or productive. And that, I believe, is the literal definition of psychosis: to live and act on the basis of a tacit, untested, unsuccessful, harmful, self-serving, or unproductive metaphor.

Theory and research—and the connection between the two—are at the center of what the *Journal of Museum Education* has been trying to do since its inception as *Roundtable Reports* 30 years ago. So, too, has been evaluation, their somewhat distant cousin. Evaluation is what allows us to learn whether, prospectively (i.e., formative evaluation), the form of what we are about to do matches the function we intend it to serve and, if not, what can be done about it. Retrospectively, summative evaluation allows us to describe what happened and, presumably, learn from it. The goal is to help museum professionals make explicit—and verifiable—formulations of, say, the relationship between visitor behavior and learning—whatever we mean by that—and museum practice, what we actually *do*. What do we think is happening, why does it happen, how do we know?

To the triumvirate of theory, research, and evaluation I might add a fourth element: Donald Schoen's concept of reflective practice, to use the phrase introduced to the museum field some years ago by Mary Ellen Munley—to rather puzzling controversy, it might be said. We may not as busy practitioners have—or feel—much need for theory or much time for research, but we are often required to conduct or direct evaluations. We have an obligation—and an opportunity—to be revising what we do on the basis of what we find out. We are also obliged to reflect on what we do as we grow and change as individuals and as professionals and as the culture changes around us. Anyway, what's the alternative—and what fun would that be?

Where theory and practice meet—where, in fact, almost every article in this part is to be found—has historically been the least busy intersection in the field. It is only in the last decade or so that it even became necessary to put a traffic light there. For me, what is most interesting in this part are the controversies and the evidences of rethinking and revision on the part of our authors. My point is: Theory doesn't just guide practice and color how we think and how we do things—theory *is* practice. After all, to behave differently, you'd have to think differently, wouldn't you? How can you think differently unless you revise your theory?

The field as a whole—as opposed to individuals—has historically had great difficulty learning from experience in this way. There are many historical and sociological reasons why this has been the case and why progress in the development of a viable theory has been so slow, fitful, and filled with excursions up blind alleys. My personal view is that the almost total lack of a body of a critical literature, both lay and professional, has been a major contributing factor; where, until very recently, have we had the museum equivalent of the *Cahiers du Cinema*, or even Siskel and Ebert?

Another factor has to have been the persistent tendency—dare I say preference?—on the part of museums to treat their visitors as ciphers, waiting for us to inject meaning in their previously empty lives, all evidence to the contrary notwithstanding. What I find so refreshing about the articles in this part—which stand in for a rather larger body of writing in the *Journal* and elsewhere—is their humility. They embody the belated recognition that, like it or not, visitors carry all sorts of meaning with them. We ignore this to the detriment of those we say we seek to serve and, we have learned, at our peril. So, on the evidence of these articles, our paradigm has shifted. Or, like Woody Allen, for whom success meant failure with a better class of woman, we have progressed to a higher order of ignorance. This is progress.

Perhaps we could not figure out how to turn our ideas into theories—or which forms of research could corroborate or disprove them. Perhaps we needed the stimulus of external scrutiny, in the form of meaningful exhibition criticism, for example, or the kinds of accountability expected of us by funding agencies. Perhaps we needed a think tank. Perhaps we needed to be liberated from constrictive cognitive models borrowed from educational psychology and other disciplines. Perhaps we needed simply to borrow more broadly—and more analytically—from a wider range of disciplines, as recently we have finally done.

Let me suggest a few of the many reasons for this recent relative success of the struggle by museums and museum people, especially the visitor research and evaluation community and, of course, the educators, to shed this form of pathology. One may have been the growing sense that museums are in a fierce competition with other forms of leisure and cultural activity, at a time of continual—albeit, self-reported—decline of free time. Then, too, as the stakes and the costs have risen, more intense scrutiny and a greater emphasis on measurable results were inevitable. Beyond this, the degree of accountability expected by funding sources and by the public has risen by quantum steps.

As competition has increased for the public's scarce leisure time and for scarce financial support, museums have sought to expand beyond their traditional markets. Traditional audiences simply have less time to give and value it more highly. And now there's more competition for that time. If museums were asking new audiences to spend valuable free time with them, those museums have needed a good reason why those audiences should, especially if they have rarely or never done so before.

At the same time, these same leisure-challenged Americans generate two or more new museums a week, even as many existing museums merge, go dormant, or scale back their activities. Why? It would appear that Americans, who create museums so feverishly while allowing others to wither or die, have an ambivalent—and ambiguous—relationship with them. In Brian de Palma's *Dressed to Kill* a gallery in the Philadelphia Museum of Art stands in for the Metropolitan Museum of Art. Are we supposed to think that museums look pretty much the same once you get inside, if you ever do? Surely people know better—don't they?

Well, museum people know that museums are not the same and that their uniqueness is what makes them interesting workplaces. We assume that this is also what makes them interesting places to visit. But what do visitors and, in particular, nonvisitors think about that? Are they looking for the same kind of "flow experiences" that brought us into the field in the first place, a chance to experience total immersion, to connect to something larger than themselves? Museums offer, we believe, a kind of grace, liberation from drudgery, anxiety, and the tyranny of the mundane. Is that what they want? I would argue that at some level, historically and still, most museum people believe in their heart of hearts that the core of our enterprise is about this liberation, this offering of grace.

The growing knowledge base allows us to understand better what keeps people out. It also enables us to know what they bring in with them—the awe and wonder and serenity many derive from the *physical* environment museums create, the light, openness, serenity, power, space, warmth, cleanliness, meticulousness, artfulness or drama, the careful and attractive presentation of the objects themselves—or the innerness, the intimacy and privacy— or the value they attach to the treasures of civilization, to human creativity— or the chance to touch base with something fundamental—or the sense of seamlessness in the experience—or the need to experience something authentic, genuine, unmediated—or the storytelling structures growing out of a core of meaning—or the chance to be alone—or the chance to be together—or the chance to be alone together—or the chance to be adventurous or unadventurous—or the sense of connectedness—or the context, the way of looking at things anew—or the leisurely tempo—or the space and time for oneself—or the returning to favorite rooms and galleries, favorite objects—or the chance to do very little at all.

I used to think museums took themselves too seriously. I have come to think that they may not have taken themselves seriously enough. People have spoken to me of museum exhibitions that have given them unique, once-in-a-lifetime experiences that were life-transforming events. I have been told repeatedly of mystical or religious experiences of great power, of enveloping or upwelling emotions of great intensity felt in museums or museumlike places. For these emotional events their whole life's experience up to that point prepared them; somehow the museum managed not to spoil it. In many cases, the museum seemed as much to release as to create the experience.

A museum visitor once said to me, "I think you could have a museum for each mood, from the reverent to the playful. You can't really design one museum that would meet everyone's needs all the time." Can't you? Probably not. Is that why we have 12,000 museums?

It still stuns me to hear museums spoken of as filling needs. Clearly, however, we are just discovering what those needs are and how, often inadvertently, we have been responding to them. The growing sophistication of the research and the growing complexity of the theorization we are applying to the problem of the visitor are heartening. Museums appear to be as important to a substantial segment of the public, in tangible and intangible ways, as the public is to us. And while people are not uncritical of us, it appears for many of them to be a lover's quarrel, which is all the more reason for us to pay careful attention.

As we have lately done. The metatheory that so many have awaited so long seems attainable now somehow, if not exactly closer—as I say, a higher order of ignorance prevails. The contributors to this part have enriched a conversation that will keep us busy for quite some time. We are, finally, seeking to comprehend the meaning from without.

Theory

A Framework for Organizing a Cumulative Research Agenda in Informal Learning Contexts

Leona Schauble, Gaea Leinhardt, and Laura Martin

For the past half-century, museums, zoos, botanical gardens, and historical reconstructions have been deliberately fashioning a change in their institutional identities. These institutions have been shifting from a singularly inward-looking role as repositories for the display of valued objects, organisms, or artifacts, toward a multifaceted, outward-looking role as hosts who invite visitors inside to wonder, encounter, and learn. Although this shift has been under way for many years, and in spite of the sustained and persistent efforts of a few committed researchers from both the museum and university communities, a field of research on informal learning in museums has not yet cohered.

This lack of coherence exists in part because of an overriding concern in museums with the evaluation functions of research—an understandable concern, but not one that has been grounded in theory or motivated by the goal of constructing a cumulative knowledge base. The lack of coherence is exacerbated by the fact that the learning research community has until recently paid scant attention to informal contexts. The inattention persists because researchers in psychology and education tend to work from assumptions and methods originally developed to explore learning in laboratories and schools. These assumptions and methods are often inadequate for the very different learning challenges and opportunities in museums. For example, museums do not, by and large, aim exclusively or even primarily for improvement on measures of subject matter knowledge but instead tend to emphasize wider goals better captured by terms like enculturation, development, attitude, and socialization. In a museum, each visitor's "treatment" is unique, because museums afford choice and variability in learning rather than mastery of a common curriculum. Moreover, learning effects of a museum visit may have a very long "cycle time," sometimes emerging years after the encounter occurs. These features make museum learning very difficult to track with the methods and approaches familiar to most researchers. Finally, for many learning researchers, the prototype of learning remains "school learning," and museum learning does not fit this prototype very well.

Yet recently, it seems, there has been a steep increase in the number of fruitful collaborations that have sprung up between museum professionals and learning researchers working together to address these challenges. In the spirit of contributing to this newly blossoming exchange, we introduce here a theoretical framework for research on processes of learning in museums. The framework has been developed to organize the common work of members of the Museum Learning Collaborative (MLC), a partnership sponsored by the Institute of Museum and Library Services. The MLC serves as a common forum for researchers and practitioners interested in learning—broadly construed, to include all forms of meaningful personal change—in informal contexts. These environments span an array of domains, from art and history to natural history and science, and in the future, we expect this variability to grow. Members of the collaborative also work in a wide variety of contexts, including universities, art museums, history museums, children's museums, science museums, zoos, historical reconstructions, arboretums, and botanical gardens.

The purpose of the partnership is to develop and then pursue together a

---

Theory highlights the questions and issues worthy of exploration, points to what is central in the research findings, and provides the integrating frame that serves to define a coherent portrait from a series of independent investigations.

---

research agenda that can support the development of a cumulative body of knowledge on museum learning, one that will build over time and become increasingly generative and generalizable. As it grows, such a knowledge base will transcend the concerns of museums to inspire new issues and questions about the nature of learning itself. To pursue such an agenda together, we need agreement on a broad but well-defined theoretical framework. Theory is essential to keep such an enterprise from spinning off into a mere collection of unrelated investigations, because theory highlights the questions and issues worthy of exploration, points to what is central in the research findings, and provides the integrating frame that serves to define a coherent portrait from a series of independent investigations.

Theoretical Approach: Sociocultural Framework
After initial reflection, we concluded that the guiding theoretical framework that could best organize our common research agenda is sociocultural theory. Sociocultural theory emphasizes that meaning emerges in the interplay

between individuals acting in social contexts and the mediators—including tools, talk, activity structures, signs, and symbol systems—that are employed in those contexts. Individuals both shape and are shaped by these mediators. A unique aspect of humans is our propensity to invent with the instruments of our own development. In our view, this focus on mediators is a perspective that is very congenial to museums, which have long honored symbolic and cultural meanings, signs, and tools. This view also emphasizes the importance of culture, environment, and history in every learning context and every learning event. These general ideas are reflected in the work of both classical theorists (e.g., Luria 1976; Vygotsky 1978) and contemporary researchers in human learning (e.g., Carpenter and Lehrer 1999; Cobb 1994; Lave and Wenger 1991; Wells, Chang, and Maher 1990).

Sociocultural theory suggests that understanding a phenomenon entails understanding its development. Thus, understanding learning means studying in detail how it unfolds. According to this perspective, human thinking is formed by the talk, tools, symbols, artifacts, histories, and activity structures that are its milieu. Rather than explaining variability in learning primarily by positing differences in individuals' propensities and talents, sociocultural theory turns our attention to questions such as: What kinds of activities are supported in this place? What forms of talk are expected? How do tools and symbols support forms of thinking that otherwise could not occur? These issues and questions are particularly fruitful for people—such as educators, exhibit designers, and teachers—who are interested not only in understanding learning but also in engineering productive forms of it.

These features of sociocultural theory imply three main ways in which it can guide learning research in museums toward questions or perspectives that are consistent with the unique nature of learning in these contexts. Specifically, this perspective throws light on the variability of learning, processes of learning, and the role of learning in personal history and the pursuit of meaning.

Sociocultural theory can span the wide variety of informal learning contexts that museums provide and their diverse populations of visitors. Unlike some other theories, it emphasizes the importance of accounting for variability as well as commonalities in visitors' learning. Important forms of variability for study include the experience, knowledge, and interests that visitors bring to museums; the kinds of activities and pathways in which visitors engage during their visits; and the means by which museums contribute to their evolving ways of knowing and responding to the world.

Sociocultural theory focuses on processes of learning, not simply its outcomes. An exclusive concern with learning outcomes implicitly assumes that learning is a kind of "product" and that visitors are containers who carry that product out with them when they leave the museum. Such a metaphor is problematic, given contemporary theories of learning and given the overwhelming variability of what visitors engage with and do in museums. Matusov and Rogoff (1995) suggest that it may be fruitful instead to refocus our attention away from these "products" and toward characterizing the range of the forms and functions of visitors' activity that takes place in museums. How can the learning activities that occur in these environments best be encouraged, fostered, and deepened so that they afford increasing levels of opportunity for future growth?

Third, sociocultural theory is *developmental,* in two different senses—in its methods for tracking change over time and in its emphasis on identifying the role of meaningful encounters and events in the sweep of a person's life history, including investigation into how that meaning may shift at different points in the life span (e.g., Baltes 1978). A developmental approach suggests the value of studying learning over a longer duration than the typical one-trial experiment; identifying relationships between visitors' long-term interests and goals and the museum; and studying the role of important social units, such as peers, families, and communities, in an individual's experiences with the museum.

The final criterion for a useful theory, one that winds through all three mentioned above, is that sociocultural theory foregrounds meaning, not just behavior. Museums are places of signs, symbols, culturally significant artifacts, tools, and activities. Learning entails meaning-making, and it is difficult to think of institutions that more self-consciously value this conceptualization of learning than museums. A focus on meaning highlights the multiplicity of forms of adaptiveness that are characteristic of individuals with widely varying environments, histories, and cultures. What counts as intelligent behavior depends on the mix of values and resources that the culture affords, so the origins of intelligence should be sought in social interaction rather than solely in the heads of individuals. Such a view emphasizes the social roots of cognition and draws attention to places like museums, where people come together in a public place to encounter objects, events, and symbols of particular cultural value.

Three Integrating Themes

This is obviously a very broad guiding theoretical foundation, and from it, we could presumably derive many "big issues" for study. To organize our work together and thus accelerate our progress in the initial years of our collaboration, the MLC partnership has decided to focus on three major integrating themes that follow from the framework. These are: (1) learning and learning environments; (2) interpretation, meaning, and explanation; and (3) identity, motivation, and interest. Our intent is to address each of these inter-related themes with a variety of studies that span different contexts and vis-itor populations. None of these themes is unknown to the museum commu-nity, and as we introduce each below, we illustrate its meaning by providing examples from learning research that has already been conducted or is being conducted in informal learning environments. What is new is the ambition of agreeing on an organizing framework that clarifies the theoretical assump-tions and interrelations among the disparate studies so together we can begin to build toward a body of work that is more than the sum of its discrete parts.

Learning and Learning Environments

The first theme articulates the interrelations between learning and the design of learning environments. Within this theme, we address the variety of ways in which text, images, models, and activities serve as mediators of and supports for learning. Equally important, we explore ways that the findings from these studies can influence the development and design of informal learning contexts. This theme regards the design of learning environments and the study of learning as best proceeding hand in hand. Brown (1992) has suggested the term "design experiments" for studies in which researchers try to understand learning by iteratively developing theoretically based educa-tional interventions and then systematically studying them. Design experi-ments typically proceed in cycles; that is, the initial design is informed by theory, and the theory, in turn, is informed by results, redesign, and further study. The premise of a design approach is that understanding how people learn depends on being able to study processes of learning in environments that actually support learning. Such environments do not naturally occur (e.g., they are not like trees or tigers); people have to construct them. Hence, the design needs to be motivated by a clear vision of what it means to learn. If it is not, there is no good reason to expect that learning, the presumed tar-get of study, will occur.

One advantage of such design experiments is that they avoid the common practice in research of artificially decomposing the system under study into a collection of "factors" that fail to capture important properties of the original whole. For example, a design researcher studying labels within a gallery would be unlikely to try to develop a general set of principles about the best ways of designing effective labels, because a design/systems perspective sug-gests that what counts as an effective label cannot be decided apart from con-cern for the gallery where the labels will appear, who is expected to read them, the function they are to serve, and the message they convey. Regarding research as a design profession has the additional advantage of focusing research questions directly on the tools and artifacts that are employed in the process of design. What are the categories of "design tools" (e.g., Carpenter and Lehrer 1999) that a gallery designer has at hand? Developing a reasonably complete list would be a valuable and intellectually challenging enterprise, but without pretending to do so, we can assume that a person starting such a list might begin by writing down activity structures, social interactions, written text, environments that the visitor enters, narratives, and conversations. This embryonic list illustrates how design research throws light on the very aspects of museums that are most useful for staff to reflect about, because these are the "design tools" that staff have at their disposal.

Design experiments may seem familiar to the museum community; the general approach is consistent with the idea of conducting research on prototypes that will eventually be revised on the basis of the findings. However, unlike much "formative" research, design experiments are explicitly concerned with learning; hence, they emphasize the importance of grounding both the design and the research in issues fundamental to learning.

For example, the design of the *Construction Site* exhibit in the ScienceWorks Gallery at the Children's Museum of Indianapolis was explicitly motivated by a series of studies on children's understandings (and misunderstandings!) of simple machines (Lehrer and Schauble 1998; Lehrer et al. in press; Metz 1991; Penner, Giles, Lehrer, and Schauble 1997; Penner, Lehrer, and Schauble in press; Schauble and Lehrer 1995). Collectively, these studies suggested that elementary school children often fail to see what is before their very eyes when they inspect devices that include gears, levers, and inclined planes. Instead, their expectations and interpretations tend to be driven by familiar mental schemes about the way things usually work. For example, in the context of inspecting chains of gears on a gearboard, children often report that all the gears turn in the same direction, regardless of their configuration or relative size, because "Things move in the direction they are pushed and don't move any faster than the thing that pushes them." The purpose for the *Construction Site* was to provide an environment in which children's extended symbolic play (at being construction workers who operate bulldozers, dump trucks, and giant cranes) would bring them into contact with the need to take actions that highlight important ideas about machines. These might include, for example, negotiating trade-offs between distance and effort in driving wheelbarrows filled with foam "rock" to a dump site over alternative ramps (one steep but short, another shallow but long), or transforming motion through hand levers to giant wheels to move a heavy bulldozer (Schauble and Bartlett 1997).

Interpretation, Meaning, and Explanation

The second major MLC theme emphasizes interpretation, meaning, and explanation as processes and products of social interaction in museums. This theme presses on the issue of dialectics among curator, institution, and viewer, and acknowledges that meaning is inherently social. Museums are places of dialogues. There are implicit dialogues between the display or art object and the viewer, and explicit dialogues between the curator/designer and the viewer/participant, or between docents and multiple participants. These dialogues may range in explicitness from mood or hint to detailed explanation. For example, contrast an exhibit of an Egyptian mummy that is carefully designed to elicit a mood of reverence and respect with an interpretive live animal show featuring local snakes and explaining facts about their growth, eating habits, and reproduction to a group of assembled visitors. Of course, even when visitors come "alone" to informal learning contexts, this dialectic quality is ever present, as the visitor interacts with the meanings and intentions of the exhibit "author." Dialogues also reflect a range of directiveness, from mere invitations to respond internally to general suggestions that can be pursued in many ways, to invariant sequences of prescribed actions. How do visitors learn to participate in these many forms of dialogue? What happens when visitors' expectations do not match those of the designers, and the conversation breaks down? For example, Siegler's (in preparation) research explores how parents attempt to interpret analogic models in museum exhibits to their children and documents the breakdowns in learning that result when there are mismatches or incomplete matches between the objects and relations in the model and the objects and relations in the phenomenon being modeled. Within this general theme, then, we address the ways in which individuals and groups make sense of their experiences within the museum.

Under this theme, we also include investigations of the nature of intentions and social interactions among viewers, and between viewers and the museum. The agenda includes research on patterns of intergenerational, intragenerational, interviewer, and even intraviewer interactions that lead to interpretation. For example, a number of studies have analyzed how and whether social interactions in visiting family groups contribute to this interpretive process (Crowley and Callanan 1997; Leichter, Hensel, and Larsen 1989). Using a body of studies on the development of scientific reasoning as a foundation, Gleason (1997) studied parent-child dyads working together on an open-ended, self-directed scientific experimentation problem very much like the activities frequently featured in science and children's museums. The findings revealed that parents worked actively and effectively to support their children's experimentation strategies but also missed some important opportunities to assist in aspects of their children's reasoning where they did not realize that children were experiencing difficulties. Identifying precisely where and how parents provided (or failed to provide) assistance gave specific clues for exhibit designers about just what parents needed to know to foster their children's learning effectively in experimentation contexts.

Another kind of study that would fit within this theme is research that considers the intentionality of an art museum's display of work and contrasts it with the typical visitor's understanding of the features, problems, and goals of a particular artist. Research on explanations in a variety of learning and teaching situations suggests that to be effective, instructional explanations require an understanding of the query or problem being explained (Leinhardt 1993; Leinhardt and Schwarz 1997). However, the artist, the curator, and the visitor may well have quite different understandings of "problem" (Leinhardt and Young 1996). A naive visitor may feel that the main problem for an artist such as Wyeth or Homer is to paint a moving and representationally accurate picture. Further, the visitor may believe that the main purpose or intentionality of the curator is to show the picture in a way that makes it easily visible. The curator, in turn, may see the problem to be "explained" as one relating to the artist's role in the larger sweep of artists of that time and place. So the curator may choose to explain this problem through arrangements that reflect the way in which the artist handled light or mass over time. Or the curator may wish to explain the technical difficulty that the artist dealt with in specific aspects of a painting by showing multiple sketches in several media of the "same" problem and its attempted "solutions." Does the visitor's sense of task and problem change as a result of these implicit and explicit explanations?

Identity, Motivation, and Interest

The final theme considers how museum experiences both depend upon and change the ways that people see themselves as learners of history, art, or science; as historians, artists, or scientists; and as members of cultural groups with a rich past and an open future. How and what people learn in museums are very much a function of their motivations (why they have come there), their interests (enduring propensities to engage with a topic), and their sense of identity (who they think they are in relation to museum offerings). Identity, motivation, and interest are closely interwoven in people's behavior, although it may be helpful to analyze them separately in research.

Within this theme, one might consider the role of narrative in engaging interest. Many art and history museums use this technique dramatically, although research on its impact is not widely acknowledged. There is an issue about learning here that is deeper than the appeal and efficiency of the form. Cognitive research shows that, universally, people can mentally organize information effectively if it is recounted to them in a story (Mandler and Goodman 1982; Mandler, DeForest, Scribner, and Cole 1980). Even children learn and remember technical information if it is presented as integral to a compelling plot (Children's Television Workshop 1993).

Researchers also recognize that people tell themselves stories about their experiences and that these stories knit the meaning and significance of events they encounter (Bruner 1996; Cortazzi 1993; Feldman, Bruner, Kalmar, and Renderer 1993). For example, the Arizona Science Center's preliminary work finds that many nonscientists have a very different view of the field than do scientists. In a sense, members of the lay public have very different personal stories about science, which may lead to barriers in their understanding. Furthermore, the fact that the canonical organization of science is in models rather than narrative may also raise challenges to comprehension. To explore these issues, the Arizona Science Center, supported by the National Science Foundation, has been investigating the role of narrative in engaging the interests of diverse audiences. Four science-oriented stories about solar energy were written by Native American, African American, Hispanic, and feminist writers in collaboration with scientists and science writers. The stories, which have been tested for audience appeal, next will be made available under controlled conditions to people visiting the solar energy exhibits at the center. Visitors will be observed as they use the story material and interact with related exhibits, to track engagement level, verbalizations, and physical interaction. Recall and reasoning tests will be administered afterward, and follow-up phone interviews will examine the longer-term impact of the narratives on comprehension of and interest in the exhibit topic. Additional studies in this genre may examine the use of stories in other kinds of museums as well, including art and history museums.

These three themes, then—learning and learning environments; interpretation, meaning, and explanation; identity, motivation, and interest—summarize the thrust of our common agenda. Although some studies fit smoothly within one of these overarching themes, at least as many studies will cross their boundaries. For example, one can hardly imagine an effective learning environment that is not concerned with interpretation and visitor interest. In our view, these interconnections are important because they call attention to the relationships among learners and environments in the context of meaning-making. A comprehensive research program on informal learning would do well to focus explicitly on those interconnections and regard them as especially fruitful junctures for study.

Conclusion

A consistent challenge for informal learning contexts has been the need to establish that visitors learn—that is, show enduring changes in their knowledge; their relationship to or attitudes about art, history, science, nature, or aerospace; and their willingness to make that relationship a long-term prospect, one that continues to deepen and change. However, this challenge has not been met successfully by simply importing the existing assumptions and methodologies of learning research. Yet learning research itself is changing. Many researchers are noting that unless research and theory are brought into serious and sustained relationship with authentic practical problems, they threaten to become dangerously specialized, professionalized, and inbred. Equally important, the wider the range of practical problems and environments in which researchers engage, the more likely it is that assumptions will be challenged in a healthy way, theories will be expanded and elaborated as they are required to do more "work," and formulations that are elegant but unfounded will be weeded out. It follows that a healthy research community is one that engages a diverse set of complex environments. Thus, in our view, formulating and pursuing an agenda together are likely to foster growth in both communities if we can agree on a direction broad enough to be inclusive but focused enough to get us somewhere together.

Journal of Museum Education 22, nos. 2 and 3 (1997): 3–8.

References

An annotated bibliography of research on informal learning as well as research updates on the Museum Learning Collaborative's progress may be found on the Web site, http://mlc.lrdc.pitt.edu/mlc/

Baltes, P. B. 1978. *Life span development and behavior.* New York: Academic Press.

Brown, A. L. 1992. Design experiments: Theoretical and methodological challenges in creating complex interventions in classroom settings. *Journal of the Learning Sciences* 2, no. 2:141–78.

Bruner, J. 1996. *The culture of education.* Cambridge, Mass.: Harvard University Press.

Carpenter, T. P., and R. Lehrer. 1999. Teaching and learning mathematics with understanding. In *Mathematics classrooms that promote understanding,* edited by E. Fennema and T. A. Romberg. Mahwah, N.J.: Erlbaum.

Children's Television Workshop. 1993. Children's comprehension of literacy strategies in *Ghostwriter.* New York: Children's Television Workshop.

Cobb, P. 1994. Where is the mind? Constructivist and sociocultural perspectives on mathematical development. *Educational Researcher* 23, no. 7:13–20.

Cortazzi, M. 1993. *Narrative analysis*. Washington, D.C.: Falmer Press.

Crowley, K., and M. A. Callanan. 1997. Shared scientific reasoning in everyday parent-child interactions. Paper presented at symposium, Multiple-space Search in Scientific Reasoning: Developmental Implications. Biennial meeting of the Society for Research in Child Development, Washington, D.C.

Feldman, C., J. Bruner, D. Kalmar, and B. Renderer. 1993. Plot, plight, and dramatism: Interpretation at three ages. *Human Development* 36, no. 6:327–42.

Gleason, M. 1997. Parent-child scientific experimentation: Observations of interactions. Master's thesis, University of Wisconsin, Madison.

Lave, J., and L. Wenger. 1991. *Situated learning: Legitimate peripheral participation*. Cambridge, England: Cambridge University Press.

Lehrer, R., and L. Schauble. 1998. Reasoning about structure and function: Children's conceptions of gears. *Journal of Research in Science Teaching* 35(1): 3-25.

Lehrer, R., L. Schauble, S. Carpenter, and D. Penner. In press. The interrelated development of inscriptions and conceptual understanding. In *Symbolizing and communicating in mathematics classrooms: Perspectives on discourse, tools, and instructional design*, edited by P. Cobb, E. Yackel, and K. McClain. Mahwah, N.J.: Erlbaum.

Leichter, H. J., K. Hensel, and E. Larsen. 1989. Families and museums: Issues and perspectives. *Marriage and Family Review* 13:15–50.

Leinhardt, G. 1993. Instructional explanations in history and mathematics. In *Proceedings of the fifteenth annual conference of the Cognitive Science Society*, edited by W. Kintsch. Hillsdale, N.J.: Erlbaum.

Leinhardt, G., and B. Schwarz. 1997. Seeing the problem: An explanation from Polya. *Cognition and Instruction* 15, no. 3:395–434.

Leinhardt, G., and K. Young. 1996. Two texts, three readers: Distance and expertise in reading history. *Cognition and Instruction* 14, no. 4:441–86.

Luria, A. R. 1976. *Cognitive development*. Cambridge, Mass.: Harvard University Press.

Mandler, J., M. DeForest, S. Scribner, and M. Cole. 1980. Cross-cultural invariance in story recall. *Child Development* 51:19–26.

Mandler, J., and M. Goodman. 1982. Remembrance of things parsed: Story structure and recall. *Cognitive Psychology* 9, no. 1:111–51.

Matusov, E., and B. Rogoff. 1995. Evidence of people's development from people's participation in communities of learners. In *Public institutions for personal learning: Establishing a research agenda*, edited by J. H. Falk and L. D. Dierking, 97–104. Washington, D.C.: American Association of Museums.

Metz, K. 1991. Development of explanation: Incremental and fundamental changes in children's physics knowledge. *Journal of Research in Science Teaching* 28, no. 9:785–97.

Penner, D. E., N. D. Giles, R. Lehrer, and L. Schauble. 1997. Building functional models: Designing an elbow. *Journal of Research in Science Teaching* 34, no. 2:125–43.

Penner, D. E., R. Lehrer, and L. Schauble. In press. From physical models to biomechanics: A design-based modeling approach. *Journal of the Learning Sciences*.

Schauble, L., and K. Bartlett. 1997. Constructing a science gallery for children and families: The role of research in an innovative design process. *Science Education* 81:781–94.

Schauble, L., and R. Lehrer. 1995. The development of model-based reasoning. Paper presented at the annual meeting of the National Association of Research in Science Teaching, San Francisco, Calif.

Siegler, J. In preparation. Analytical thinking in museums: How parents help children interpret models.

Vygotsky, L. 1978. *Mind in society: The development of higher psychological processes.* Cambridge, Mass.: Harvard University Press.

Wells, G., G. L. Chang, and A. Maher. 1990. Creating classroom communities of literate thinkers. In *Cooperative learning: Theory and research,* edited by S. Sharan, 95–121. New York: Praeger.

Situated Motivation and Informal Learning

Scott G. Paris

The purpose of this article is to discuss the role of motivation in informal learning, partly as a complement to the other approaches to informal learning in these two special issues and partly because of the importance of examining the causes and outcomes of learning wherever it occurs. Various motivational processes can serve as useful guides for researchers, educators, and exhibit designers in museums.

Contextual Views of Learning and Motivation

Falk and Dierking (1992) proposed an interactive experience model of learning that results from the intersection of three contexts in museums: the personal, the social, and the physical. The central point of this view of learning is that no single context is sufficient to explain what people take away from their museum experiences. Current theories of learning and motivation are compatible with this approach because they emphasize a person's interactions with other objects and people in a specific situation. Indeed, the unit of analysis in many sociocultural theories is the person in a situation engaged in an action, very much like a museum visitor engaged in exploring and understanding exhibits. The contextual bases for understanding learning were the foundation for early studies of "situated learning" by Brown, Collins, and Duguid (1989), "apprenticeship" by Rogoff (1990), and "legitimate peripheral participation" by Lave and Wegner (1991). Schauble, Leinhardt, and Martin (1997) and Crowley and Callanan (1998) elaborate these social-contextualist approaches.

I suggest that motivation can be analyzed as "situated" in a manner that is analogous to contemporary social-contextual views of learning. Whether a person pursues his or her interests while meandering through a museum, asks questions, picks up objects, reads exhibit labels thoroughly, and so forth is not simply a function of whether the person "has" adequate motivation, because motivation does not vary in amount as much as it varies in the likelihood of expression in specific situations. It follows that the situational elicitation of motivation will have an influence on the content and degree of visitors' learning. The two essential features of motivation are direction and vigor of behavior. What factors influence the direction, goals, and choices of visitors, and what factors influence the vigor, effort, and persistence of people's behavior in museums? Several processes are fundamental for understanding motivation that is "situated" or embedded and elicited in specific settings (Paris and Turner 1994). The motivational processes are presented in an easily remembered format; they all begin with the letter C—constructing meaning, choices, challenges, control, collaboration, and positive consequences.

Constructing Personal Meaning

Many accounts of learning note that people learn best when they actively manipulate the information to be learned and when that information builds on previous knowledge. However, a less emphasized aspect of constructive and active learning is the motivation supplied by connecting new learning with the individual's interests, background knowledge, and emotionally valued topics (Csikszentmihalyi and Schiefele 1992). For example, a visit to a medical exhibit may be especially meaningful if the visitor has a related health condition, or a visit to an art exhibit may be a moving experience if the

---

Various motivational processes can serve as useful guides for researchers, educators, and exhibit designers in museums.

---

visitor knows something about the artist's life. In project-based learning in schools, teachers may provide "driving questions" about the topic or may relate the topic to students' personal experiences in order to motivate their independent investigations (Blumenfeld et al. 1991). In a similar vein, museum visitors often bring with them their own questions, issues, and interests that impel them to explore exhibits. The key similarity is that, in both settings, people are motivated to learn more about topics that have personal relevance and utility.

"Motivated to learn" may not adequately characterize the actions of all visitors, though, because it suggests that learning is limited to acquiring new information. For many people who visit museums, zoos, botanical gardens, and similar places, their motivation may be to construct, elaborate, and relive their personal experiences. They may "learn" more about themselves and their experiences through reflection inspired by exhibits and moods stimulated in these settings. The construction of personal meaning may also involve reminiscing and finding comfort in recollections stimulated by exhibits because people are challenged to find and make meaning in these contexts that bring a sense of self-fulfillment (Kaplan 1995; Silverman 1995). These affective reactions and restorative feelings of peacefulness may represent a neglected aspect of learning: emotional adaptation and aesthetic appreciation. They are deeply motivating because they may rekindle memories, embellish previous knowledge, and extend understanding in idiosyncratic, personal ways. These ephemeral aspects of learning that museum educators notice among their visitors are not ordinarily included in theories of learning that emphasize facts, concepts, and analytical thinking. However, personally constructed meanings are often the compelling reasons for the visit in the first place and the most salient memories for years after. Understanding such aspects of informal learning can expand the understanding of learning in more formal contexts, such as school, where emotional, personal, and aesthetic reactions are often overshadowed by cognitive acquisitions.

Choices

When students have opportunities to choose what they learn and how they demonstrate their mastery, they expend more effort learning the material. Interest in a topic involves both feeling-related characteristics, such as enjoyment and involvement, and value-related characteristics, such as attributing significance to an activity (Schiefele 1991). When people attribute positive values and feelings to particular courses of action, they are likely to choose them and pursue them vigorously (Pintrich and DeGroot 1990). Many tasks in school are closed as opposed to open-ended. Closed tasks do not allow students freedom to explore topics, and they engender little persistence when the correct answer is not known. In contrast, open-ended tasks, such as problem-based learning and hands-on science activities, allow students to explore information according to their interests and familiarity. Open-ended tasks stimulate students' curiosity and invite participation. A hallmark of museum exhibits is their open-endedness; visitors are free to approach, engage, and persist at their own pace. When students in school or visitors in museums have choices, they demonstrate persistence in the face of difficulty, more commitment to the task, and greater self-regulation (Covington 1992; Paris and Cross 1983).

Museum visitors have many kinds of choices, but perhaps the most important concerns their goal orientation. Motivational theorists have contrasted two types of goal orientations—mastery and performance—and noted the consequences for people's behavior (Anderman and Maehr 1994). People who have a mastery orientation believe that effort is critical for their own success. They take risks, exhibit creative and effective strategies, and pursue the completion of the task for the sake of learning and doing their best. In contrast, people who have a performance orientation believe that success is defined by outperforming others. They strive to complete the task quickly, avoid challenging tasks, give up in the face of difficulty, and attribute failure to personal inadequacy (Dweck and Leggett 1988). As you might expect, people who have mastery orientations in academics, athletics, and other endeavors are more confident, satisfied, and higher-achieving than people with performance goals in those situations.

These different goal orientations are also evident in museums. Performance goals are revealed by children filling out required worksheets without thinking as they pass by exhibits on a field trip or by families dutifully taking their children to every single exhibit in a perfunctory manner. We saw children in a hands-on science museum who undermined their own learning opportunities with performance goals (Paris et al. 1994). We watched hundreds of children in grades 1–8 visit the second floor of the museum, a huge open room with more than 50 exhibits. Most of them raced from one exhibit to the next, spending less than a minute at most and less than 20 seconds at many. They turned handles, pushed buttons, pulled ropes, and sped on to the next exhibit. Their motivation displayed free choice, but their behavior seemed directed at "making things happen" or, at best, understanding how to make each exhibit work rather than why it operated as it did. Some may call this a performance goal; others may call it a procedural, as opposed to a conceptual, orientation to the exhibits. Still others might say it is an expected response pattern when you turn loose a class of students with limited time to see many interesting exhibits. Regardless of the reason, all three factors diverted children's motivation from understanding, exploring, and learning about the exhibits. Exhibit designers might examine visitors' reactions to determine if exhibits promote a performance orientation or a mastery orientation among visitors, because the more thoughtful mastery orientation leads to a deeper appreciation of the exhibit and museum experience.

Challenges

Some tasks appear too difficult, and people avoid them because the chances of success are low. Other tasks are so easy that people shun them because there is no pride in completing them and great potential embarrassment in failure. People gauge the degree of challenge that tasks provide and, depending on the situation, may choose to engage in moderately difficult tasks to confirm or enhance perceptions of their competence and self-efficacy (Clifford 1991; Schunk 1989; Zimmerman 1989). For example, Csikszentmihalyi and Hermanson (1995) assert that flow experiences are optimal when environmental challenges are in balance with the individual's skills and abilities. This "fit" with abilities is critical because activities that are too difficult lead to frustration and activities that are too easy lead to boredom (Rohrkemper and Corno 1988).

Museums provide many opportunities for individualized challenges to visitors. The challenges might be given by docents or staff who ask questions of visitors or challenge them to try their hand at an exhibit. Or an exhibit may invite visitors to test their skills against other visitors or against normative expectations for speed, accuracy, and so forth. We found that even the physical arrangement of an exhibit may invite participation because people "see" the challenge that it poses. For example, in one study, we observed that when the pieces of a tangram were partially assembled, visitors were more likely to approach the puzzle and complete it compared to another tangram alongside it that was either fully disassembled or fully completed (Henderlong and Paris 1996). In the same study, we observed a similar effect with wall mazes that visitors could construct to allow a ball to roll along the path. Something about the partially completed maze seemed to challenge visitors to complete it more than a maze that was complete or disassembled. Maybe there was a need for closure, maybe visitors thought that it was "doable" because someone else had done it halfway, or maybe the task was clear and the challenge was just high enough that successful completion led to feelings of pride and satisfaction.

Some tasks invite participation because they are perceived as challenging. Other situations allow visitors opportunities to adjust task difficulty in order to provide reasonable challenges. Then they learn to select and adjust their goals and to take pride in success based on their efforts. Some motivational theorists emphasize that the value of risk taking in the face of challenge depends on the likelihood of failure and the interpretation of failure. For example, Clifford (1991) has described "constructive failure" as opportunities to learn the value of persistence and alternative strategies to accomplish a goal. Positive adjustments to failure events have been referred to as "adaptive learning" because the experiences can stimulate strategies that can be enacted and lead to new levels of perceived efficacy and competence (Rohrkemper and Corno 1988). In this view, visitors may approach museum exhibits that provide reasonable challenges and opportunities to confirm one's competence, but the exhibits need to be designed so that visitors do not feel frustrated if they persist and use good strategies. When adaptive strategies pay off with success, visitors feel a sense of accomplishment in the face of a meaningful challenge.

Control

It is ironic that one of the goals of education is to foster independent learning, yet students are often given few opportunities to select and control their own learning environments. In contrast, museums and community contexts for informal learning place a premium on the individual's self-control. A critical issue for museums is how to nurture autonomous learning, respecting the individual's control of what exhibits are visited and how they are engaged, yet still encourage thorough exploration of the themes, issues, and exhibits. Many museums are meeting this challenge through inquiry-based learning activities including tours stimulated by docents, maps, audiocassettes, and problem-based searches for information.

A key feature of these activities is the opportunity to exercise control using navigation and selection skills, time management, planning, and learning strategies. Open-ended tasks, such as museum explorations, information searches, and cooperative problem-solving, require people to make plans and persevere. Thoughtful engagement in tasks requires strategies that control intentions and impulses to avoid distractions and remain committed to one's selected goal (Corno 1989). These essential skills for museum exploration are analogous to many of the independent learning skills that students need in middle school and high school. They can be nurtured through appropriate experiences in informal learning situations that cede control to students. Thus, self-controlled learning on field trips and museum visits can facilitate self-controlled learning in school.

Part of the appeal of museums for visitors of all ages is the freedom to explore a variety of exhibits, artifacts, and programs, which often inspires a sense of discovery and wonder that motivates further exploration. Visitors' control of the environment makes them active seekers of information and meaning. They make choices and adjust challenges according to their own moods, interests, goals, and knowledge. The motivational power of self-controlled exploration of a stimulating environment should not be underestimated. In school, these feelings have important motivational consequences. For example, Ryan and Grolnick (1986) found that children who perceive their classrooms as promoting autonomy reported greater interest in their schoolwork, greater perceived confidence in school, and generally positive views of their self-worth. Museums that encourage self-controlled learning may provide similar benefits for the attitudes and perceptions of visitors.

Collaboration

Social interaction is motivating in several ways. First, people stimulate each other's imaginations. Questions, comments, and new ideas introduce elements of surprise that pique curiosity and encourage further exploration. Collaboration encourages discussion and social negotiation of ideas so that visitors explore alternative perspectives, methods, and solutions. Second, collaboration promotes teamwork and social cooperation. Social goals are more motivating than performance or ego-centered goals. Motivation is enhanced when working with others because there is an obligation to the group and a shared goal of learning together. Third, there are social supports for task completion that enhance effort allocation from individuals. More simply, people work harder in groups, and productive social interactions promote positive concepts about the activity. Fourth, when people work together, they provide models of expertise that others can emulate. Children or novices at a task can watch skilled people and learn through observation and modeling. This is part of the "legitimate peripheral participation" emphasized by Lave and Wegner (1991). Fifth, peers provide benchmarks for monitoring one's own level of accomplishment, which may in turn increase the belief in self-efficacy. Watching others may persuade the observer that "I can do that, too" or "I'm pretty good at this." Mentors, docents, and tutors provide encouragement as well as models, and their support is often essential for maintaining people's effort and feelings of accomplishment.

Consequences of Learning

Closed tasks in schools focus on correct answers in the same ways that some visits to museums are limited to answering "What is it?" or "Did you see everything?" Such narrow views of learning are countered by open-ended activities that allow students and museum visitors greater choices, challenges, control, collaboration, and construction of personal meaning. People take away different consequences from closed and open-ended activities. When students are working to obtain the correct answer, they focus on right and wrong, number correct, and scores on tests—common denominators of extrinsic motivation and performance goals. Students rarely take pride in their effort or accomplishments under these circumstances. In contrast, when visitors in museums work to understand, they focus on the processes of learning, the ambiguities of problems, and multiple perspectives on objects. These mastery-oriented approaches to self-discovery foster feelings of pride and self-efficacy that are based on the person's efforts and adaptive strategies.

We observed these positive feelings of self-efficacy in an activity called "If I Had a Hammer," which was conducted at the Henry Ford Museum & Greenfield Village. This field trip activity for grades 4–8 was designed by Perry Wilson "to help students apply skills they are learning in school to a real-life activity" (Lantos 1994, 14). The program has been adopted by the National Building Museum and, with sponsorship from Home Depot, is offered at museums around the country. The two-and-a-half-hour activity involves assembly of a small house and emphasizes teamwork, planning, and problem-solving. During the activity, participants are given information about mathematics, engineering, ecology, history, and architecture. Nearly all the participants were excited by the activity because it was a novel challenge with a tangible outcome. They were proud of their accomplishments and saw the relevance of problem solving and teamwork. Clearly, they had fun, felt proud, and displayed their confidence in using the tools and building the house. These consequences motivate children to learn more about building things and also motivate them to return to the museum.

Designing Motivating Situations

The challenge facing educators in schools and museums alike is to create environments that nurture learning and discovery. This task may be easier to accomplish in informal learning contexts where the objects, exhibits, and programs are arranged in an open landscape that invites exploration. Museum environments foster intrinsic motivation and sustained engagement because they promote construction of personal meaning, permit choices, provide challenges, foster personal control over learning, invite collaboration, and lead to feelings of pride and self-efficacy. These principles of intrinsic motivation provide some guidelines for creating effective, motivating learning environments in schools and museums and illustrate how informal and formal learning situations can reinforce each other.

A museum program that exemplifies these principles was "Hands-On Biology," designed by the Ann Arbor Hands-On Museum in Michigan with the support of the Howard Hughes Medical Foundation (Paris, Yambor, and Packard 1998). This six-week curriculum for grades 3–5 matched state-mandated educational objectives and fostered hands-on experiences with plants, animals, and scientific equipment. A primary goal was to increase the participation and interest of girls and minority students in science through engaging laboratory activities and guidance from female and minority college students.

"Hands-On Biology" was a partnership among museum staff, teachers in local schools, and a university. The museum provided the teacher, the biology curriculum, and materials such as discovery boxes and living exhibits. The university provided mentors and research expertise. Teachers volunteered for the project, and they learned how to conduct inquiry-based science lessons and use community resources to enhance their teaching.

Students could choose laboratory activities, build on their own previous experiences with plants and animals, and create personal projects. They were offered a variety of activities, such as exploring exhibits, using microscopes, reading books, or performing experiments, so that they could select challenging tasks. The college student mentors provided a scaffold for these experiences, allowing the younger students to work independently but supporting them in achieving success. They also encouraged the students to question their previous assumptions and about biology. Students were responsible for choosing laboratory activities, creating and monitoring their own projects, and completing their portfolios. The teaching style was enthusiastic, not authoritarian, and students knew they had control of their activities and learning.

The data indicated that students' attitudes about science were even more positive after the program, and their problem-solving skills and knowledge about biology improved substantially. Girls in particular showed very positive attitudes and learning. The culminating project exhibited at "Family Biology Night" also promoted their feelings of accomplishment and self-competence. Here is a description of a lab activity written by a college student mentor:

> This lab was successful because the various activities were set up as mysteries. For instance, one activity was talking about how a whale is protected from the cold temperatures below the ocean's thermocline. An ice-cold bucket of water allowed the children to feel the coldness of deep ocean water. Each student was then able to put his or her hand in a "blubber glove" that demonstrated the insulating effect of a whale's inner blubber. The children made many great guesses why a whale can survive in the cold water, and each child showed excitement when the phenomenon was explained.

"Hands-On Biology" was conducted for four years at more than a dozen schools and had similar positive impact on students and teachers.

One implication of its success is to underscore the value of partnerships that combine the resources of universities, museums, and schools. Universities can increase their service learning by involving undergraduates in school outreach programs. Museums have creative educational staff members and physical resources that can augment school curricula if teachers have access to them and are shown how to incorporate the materials. Collaborating teachers can work with highly trained and motivated aides as well as new knowledge and methods, and they can help connect school and museum programs effectively.

Conclusions

Museums invite learning and discovery in many ways. This article has described some key motivational processes that give direction and vigor to learning. The processes are derived largely from research in schools with students, but they can be extended to museum settings and visitors of all ages.

Part of the challenge for both educators and researchers in the future is to integrate various situations for learning into lifelong opportunities that reinforce each other. These situations will be effective if they promote the motivational processes embodied in constructing personal meaning, making choices about goals and engagement, adjusting challenges, taking responsibility and control for self-directed learning, collaborating for joint goals and teamwork, and deriving positive consequences from learning such as feelings of pride, efficacy, and accomplishment. Our challenge is to design, create, assess, and revise these opportunities for learning.

Journal of Museum Education 22, nos. 2 and 3 (1997): 22–27.

References

Anderman, E., and M. L. Maehr. 1994. Motivation and schooling in the middle grades. *Review of Educational Research* 64:287–309.

Blumenfeld, P. C., E. Soloway, R. W. Marx, J. S. Krajcik, M. Guzdial, and A. S. Palincsar. 1991. Motivating project-based learning: Sustaining the doing, supporting the learning. *Educational Psychologist* 26:369–98.

Brown, J. S., A. Collins, and P. Duguid. 1989. Situated cognition and the culture of learning. *Educational Researcher* 18:32–42.

Clifford, M. M. 1991. Risk taking: Theoretical, empirical, and educational considerations. *Educational Psychologist* 26:263–97.

Corno, L. 1989. Self-regulated learning: A volitional analysis. In *Self-regulated learning and academic achievement: Theory, research, and practice,* edited by B. J. Zimmerman and D. H. Schunk, 111–41. New York: Springer-Verlag.

Covington, M. V. 1992. *Making the grade: A self-worth perspective on motivation and school reform.* Cambridge: Cambridge University Press.

Crowley, K., and M. Callanan. 1998. Describing and supporting collaborative scientific thinking in parent-child interactions. *Journal of Museum Education* 23, no. 1: 12–17.

Csikszentmihalyi, M., and K. Hermanson. 1995. Intrinsic motivation in museums: Why does one want to learn? In *Public institutions for personal learning: Establishing a research agenda,* edited by J. H. Falk and L. D. Dierking, 67–77. Washington, D.C.: American Association of Museums.

Csikszentmihalyi, M., and U. Schiefele. 1992. Arts education, human development, and the quality of experience. In *The arts, education, and aesthetic knowing,* edited by B. Reimer and R. Smith, 169–89. Chicago: University of Chicago Press.

Dweck, C., and E. Leggett. 1988. A social-cognitive approach to motivation and personality. *Psychological Review* 95:256–73.

Falk, J. H., and L. D. Dierking. 1992. *The museum experience.* Washington, D.C.: Whalesback Books.

Henderlong, J., and S. G. Paris. 1996. Children's motivation to explore partially completed exhibits in hands-on museums. *Contemporary Educational Psychology* 21:111–28.

Kaplan, S. 1995. The restorative benefits of nature: Toward an interactive framework. *Journal of Environmental Psychology* 15:169–82.

Lantos, L. 1994. If they had a hammer. *Museum News* 73, no. 2:14–15.

Lave, J., and E. Wegner. 1991. *Situated learning: Legitimate peripheral participation.* Cambridge: Cambridge University Press.

Paris, S. G., and D. R. Cross. 1983. Ordinary learning: Pragmatic connections among children's beliefs, motives, and actions. In *Learning in children,* edited by J. Bisanz, G. Bisanz, and R. Kail, 137–69. New York: Springer-Verlag.

Paris, S. G., W. P. Troop, J. Henderlong, and M. Sulfaro. 1994. Children's explorations in a hands-on science museum. *Kamehameha Journal of Education* 5:83–92.

Paris, S. G., and J. C. Turner. 1994. Situated motivation. In *Student motivation, cognition, and learning: Essays in honor of Wilbert J. McKeachie,* edited by P. Pintrich, D. Brown, and C. Weinstein, 213–37. Hillsdale, N.J.: Erlbaum.

Paris, S .G., K. M. Yambor, and B. W.-L. Packard. 1998. Hands-On Biology: A museum-schools-university partnership for enhancing children's interest and learning in science. *Elementary School Journal* 98, no. 3.

Pintrich, P., and E. DeGroot. 1990. Motivational and self-regulated learning components of classroom academic performance. *Journal of Educational Psychology* 82:33–40.

Rogoff, B. 1990. *Apprenticeship in thinking: Cognitive development in social context.* New York: Oxford University Press.

Rohrkemper, M., and L. Corno. 1988. Success and failure on classroom tasks: Adaptive learning and classroom teaching. *Elementary School Journal* 88:297–312.

Ryan, R. M., and W. S. Grolnick. 1986. Origins and pawns in the classroom: Self-report and projective assessments of individual differences in children's perceptions. *Journal of Personality and Social Psychology* 50:550–58.

Schauble, L., G. Leinhardt, and L. Martin. 1997. A framework for organizing a cumulative research agenda in informal learning contexts. *Journal of Museum Education* 22, nos. 2–3: 3–8.

Schiefele, U. 1991. Interest, learning, and motivation. *Educational Psychologist* 26:299-323.

Schunk, D. H. 1989. Social cognitive theory and self-regulated learning. In *Self-regulated learning and academic achievement: Theory, research, and practice,* edited by B. J. Zimmerman and D. H. Schunk, 83–110. New York: Springer-Verlag.

Silverman, L. H. 1995. Visitor meaning-making in museums for a new age. *Curator* 38:161–70.

Zimmerman, B. J. 1989. Models of self-regulated learning and academic achievement. In *Self-regulated learning and academic achievement: Theory, research, and practice,* edited by B. J. Zimmerman and D. H. Schunk, 1–25. New York: Springer-Verlag.

REFLECTIONS

The museum community devoted considerable energy during the 1990s trying to document the value of visitors' experiences, largely in terms of learning. In turn, the focus on learning has stimulated conceptual and methodological discussions about the nature of learning, how to assess it, and how to promote it in informal settings. Besides producing some frustration with traditional accounts of learning and the importation of ideas from formal education, these discussions have generated new ideas about visitors' experiences that capitalize on the unique features of informal environments. Two consequences for future research seem likely. First, theories of learning will be reconceptualized with context as the foreground for interpretation and with notions of how experiences change people that are broader than the simple addition of knowledge. Second, analyses of learning beg for analyses of motives, and I expect more research on visitors' motivation to be connected with analyses of experiences.

—*Scott G. Paris*

Constructivism in Museums: How Museums Create Meaningful Learning Environments

Kodi R. Jeffery

The role of museums has changed . . . from merely exhibiting objects to interpreting them and finally to encouraging visitor interpretation. Museums give visitors firsthand experiences with objects that can involve looking, handling, interacting, or actually experimenting. In many ways, museums provide some of the most *real* learning experiences people ever encounter. . . .

As museums have changed, so have their educational goals. Originally there was no such thing as a museum educator, although people probably assumed they were learning something from their museum visits. Now we conduct research seeking to quantify and enhance visitor learning. Educational research has also been conducted in more formal settings, and many theories of formal and informal educational research are coming closer together.

Such is the case with constructivism. Jean Piaget, often considered the father of constructivism, performed detailed studies on how children learn. He believed that individuals develop "cognitive structures" and that in order to learn, children must accommodate, or internalize, their experiences, fitting them into this pre-existing framework (Touchette 1990). Piaget and D. P. Ausubel, another early constructivist, emphasized the importance of prior knowledge in new learning. Ausubel's dictum, well known among science educators, provides a basis for constructivism and meaningful learning theory.

> If I had to reduce all of educational psychology to just one principle, I would say this: The most important single factor influencing learning is what the learner already knows. Ascertain this and teach him accordingly. (Ausubel, Novak, and Hanesian 1978, iv)

These theorists provided a jumping off point for constructivism. Since their initial work, learning theory has taken leaps and bounds, and constructivism has become a well-developed theory.

Constructivism

So just what is constructivism anyway? . . . Constructivist theory holds that prior knowledge is of primary importance. Learners come to us with a wealth of knowledge already organized. It is upon this knowledge structure

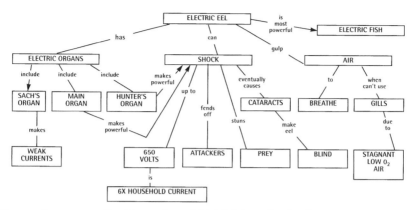

Figure 1. Concept maps, like this one of an exhibit label about electric eels, represent an individual's understanding of a given topic. They may also be useful guides as we plan our exhibits and seek to link them to each other and to our visitors' prior knowledge and experience.

that learners hang new information, creating new links to their pre-existing knowledge. The more links created, the more stable this new knowledge will be. Individuals learn when they modify existing conceptual structures, creating new links and integrating new concepts. To learn meaningfully, a person must choose to integrate new knowledge into his or her conceptual structure, relating the new material to pre-existing knowledge and experiences (Novak and Gowin 1984).

Rote learning, on the other hand, may be arbitrarily incorporated into an individual's knowledge structure without forming links to other concepts and propositions. Because individuals who learn meaningfully must mesh old knowledge with new, they may have to restructure and rearrange previously linked concepts. Although this form of knowledge acquisition requires more effort than rote learning, the resulting concepts are more stable and more accessible, since they are linked to a greater number of other concepts and propositions.

We do, of course, have to start somewhere when we build knowledge, and sometimes we start out learning things by rote rather than building upon pre-existing knowledge. Nevertheless, this type of learning may later be incorporated into a knowledge structure, perhaps even providing a basis on which further knowledge is built. But if we never build upon or explore relationships to that original rote learning, it will never become meaningful and will likely be lost somewhere in our minds, as are so many of the isolated facts we once memorized for a long-forgotten exam.

Some constructivists . . . believe that there is no such thing as an objective reality. Rather, they claim that knowledge exists exclusively in the mind of the learner. Thus all knowledge is "equal" insofar as it enables a person to learn to live with the people, objects, and society around them (von Glasersfeld 1996). This view is considered to be a radical constructivist view, and many constructivists, myself included, believe instead that there is an objective reality by which we may judge many things. As a science educator, I feel it is important for students to construct valid scientific knowledge about the world around them, and I work to facilitate that construction. I do not wish to suggest that *all* knowledge is either "right" or "wrong": clearly we cannot claim that there is only one correct way to create art, for example. But in many areas there is a currently accepted knowledge base that learners need to understand to function in and contribute to our world.

If knowledge may be structured into a valid or "correct" form, so may it also be structured into an incorrect form, holding misconceptions. Misconceptions may be firmly held and difficult to dislodge and replace. If an individual has put a great deal of effort into building a knowledge structure, and if the misconceptions are held in a central, heavily linked position, dislodging them will require a major reconstruction. Many people repeatedly reject new information because they cannot find a way to mesh it comfortably with their pre-existing knowledge. Schauble, Leinhardt, and Martin (1997) describe how children may ignore their own senses, interpreting their experiences in favor of the incorrect and contradictory mental schemas they have previously created.

Resnick (1983) suggests three conclusions from cognitive science research:

1. The capacity to learn at any given time is limited.
2. An individual constructs meanings, and this ability to construct meanings is influenced by prior knowledge.
3. Individuals often employ and invent rule-directed procedural devices to expand their capacity to learn and to construct meanings.

Making meaning is, therefore, an active process in which the learner consciously links new knowledge to old. Teachers linking concepts from various lessons can help students learn to construct chunks of information (Duschl 1990). Museums may also help in knowledge construction by providing opportunities for visitors to build links to their pre-existing knowledge. Whenever a museum links concepts to each other or to experiences familiar to visitors, meaningful learning is enhanced. In addition, the museum experience itself may provide a basis upon which new knowledge can be constructed.

Concept Mapping

One tool that has developed out of constructivist theory and that may also help explain it is concept mapping. Concept mapping is a metacognitive tool developed by Novak (1979) and designed to represent a person's knowledge structure. Figure 1 shows a concept map depicting all the information presented in an exhibit label on electric eels. Links between concepts form propositions that explain the relationship existing among these concepts (e.g., concept—linking words—concept). The more propositions a mapper can construct around a specific concept, the more complete will be his or her knowledge about that concept. Thus mappers could represent a significant portion of their knowledge of a topic by constructing as many propositions as possible for a given concept.

Because each individual's knowledge and experiences are different from those of any other individual, each map will be different. Maps show the relationships formed by a person through a lifetime of experience. Since maps vary so much with the content selected by the individual, there is no one "right" map. Nevertheless, maps do provide enough similarity of structure that they may be compared, and the propositions may be judged as valid or invalid according to standards of currently accepted knowledge.

Concept maps are arranged hierarchically, with the most important or superordinate concept at the top of the map. The maps flow downward through various underlying concepts. Evidence shows that the brain also

---

To create a truly constructivist setting, museums must develop exhibits that get visitors involved, relating to them, to their lives, and to their past experiences.

---

stores information hierarchically, and thus a concept map may provide a two-dimensional picture of an individual's cognitive structure (Hooper 1990). Examples help learners link concepts to their experience in the real world. The more experiences learners have, the more potential examples they have to link to their knowledge and to make their learning meaningful.

Concept maps focus on the understanding of one superordinate concept, but a complete map is somewhat like a rubber sheet. One could lay out the map on the sheet, picking up one of the concepts and having the rest fall around it into a new map with a different superordinate concept. Likewise, our knowledge structures may link many concepts, but at any given time we may focus on one of those concepts, exploring our knowledge of it and, perhaps, adding to or restructuring it.

Semantic Networks

Semantic networks are another, related way to represent knowledge structures. Unlike concept mapping, semantic networks provide no hierarchy. They are also not limited to two dimensions. Computer programs allow us to map knowledge in n-dimensional space. Only individual portions of the network (slices) are seen two-dimensionally. Each concept may be linked to many others, and the relationships are bidirectional.

Semantic networks do not require that representations be words; they may also be such things as images, text, and sound. As museums encourage exploration and experiences with objects, much of the "knowing" resulting from a museum experience may be in one of these less-standard forms. Semantic networks even permit affective knowledge and experiences to be represented, and feelings and emotions may well be the factors that make a museum experience so meaningful.

Nets have the ability to integrate ideas across a large knowledge base. They may be constructed rapidly, and various elements (concepts, propositions, and relations) may be easily located and listed. Concepts about which a learner has a great deal of knowledge will be more deeply "embedded" in a net. But their size and multiple dimensions make them difficult to grasp in a clear overview. Thus it is helpful to combine nets with tools such as concept maps to more accurately represent an individual's understanding and promote learning, teaching, and research efforts (Fisher 1990).

Semantic networks and concept maps are representations of the cognitive structures that exist in an individual's mind. They are useful for picturing the types of associations that occur in the mind, but they are, of course, simplified versions of much more complex structures. Each may be used both as an assessment of understanding and as a learning tool in itself, since creating these structures requires a learner to assess his or her understanding of a subject and give it meaningful form. We can use these tools to help us understand what types of knowledge many of our visitors have upon entering our museums (or construct within them), but to do this, we must make sure the visitors are involved in constructing maps of their own understanding. This could be done by actually inviting visitors to participate in a study, or perhaps it could also be observed through some sort of display in which visitors put together a "puzzle" or participate in a quiz/game on a computer.

We can also use these tools as models in designing our museums by seeking ways to link our exhibits and activities to themes meaningful to visitors. Although visitors may not buy into our themes, they may still recognize some commonalities within our exhibits. And if any exhibits relate to a visitor's prior knowledge, the themes and links we have provided may help that visitor understand and create links to his or her cognition structure.

Constructivism in Museums

Museums may be the perfect environments in which to use constructivist theory and observe meaningful learning. Falk and Dierking (1992, 114) suggest that "museums are excellent environments for meaningful learning because they offer rich, multi-sensory experiences." These environments offer an intimate involvement with perceptible and tangible objects, whether natural or human-made, creating an impetus for change in the personal meaning of experience. Certainly many of life's experiences offer us similar intimate contact with objects, and they may, indeed, result in some constructive learning, but only in a museum setting can visitors have so much contact with so many and such a large variety of objects. Museums also have the opportunity to give direction to visitors' experiences, creating interactive situations that allow visitors to have experiences they would not have in a different environment.

Falk and Dierking (1992) have identified three contexts that interact to form the museum visit: . . . personal, social. and physical. These contexts become crucial in understanding the role of constructivism in museums. It is perhaps the uniqueness of the environment and the interaction of these various contexts that creates such an effective environment for meaningful, constructive learning. The personal context includes each individual's prior knowledge; the social context allows visitors to learn from and help each other; and the physical context provides the material to be explored. Many visitors come in family groups or other groups that have a great deal of common experience and knowledge. Group members can remind each other of past experiences relevant to the subject matter at hand. Hilke (1988) argues that families have been in the business of learning together for years. They bring many resources that help them create meaningful learning experiences. The groups Hilke observed remained remarkably focused on the museum displays and exhibited many behaviors geared toward knowledge acquisition. The most frequent behaviors involved doing hands-on activities or looking at exhibit objects rather than reading or listening; evidently visitor groups were pursuing strategies that focused on creating actual experiences with the objects in the museum. In addition, visitors tended to pursue their personal strategies over cooperative strategies, although they were still bound to the group, and they broadcast information to other group members. Crowley and Callanan (1998) explain that children who share their learning with others are more likely to be able to transfer their new knowledge to subsequent problems. This sharing of experiences may encourage people to compare new information to their previous conceptions. Visitors may be more likely to struggle for links to their past experiences, perhaps grasping for those experiences previously shared with family or friends to create a mutual background and seek a consensus with other group members. As visitors share and possibly even "relive" their experiences, they may build more links between their past and the activities that prompted their current discourse.

Museums have focused on object-oriented education for years—a style that facilitates constructive learning. Only recently have formal educational institutions recognized and begun to emphasize the value of firsthand experience in learning. Nevertheless, we need to acknowledge that although museums focus on objects, the mere presence of objects does not guarantee meaningful, constructed learning. People construct knowledge from all types of experiences, whether they are actually manipulating something, reading about it, talking about it, or even hearing someone else talk about it. The key to constructivism is not in what one does with the hands but what one does with the mind. In using constructivist theory to develop our museums, we must not take for granted the fact that we have wonderful objects that invite meaningful experiences. It is how we present those objects, how we allow visitors to interact with them, and how we help visitors relate those objects to their prior knowledge that will determine visitor learning.

Over the years, many researchers have attempted to study the learning that results from experiences in museums. Koran, Koran, and Foster (1988) contend that there are numerous types of visitor learning, including factual knowledge, conceptual knowledge, process knowledge, curiosity, heuristics of the above categories, and affective learning. Some researchers, after conducting true/false or multiple choice tests, determined that museum visitors do not take away any cognitive gains. Thus, many museum professionals have begun to emphasize the affective learning that takes place instead, perhaps because that is easier to observe. But just because we have had a difficult time in sorting out the cognitive gains of visitors does not mean that there are no cognitive gains. Indeed, perhaps it is the interaction of the cognitive and the affective realms that makes museums such uniquely powerful learning institutions. The studies that have attempted to quantify cognitive museum learning by giving tests to visitors presuppose that the visitors recognize and accept the exhibit theme intended by the designers and educators. Hilke (1988) has shown that visitors are more likely to follow their own agendas, focusing on exhibits and concepts of interest to them or with which they have previous experience. Instead of making connections among various parts of an exhibit, visitors seek relationships to their own knowledge and experiences.

Implications

Museums already have the requisites for constructivist learning. They offer free choice environments in which visitors can experience various materials in a number of different ways. But just because learning situations are offered does not make the environment necessarily constructivist. Visitors must be brought into the experiences somehow, and they need to find their own meaning from the exhibits. A tour full of facts and objects may be interesting—and it may even offer visitors some exposure to experience—but visitors still may not really construct much knowledge from it. The visit might be enjoyable, even memorable, but visitors may learn little more than that the museum is an interesting place worth visiting again. Some few facts might be remembered for a time, but there is very little true construction of knowledge.

To create a truly constructivist setting, museums must develop exhibits that get visitors involved, relating to them, to their lives, and to their past experiences. Hilke (1988) argues that designers must anticipate visitors' common questions and interests to create successful exhibits. But even that anticipation may be inadequate, since visitors often neglect to read labels. In my study of family groups visiting a public aquarium, visitors recalled with great excitement an exhibit about electric eels. Specifically, visitors recalled experimenting with the "finger tingler," an exhibit at which they could give themselves (or others) a mild electric shock. Labels clearly explained that the shock was very mild and that an electric eel can give a jolt of 650 volts, potentially killing its victim. Nevertheless, fully half the visitors I interviewed believed that they had felt, by using the finger tingler, what it would feel like to be shocked by an electric eel! Despite the fact that visitors were actively engaged and interacting with the exhibit, despite the fact that their experience was memorable and fun, they came away with a potentially deadly misconception (Jeffery and Wandersee 1996).

In creating a constructivist museum, exhibit designers and museum educators need to work together to give visitors experiences that closely relate to the material we hope to teach. We need to realize and accept that visitors will follow their own agendas and construct their own knowledge structures. But we also need to be aware of the potential misconceptions that might arise from our exhibits and attempt to minimize them. Formative evaluation can certainly expose some of the interpretations visitors could construct from our exhibits and thus help us avoid fostering misconceptions.

In addition, we must find ways to reach visitors, building bridges to their past experiences and knowledge. It is important to remember that although we may provide wonderfully linked exhibits, we are imposing our own themes on them. Visitors may not be able to follow our themes, but they will seek ways to incorporate our exhibits into their own themes. If we can facilitate this incorporation, we will be helping visitors create mental links that are meaningful to them. Tools such as concept maps and semantic networks may provide us with glimpses of what visitors find meaningful and what common visitor themes may be, thus enabling us to incorporate those patterns as we develop exhibits.

Some visitors, of course, will note a theme or partial theme running through an exhibit, especially if it has some relevance to them. Our themes may help them build some additional knowledge and make more sense of the exhibit by providing links among different exhibits. Even if a theme is not actively recognized by a visitor, it may still provide some direction to exhibits. Without themes, visitors may find themselves in so much chaos that it reduces their ability to make sense of an exhibit.

Museums can also help create cognitive gains indirectly by providing experiences upon which visitors can later build new knowledge. The Project 2061 report on biological and health sciences argues that biology must first be experienced before it can be properly learned and appreciated (AAAS 1989). Museums are one place where people can gain that experience. In addition, museums can provide background information necessary for people to understand more complicated concepts. We have identified protoconcepts that may prepare students to study and understand evolution at a later date (Jeffery and Roach 1994). Museum exhibits could likewise prepare visitors to learn about a variety of related topics by giving them experience with simplified, preparatory material upon which they could later construct a valid knowledge structure.

Conclusions

Museums are ideal constructivist learning environments. They allow visitors to move and explore freely, working at their own pace. They encourage group interaction and sharing. They allow personal experience with real objects. They provide a place for visitors to examine and expand their own understanding. As museum professionals, it is our job to build and enhance these environments to pull the visitors into the experience, allowing them to explore in ways that pique their curiosity and encourage them to investigate and make comparisons to their own lives and experiences. Programs and exhibits must be carefully crafted and tested to assure that they enhance visitor knowledge and/or feelings without encouraging misconceptions. We may not always be able to teach just what we want, as we must accept that visitors will guide their own learning and choose how to incorporate their new experiences into their pre-existing knowledge structures. But we can facilitate that learning by creating environments where visitors will question their knowledge structures, adding to or rebuilding them as necessary.

Journal of Museum Education **23, no. 1 (1998): 3–7.**

References

AAAS. 1989. *Biological and health sciences: Report of the Project 2061 phase I biological and health sciences panel.* New York: American Association for the Advancement of Science.

Ausubel, D. P., J. D. Novak, and H. Hanesian. 1978. *Educational psychology: A cognitive view.* 2d ed. New York: Holt, Rinehart, and Winston.

Crowley, K., and M. Callanan. 1998. Describing and supporting collaborative scientific thinking in parent-child interactions. *Journal of Museum Education* 23, no. 1: 12–17.

Duschl, R. A. 1990. *Restructuring science education: The importance of theories and their development.* New York: Teachers College Press.

Falk, J. H., and L. D. Dierking. 1992. *The museum experience.* Washington, D.C.: Whalesback Books.

Fisher, K. M. 1990. Semantic networking: The new kid on the block. *Journal of Research in Science Teaching* 27, no. 10:1001–18.

Hilke, D. D. 1988. Strategies for family learning in museums. In *Proceedings of the First Annual Visitor Studies Conference,* edited by S. Bitgood, J. T. Roper Jr., and A. Benefield, 120–25. Jacksonville, Ala.: Center for Social Design.

Hooper, C. 1990. What science is learning about learning science. *Journal of NIH Research* 2, no. 4:75–81.

Jeffery, K. R., and L. E. Roach. 1994. A study of the presence of evolutionary protoconcepts in pre–high school textbooks. *Journal of Research in Science Teaching* 31, no. 5:507–18.

Jeffery, K. R., and J. H. Wandersee. 1996. Visitor understanding of interactive exhibits: A study of family groups in a public aquarium. Paper presented at the meeting of the National Association for Research in Science Teaching, St. Louis, Mo.

Koran, J. J., M. L. Koran, and J. S. Foster. 1988. Individual differences in learning in informal settings. In *Proceedings of the First Annual Visitor Studies Conference,* edited by S. Bitgood, J. T. Roper Jr., and A. Benefield. 1:66–72. Jacksonville, Ala.: Center for Social Design.

Novak, J. D. 1979. Applying psychology and philosophy to the improvement of laboratory teaching. *American Biology Teacher* 41, no. 8:466–74.

Novak, J. D., and D. B. Gowin. 1984. *Learning how to learn.* New York: Cambridge University Press.

Resnick, L. 1983. Mathematics and science learning: A new conception. *Science* 220:477–78.

Schauble, L., G. Leinhardt, and L. Martin. 1997. A framework for organizing a cumulative research agenda in informal learning contexts. *Journal of Museum Education* 22, nos. 2–3:3–8.

Touchette, N. 1990. Piaget's stages. *Journal of NIH Research* 2, no. 4:76–77.

von Glasersfeld, E. 1996. Footnotes to "The many faces of constructivism." *Educational Researcher* 25, no. 6:19.

Further Reading

Mintzes, Joel J., James H. Wandersee, and Joseph D. Novak, eds. *Teaching science for understanding: A human constructivist view.* San Diego, Calif.: Academic Press, 1998.

Osborne, Jonathan F. "Constructivism in museums: A response." *Journal of Museum Education* 23, no. 1 (1998): 8–9.

Constructing Informed Practice

Danielle Rice

I am indebted to Kodi Jeffery-Clay's (1998)succinct and helpful definition of constructivism and her discussion of how constructivism applies to museum education. It is clear from the picture she paints that constructivism can be applied to museum-based learning in a variety of ways. As the hottest thing in the museum education field, constructivism seems like a "good thing," a theory that museums would naturally want to embrace. It is therefore not surprising to find a number of museum professionals claiming, as Jeffery-Clay does, that museums are ideal constructivist learning environments. However, is it productive for museum educators to get behind theories such as constructivism merely to justify existing, time-proven practices, or would it be more useful to challenge and refine existing practices against the backdrop of a variety of educational theories?

The argument that museums are ideal constructivist environments because they are multisensory and invite interaction with other people as well as with real objects seems somewhat limited. By this definition, the world and everything in it is an ideal constructivist learning environment. Jeffery-Clay seems to equate hands-on experiences with constructivism, whereas the real issue is not necessarily how people interact with physical objects but rather how they use their minds to construct meanings or make sense of the objects in museums.

One can argue that museums are, in fact, far from ideal constructivist environments because they are highly artificial settings that intentionally impose an ordered framework on the natural disorder of things found in the real world. They are designed to structure and represent reality in their own terms. With their roots in 18th-century enlightenment thinking, museums—along with the encyclopedias and dictionaries that are also the products of that time—are the outcome of an optimistic world view that knowledge is objective and therefore measurable and quantifiable.

Most museums today still collect, classify, and order in much the same way that they did in the 18th century. They use their exhibitions and displays to develop narratives about the way things are to be understood. In zoos, animals are arranged according to species; in art museums, the chronology of art history provides the main story thread. Many natural history museums are organized according to different departments of knowledge, thus implying that this kind of compartmentalization is rational and scientific. Even the most hands-on, exploration-based institutions, the ones that raise more questions than they answer, organize their exhibits according to certain broad themes or areas.

One of the significant differences between museums today and museums a century ago is that, for the most part, museum professionals no longer consider that the narratives told in museums are the absolute truth. As Lisa Roberts (1997) so aptly points out, museum workers today, and particularly museum educators, are keenly aware that because museums "construct" their own versions of reality, they may help or hinder visitors from developing their own interpretations. The museum's construct may lead visitors to greater consensus and shared understanding, or it may not.

The task of museum educators has changed over the years as a result of these new ways of thinking about knowledge. In the past, educators functioned primarily to present the museum's version of reality to the visitors we

---

Theories are useful not only insofar as they justify practice, but rather as they reform, improve, and invigorate it.

---

encountered through various lectures and tours. With the new awareness—gained in part from constructivist theory—that institutions such as museums construct consensual meanings and that individuals construct personal ones—has come a new responsibility for museum educators. Now, instead of merely presenting the institutional perspective to visitors, we attempt to navigate between the museum's construction and visitors' ways of knowing. This navigating takes many forms and includes using the research about how visitors interact with exhibits to reform the design and interpretation of those exhibits. Most often, the navigating is still done in the interest of getting visitors to adapt to the museum's version of reality rather than the other way around.

One of the big challenges to museum education in recent years has been the rampant relativism that results from maintaining that no one meaning is privileged over another. I was relieved to find that Jeffery-Clay characterizes this kind of thinking as an aspect of radical, rather than mainstream, constructivist theory. In art museums, this relativism has been more pronounced than in science museums, perhaps because, when it comes to art, people are more willing to accept that art lends itself to a broad range of interpretations. Thus if people construct ideas about art that are incorrect by the standards of museum professionals, this is deemed a less serious problem than if they form incorrect ideas about science. Indeed, in recent art museum education practice there has been a pronounced trend toward a type of teaching that asks visitors open-ended questions which lead them not to a predetermined interpretation of a work of art but rather to examine their own cognitive process and attitudes. While this pedagogy may stimulate more thoughtful engagement with art, it can also be misused by museum educators to abdicate the responsibility of actually teaching visitors about the broader, consensual understandings that constitute an informed perspective.

I am surprised not to find in the recent debates about constructivism and museums a theory that I have found useful for many years and one that seems to fit in perfectly with the tenets of constructivism. I am referring to the notion of "cognitive dissonance," the essence of which was defined by George Miller (quoted in Peckham 1978, 101) as the tension that results as "the organism struggles to reduce the mismatch between its own criteria and perceived reality." In other words, the "criteria" correspond to those structures that are the basis upon which people construct meaning. Cognitive dissonance is what happens when a person is confronted with an object or piece of information that does not fit into his or her pre-existing structures. When the mismatch occurs, most people are tempted to reject the perceived reality and stick to their own structure, thus reducing the cognitive tension. This reaction is perhaps one of the reasons that science educators find it so difficult to teach people something that mismatches a pre-existing, or "common-sense," view of science.

The usefulness of cognitive dissonance was developed into a theory of art by Morse Peckham (1965). Working to resolve some of the very real tensions caused by the confrontational pop and conceptual art of the time, Peckham concluded that the role of art was to train people to endure cognitive dissonance as a necessary preliminary to problem perception and meaningful innovation. Thus, when a viewer is confronted with an art object that does not immediately fit neatly into her definition of art—as is so often the case with innovative contemporary art—the encounter becomes meaningful when the viewer resists the temptation to reject the object as "not art." As mediators, museum educators can work to help viewers live with the ambiguity of not knowing while they explore a large variety of options and interpretations. This goal seems entirely in keeping with constructivist educational theory.

Museum education has traditionally been a very practical field that rarely articulates the theories underlying its practice. For this reason museum educators are often criticized by their colleagues in academic settings, and, feeling somewhat vulnerable, we rush to jump on the latest theoretical bandwagon before fully understanding its implications. Constructivism does indeed seem to be a useful cluster of theories with broad applicability to museum education. But it is important to remember that there are other theories to be explored as well.

Ideas coming out of anthropology and rhetoric, for example, have invigorated educational theory with a neo-pragmatist approach that sees learners as belonging to particular cultures or discourse communities. In this theoretical framework, educators, instead of considering how people construct knowledge, have to be concerned with issues of task, specifically with questions such as what we want to accomplish with this specific audience at this specific moment. Because museums are more and more being used as recreational, leisure-time, social environments, not all people come to museums to learn. Thus in some situations the task of museum educators may be to move people who have come with a different agenda into becoming learners.

In the real everyday work of museum education, theories such as constructivism and neo-pragmatism should be welcomed, debated, experimented with. But no one theory should be embraced as the one and only ultimately defining one. For in the end, theories are useful not only insofar as they justify practice, but rather as they reform, improve, and invigorate it.

Journal of Museum Education **23, no. 1 (1998): 10–11.**

References

Jeffery-Clay, K. 1998. Constructivism in museums: How museums create meaningful learning environments. *Journal of Museum Education* 23, no. 1: 3–7.

Peckham, Morse. 1978. Art and disorder. In *Esthetics contemporary,* edited by R. Kostelanetz. New York: Prometheus Books.

Peckham, Morse. 1965. *Man's rage for chaos.* Princeton, N.J.: Princeton University Press.

Roberts, Lisa. 1997. *From knowledge to narrative: Educators and the changing museum.* Washington, D.C.: Smithsonian Institution Press.

Further Reading

Rice, Danielle. 1993. The cross-cultural mediator. *Museum News* 72, no. 1:33–41.

Rice, Danielle. 1995. Museum education embracing uncertainty. *Art Bulletin* 77, no. 1:15–20.

For a bibliography on visual thinking strategies, visit the Visual Understanding in Education Web site at: www.VUE.org/documents/index.html.

Exhibitions as Educators; or, The Mundane and Magnificent Art of Stringing Beads

Signe Hanson

I've just spent seven hours reading exhibition proposals for a government funding agency, and I am up to here with aggressively ambitious educational goals and pedagogically occluded verbiage. The authors of each fat proposal promised that they would prove beyond a shadow of a doubt, using scientific methods of evaluation, that their exhibition would accomplish each and every one of these goals. Real learning about incredibly complicated topics would truly take place, and the exhibition would change the lives of children and adults as well as solve the dismal problems of teachers and inner-city school administrators.

Time passes. It's now 24 hours and one workday later. Reason has returned along with memory. I remember struggling over educational goals for exhibitions like these myself, struggling to reconcile rhetoric and reality as I perceived it. Were visitors really getting anything out of our exhibitions? How could we tell? The gap between our aspirations and what seemed to be happening in the museum was at best disappointing. As a designer, I despaired when curators or exhibit developers gave me lengthy educational rationales for doing exhibitions their way, for passing over the elegantly simple yet theatrical presentations I was proposing. As a fledgling administrator charged with taking the broader view, I strove to delete "eduspeak" from my writing and conversation and learn more about the experiencing, discovering, intuiting, messing about, reading, and synthesizing behaviors that I saw around me.

Over time I have created a metaphor for the way I think learning takes place in museums—and in the rest of life as well. This metaphor has to do with the stringing of beads. Consider that life's single experiences are like single beads not yet strung together in linear form. And consider that a visitor to an exhibition might well collect a pocketful of experiences, or beads, to take home. These beads are different for each visitor, chosen from among the many possibilities we exhibitors have wittingly or unwittingly provided. Visitors collect beads eccentrically and personally, picking what they will and stubbornly overlooking some of our proudest exhibition constructs or techniques.

Sometimes a visitor will choose several similar beads, see the related points in an exhibit, and string those beads together on a clear monofilament of cognition (the oft-mentioned "aha!" event). On the other hand, he or she may simply see one thing that sparked curiosity (a bead!) and then go off to find the restroom or visit the gift shop.

These beads join other beads already in the pocket. Perhaps others are picked up at home, work, or school. They may or may not be particularly related. And at some point—maybe right away, maybe far in the future—the visitor sorts and organizes a number of beads from the collection into a linear necklace strung on a thin thread of knowing. This necklace is worn proudly until the wearer needs to restring it with other beads and other experiences, to make new necklaces and draw new conclusions. This is learning, and it is more often than not a process, not an event with edges.

In this fashion, it is possible for a child to blow soap bubbles in her backyard, sit in soap bubbles in her bath, blow giant soap bubbles at a bubbles exhibit at a science center, "know" kinesthetically the tolerances of soap films before she can wrap words around the knowing, and see the iridescence on a bubble as well as on an oil slick or the back of a blackbird. And if in a high

---

Knowing the visitor requires learning to listen intently, to take time out of hectic schedules to go back and listen again, to be willing to hear as well as listen, and to put off doing until we have heard.

---

school physics class she strings together a necklace on a sturdy cord that the teacher calls "surface tension," she may later, as an adult, restring some of those beads onto a lighter twine at the sight of the iridescent glaze on a Japanese tea bowl.

But if this collecting of beads, this process of learning, occurs throughout our lives and in all sorts of places, what is unique about the part museums can play in the process? The nature of the museum visit is, of course, our greatest asset and our greatest educational challenge. Museums offer informal, one-time access to exhibitions by people who are of various ages, backgrounds, levels of tiredness or hunger; who come alone or in groups, at only roughly predictable times, and with agendas of their own; and who may stay if they are captivated by something but will drift away instantly if they are not. We don't get many second chances. How do we hook them, and how do we keep them?

For starters, fascinating things are our primary resources. In our exhibits we can offer our audiences objects they will never see in the rest of their world. The trick is to show these things in compelling ways, yet in ways that allow the visitor to connect the experience to other learning experiences, to extend and continue the learning beyond the museum walls.

Second, Urie Bronfenbrenner was absolutely right when he said on the PBS series *Childhood*, "The most powerful and attractive aspect of any environment to human beings is *other* human beings." To truly compel the visitor, both the exhibition and the staff who interact with the public must serve as teachers. While exhibitions at baseline must be safe when there are no staff in them, we know beyond a doubt that we can provide much richer content in much more flexible ways when staff are on the exhibit floor. We probably underestimate, and certainly underfund, the role of "temporary mentor" in museum learning. Many of the things I have enjoyed learning the most were things I learned through other people with whom I had a fleeting interaction that piqued my curiosity: the paintings of Nicolas de Staël, a Navajo sand painting, how to trellis a grape arbor.

It seems to me that because of fiscal pressures and the perceived need to be relevant to broader audiences, some museums may be evolving into something related to, but pointedly not, community centers. One of the signs of this evolution is a growing interest in volunteer staffing programs, some of which have the goal of broadening the ethnic, racial, and economic base from which volunteers are recruited. If this works, we will not only have more trained and enthusiastic people on the exhibit floor, but we will have widened the perspectives and voices to which visitors and other staff can have access.

The notion of widened perspectives is key. Since education in exhibits is a highly personal event for the visitor—based on what he or she brings to the exhibit as well as what the exhibit provides—it stands to reason that the richer the bead choices available, the more likely we are to tap into visitors' individual learning styles and abilities. This argues for more exploration of ways to enrich the content of museum exhibits. The designer in me sighs. There goes that simple, elegant story line. That means we have to let the curators and exhibit developers come in with all those tangled ideas and multiple voices, that we have to live until late in the exhibition process with unresolved issues and uncertainties.

That may be true, but it is also a great opportunity for designers to team up with people of different skills and bring to the mix the thing we do best: showmanship. The nature of the museum visit requires that we use all the available lures and baits to catch and keep the visitor's interest. We should use all our skills to show those beads to the greatest advantage. We should pick our beads carefully, show astounding, beautiful, rare, incredibly ugly, historical, or widely diverse beads. We should let the light shine through them, show the bottoms as well as the tops of our beads, let them tell their own stories.

Do the rest of my colleagues on an exhibit team share this vision? Probably partially, but they are, I hope, trusting me as the designer to work out the colors and the lights and the bottoms of the beads. They have their own concerns. In the best situations, there may even be a certain positive tension between our respective advocacies. I think the best exhibition pros think broadly about their own positions within exhibit teams and respect, use, and sometimes learn the skills of the other group members. And when it really works, all of us have been focused intently on getting that bead into the visitor's pocket.

That's where it all begins and where it ends when we're talking about museum education—with the visitor. We are all in our own ways educators, and like all good teachers we need to remember that you cannot force-feed information and make learning happen. It requires the active participation of the learner.

Research on learning and evaluation in informal situations like museums teaches us that we need to listen not only to our professional colleagues but also to our visiting public. If there is anything I'd like to change in the general consciousness of exhibition professionals, it is that the visitor must be sitting on that team with us. We need to know who the visitors are, what they know about specific topics, what they want to know, and how learning might or might not happen. Knowing the visitor requires learning to listen intently, to take time out of hectic schedules to go back and listen again, to be willing to hear as well as listen, and to put off doing until we have heard.

That's another kind of learning that goes on in museums, isn't it?

Journal of Museum Education 17, no. 3 (Fall 1992): 8–9.

Making Meaning Together: Lessons from the Field of American History

Lois H. Silverman

Over the last few years, the field of American history has witnessed an explosion of interest in how contemporary individuals understand and use the past. In 1989, the leading scholarly publication in the field, the *Journal of American History*, devoted a special issue exclusively to the topic of history and memory;[1] prestigious universities have held conferences with titles like "History and Memory" and "How We Learn History: The Past, the Classroom, and Society"; and in 1990, a group consisting primarily of historians founded the Center on History-Making in America, an interdisciplinary initiative at Indiana University that promotes and conducts research on people and the past. While those who call themselves "public historians" have long been interested in citizens' encounters with history, much of the recent movement has gone beyond professionals theorizing about the experiences of others to include gathering and analyzing empirical data such as the attitudes and behaviors of contemporary Americans. These data have allowed scholars to document the range of ways in which people make meaning of the past and explore the workings of memory, narrative, and historical consciousness. Fueling this trend is some serious "reflective practice" in what has been one of the most authoritarian of academic disciplines. The results are a growing concern among some historians with the audiences of history and an increasing desire to see the discipline become more democratic, relevant, and meaningful to a wide range of citizens. What's this got to do with museum education?

Those who work in history museums, historic sites, and historic houses may already be familiar with this movement, given its potential impact on the interpretation of history. Since the concept of the past is an integral component of many other disciplines, including art, archeology, and science, the importance of this work is clearly not limited to institutions with "history" in their titles. Indeed, a growing understanding of how people make sense of the past is likely to influence the interpretation of art, archeology, and other fields. Yet the connection of this work to museum education is at once more subtle and more complex than the issue of subject matter. The movement afoot in the theory and practice of history is a mirror of quite similar—and fundamental—

issues and challenges facing museology today: What is the nature of interpretation? Who makes meaning? How? How might we move beyond the dichotomy that separates "professionals" from "laypersons" to more beneficial and inclusive ways of interacting? How can we revitalize the field and its institutions so that they might serve as tools for all people? Given new understandings of interpretation and of audiences, what new or revised skills might we need to accomplish these goals? As a museum educator, audience researcher, and director of the Center on History-Making in America, I have been amazed to see firsthand how similar are the challenges that face history and museology today—and many other fields of knowledge as well. In the next few pages, I'd like to offer an overview of recent developments in American history and illustrate how similar application of the meaning-making paradigm and related ideas to museum education can help us to create more inclusive and democratic museums—model institutions for a functional and healthy multicultural society. In short, here are some lessons from history for museum education in the present.

The Paradigm of Meaning-Making: Recalling the Nature of "Interpretation"

As this issue of the *Journal of Museum Education* illustrates, the American academy is clearly in the midst of a powerful paradigm shift to embrace the notion of "meaning-making." This paradigm seems to have emerged as a response to and means for dealing with the country's changing cultural landscape and the fact that multiple and often conflicting points of view indeed exist and clash in our society. In the field of communications, many scholars now believe that communication does not occur in a linear fashion, with one active party conveying information to a passive other, but that communication is a process in which meaning is jointly and actively constructed through interaction. Developed further in the work known as cultural studies, this notion has surfaced in a variety of other fields as well. While differences do exist in approaches to the notion, most share the growing belief that people who are communicating negotiate power and authority in the making of meaning.

This paradigm has profound implications for history. Long considered by many to involve the expert retrieval of objective truth, recovered through documentable evidence by highly trained individuals, the meaning-making paradigm offers a powerful reminder that history, when viewed as a process, is an *interpretation*—a story or perspective that is crafted, albeit with expert documentation, by certain people for certain ends. And even though the historian might communicate his or her particular interpretation with authority, another person who encounters it may yet make very different meaning of it from that which the historian intended. Thus while historians may continue to be the most recognized and valued presenters of the past in our society, their products are interpretations, which can then be interpreted further by those who read them. It seems increasingly clear that professionals and citizens "share authority" for constructing meaning of the past.[2] It is no wonder that growing numbers of historians are working to understand the ways that audiences think and interact with history.

Much of the same may be said for museum educators, for, like historians, the act of "interpretation" is our raison d'être. And like our fellow "keepers of culture," we seem to have lost sight of the meaning of the term "interpretation" as a viewpoint or particular understanding and have defined it instead in our minds and in the minds of many visitors as immutable truth, operating as if the results of our work can and must be experienced in just one way. Like historians, museum educators do not need to abandon the role of purveyors of excellent interpretation. The paradigm of meaning-making simply opens the door for museology, as well as history, to consider some desperately needed expansion.

Who Does It and How? Everyperson His or Her Own Historian

At the core of the recent movement in history is the revival and advancement of a concept expressed eloquently, accessibly, but unfortunately in gendered language by Carl Becker in 1932: "Everyman his own historian." Arguing that all history is essentially the same, whether it is about military figures or everyday life, Becker shows that all people regularly use knowledge of the past to various ends in the present and in the process exercise research skills that are similar to those of the "expert" historian.

> If the essence of history is the memory of things said and done, then it is obvious that every normal person, Mr. Everyman, knows some history. . . . Mr. Everyman, as well as you and I, remembers things said and done and must do so at every waking moment.

Becker also recognized the social nature of the meaning-making process. History is

> an imaginative creation, a personal possession which each one of us, Mr. Everyman, fashions out of his individual experience, adapts to his practical or emotional needs, and adorns as well as may be to suit his aesthetic tastes. In thus creating his own history, there are, nevertheless, limits which Mr. Everyman may not overstep without incurring penalties. The limits are set by his fellows. If Mr. Everyman lived quite alone in an unconditioned world he would be free to affirm and hold in memory any ideal series of events that struck his fancy, and thus create a world of semblance quite in accord with the heart's desire. Unfortunately, Mr. Everyman has to live in a world of Browns and Smiths . . . which has taught him the expediency of recalling certain events with much exactness.[3]

Building on these ideas in recent work, David Thelen and others have coined and promoted the term "history-making" to refer to all the different ways humans interpret or make meaning of the past, from "reminiscence beside a fireplace or restoration of a piece of furniture"[4] to the writing of books and the production of exhibits and documentaries. The concept of "history-making" joins the notion of history as process with the meaning-making paradigm. Two important effects of this concept are to further Becker's effort to democratize history activity and to suggest that understanding the ways people make history is a critical step in understanding how meaning about the past is negotiated.

Indeed, recent empirical studies in a number of fields illuminate the pervasive and varied ways in which ordinary people relate to the past. Using ethnography, for example, Henry Glassie studied an Irish community called Ballymenone and described how people interpret the past by telling stories, arranging their household goods, and going about their everyday occupations. Drawing upon sociology and communications theory, Tamer Katriel and Thomas Farrell examined the making and using of scrapbooks for pleasure,

---

The paradigm [of meaning-making] broadens our notion of the museum educator's role to be one who is knowledgeable in the ways people make meaning of objects and skilled in facilitating dialogue and negotiation.

---

reminiscence, communication, and the maintenance of relationships.[5] Other explorations of history-making activity can be found in the literature of psychology, anthropology, and communications.

As Thelen describes, understanding the range of ways that people make meaning of the past and using that broad spectrum as the basis for public history can open the door to new directions in exhibits, textbooks, activities, films, and other media that might indeed excite and involve Americans in history.[6] Research as well as reflective practice in public history has shown that many of the ways people relate to the past in their everyday lives are quite active and integral components of the ways they make sense of interpretations about the past presented to them by historians in museums, theaters, and classrooms. Such expansion, therefore, seems not only logical but necessary if historians wish to communicate meaningfully with the public.

While this philosophy can lead to exciting new projects and programs, it can also help to explain the success of certain techniques and practices. For example, many historians wondered why Ken Burns's television film *The Civil*

War was so popular and successful in the eyes of the public. To explore how viewers made sense of the series, David Glassberg analyzed 444 letters received by Ken Burns in response to the film. The letters suggest that those writing viewed *The Civil War* most often in the context of their own family history but also in the content of their previous television watching experiences and their previous knowledge of the war. Glassberg concluded that Burns's series created "spaces for sharing information," which "viewers filled with stories," and that the letters and diaries "made viewers feel closer to the process of history-making, not passive and removed."[7] In sum, *The Civil War* encouraged and supported some of the personal ways people relate to the past far more effectively than have many documentaries before it.

Who and How? Everyperson His or Her Own Interpreter

What about museum education? Once again, we may see our field mirrored in the history movement, but there's a lesson to be learned from Becker: namely, everyperson his or her own interpreter. Like history, making meaning of objects is something we do all the time, not just in museums and not just those of us who get paid for it. Whether art, history, science, anthropology, popular culture, or kitsch, we each exercise a variety of skills—including identification, description, and evaluation—that are similar to those of the museum professional in responding to objects in most contexts. Like history-making, those processes are social; the meanings we make are influenced and constrained by other people, including those with whom we participate in relationships and social groups.[8] And as is the case with history-making, there exists a range of ways in which we respond to and make sense of objects: we reminisce about them, imagine and fantasize with them, worship and revere them, treat them as symbols, react unconsciously to them, and use them to tell stories to others—often on topics having little to do with the museum's intended "messages." Many of these ways of relating to objects are typically deemed "naive" and inappropriate behavior in museums. Yet our own experiences and recent research attest to the fact that such behaviors can be integral parts of the museum experience, important and satisfying to many visitors. As in the case of history, it seems that understanding the range of ways that people make meaning of objects and using that broadened spectrum as the basis for museum programs and exhibits can open the door to more democratic practices in museums. Such practices can provide opportunities to model and communicate basic values such as pride, respect, and tolerance that grow increasingly crucial for the functioning of multicultural society.

Literature on objects in anthropology, sociology, psychology, communications, ethnic studies, and folklore can help to stimulate our thinking along these lines. Communications research, for example, certainly sheds light on the ways in which people relate to objects as symbolic of values and mnemonic of stories that express those values. In a case study of a rural Pennsylvania community, for example, Christopher Musello examined the use of family objects within the daily lives of community members. He found that families use their possessions to symbolize important people and events and to pass on family values embedded in stories.

> Furnishings are largely dependent for their interpretation on the rounds of talk they generate and support about the range of references they embody. In conjunction with talk, they are employed to stimulate and facilitate the transmission of . . . accounts of people and events.[9]

We know that visitors engage in such storytelling in museums all the time. Should that activity and those meanings continue to take second place to the interpretations of museum staff? The popularity of comment books, self-made videos, and computer databases for visitor input in more and more museums suggests otherwise. Understanding the many ways we make meaning of objects in our culture may in fact help us see a wider range of behaviors that museums could be supporting and promoting. In so doing, museums could become cultural havens for, as well as models for, the respectful exploration and exchange of ideas.

Beyond Expert and Novice: Understanding Similarities and Differences

Recognizing the spectrum of history-making activity and the ways that people relate to objects offers hope that we might move beyond the often condescending and limiting dichotomy of professional-expert/layperson-novice that still exists in history and museology alike. Letting go of judging responses as "right" or "wrong" can provide room for something more. But what?

To move toward a practice of history that is more inclusive and democratic, Thelen argues for the need to understand the *similarities and differences* in the ways that people interpret and use the past as a means to create new dialogues among all history-makers.[10] Through the exchange of opinions, reactions, and perspectives, multiple viewpoints and meanings can be explored.

Stuck in the expert/novice linear communication model, some historians do not think to encourage such dialogue or see its great potential for educating about diversity. Michael Frisch relates one such missed opportunity at the point at which history was being presented to the public: an experience of attending a labor history symposium with academics, trade unionists, and community people. The symposium featured the presentation of oral history interviews about steelworkers' strikes organized in the 1930s.

> It was not clear until one overheard comments in the lobby, however, that people had seen it very differently: many of the academics heard in the tapes evidence of the pervasiveness of class conflict and a call to militance inspired

by labor's heritage of struggle. But the trade-unionists seemed to come away with a very different message: recalling the "bad old days," they said, made them appreciate the distance between then and now, as measured by their current no-strike contracts, grievance procedures, and pension benefits. But the interviews had not focused on such messages in either sense, and the program offered no opportunity or framework for discussing, contrasting, and evaluating the connection of this particular past to the present. . . . The program ended where it should have begun.[11]

If different voices were to share "interpretive" authority from the start of the process of creating history, there is hope that common ground might also be forged and methods developed for supporting multiple points of view. A new, more inclusive vocabulary could become a shared goal, as well as less judgmental criteria for comparing perspectives. New frameworks and techniques for the practice of history, born of "shared authority," might then emerge. Thelen offers the idea of a history textbook in which

> teachers, government officials, community activists, history buffs, stamp collectors, farmers, and school children would discuss and negotiate its content. In the course of listening to each other, they might construct a new historical experience.[12]

It is not hard to fantasize the challenge and excitement of such a project or the ideas and educational approaches that could result from such dialogue and others like it.

Museums and Dialogues

In creating museum exhibits and programs that interpret objects, it is similarly time for museum educators to take further steps beyond the expert/novice dichotomy to create more effective ways to share authority for the making of meaning in museums. As in history, such steps can be facilitated by affording more opportunities to explore and promote differences among perspectives while also working toward the creation of expanded but common ground.

In the realm of products, such as exhibits and programs, we have laid some important groundwork already, through the growing use of feedback books, computer databases, and other mechanisms for incorporating diverse visitor responses. But in addition to such techniques that provide a relatively small space for visitor choices, imagine: a gallery with the explicit goal of fostering the sharing and exchange of various perspectives on objects; an exhibit that makes equal room for other "interpreters" by giving visitors space and materials to create and add labels and other devices for communicating their interpretations to others, including suggestions to others on how to relate to the object as they do; a museum program that begins, as Frisch suggested, with audience members' multiple interpretations of what they've seen and then challenges visitors and staff alike to truly understand each other's perspectives.

In the realm of process, or the ways in which we create exhibits and programs, we also have experience on which we can build in our efforts to create expanded dialogues. In many museums, tremendous gains have come from the difficult but rewarding work of using teams, community advisory groups, and focus groups in planning and design. It's time to explore further what such groups could look like, what purposes they could serve, and how they would operate. How about casting our nets wider than staff and community membership and involving individuals who make meaning of objects in many different ways? How about, as Thelen suggests for history, convening a group to discuss the vast "meaning of things," in which teachers, collectors, shamans, the elderly, anthropologists, shopkeepers, museum educators, children, and others would discuss and negotiate the content of an exhibit and, in the process, construct new experiences with objects?[13]

What might the outcome be? While it's hard to know in advance, negotiation specialists suggest that shared authority for a group goal is likely to produce common ground.[14] Could museum exhibits and programs find such common ground? The popularity of Fred Wilson's exhibits suggests so. While largely the vision of one individual, Wilson's unique installations suggest the great potential museums have to be places that can transcend differences as well as communicate about them. As Donald Garfield describes Wilson's philosophy, "The key element for Wilson is to let the *shared humanity* of the museum, its collections, and visitors come through." As Wilson explains:

> Even the most standard exhibition can be more human. Because you are human. The people who organize exhibitions are human. If they . . . tap into what led them to get excited about museums in the first place, and put THAT out there along with the scholarship, that is how to reach people.[15]

While individual artists or museum educators may well possess the sensitivity and skill to hypothesize what constitutes "shared humanity," imagine the challenge and potential rewards of seeking answers to that question through broad dialogues among diverse groups. And imagine developing exhibits and programs that reflect those answers as well as the processes involved in finding them!

On the Role of the Museum Educator

What new or revised skills do we need to accomplish these goals? How might we rethink the role of the museum educator as a result? While the field of history has not yet imparted much advice in this realm, the paradigm itself broadens our notion of the museum educator's role to be one who is knowledgeable in the ways people make meaning of objects and skilled in facilitating dialogue and negotiation.

As we move from a model of the museum professional as exclusively a one-way expert communicator to one who participates and facilitates in shared processes of meaning-making, these needs become clear. While subject matter knowledge, excellent interpretive abilities, and the ability to communicate information clearly and effectively are and will always be necessary skills for museum educators, we will increasingly need to understand the diverse ways that people make meaning of objects if we hope to support these perspectives effectively. While the field of museum visitor studies offers great insights and new developments, we must also look toward research and observations on the role of objects in our lives from psychologists, folklorists, artists, religious leaders, anthropologists, poets, collectors, historians, novelists, and our friends, relatives, children, and selves. What more could museums do and be?

To truly support, encourage, and promote dialogues in museums, museum educators (and others) must also hone our skills as *facilitators*—learning and improving in the areas of listening, supporting, prodding, and negotiating—skills that grow increasingly vital to the functioning of a multicultural society. Many of these skills have long been the hallmark of a good educator in any context; yet focused on communicating the "museums' message," we may have lost sight of their importance. In this area, too, we may look to literature on conflict resolution, therapy, counseling, and management as well as to firsthand experience and experimentation, for guidance and inspiration.

To preserve differences, to facilitate mutual respect, and to forge the discovery of "shared humanity" are tremendous challenges that face the field of history—and nearly every other realm of our society today. What better place to uphold these goals and model paths to their accomplishment than museums, the places that house objects of so many different meanings?

Journal of Museum Education 18, no. 3 (Fall 1993): 7–11.

Notes

1. *Journal of American History* 75, no. 4 (1989): entire issue

2. Michael Frisch, *A Shared Authority: Essays on the Craft and Meaning of Oral and Public History* (Albany: State University of New York Press, 1990).

3. Carl L. Becker, "Everyman His Own Historian," *American Historical Review* 37, no. 2 (1932): 223, 228.

4. David Thelen, "History-Making in America," *Historian* 53, no. 4 (1991): 631.

5. Henry Glassie, *Passing the Time in Ballymenone: Culture and History of an Ulster Community* (Philadelphia: University of Pennsylvania Press, 1982); Tamar Katriel and Thomas Farrell, "Scrapbooks as Cultural Texts: An American Art of Memory," *Text and Performance Quarterly* 11, no. 1 (1991): 117.

6. Thelen, "History-Making in America."

7. David Glassberg, "'Dear Ken Burns': Letters to a Filmmaker," *Mosaic* 1, no. 3 (1991): 8.

8. Lois Silverman, "Of Us and Other 'Things': The Content and Functions of Talk by Adult Visitor Pairs in an Art and a History Museum" (Ph.D diss., University of Pennsylvania, 1990).

9. Christopher Musello, "Family Houses and Personal Identity" (Ph.D. diss., Annenberg School for Communication, University of Pennsylvania, 1986), p. 388.

10. Thelen, "History-Making in America."

11. Frisch, *Shared Authority*, p. 190.

12. Thelen, "History-Making in America," p. 648.

13. Ibid. See also Mihali Csikszentmihalyi and Eugene Rochberg-Halton, *The Meaning of Things: Domestic Symbols and the Self* (Cambridge: Cambridge University Press, 1981).

14. Roger Fisher and William Ury, *Getting to Yes: Negotiating Agreement without Giving In* (New York: Penguin Books, 1981).

15. Donald Garfield, "Making the Museum Mine: An Interview with Fred Wilson," *Museum News* 72, no. 3 (May/June 1993): 49, including quotation from Fred Wilson.

Why the "Public Understanding of Science" Field Is Beginning to Listen to the Audience

Bruce V. Lewenstein

I come to this discussion about museum education not as a museum person but as a science writer, teacher, and researcher in the general field of "public understanding of science." In this field we are driven by many of the same concerns, and face many of the same issues, as people in the museum field:

- Our topic is a fundamental component of modern culture.

- The details of our subject matter are often complex, jargon laden, and of (apparently) little immediate interest outside a narrow professional world.

- Though we (whoever "we" may be) are often excited and enthralled by our subject, studies routinely show that the public (a term to be defined later) lacks knowledge that we believe to be necessary for leading a full life.

- For our subject to continue to progress, we must excite young people into supporting the field and recruit them into relevant careers.

- Attempts to communicate our topic are often driven by the concerns described above, and we are constantly searching for "better" ways to get our message across.

Consider these generic statements in light of your favorite museum topic—science, art, nature, history, and the like—and you will, I suspect, find them equally relevant to your own concerns.

In this article, I will discuss the current state of public understanding of science activities, putting special emphasis on how reformulations of the issues listed above can help us find better ways of conceptualizing what our task should be. Those reformulations should apply to all of us in the "understanding" business, whatever our subject matter.

Public Understanding of Science as a Field

Public understanding of science activities began in the Middle Ages, but the field as we know it developed after the scientific revolution of the 17th century, when natural philosophy evolved into a series of specialized intellectual inquiries that required a dedicated, essentially full-time commitment to understand them. By the middle of the 19th century, when the term "scientist" was first used, such fields as physics, chemistry, biology, astronomy, and geology were becoming professionalized; the knowledge developed in fields was no longer readily accessible to people who were not members of profession.

Thus a new form of activity arose called "popularization." In the 19th century, at least four different strands of popularization developed. First, leading scientists often wrote clearly and persuasively about science, both to explore philosophical issues and to proselytize for the scientific approach to the world. Second, industrial revolution complaints about the lack of science literacy among the public led to the creation of mechanics' institutes, pulp magazines, and other media intended to inculcate the lower classes in the means and ideology of the science-based world. Third, throughout the century, public demonstrations and itinerant lecturers began to fill the needs of the masses eager for education and entertainment. Fourth, museums in their modern form began to appear, both as collections of research materials and as cabinets of curiosity intended to appeal to the masses.

In the 20th century, new producers of popularized science emerged. Scientific societies and voluntary organizations devoted to particular diseases developed sophisticated public information offices. Beginning in the years

---

The deficit model is based on a particular, academic, knowledge-based definition of science. But the public's version of science is more sprawling.

---

after World War I, journalists began to specialize in science. The first of the new "experience science" museums—the precursors of today's interactive science centers—was developed in the 1930s. In the 1950s and 1960s, the environmental movement emerged. Finally, government and educational agencies periodically recommitted themselves to science education and science literacy, especially after World War II, after Sputnik, in the late 1970s, and again in the late 1980s.

Virtually all these historical contexts for popular science have involved proselytization and commitment to showing the public the benefits of science. "Public understanding of science" has meant public appreciation of the benefits science provides society.[1]

Traditional Ways of Thinking

The people who have been concerned about public appreciation of science have almost universally believed that the problem is insufficient appreciation. In particular, they have focused on the public's lack of information and knowledge about science.[2] Their efforts to popularize science were justified as attempts to address the problem by improving the flow of information from a presumably "correct" source to a presumably eager but ill informed or misinformed audience.

For example, throughout most of this century, scientists and others have periodically decried the growing problem of public understanding. The modern world required knowledge of science and technology, the sages asserted, but people didn't seem to know what they needed to know. This complaint was heard in the mid-1910s, the mid-1940s, the late 1950s, and the late 1970s, and we hear it now.[3]

New initiatives to address the problem—magazines, lecture tours, institutions—resulted, often focusing on presenting "more" and "better" information to the public. For example, in reaction to concerns of the 1950s, science journalists created the Council for the Advancement of Science Writing in 1960 and quickly characterized its mission as increasing "the quantity and quality of scientific information in the public press."

Many of the people who developed the great science museums and science centers in this century were also responding to the cries for more scientific information for the public. They were either senior scientists who chose to devote part of their efforts to science education and exhibition (such as Frank Oppenheimer, founder of the Exploratorium) or educators and missionaries for science who saw science museums and interactive science centers as a way of proselytizing for science (such as Waldemar Kaemppfert, first director of the Chicago Museum of Science and Industry and later science editor of the *New York Times*).[5]

Beginning in the 1950s, a series of surveys of public attitudes toward science showed that the public "demanded" more information about science. And since the 1970s, a biennial survey of public knowledge of science sponsored by the National Science Foundation has produced the tremendously valuable data that are at the heart of the frequently cited statistic that only 20 percent of the American public pays any attention to science and only 5 percent can be considered "scientifically literate."[6]

The logic behind these surveys—the logic of solving a problem by first identifying the lack of knowledge—has been called the "deficit" model of public understanding.[7] Based on a linear model of communication, which assumes that information (and knowledge) flows from the lab bench to the scientific community to the public, the deficit model has led to "magic bullet" approaches to improving science communication. These approaches focus on issues like readability, simplification, and accuracy. If only these problems can be solved (the argument goes), then the public will learn about science.

My sense from discussions with museum educators is that the same arguments can apply directly to most museum education situations. The problem is that the public doesn't know enough about the subject, and so we need to focus our efforts on increasing the public's knowledge.

Newer Understandings of "Understanding"

Clearly, the deficit approach has much to recommend it. It focuses our attention on communication techniques, forcing us to consider language and technical detail as we construct our mass media stories, museum signs, educational films, or other products. But recent work in the history and sociology of science has also shown the great weakness of the deficit approach: it places science on a pedestal and fails to recognize the knowledge the public does have. The critique of the deficit model has two parts: one points to the institutional imperatives behind the traditional way of thinking, and the second redefines the issues from the audience's perspective.

Institutional Imperatives

While we like to think of scientific knowledge as impersonal and objective, much recent scholarship has shown how often institutional factors affect the course of science. Funding, institutional goals, political disputes, and so on shape not only what science gets done but, at least according to some analysts, even the findings.[8] Studies of science journalism and other areas of public understanding of science have only begun to identify how popularization activities maintain the traditional model of science—clearly an area that needs to be addressed.[9]

Nor do we know a great deal about how these institutional influences affect museum education. Sharon Macdonald and Roger Silverstone have shown that various institutional factors inherent in museum practice led the Science Museum (London) to downplay concerns about food safety in a major exhibition on food. But they are careful not to claim that the limited attention to food safety controversies was simply a response to the exhibit's sponsorship by the food industry.[10] The details of how institutional pressures affect museum presentation still need to be worked out.

The Role of the Audience

The second critique of the deficit model—and ultimately the more important one—is that we know very little about how the audience creates its own meanings for science stories or exhibitions. The traditional focus on problems has led to much knowledge of how science stories in the mass media are shaped and constructed;[11] but the same focus has left the audience part of the picture more fuzzy. We simply don't know how members of the public mesh new information about science into their existing beliefs and knowledge.[12]

In the science museum world, the situation is a little less clear. Visitor studies, of course, have been staples of the field for generations: one bibliography lists nearly 1,400 citations from 1887 to 1979.[13] But until a few years ago, those valuable baseline studies went little beyond counting and characterizing the audience. Now, both in science museums and in other kinds of museums, researchers are beginning to explore what meanings, what *understandings*, visitors take away.[14] The fruits of these new labors are still to come. We are still integrating our understanding of studies that compare the experiences of novice visitors with those of more practiced visitors and studies that compare the meanings people derive with the information the museum presents.

Nevertheless, the concern with audience interpretations is a key lesson from recent work in the public understanding of science.[15] Audiences are not passive receivers of information but active creators of meaning who add new information to the understandings and expertise they already have from previous life experiences. Thus, for example, sheep farmers in the Cumbrian hills of England reacted skeptically when government officials tried to tell them how to market their sheep after radioactive fallout from the Chernobyl nuclear power accident contaminated the herds.[16] The farmers recognized from experience the likelihood that technical information would change. More important, they knew that their own expertise in farming was deeper and more relevant than government pronouncements that clearly did not recognize the daily realities of life in the hills.

Additional case studies reinforce the point. Whether the example is how communities respond to local toxic contamination, how investors make sense of rapid developments in high-temperature superconductivity, or how readers respond to tabloid newspaper stories about science and health mixed in with Hollywood gossip and three-headed babies, the lessons from the public understanding of science literature are clear: we must turn our attention from producing information intended to remedy a deficit and toward understanding what the audience does with the information we provide.[17]

One consequence of this turn is that we need to define our audiences more clearly. The public isn't really one audience but an amalgamation of many audiences. The public, for example, may not be interested in the details of groundwater contamination. But in a community affected by that problem, 60 to 80 percent of the audience—even those with only high school educations—can respond correctly to graduate-level toxicology questions.[18] As another example, until recently, I had only a general knowledge of arthritis. But when I was diagnosed with a mild case of the disease, I quickly acquired a lot of knowledge about nonsteroidal anti-inflammatory drugs—knowledge that I soon discovered many other arthritis sufferers shared. We compared effectiveness, side effects, prices, and so on.

The point is that audiences are constantly forming, shaping, and reconstructing themselves, often around technical issues of immediate concern.

Recognizing this segmenting of the audience—a major achievement of the business world in recent years—is necessary for us to gain insight into how individuals and groups of individuals make sense out of the materials that we produce as professionals in the field of public understanding.

Whose Understanding?

There is one danger in switching to the public's perspective. If we allow the public—whatever public we mean—to define for us what we say and how we say it, are we abrogating our responsibility to use our knowledge of a subject to shape the public's understanding? That is, if we believe science is important—and by science we mean basic research of the sort conducted in university laboratories—are we wrong to let the public's interest in UFOs, cancer cures, and dinosaurs rejuvenated from ancient DNA define how we approach museum exhibition? (The same questions can be posed, of course, for art, community history, or any other museum topic.)

This article is not the place to argue through the implications of taking the audience's perspective on our subjects. But I believe there is a middle ground between high-culture arrogance and new-age credulousness. We *must* let the audience help us shape our presentations, for if there is any lesson of the 1980s, it is that marketing works. On the other hand, *we* are the ones who choose our topics and materials, not the audience. Thus the audience-driven presentation is constrained by the materials we bring to the occasion. Our goal must be to craft interesting, engaging, educational exhibits within the limitations that "truth," as we understand it, allows.

What Comes Next?

Recent work in the public understanding of science leads to several research, political, and practical agendas. Though those agendas cover the full range of activities in public communication of science and technology (newspapers, television, museums, community groups), they are also transferable, I suspect, to a cross-section of museums representing far more than science.

Research Agendas

Clearly, we need to know more about our audiences—not just who they are, how often they read us or come to us, and with whom they discuss us or visit us, but also why they read or come and what they do with the information they get from us. We also, of course, need to know more about those who *don't* come to us and those who leave us quickly, bored or frustrated by what we have presented. We need to understand the relationship between the information and images we present and those that exist in the world of potential readers and visitors. To ask these questions requires that we continue the trend—both in public communication of science research and in museum studies—of going beyond counting readers or visitors. We need to continue to increase our inclination to act as anthropologists, following people around and discovering how they make meaning out of their world.

One consequence of this research program will almost certainly be that we have to reconsider how we define science (or whatever subject interests us). The deficit model is based on a particular, academic, knowledge-based definition of science. But the public's version of science is more sprawling, less fixed in its boundaries. We must do our research with care here, learning what the public means by science without losing our own vision of what *we* mean. The same is true for any topic in the "understanding" business.

Political Agendas

If we accept that the audience shapes our approach to understanding, we will be putting the audience in charge of our activities. In the words of a perhaps-fading fad, we will be empowering the audience. That's a scary thought for scientists, journalists, artists, museum curators, and others who have traditionally considered themselves as the repositories of knowledge and keepers of culture. To turn authority over to the audience is antithetical to the roles we've defined for ourselves as protectors of culture.

Yet we must learn to give up power and authority, terms that suggest why I call this a political agenda: not because we necessarily want to let the masses rule, but because if we don't turn over authority, we will become increasingly isolated from the very audiences we are trying to reach. I am not calling for radical overthrow of the status quo. Instead, this is a middle-of-the-road call for accommodation among groups with very different definitions of what is important in life. The conclusions in the American Association of Museums' *Excellence and Equity* report seem to me a good start toward achieving these political agendas.[19]

Practical Agendas

These research and political issues lead us to several practical conclusions. Newspaper stories, magazine articles, television dramas—and museum exhibitions and programs—cannot be about what *we* think is important. They must be defined by what the *audience* thinks is important. Only then will they open the door that lets us reach in and show them the beauty that makes us care about their understanding. Our programs should be guided not by concerns about public knowledge deficits but by public interests. Equally important, we should judge our success not by how much the public improves but by how interested they are. And since interest is harder to measure than specific levels of knowledge, we need to reconsider many of our evaluation techniques.

Conclusion

Movements in the field of public understanding of science have led us to a greater appreciation of the audience's role in our activities. But now we face the difficult task of reorienting our activities to acknowledge that role. We cannot say, "The audience is important" and then continue to focus on how to provide clear, direct, simple explanations of technical subjects. Instead, we have to say, "What is it that the public wants?" and then turn our efforts in that direction. The same lesson, I believe, can be useful throughout the museum education world.

Journal of Museum Education 18, no. 3 (Fall 1993): 3–6.

Notes

1. Bruce V. Lewenstein, "Public Communication of Science and Technology: The Historical Goal," paper presented to Conference on Policies and Publics for Science and Technology, Science Museum, London, April 1990.

2. Christopher Dornan, "The 'Problem' of Science and the Media: A Few Seminal Texts in Their Context, 1956–1965," *Journal of Communication Inquiry* 12, no. 2 (1988): 53–70.

3. John Burnham, *How Superstition Won and Science Lost: Popularizing Science and Health in the United States* (New Brunswick, N.J.: Rutgers University Press, 1987); Robert Hazen and James Trefil, *Science Matters: Achieving Scientific Literacy* (New York: Doubleday, 1991); Marcel C. LaFollette, *Making Science Our Own: Public Images of Science, 1910–1955* (Chicago: University of Chicago Press, 1990); Bruce V. Lewenstein, "Was There Really a Popular Science 'Boom'?" *Science, Technology and Human Values* 12, no. 2 (Spring 1987): 29–41; Lewenstein, "The Meaning of 'Public Understanding of Science' in the United States after World War II," *Public Understanding of Science* 1, no. 1 (1992): 45–68.

4. Lewenstein, "Meaning of 'Public Understanding,'" p. 58.

5. Victor J. Danilov, *Science and Technology Centers* (Cambridge, Mass.: MIT Press, 1982); John Durant, ed., *Museums and the Public Understanding of Science* (London: Science Museum and COPUS, 1992); Hilde Hein, *The Exploratorium: The Museum as Laboratory* (Washington, D.C.: Smithsonian Institution Press, 1990).

6. Jon D. Miller, *The American People and Science Policy: The Role of Public Attitudes in the Policy Process* (New York: Pergamon Press, 1983); Miller, "Scientific Literacy: A Conceptual and Empirical Review," *Daedalus* 112, no. 2 (1983): 29–48; National Science Board, "Public Science Literacy and Attitudes Towards Science and Technology," in *Science and Engineering Indicators—1991*, ed. National Science Board (Washington, D.C.: U.S. Government Printing Office, 1991), pp. 165–91.

7. John Ziman, "Public Understanding of Science," *Science, Technology & Human Values* 16, no. 1 (Winter 1991): 99–105.

8. James Petersen et al., eds., *Handbook of Science, Technology, and Society* (Newbury Park, Calif.: Sage, 1994).

9. Bruce V. Lewenstein, "Science and the Media," in ibid.

10. Sharon Macdonald and Roger Silverstone, "Science on Display: The Representation of

Scientific Controversy in Museum Exhibitions," *Public Understanding of Science* 1, no. 1 (1992): 69–87.

11. Sharon M. Friedman, Sharon Dunwoody, and Carol L. Rogers, eds., *Scientists and Journalists: Reporting Science as News* (New York: Free Press, 1986); Dorothy Nelkin, *Selling Science: How the Press Covers Science and Technology* (New York: W. H. Freeman, 1987).

12. Marcel C. LaFollette, "Beginning with the Audience," in *When Science Meets the Public*, ed. Bruce V. Lewenstein (Washington, D.C.: American Association for the Advancement of Science, 1992), pp. 33–42.

13. Denis Samson, Bernard Schiele, and Pierre di Campo, eds., *L'evaluation museale publics et expositions* (Paris: Expo Media, 1989).

14. Durant, *Museums and the Public Understanding of Science.*

15. The same concern is evident in recent museum work; see Danielle Rice, "The Cross-Cultural Mediator," *Museum News* 72, no. 1 (January/February 1993): 38–41.

16. Brian Wynne, "Sheep Farming after Chernobyl: A Case Study in Communicating Scientific Information," *Environment Magazine* 31, no. 2 (1989): 10–15, 33–39.

17. Phil Brown and Edwin J. Mikkelsen, *No Safe Place: Toxic Waste, Leukemia, and Community Action* (Berkeley: University of California Press, 1990); Helga Nowotny, "Scientific Knowledge Transformed: The Hybrid Space of Public Discourse," *Public Understanding of Science* 2, no. 4 (1993): forthcoming; William A. Evans et al., "Science in the Prestige and National Tabloid Press," *Social Science Quarterly* 71, no. 1 (1990): 105–17; Gerald Hinkle and William R. Elliott, "Science Coverage in Three Newspapers and Three Supermarket Tabloids," *Journalism Quarterly* 66, no. 2 (1989): 353–58.

18. J. Fessenden-Raden, J. Fitchen, and J. Heath, "Providing Risk Information in Communities: Factors Influencing What Is Heard and Accepted," *Science, Technology and Human Values* 12, nos. 3/4 (1987): 94–101; Clifford W. Scherer and J. Paul Yarbrough, "Media Focus, Personal Dispositions, and Activation of Health Risk Reduction Behavior: A Longitudinal Study," paper presented to conference on Science Communication: Environmental and Health Research, University of Southern California, Los Angeles, December 1989.

19. American Association of Museums, *Excellence and Equity: Education and the Public Dimension of Museums* (Washington, D.C.: American Association of Museums, 1992).

Further Reading

Beetlestone, John G., Colin H. Johnson, Melanie Quin, and Harry White. "The Science Center Movement: Contexts, Practice, Next Challenges." *Public Understanding of Science* 7, no. 1 (1998): 5–26.

Bradburne, James M. "Dinosaurs and White Elephants: The Science Center in the Twenty-First Century." *Public Understanding of Science* 7, no. 3 (1998): 237–53.

Gregory, Jane, and Steve Miller. *Science in Public: Communication, Culture, and Credibility.* New York: Plenum Trade, 1998.

Irwin, Alan, and Brian Wynne, eds. *Misunderstanding Science? The Public Reconstruction of Science and Technology.* Cambridge, England: Cambridge University Press, 1996.

Ongoing scholarly work can be followed in the journal *Public Understanding of Science*, Bruce Lewenstein, editor, Department of Communication, 321 Kennedy Hall, Cornell University, Ithaca, N.Y. 14853; pubscience@cornell.edu.

REFLECTIONS

While the traditional concerns for "better" communication remain, much additional research has strengthened the belief that we must understand the audience's perspective. Rejections of the "deficit" model have become formulaic in many articles, as more researchers focus on the "local, situated knowledge" when looking at public understanding of science issues. The science museum world has paid some attention to these new perspectives, but much of the day-to-day work in the field is still concerned with how best to convey information to the "general" public. In light of my caution that "listening to the audience" does not require passive acceptance of audience perspectives, I should note the controversy that erupted over the Smithsonian Institution's *Science in American Life* exhibition. The exhibition tried to take the more nuanced perspective I suggested and was roundly criticized by many working scientists as "anti-science"; the American Chemical Society, after paying $5 million to sponsor the exhibition, formally cut its connection to it. Yet a careful visitor study by the Smithsonian's evaluators showed that the exhibition actually spoke quite directly to visitors' beliefs in science and strengthened their already strong support for science.

—*Bruce V. Lewenstein*

The Personal Past in Public Space

David Carr

Every life writes a text with hidden pages, some unreadable even to their author. But there are illuminating moments in museums, found in no other places, when such pages become visible and their messages become clear. An object suggests an idea we have not encountered in years. An exhibition holds a theme that touches our forgotten schooling. We see an image of a past time and place, and we recognize it as the experience of our family, or of a family like our own. The challenge for an educative museum is to create a situation where communication is valued and context invites and illuminates memory without compromising the authenticity of content.

At the edge of the 21st century, the theme of remembering (and related themes of narrative, reconstruction, and conservation) appears at the center of our common search for an understanding of the 20th. Especially in the current observances of World War II from a half-century's perspective, the idea of memory dominates the details of memories. We analyze the meaning of memory even as we listen to those who recall their experiences of D-Day and the *Enola Gay*, of Iwo Jima and Dresden. Tensions between recorded history and living memory meet in debate, and at stake is the ownership of the past.

In the case of the Smithsonian's reduction of the *Enola Gay* exhibit, the idea of a public story surrounded by engaged critical thinking was made impossible. The most meaningful recognition to come from that sad encounter between veterans and historians must not be lost. History can be seen as my possession, my knowledge, and my identity—a living relationship defined more by personal integrity and the need to reconcile stark and traumatic experiences than by scholarship. The most authentic story of the bombing may be what people think of it, how they own it, how it has become a transforming part of them. It is the story they tell themselves in order to live peacefully with the past. And these human stories of personal possession must be regarded with the deepest respect because, in some way, such memories are all, always, true.

We have seen how powerfully a crafted and burnished personal memory can stand among artifacts, assert itself, and demand that attention be paid.

One scholar described this power as the "inevitable tension between the commemorative voice and the historical voice when history becomes the focus of a public exhibit or ceremony."[1]

It is not my purpose to advance or resolve this debate, but to contemplate the value of individual memory to the museum. Recent controversy aside, there is no more likely place than the museum for the meeting of recorded history and living memory. Here the reconstructed records of scholars and the crafted memories of witnesses can intersect to create a productive forum. Here multiple truths can be expressed. Here, where memory is respected evidence, a human repertoire of experienced narratives and authentic stories can be told. In the museum, history can be practiced as it is understood by its scholars and held by its witnesses—each kind of knower touching and telling the truth differently.

The crafted memory appears in the voice of the witness, unique and intimate. I think of my own father's World War I stories of biting lice and acrid gas; I think of my mother's screaming memory of horses in a burning barn. For each of them the crafted memory was kept alive to be revisited and augmented over time. The crafted memory is one we work to keep actively in

---

Memory transcends the bland narrative and the perfunctory label; it can deepen and extend the human presence in things.

---

mind in order to remind ourselves of the story that happened to us and brought us here. Whatever its verity as a report, the crafted memory is true in the sense that all caringly constructed narratives hold a truth for their narrator. The crafted memory is recollected and held, and possibly offered, as a small carved treasure is held in the palm of the hand.

What such memory means for the museum is not difficult to see. Evoked in the museum, individual memories are momentary mirrors; they inspire an instant of reflection and recovery. When a living memory is recovered and shared among companions, what is transmitted is the integrity of an observation and the intensity of its personal contexts.

Memory transcends the bland narrative and the perfunctory label; it can deepen and extend the human presence in things. Here are two encounters with living memory, one with a human witness and the other with an object that was a kind of inanimate witness. Both, a half-century later, come out of the Holocaust.

In 1992, while consulting at the Children's Museum of Indianapolis, I saw a traveling version of the child's-eye view of the Holocaust, *Remember the Children: Daniel's Story,* for the second time. I entered the exhibition with well-informed understanding. Many books and essays on my shelf, many films and photographs, and knowledge cultivated over 20 years accompanied me; and I had seen this exhibit a year before, in New York. Seeing it again in Indiana, I reviewed the familiar images, words, and sounds, comparing one installation to another, wondering how the midwestern eye interpreted this narrative two years before the story of Schindler's list was well known across America. In this setting, several local Jewish guides assisted. The spaces were more open, less constrained and discontinuous than they had been in New York. Here one had an opportunity to know the sense of Daniel's *passage* better. His family's fate, somehow, was clearer.

I joined a guide and his group in the ragged and dim simulation of a ghetto; he spoke of the privations and scarcities experienced in rooms such as these. But this simulated interior, I thought, could never fully simulate the fear—the grave knowledge of the exterior world—that must have been rampant in such real spaces. We moved beyond this room, to a space with a wall-sized photographic mural of a camp. The guide—in his late 60s, articulate, with barely an accent—alluded to the railroad cars in the photograph and to the small humans in the image. "Look there," he said. "I am one of those in the photograph." And he went on to tell about his job in the camp: collecting luggage and other possessions newly arrived with their owners and separated from them.

He spoke a few more sentences and then said, "Perhaps you have not seen something like this." And he rolled up his jacket sleeve, then his shirt sleeve, to show a tattooed number just above his wristwatch. He went on to talk more about his life in the same voice. Later I read about him in an adjacent photographic study, and about his lost parents and siblings. I thought again about what I felt to be missing in the simulated ghetto rooms—that grave knowledge of the exterior world—but the presence of a witness and the authority of his voice had filled my experience completely.

Talking about this moment later to my students, my voice was unexpectedly heavy and quite unsteady—in fact I had to stop talking about the experience—not with new knowledge of my own, but with the sudden transformation of the narrative, the change in information I had experienced that day through the eyewitness memories of my guide. In him I had encountered a dedicated conservator of memory caringly crafted out of an experienced nightmare. No narrative I had command of, either on my shelves or in my thoughts, had the weight of this encounter. And no exhibition, not even the United States Holocaust Memorial Museum itself, could fully capture and present the power of his rolled-up sleeve.

The second encounter is told in a story by the contemporary German writer Erich Fried, "My Doll in Auschwitz."[2] The writer visits Auschwitz in 1967, fearful and uncertain. The night before his journey, he reads in preparation, "as a help against anxiety and against the shivering." He is prepared by his reading to acknowledge and verify what he sees—the "unbearable became for a few seconds almost bearable. . . . I had expected the mountain of shoes, I had also read about it and seen photos." The writer moves on, seeing pile upon pile of remaining possessions, remnants of the dispossessed in Auschwitz. Then his memory is present in a sudden way.

> Even more surprising was the mountain of children's toys. I could not remember ever having read anything about it. . . . Or had I quickly wanted to forget it? Apart from that I had children myself, and that didn't make it any easier. . . .
>
> Somewhat helplessly I looked at the pile of toys, partly damaged, partly well-preserved. Suddenly I saw Moritz. Moritz was about ten inches high, red haired, with a green jacket and green trousers. He was on wheels, so that when he was pulled along on the string, he alternately bent forward and leant back. At the same time he also swung his arms and legs. It wasn't me pulling him along on the string; I was separated from him by a glass barrier, but I knew exactly. It was a reunion. Moritz had been my own doll, broken when I was four years old, but now completely undamaged. As a child I had of course never considered that Moritz was mass produced. I cannot remember either ever having seen a second Moritz in a toy shop or in the park where I played. Only in Auschwitz, more than forty years after my doll was broken, did I see its double.
>
> From this moment on Auschwitz had a new dimension for me. It was no longer just the unimaginable other, the completely alien and dead, instead something strangely familiar had emerged out of the emptiness and emerged again and again.

The writer then sees the familiar in all Auschwitz objects; he encounters his own possessions in the possessions of the dead, and he rediscovers knowledge of objects he had lost. "I had never thought about them again, but now, in Auschwitz, they were old friends."[3]

From my guide in Indianapolis, I learned that memory is embodied, that it exists in the person. Offered as evidence among objects, memory has a deep and disproportionate power to instruct and awaken the experiences of others. Erich Fried's remembrances as a visitor in the concentration camp are unexpected; they are moments when he sees as if into a mirror or an album and finds a sudden, entire world of intimate connections. It is of course a wholly interior world, but to Fried it was invisible, and unbearable, until the encounter with his doll in Auschwitz. He wrote, "Such details can make possible a leap from one's own fear and dread to insights and reflections, and even lead to overcoming fear with the help of what one was most afraid of."[4]

Lessons for the practice of education in these two stories may be difficult, but worth stating. Perhaps every exhibition needs a forum, a place for the expression and communication of memory and observation. Throughout the museum, apart from the identifications of objects and contexts, it may be useful to emphasize the continuities of things, the threads and ribbons that interlace artifacts with their human observers. Perhaps, among these observers, there will be a witness who feels invited to speak up and offer an example from the personal past in the public space.

There is power in reconstructing the everyday lives of objects through memory and human presence. For every visible thing, there is an invisible context that needs to be evoked, or rescued from where it lies silently in human experience.

Journal of Museum Education 20, no. 2 (Spring/Summer 1995): 3–5.

Notes

1. Edward T. Linenthal, "Can Museums Achieve a Balance between Memory and History?" *Chronicle of Higher Education*, February 10, 1995, p. B1.

2. Erich Fried, "My Doll in Auschwitz," in *Children and Fools* (London: Serpent's Tail, 1992), pp. 49–62.

3. Ibid., pp. 51–52.

4. Ibid., p. 58.

Further Reading

Baxter, Charles, ed. *The Business of Memory*. St. Paul, Minn.: Graywolf Press, 1999.

Kotre, John. *White Gloves: How We Create Ourselves Through Memory*. New York: Free Press, 1995.

Schachter, Daniel. *Searching for Memory: The Brain, the Mind, and the Past*. New York: Basic Books, 1996.

Smith, Frank. *To Think*. New York: Teachers College Press, 1990.

This essay was based on evidence in both experience and literature that the museum user carries a private record of images, themes, and texts, the building materials that configure memory. I had also come to understand that the individual is always working on that record: sorting, rearranging, juxtaposing, reinterpreting, justifying, even denying its parts—or its powers over feelings. These examples were particularly resonant for me, since I had worked with the Jewish Museum in New York, had read several strong Holocaust memoirs, and knew the topic to be among my own unfinished issues. Now, as then, I begin from the premise that memory should be seen as a form of art. I ask museum professionals to consider the questions: Once the authentic personal memory is evoked, what shall we do with it? How should the museum express its respect for the integrity of memory while assisting in the construction of new frames for it? What does it mean to be the one who remembers?

—David Carr

Research and Evaluation

Professionalism and Research in Museum Education

Annie V. F. Storr

In 1990, the Museum Education Roundtable instituted the annual Research Colloquium as an experiment in professional development. The purpose was to encourage advanced thinking about small and large questions in the field by providing a forum for some of the best of these questions as developed presentations.

MER's Research Colloquium is now a continual process for the mutual support of museum educators who undertake ongoing, often independent, study of concepts or questions that reach beyond the limits of a specific public service project or an annual schedule of interpretive programs. Research in museum education is as varied and rich as the disciplines represented in our museums, from philosophical inquiry into an abstract question of professional values to high-tech proof of a working hypothesis. There is room for both qualitative and quantitative analysis. The central goal is systematic critical thinking in its many forms. The experience of the last two years confirms my belief that this broad research and analysis are absolutely vital to sustained growth for many individual educators and to our profession's collective maturity and institutional standing.

Museum education is a thinking person's career. Most of us were drawn into it because we not only love objects but also possess a flair for ideas. Mental work and mental play are at the heart of what we do. We use them constantly, often unconsciously, to design creative interpretive programs, to teach, and to understand our role within the larger order of things. Above all, by exercising our minds energetically, we model the benefits of an engaged, thoughtful relationship to the world.

As museum education matures as a thinking person's profession, it is becoming both possible and necessary to advance its intellectual aspects. The firmer the theoretical base and the deeper our accessible reserves of information and ideas, the stronger the profession becomes. Our widening circle possesses more and more years of cumulative, varied experience. The recent increase in the number of good books and in-depth seminars shows that both the demand and the talent exist for marked advances in critical thinking about the issues that face us. We are learning an enormous amount by borrowing the lessons of sociology, psychology, cultural studies, and political science. While maintaining the flow of ideas from these sources, we are more ready than ever to shape the distinct intellectual disciplines of museum education.

The key to real intellectual advancement is activating individual minds. New ideas are often best inspired by the collegial exchange at which museum educators tend to excel. Those first ideas, however, are almost always carried through to their most valuable conclusions by one person. If genius is 10 percent inspiration and 90 percent perspiration, one persistent individual usually sweats the most. In addition, whether pursued actively or left to simmer at the back of the mind, the cutting-edge ideas in any profession also usually require the passage of time to ripen. Breakthroughs generally involve shifts in perspective, and so—paradoxically—they are likely to flash to mind at 3 A.M., during vacation, or on retreat. Once an idea has begun to take shape, then its originator almost invariably benefits from the feedback of peers to fill gaps, clarify points of the argument, and reroot the implications of the concept in practice.

The firmer the theoretical base and the deeper our accessible reserves of information and ideas, the stronger the profession becomes.

To promote original thinking, we need to provide a number of conditions. The changes required to create these positive conditions need not be grand or ambitious. However, some of them involve patterns not already built into existing museum education departments and programs.

We can do a lot by altering the way we think about things we already do well. Museum educators tend to be good problem solvers, skillful users of resource facilities, habitually active learners. We know how to make an argument for worthwhile initiatives, and we are communicators above all. But, for a variety of reasons, we simply haven't yet made the conceptual leap that combines exactly these talents and applies them to building up our professional discipline through formal and informal research.

Once we see ourselves as thinkers as well as doers, the first steps to making the conceptual leap become clearer. The structure of our jobs does not often encourage long-term inquiry, but there are signs of change, and the impetus to cultivate the change has to come from us. Here are a few suggestions for individuals to try out as a complement to hands-on work and others for groups, departments, or museums to consider collectively. All are aimed toward the practice of consciously disciplined learning, critical thinking, and the professional exchange of ideas:

For individuals:

•For your own files, in-house memos, or the local paper, write reviews of new exhibitions or conferences that push beyond description to probe an issue presented by the subject matter or approach.

•Collect all your records (working files, program evaluations, clippings) on a related subject from time to time, and look at them as raw research materials in their own right. What have you discovered generally from three years of specific projects? For example, what is the state of the art in exhibitions about trash? Why is the adolescent audience increasing in your museum? Is it happening elsewhere? How do changes in the themes outlined in docent manuals actually affect tours? Even if you don't carry out a research project, the exercise is stimulating. If you do, the first three pages of data, ideas, and questions you sketch out are the draft of material that is valuable to your colleagues.

•Reconnect with your own educational roots. Stop periodically to ask yourself, What does my background as a _____ tell me about this situation? How would basic principles of (for example) sociology or educational theory help me answer this question?

•Whenever you hear yourself saying, "You know, I have been thinking about_____ for a long time," stop *before* you say, "but I haven't done anything with it." Instead, *write down* an outline of what you have been thinking. Having thought about something for months or years is not having "done nothing." You are already a crucial step ahead of everyone else who hasn't had your experiences and hasn't been mulling them over.

•Get in the habit of finishing every project report and grant report with a page on "wider implications" and "questions for further study." Send a copy to five colleagues with diverse interests for their comments.

•Submit presentation proposals to existing academic conferences. A number of fields have recently shown increased interest in "crossover" topics from museum personnel.

For groups:

•Start a reading group or study circle in which members take turns giving presentations on a variety of topics, followed by discussion. In this arena, stick to analyzing issues; avoid showcasing current projects.

•Start a local or regional colloquium with peer review of proposals.

•Encourage education staff to participate in in-house or local research circles—monthly lecture series, brown-bag lunches—that have usually been attended mostly by collections curators. Ask for program summaries in staff meetings.

•Work out ways that staff members can have uncommitted hours or release time to collect data, think, or write.

•Acknowledge achievements in museum education studies with notices in museum newsletters and staff meetings. Consider instituting a regular award for the best contribution to museum education research.

•Include practice in professional research and original critical thinking in training programs and in-house professional development sessions.

As museum educators, we stand to become professionally stronger, smarter, and more confident of our reasons for what we do if we build self-study and critical thinking into the very fabric of our work. The rapid growth in the first years of MER's Research Colloquium combines with many other signs to indicate that this is the time to make active efforts, as individuals and institutions, in the direction of formal and informal research in the field.

Journal of Museum Education 17, no. 3 (Fall 1992): 20–21.

Questioning the Entrance Narrative

Zahava D. Doering and Andrew J. Pekarik

There has been considerable discussion in the pages of this journal and else-where about what we would like to see visitors learn from museums and how we can influence their behavior and responses. Much less attention has been paid to what individuals already know when they enter the museum. Museum visitors are not "blank slates" on which we write. They attend a museum or an exhibition usually because they already have some level of interest in the sub-ject and some knowledge and opinions about it.

The internal story line that visitors enter with, which we can call their "entrance narrative," has three distinct components:

•a basic framework, i.e., the fundamental way that individuals construe and contemplate the world

•information about the given topic, organized according to that basic framework

•personal experiences, emotions, and memories that verify and support this understanding.

This model suggests that the most satisfying exhibitions for visitors will be those that resonate with their experience and provide information in ways that confirm and enrich their view of the world.

Although we have not attempted in our research to identify differences in the ways that museum visitors think about the world, we have indirect evi-dence of its importance. Museums do not draw all segments of the population equally. The primary factor in predicting whether an individual is likely to visit a museum of any kind is level of formal education. We hypothesize that this association reflects the influence of formal education on the way that indi-viduals encounter and think about the world and their place in it.

The effect of the second component of the "entrance narrative," the spe-cific knowledge and opinions visitors bring to the subject, is more easily meas-ured. Depending on the individual, the type of museum, and the exhibition, the level of a visitor's knowledge can range from expert to complete novice. The priority of particular opinions in the minds of visitors depends upon their personal experiences, including their awareness of current events and the climate of public thinking on related issues, particularly as discussed in the media. Moreover, not all visitors feel secure either in their knowledge or in their opinions.

When visitors encounter the contents of an exhibition, they necessarily place them within the narrative that they have previously constructed to explain objects and ideas of this type. They may not want to learn much more specific detail than they already know, and they certainly do not intend to have their narratives radically revised. Instead, they want their narratives to be confirmed. In fact, visitors want validation so strongly that if the exhibition story departs in only minor ways from their expectations, they are likely not to notice the areas of difference. If the museum's narrative unexpectedly and explicitly differs in major ways from their own views, adult visitors are likely to be rather upset and may even act upon their feelings by writing long, angry comments in the visitor's book, sending letters to the local press, or canceling their membership in the "misguided" institution. If the museum's narrative supports and encourages their views, however, they leave the museum delighted and confident, with a renewed sense of empowerment and a heightened respect for the importance of the subject and their appreciation of it.

We hypothesized that the most satisfying museums or exhibitions will be those that resonate with visitors' entrance narratives and confirm and enrich their existing view of the world.

The experience of most museum visitors thus tends to be subtle, incremental, and supportive. Museums, as perceived and used by their current audiences, are instruments of stability, not revolution. In this way, perhaps, they parallel the implicit goals of the formal education system. Whether they intend to or not, successful museums will both reflect and subtly influence the viewpoints of the culture by reinforcing and supporting the views of those both sympathetic to and relatively knowledgeable about a particular subject.

People want to leave museums satisfied with themselves and their beliefs. In this regard, museum visiting, one among many leisure-time options, is seen as a respite from normal life, a time to "recharge" one's perspective on the world. At the same time, audiences also want museum visits to be inspirational and uplifting, emotionally developmental in some way.

Museums have traditionally identified this inspirational aim as a key component of their educational missions. One of the founding fathers of museum education, John Cotton Dana, wrote in 1925 that "a good museum *attracts, entertains, arouses curiosity, leads to questionings*—and thus promotes learning."[1] This sequence is closely linked to the emotional component of the visitor's experience. We have come to believe that emotional response plays a central role in the museum experience and are now studying it in greater detail.

Validation and Education

For practical reasons, we cannot expect to assess precisely the impact of a museum visit on what takes place outside the museum months or years later. Too many other factors, random and uncontrolled, also become potential motivators. The museum visit is generally one experience among scores or hundreds or thousands that ultimately lead to some action or response that, in turn, reflects the kind of movement we associate with educational impact.

Very often the museum experience plays a supportive role in this dynamic whereby innumerable experiences coalesce into a desire for action or change. When the museum visitor seeks confirmation and validation, a detail in an exhibition resonates in the mind or heart of the visitor because of some prior connection with that idea, image, or object. It, or something like it, was already part of the visitor's entrance narrative. To see it now, perhaps for the first time in person, highlights and underscores that part of the story and the things it represented in the visitor's mind.

Although, as Dana said, the attraction of the object may lead to questioning, the goal of that questioning is usually to place that thing even more firmly within the visitor's established entrance narrative. The mind naturally seeks resolution, consistency, and wholeness in its internal construction of the world. What stands out is investigated primarily so that it can be absorbed into a new, perhaps modestly revised, understanding. Things that don't fit, that cannot be resolved, are usually deeply disturbing and are generally avoided and forgotten or distorted until they do fit.

We must be somewhat cautious in linking this process of validated understanding that is characteristic of the museum experience to the idea of educational impact. If we decide that we are content to define educational impact as an emotionally powerful confirmation of visitors' entrance narratives, we will find most of our museums to be very effective and held in high social regard as sources of authoritative confirmation.

The issue of how to define educational impact is particularly important for Holocaust museums. More than any other museum type, Holocaust museums portray ideas and events that are fundamentally incomprehensible. In the end, no narrative can fully account for them—neither the entrance narrative of the visitor nor the story line of the museum. Each, though, inevitably gropes for a version that will make sense, that seems reasonable, clear, graspable. The places where those narratives fail are easily ignored, by both the visitor and the museum, because they seem to deny the act of understanding itself.

What exactly happens when the visitor encounters some object in the museum that can be placed within that individual's entrance narrative? One possibility is that in the process of encountering the object, now underlined in the mind, the object may come to stand so strongly for the part of the story in which it figured that the story line itself is not so much enriched as fossilized. James Young writes in *The Texture of Memory* that

> remnants of our historical past have long come to stand for the whole of events. . . . Too often, however, these remnants are mistaken for the events from which they have been torn: in coming to stand for the whole, a fragment is confused for it. Authentic historical artifacts are used not only to gesture toward the past, to move us toward its examination, but also to naturalize particular versions of the past. . . . At such moments, we are invited to forget that memory itself is, after all, only a figurative reconstruction of the past, not its literal replication.[2]

In other words, instead of leading us toward questioning that will, in turn, bring about an adjustment in and engagement with what we know, the interesting object can just as easily move us toward a rigid, simplified understanding that may ultimately be more satisfying precisely because it requires less of us.

As Young goes on to say:

> Museums, archives, and ruins may not house our memory-work so much as displace it with claims of material evidence and proof. Memory-work becomes unnecessary as long as the material fragment of events continues to function as witness-memorial. Are we delegating to the archivist the memory-work that is ours alone? Do we allow memorials to relieve us of the memory-burden we should be carrying? The archivists' traditional veneration of the trace is tied directly to their need for proof and evidence of a particular past. But in this they too often confuse proof that something existed with proof that it existed in a particular way, for seemingly self-evident reasons.[3]

When Young uses terms like "memory-work" and "memory-burden" he emphasizes the difficult, unresolved character of all attempts to understand the Holocaust. Museums are not especially well suited to this kind of effort. By the voluntary nature of the visit, the pull toward the validation and confirmation of the entrance narrative, and the implicit desire for an established, authoritative, static resolution, the museum experience tends to move away from the dynamic, tense confrontation of irreconcilables. The museum is generally conceived as a place of settled understanding, not as a place of active conflict.

For that matter, the same desire for a clear, simple answer to even the most difficult question is characteristic of the formal education system as well. Bill Parsons of the United States Holocaust Memorial Museum, in talking to us about his experience teaching the Holocaust in the classroom, pointed out that he always worked to maintain the tension between the particular and the universal, to deliberately keep understanding from reaching stability. But most teachers find this path extremely difficult and want to arrive instead at an agreed truth.

In the minds of many visitors, museums seem to stand for the embodiment of this agreed truth. They present themselves as temples of knowledge, erected and maintained by true experts who embody the state-of-the-art understanding of their subject matter. Visitors do not generally expect museums to debate the significance or meaning of their contents or to embody a wide range of conflicting viewpoints. In fact, most people are inclined to go to the other extreme and accept the presumed importance and significance of any object acquired by the museum, even if they themselves cannot see why it matters.

Some museum staff may be tempted to see their educational mission as the communication of this agreed truth to visitors. Would you accept this as educational impact? If visitors enter your museum, adjust their entrance narrative to align it more closely with the museum's story line, and leave it at that, would you be satisfied? Under those circumstances, would you accept the absence of deeper questioning?

How are we to account for the fact that, as Young points out, "the historical meanings we find in museums may not be proven by artifacts, so much as generated by their organization?"[4] Yet visitors give very little attention to who set up an exhibition. They generally tend to receive museum presentations as objective truth rather than as the informed speech of an individual or group of individuals with particular perspectives and intentions. The museum visitor, an educated individual who is normally alert to the special interests of advertisers, the intentions of authors, and the selective sources of all kinds of speech, typically sets all such cautions aside when entering the museum. Only when the museum's story line deviates in radical ways from the visitor's own entrance narrative is that individual likely to become conscious of the fact that exhibitions, too, have authors, and those authors, in turn, have interests to serve.

Today, most of us consider it an important part of the task of education to teach individuals to question the sources of their understanding. Only in museum education do we still encourage visitors to accept the authority of the institution. No one has yet devised a way for museums to systematically lead their visitors to question their own authority, for even in attempting to do so they seem to propose only a still more authoritative, more up-to-date position. How could museums foster the kind of tension that teachers like Bill Parsons have found so educationally effective?

For example, Edward Linenthal recounts how political pressure affected the discussion of Armenian genocide in the United States Holocaust Memorial Museum. He concludes, "In the past decade, official memory was receptive to the Holocaust and not to the memory of Armenian genocide, thereby weakening one of the stated virtues of remembering the Holocaust."[5]

Consider this: Which would be a better indication of the educational impact of that museum, the visitor who accepts the museum's presentation of Armenian genocide or the visitor who rejects it as wholly inadequate? Would you prefer education to mean that the visitor accepts everything that your museum says and gives it the same weight and emphasis that the museum does? Or would you prefer that visitors become engaged with the presentation, question it, and struggle with it intellectually and emotionally?

Conclusion

Whenever, as researchers, we attempt to address the experience of museum visitors, we, too, begin with a kind of entrance narrative of our own, a pre-existing model of how we believe visitors think and behave. Although we feel most comfortable and confident when our research results confirm this model, real learning takes place only when the model doesn't fit. Increasingly we have focused on those weak points, noting that most of them are concentrated around the ideas and motivations with which visitors enter the museum. We simply don't know enough about how people view their museum-visiting activity. Until we clarify this question, we will not be in a good position to know what they come away with either. In the meantime we must probably accept that, as long as learning continues, the result is not likely to be an agreed truth but rather a constant state of tension, marked by refined questioning and continuous revision. It is precisely through such apparently hopeless efforts that we come to better comprehend the complexity, the possibilities, the limitations, and the dangers of museum education.

Journal of Museum Education 21, no. 3 (Fall 1996): 20–23.

Notes

A complete version of this article, "Assessment of Informal Education in Holocaust Museums," which includes specific references to studies, will appear in proceedings of the conference "51 Years Later: Evaluating Holocaust Education," organized by the United Jewish Federation of Metro West and held May 12–15, 1996. We appreciate the insightful comments of William Parsons, executive officer and former director of education at the United States Holocaust Memorial Museum, and Tom L. Freudenheim, executive director, Yivo Institute for Jewish Research, and former assistant secretary for arts and humanities, Smithsonian Institution, on a draft version of the complete paper.

1. John Cotton Dana, "The Museum of Interest and the Museum of Awe," *The Museum* 1, no. 2 (April 1925): cover page. Emphasis added.

2. James E. Young, *The Texture of Memory: Holocaust Memorials and Meaning* (New Haven: Yale University Press, 1993), p. 127.

3. Ibid.

4. Ibid., p. 128.

5. Edward T. Linenthal, *Preserving Memory: The Struggle to Create America's Holocaust Museum* (New York: Penguin, 1995), p. 240.

Further Reading

Doering, Zahava, and Andrew Pekarik. "Strangers, Guests, or Clients? Visitor Experiences in Museums." *Curator* 42, no. 2 (1999): 74–87.

Pekarik, Andrew, Zahava Doering, and D. A. Karns, "Exploring Satisfying Experiences in Museums." *Curator* 42, no. 2 (1999): 152–73.

REFLECTIONS

Our research, and that of colleagues, continues to affirm the importance of the entrance narrative to understanding the experience of visitors to cultural institutions. Most recently, we have explored one facet of what visitors bring with them as they cross our thresholds: namely, expectations for specific kinds of museum experiences. We hypothesized that the most satisfying museums or exhibitions will be those that resonate with visitors' entrance narratives and confirm and enrich their existing view of the world. Through in-depth interviews, sample surveys, and analyses of visitor comments, we constructed a working list of types of museum experiences. Using this list, we now have data from visitors in nine Smithsonian museums. Analysis of the results showed that experiences can be classified into four categories:

- object experiences, which give prominence to the artifact or the "real thing"
- cognitive experiences, which emphasize the interpretive or intellectual aspects of the experience
- introspective experiences, which focus on the visitor's personal reflections, usually triggered by an object or a setting in the museum
- social experiences, which center on one or more other people, besides the visitor.

—*Zahava D. Doering and Andrew J. Pekarik*

Recalling the Museum Experience

John H. Falk and Lynn D. Dierking

In 1984, to begin addressing the issue of long-term learning in museums, we initiated a series of museum recollection studies. At the time, it seemed critical to understand memories of museums more broadly, to investigate their components, saliency, and persistence, both soon after the experience and long after. We began with a series of open-ended, ethnographic-style interviews, conducting the first 11 over a period of two years.[1] These early interviews proved so interesting and useful that we have continued to build on this line of research, as have many others. What does our work and that of other researchers reveal about museum memories?

In our early exploratory study, which intentionally included only a few subjects, general patterns about museum recollections emerged from the data:

• Individuals interviewed could place the museum visit within a social, geographical, and temporal context.

• Individuals interviewed had surprisingly good recollections of how long they had spent in the museum and often of their mental state at the time (such as being bored, enjoying themselves, or feeling hassled).

• Most individuals could recall at least a few exhibits they had seen and some specific details about them, though no individual could recall a full visit's worth of exhibits and objects.

• All individuals referred to some aspect of the museum's architecture or "feel."

• Interviews also suggested that often museum memories were bound together in highly personal ways.

Although we took care not to generalize given the number of subjects, we had a sense from this early study that people were best able to remember those things with which they already had some experience or knowledge. For example, one subject (a 54-year-old salesman) recalled a variety of facts and feelings about the *Spirit of St. Louis,* which he had seen at the Smithsonian when he was a young boy. During the interview he stated:

> The thing I remember best was seeing the *Spirit of St. Louis.* It was suspended

from the ceiling. I had heard about it in school and I marveled at the history. I was really struck by the way it was designed, the fact that it had no forward windows. I had never realized that Lindbergh couldn't even see in front of him as he flew, that he was flying blind. I was also impressed by the scalloped effect of the metal. It was such a weird, special type of plane. I remember just how amazed I was by that plane.

He had heard about the plane quite a bit in school, but he had never seen it. The combination of having prior knowledge of the plane and seeing the real object produced an indelible memory. In a similar way, other subjects seemed to recall most vividly exhibits that built upon prior knowledge rather than upon totally novel objects and ideas. The experience of seeing tangible examples of previously learned information or previously seen photographs may have played a role in producing long-term memory.

As our interest and experience in this area of research grew, we began to explore additional questions. In a study of museum professionals' recollections of early museum experiences, for example, we looked for patterns in three major categories: (1) the number of recollections for each subject; (2) whether subjects described themselves as frequent or infrequent museum visitors as children; and (3) the domains in which recollections seemed to fall.[2] In the third category, we identified eight domains that had emerged from earlier research:

1. social memories, such as who accompanied the subject on the trip and in what arrangement, such as a family or school group

2. specific recollections of exhibits or objects viewed

3. the physical characteristics of the museum, such as the architecture, size, or floor plan

4. temporal memories of the visit, such as the time in the subject's life, the time of year, or the time of day he or she attended

5. affective dimensions of the visit, such as how it made the subject feel

6. whether the memories tended to be concrete or abstract

7. whether the memories included specific details, such as what the subject wore, what he or she ate that day, whether a souvenir was purchased, and whether the souvenir was still in his or her possession

8. whether the museum recollections were bound with other memories—such as memories related to visiting that specific museum at other times—or bound to a hobby, interest, or other concrete life experience or event such as a memorable family vacation or the birth of a brother or sister.

As with our earlier study, the findings indicated consistent patterns among recollections. All individuals interviewed placed their recollections within a social, geographical, and temporal context. They recalled at least a few exhibits they saw, but mostly on a very concrete level. Most embellished their recollections with details about the architecture, the journey to and from the museum, and the food and gifts they purchased at the museum. Almost all the memories were also bound to nonmuseum memories such as family events, personal experiences, or future occurrences. The vast majority of subjects recalled experiencing strong emotional responses to their early visits, reinforcing that affect is an important dimension of museum recollections.

Despite many similarities between subjects who described themselves as frequent museum visitors versus those who said they were infrequent visitors, we observed distinct quantitative and qualitative differences. The infrequent visitors' recollections were more numerous, tended to be very specific to the particular visit recalled, and often were memories of particular exhibits. Since museum experiences are more novel for the infrequent visitor, we hypothesized that it was this novelty that helped make their specific memories so salient.

The infrequent visitors' memories also tended to be much more bound to events such as a memorable family vacation or a school field trip. In part,

---

The vast majority of subjects recalled experiencing strong emotional responses to their early visits, reinforcing that affect is an important dimension of museum recollections.

---

we felt that the vacation or field trip probably had provided the reason for going to the museum. In such circumstances, the social occasion rather than the museum in question drove the visit and hence strongly influenced the visitor's memory.

On the other hand, many individuals in the frequent visitor group indicated difficulty in recalling their "first" visit and actually suggested that the recollection might be a composite memory of several visits. For the most part, their memories were not of specific exhibits, as was the case with infrequent museum visitors, but were a gestalt of their many museum experiences.

The results of this study reinforced the idea that early museum experiences are recalled within a larger social, geographical, and temporal context, are bound into an individual's memory in often idiosyncratic ways, and form patterns that can be systematically investigated using interview methodologies. The results also reinforced the sense that visitors, particularly children, recall exhibits and objects seen in the museum but rarely recall abstract concepts or principles. This was even the case for a group of individuals who ultimately chose to work in museums.

Our next study investigated early school field trip recollections, attempting to document systematically the persistence and character of such memories.[3] We interviewed 128 individuals about their recollections of school field trips taken during the early years of their school education: 34 9- and 10-year-old children (fourth grade); 48 13- and 14-year-old children (eighth grade), and 46 adults 20 years and older (graduating college seniors).

Overall, 96 percent of all subjects could recall a school field trip: 100 percent of the 9- and 10-year-olds; 96 percent of the 13- and 14-year-olds; and 93.5 percent of the adults. Although there were age trends, there were no statistically significant differences among age groups. The most frequently recalled field trips were to historical sites or farms (28 percent); natural sites and nature centers (27 percent); zoos or aquariums (12 percent); natural history museums (11 percent); and science-technology centers (9 percent).

Among the 123 individuals who indicated a recollection of a field trip, only two could not recall any specifics. Of the remaining 121 individuals, 8 percent could recall at least one specific event, object, or exhibit; 6 percent could recall two; and 86 percent could recall three or more. There were no significant differences as a function of age. Examples of recollections were:

> I remember rows of brooms to vacuum cleaners and the different stoves, Lincoln's chair with blood. (30-year-old female recalling a fifth-grade trip to the Henry Ford Museum and Greenfield Village)

> I remember my mom giving me money in the morning for the souvenir shop. I bought a miniature swan, which I still have. (21-year-old female recalling a third-grade trip to the American Museum of Natural History)

> Our class went into some trailors [sic] and did activities. Then we switched according to the letter of our last name. We did crafts, we looked at collections of butterflys [sic], we went for a nature walk and we also had lunch in between. (13-year-old female recalling a first-grade field trip to a school-run outdoor nature camp)

> I remember we looked at insects and we looked at caterpillers [sic] on the way back it haled [sic] and poored [sic] down rain we all got soaked. (9-year-old male recalling a first-grade trip to a nature center)

We conducted a content analysis of all the specific recollections of events or experiences from the field trip. Seventy-seven percent of the recollections were related to content or subject matter; 56 percent to physical setting; 56 percent to gifts/souvenirs, food, or clothing; 55 percent to feelings about the setting; 47 percent to social aspects of the visit; and 1 percent to "life lessons/skills learned." There were no age-related differences. The data showed that the most frequently recalled experiences related to what individuals did, what they saw, with whom they had visited, what they ate, what they purchased, or how they felt about these things.

When asked if they had ever thought about the field trip experience again since their trip, 80 percent said yes; 73 percent said they had thought about it frequently and gave specifics. There were no age-related differences. Some examples of subsequent memories of earlier field trips were:

> When I came home from the zoo I planted the seed I found. It grew to be a big tree that stands in my backyard that I see every day. (14-year-old female recalling a first-grade trip to the zoo)

> Yes, when I watched my sister leave for the Smithsonian in 1st grade and when in 2nd grade we went to the Smithsonian, and when we went in 3rd grade and in 4th. (14-year-old male recalling a first-grade trip to the Smithsonian)

> I remember[ed] the tomato horn worm again because when we went to the Smithsonian we saw a tobacco horn worm in the Insect Zoo there. Also when I went to the State House [in Maryland] I remember their was [sic] carvings of tobacco their [sic]. (10-year-old girl recalling a second-grade trip to a colonial farm)

This study reinforced that early elementary school field trips were salient experiences in the lives of children. The overwhelming majority of subjects interviewed readily recalled their field trips—when and with whom they went, the journey there and back, and at least some details of what they did. There was no evidence that recollections significantly declined over time; rather, they persisted over long periods.

Since initiating this line of research with the general public, museum professionals, and school-age children, we have interviewed more than 250 individuals. It is remarkable how similar the patterns among recollections are and how much the findings support the saliency and persistence of museum memories. It is also reassuring that other researchers investigating similar questions have arrived at the same conclusions.

One investigation of kindergarten children's recollections of a field trip to an archeology museum was intended to determine if this trip would be recalled and distinguished from other trips taken during the year. In their study, Robin Fivush, Judith Hudson, and Katherine Nelson focused on the linguistic details of the children's reports and found that children were able to distinguish among trips.[4]

Even more interesting, though, is the finding that for more than a year, these children were able to recognize and pick out, in order, a series of six photographs taken on the day of the field trip. Moreover, the researchers report, "although there was a loss of detail in the children's recall of the novel occurrence, the structure of the reports remained specific and the content was surprisingly accurate."

Unfortunately, this study paid little attention to the content of the children's recollections as opposed to the form of the recollections. In general, children had a much better recollection of what they did than of where they went. In a follow-up study six years later, the children first had little recall of this field trip. With considerable cuing, however, all of them were able to remember some details.

Inez Wolins, Nina Jensen, and Robyn Ulzheimer's research on children's memories of school field trips provides a better tool for correlating memories with actual experiences.[5] Over two years, a third-grade teacher took her students on 29 field trips to 17 different institutions. The researchers were interested in the effects on recollection of the frequency of visits to a particular institution, the nature of presentations at the museum, preparation by the teacher before the visit, discussions after the visit, and the children's previous trip experiences.

The researchers were able to show clearly that children were most likely to remember trips repeated to the same museum, experiences that were meaningfully linked to the school curriculum, and experiences in which they had direct involvement or engagement. For example, one child remembered a particular aspect of a science demonstration after having been selected to participate in the demonstration. Another series of visits to the Japanese Hill and Pond Garden in the Brooklyn Botanic Garden, the Isamu Noguchi Garden Museum, and the Metropolitan Museum of Art to view Japanese art were particularly memorable because at school the children participated in a highly interactive curriculum unit on Japan in which the focal point was the construction of a Japanese garden in the center of the classroom.

Research by John Stevenson and by Paulette McManus also supports the persistence of long-term memories of museum experiences. Stevenson conducted follow-up interviews of families who had visited the Launch Pad gallery, an interactive science and technology gallery at the Science Museum, London.[6] Even after six months, individuals could readily discuss what they had seen and done during a roughly hour-long visit to the museum. Stevenson put respondents' recollections of Launch Pad exhibits into three categories. The first category was "descriptions" (60 percent of responses), which he defined as "pragmatic accounts of what the subject did with the exhibit or of the exhibit itself." Another 14 percent of responses were categorized as "feelings," or "accounts which contain sentiments such as enjoyment, surprise, annoyance, dissatisfaction, etc." The final category, with 26 percent of responses, was "thoughts," "statements containing evidence of thinking or reflecting about the exhibit in some way."

Examples of these types of recollections were:

Descriptions:

There were these brick things and there was this boat—sort of a boat about that long—and you got to make it high enough and long enough so the boat can go under.

The thing where you have to trail along on the carpet and set off an alarm.

Feelings:

It was quite amazing watching it shoot up into the air!

It was rather clever. . . . I enjoyed it.

Thoughts:

I couldn't really understand, but then, perhaps I didn't read it much. . . . I mean I understand that if there's acid in your body you act like a battery, but it wasn't really. I thought it could be explained a bit more.

It was like one of those bubble lamps, wasn't it, where the bubbles go elongated and strange shapes.

More than half of the descriptions were concerned with how individuals interacted with or observed an exhibit either alone or with others; 15 percent were about what others were doing with an exhibit. The largest group of feelings expressed (23 percent) related to subjects' feelings of fascination with specific exhibits, while only 14 percent of the feelings expressed were concerned with enjoyment alone. Thirty percent of the thoughts dealt with effects that visitors noticed and which were accurately noted. Relating the exhibit to something relevant accounted for another 23 percent of the thoughts, while 17 percent expressed a lack of understanding about the phenomenon observed.

In Stevenson's study, recollections were both prompted and unprompted. More than a quarter of all the exhibit recollections he recorded— approximately five for each visitor interviewed—were spontaneous and unprompted. Verbal prompts and photographs elicited the remaining three-quarters of the recollections. Stevenson concluded that more than half of all the exhibits mentioned by visitors were "remembered clearly and in detail." His results also documented that visitors spent considerable time thinking about exhibits, both during and after the visit. In other words, these were not "mere experiences"; there was evidence of considerable cognitive processing as a result of this museum visit.

McManus reached similar conclusions in a study of visitor memories of Gallery 33 at the Birmingham Museums and Art Gallery in Birmingham, England.[7] Gallery 33 is an innovative permanent exhibition about beliefs, values, customs, and art from around the world. In McManus's study, a sample of 136 visitors who wrote their names and addresses in the gallery's comment book were sent a follow-up letter (with a stamped envelope provided for return) asking them to write down any memories of the exhibition they might have; 30 individuals (22 percent) replied. The time elapsed between visit and recollections ranged from two to ten months, with an average elapsed time of seven months. Respondents ranged in age from under 8 to between 41 and 50.

McManus organized visitors' recollections into four categories: objects or things (51 percent); episodic events (23 percent); feelings at the time of visit (15 percent); and "summary memories" on recall (10 percent). The average number of memories generated by individuals was five. The most memorable objects in Gallery 33 were interactive videos, followed closely by masks that visitors could try on. Almost half of the memories ranged over many items in the gallery and were very individualized in preference and recollection. In fact, a good percentage of all recollections, across all categories, could be described as very personal and individualized. Examples were:

> The design of the gallery down to colours, textures, "high tech" flooring and rails, and including the layout and the relative positions of the music area, the mask area and the textiles.

> The seats, and the metal seats I did not like.

> As I was walking around I couldn't take my eyes off of the masks.

> Enjoyed being invited by Polish people to join in national dancing.

> Trying on an Egyptian mask and other masks and looking funny in the mirror.

> I visited Gallery 33 by accident as I had really taken my children to the museum to see the dinosaurs.

McManus concluded that Gallery 33 had a lasting impact on visitors, at least within the 22 percent who responded to the questionnaire. One hundred thirty-six discrete memories were found in the accounts of the visitors, who had on average visited seven months before they were asked to recall their visits. The range and depth of the memories were remarkable, particularly since they were all spontaneous; the interviewers used no form of prompting, such as gallery photographs. There was definite evidence among the respondents that a visit to Gallery 33 resulted in both positive attitudes toward the topics presented and considerable reflection after leaving the museum on the issues posed.

A number of studies in the museum literature have focused on memory but utilized methodologies other than recollection interviews or questionnaires. Although many of these studies have centered more on short-term memory and have been behavioristic in design, they do provide some additional insights into how museum memories are formed and influenced. In fact, as Amy Cota and Stephen Bitgood correctly point out in the introduction to a series of abstracts on memory presented in *Visitor Behavior*, any study that has attempted to measure knowledge gains from museum visits is to some degree a memory study.[8] Using this very broad definition of memory, literally hundreds of museum studies have assessed museum memories. Most of these studies, however, shed little insight on either the process or the products of museum experiences.

Taken as a whole, these studies of museum memory, both recollection studies and short-term memory studies, suggest that museum memories are salient and persistent and that they are influenced by the amount of time spent in the museum, the mode of presentation, the social and physical milieu, and the prior experiences and knowledge of the visitor.

Journal of Museum Education 20, no. 2 (Spring/Summer 1995): 10–13.

Notes

1. John H. Falk, "Museum Recollections," in *Proceedings of First Annual Visitor Studies Meeting*, ed. Stephen Bitgood et al. (Jacksonville, Ala.: Psychology Institute, Jacksonville State University, 1988), pp. 60–65.

2. John H. Falk and Lynn D. Dierking, "The Effect of Visitation Frequency on Long-Term Recollection," in *Proceedings of 1990 Annual Visitor Studies Conference*, ed. Stephen Bitgood (Jacksonville, Ala.: Center for Social Design, 1991), pp. 94–103.

3. John H. Falk and Lynn D. Dierking, "Assessing the Long-Term Impact of School Field Trips," in *Current Trends in Audience Research and Evaluation*, vol. 8 (Washington, D.C.: AAM Committee on Audience Research and Evaluation, 1994), pp. 71–74.

4. Robin Fivush, Judith Hudson, and Katherine Nelson, "Children's Long-Term Memory for a Novel Event: An Exploratory Study," *Merrill-Palmer Quarterly* 30, no. 3 (1984): 303–17.

5. Inez S. Wolins, Nina Jensen, and Robyn Ulzheimer, "Children's Memories of Museum Field Trips: A Qualitative Study," *Journal of Museum Education* 17, no. 2 (Spring/Summer 1992): 17–27.

6. John Stevenson, "The Long-Term Impact of Interactive Exhibits," *International Journal of Science Education* 13, no. 5 (1991): 521–31.

7. Paulette McManus, "A Study of Visitors' Memories of Gallery 33," in *Gallery 33: A Visitor Study*, ed. J. P. Jones (Birmingham, U.K.: Birmingham City Council, 1993), pp. 56–74.

8. Amy Cota and Stephen Bitgood, "Museum Studies of Memory: Selected Abstracts," *Visitor Behavior* 9, no. 2 (1994): 13–14.

Further Reading

Falk, John H. "Museums as Institutions for Personal Learning." *Daedalus* 128, no. 3 (Summer 1999): 259–75.

REFLECTIONS

In the past five years, additional museum research has confirmed both the value and importance of using long-term memories to understand the impact museums have on visitors. In addition, recent advances in the neurosciences and the cognitive sciences have permitted a greater understanding of how these findings fit within larger psychological and biological frameworks and independently validate the importance of this line of research. For example, our findings on the importance of context, and the presence of an emotional, physical, and social "stamp" on all memories, have now been independently substantiated by numerous investigators in a wide range of situations. Finally, of importance to the museum field is recent research which finds that what people remember about a museum experience immediately following their experience—for example, as they exit an exhibition—often bears little relationship to what they recall weeks, months, or years later. Thus, as the museum community comes to fully understand and appreciate the importance of meaningful assessment, every effort should be made to include the measurement of visitors' long-term memories.

—*John H. Falk and Lynn D. Dierking*

The Quandaries of Audience Research

Minda Borun and Randi Korn

With federal agencies requiring evaluation plans as part of exhibit and program proposals and corporate and foundation funders increasingly interested in accountability, the audience research field is experiencing a growing demand for services. Suddenly, there is more work than the handful of trained professionals can keep up with. We are faced with a need to train additional practitioners, specify minimum standards of competency, define a museum staff evaluator position, and sharpen our focus on the central questions for this work.

Standards of Practice

Since social science research involves talking to people, it might seem that anyone can conduct a study. Yes, anyone can talk to visitors and get a sense of what they think about an exhibit, program, or the museum as a whole, but the construction of a research study to uncover basic truths about the museum experience, or the development of an evaluation plan that gives actionable information about the effectiveness of museum presentations, requires formal training in research techniques.

The Visitor Studies Association and the American Association of Museum's Committee on Audience Research and Evaluation (CARE) offer short, one- or two-day workshops to museum professionals. The intent of these workshops is to give participants a general overview of the evaluation process, to enhance their interest in conducting audience studies, and to enable them to work more effectively with research professionals. Unfortunately, these workshops have also produced a group of people who feel that they have become "instant evaluators," and the profession is now facing a serious problem of quality control. Some of the work that is being done does not meet acceptable standards of practice.

While we certainly do not want to limit access to the visitor studies field or to make its practices seem abstruse, it is important to point out that some basic training is required before you can conduct meaningful evaluation or research. Specifically, courses in experimental methods, interviewing techniques, and statistics are necessary in order to know how to set up a study, talk to visitors, and analyze and interpret data. This is not to say that a full graduate degree is required; on the other hand, it does take more than a one- or two-day workshop.

Good research design, sampling, validity, reliability, statistical testing, and content analysis procedures are critical concerns of research and evaluation. Experimental design—the plan for a study—determines whether the data you collect will yield the information you seek. Proper sampling procedures ensure that the study group will represent the larger population you want to describe. A validity test looks to see if you are measuring what you think you are measuring. A reliability test tells you the likelihood that two independent observers will score the same event in the same way.

Statistical testing allows you to determine whether the relationships you observe are "significant" or likely to have occurred by chance. A judgment of "practical significance" considers whether the statistical difference is meaningful in the context of the questions being asked. The ability to judge practical significance comes only with experience. Finally, careful content analysis uncovers patterns in descriptive data obtained through open-ended interviews

---

We are learning what not to ask visitors and are experimenting with new questions as we piece together the complexities of the visitor experience.

---

with visitors. All these procedures require training in research methods. If careful procedures are not used in the collection, analysis, and interpretation of data, you cannot have confidence in the results of a study or in any recommendations based on the results.

Training

Closely related to the question of standards of practice is the issue of training future visitor studies professionals. If the visitor studies field is to grow and flourish, it needs a way to train new practitioners. In the past, the field has attracted primarily psychologists, with a few anthropologists and sociologists in the mix. These individuals have been through lengthy and expensive graduate training in social science research. One of the few alternatives to an advanced graduate degree in social science is to apprentice with one of the relatively small number of senior researchers in the field.

In 1986, Harris Shettel and Mary Ellen Munley conducted a survey of museum education and training programs and found that only 5 out of 56 graduate-level programs offered a course in evaluation techniques.[1] Since their study, there has been some increase in the number of museum evaluation courses offered, but they are rarely required for a degree in museum studies or museum education. There is no degree program or even concentration in visitor studies for the would-be practitioner.

Clearly, we need to begin laying the groundwork for a program of graduate training in audience research that will allow students to acquire the necessary skills and experience to carry on and expand the visitor studies field.

In-House Evaluators and the Organization Plan

Increasing numbers of museums are hiring in-house evaluators to assist with audience research and evaluation. These new staff members can fit into the museum's organizational structure in a variety of ways.

Ideally, evaluators should answer to a high-level, neutral staff member who is not aligned with any one department or project but who has the best interests of the museum in mind. If evaluations focus on products of the education or exhibits department, an evaluator should not report to the head of exhibits or education. The evaluator ought not to have a stake in the product being evaluated or be influenced, even unconsciously, by his or her supervisor's involvement with the product. Under no circumstances should the individual in charge of the project being evaluated be the individual responsible for writing the evaluator's performance review. It is best if the evaluator works in a neutral department—one removed from the planning and production of the product—and reports to a museum director, associate director, or vice-president.

Asking the Right Questions

Museum researchers are continually challenged to design and implement studies demonstrating that people learn in museums. A few decades ago, when educational researchers were trying to measure cognitive outcomes in classrooms, museum researchers were doing the same with casual visitors in the museum exhibit environment. Measuring learning and understanding its complexities were stumbling blocks in both settings.

Over the years, our understanding of how people learn has evolved and broadened to include a wide range of abilities, skills, and intelligences. In response to this broader understanding and awareness, the ways in which we provide instruction, measure impact, and evaluate the museum experience must also evolve.

What is it that we want to know about visitor experiences? The experience researchers and evaluators have accumulated over the years contributes to and supports the methodological shift many of them have made from information to meaning, from measuring to understanding, and from results to process. This shift necessitates creative data collection methods and asks alternative questions. We are learning what not to ask visitors and are experimenting with new questions as we piece together the complexities of the visitor experience.

Concerns about asking the right questions are in part related to another methodological problem: most often, budget and time constraints demand that exhibit and program evaluation occur immediately after a visit, before visitors have time to process, internalize, or reflect on their experiences. Museum experiences, however, may not be fully realized during a museum visit, nor do they end when the visit ends. Even though evaluators continue to make important contributions to the visitor studies field, one must wonder what we may be missing by not being there to ask questions when visitors reflect on an experience they had in a museum a month ago, a year ago, or five years ago. Only recently have museum researchers begun to examine long-term effects of museum visiting.

Over the next decade, with enthusiasm and determination, researchers and evaluators will work together to meet the challenge of framing the questions that will move us closer to understanding the visitor experience and to measuring multiple outcomes.

Research and Planning Strategy

Issues surrounding the audience research field will continue to evolve. This is true for any profession. Whatever the issues, they should not prevent any museum from including research in its planning strategy. Evaluation findings can be used to identify the qualities and shortcomings of particular programs and to determine whether learning and experience objectives are being met. If the museum community is concerned about its public image and the effect of its programs on visitors, these concerns should be reflected in a research and evaluation program.

Journal of Museum Education 20, no. 1 (Winter 1995): 3–4.

Note

1. Harris Shettel and Mary Ellen Munley, "Do Museum Studies Programs Meet Evaluation Training Needs?" *Museum News* 64, no. 3 (February 1986): 63–70.

Further Reading

Borun, Minda, and Randi Korn, eds. *Introduction to Museum Evaluation.* Professional Practice Series. Washington, D.C.: American Association of Museums, Technical Information Service, 1999.

The Art Museum and the Elementary Art Specialist

Denise Lauzier Stone

Art museums offer teachers an array of valuable resources with which to facilitate art education goals. These include slides, reproductions, written materials, and original works of art. To what extent do elementary art specialists use these resources? What types of art museum resources do these specialists use? How frequently do they take advantage of them? What types of museum programs do they typically request? What obstacles have they encountered in using art museums? Do teachers get involved in art museums outside the classroom? If so, in what capacity? These questions are only a few that were addressed in a national survey of elementary art specialists. The purpose of the study was to discover the relationships between art museums and schools. Resulting information sheds light on how art museum educators can improve art museum–school links. Research for the study was supported with grant money from the University of Kansas.

The Study

A 16-item questionnaire was developed and pilot tested. Questions ranged from whether respondents used museum resources to demographic information regarding teaching experience and age. A combination of closed and open-ended questions was developed to obtain a full range of information, since very little research is available on this topic.

A list of elementary art specialists was obtained from the National Art Education Association to select the sample, and 900 specialists were systematically selected for the study. The questionnaire, accompanied by an explanatory cover letter, was mailed to respondents in the spring of 1990, and follow-up questionnaires and another cover letter were sent to nonrespondents six weeks later. A total of 524 respondents completed the questionnaire, yielding a return rate of 58 percent.

The Results

The results provide a picture of the way elementary art specialists use art museums. Table 1 highlights the findings, indicating the percentage (rounded) of art specialists who responded. Additional statistics are presented in the text.

Resources Borrowed

A large group of elementary art specialists (32 percent) indicated that they borrow resources from art museums to support art education instruction in the classroom. The kinds of resources that are borrowed include slides (25 percent), reproductions (14 percent), teacher handbooks (12 percent), films (10 percent), filmstrips (5 percent), and originals on loan (4 percent).

The survey provided interesting information about the frequency with which elementary art specialists use borrowed resources. Of those who responded, 34 percent use borrowed resources annually, and 32 percent use them semiannually. Less than one-quarter (22 percent) use resources every month, and a negligible number of teachers use them every two weeks (9 percent) and every week (4 percent).

Programs Requested

The results show that the traditional museum tour is the most popular type of program requested by elementary art specialists. Almost half of the

---

The purpose of the study was to discover the relationship between art museums and schools. Resulting information sheds light on how art museum educators can improve art museum-school links.

---

respondents indicated that in the past two years they requested a tour of a museum's collections (47 percent); more than one-third reported that they requested a program based on special exhibits (38 percent); and more than one-quarter said that they asked for programs specifically tailored to their curriculums (28 percent). About 20 percent asked for programs based on selected concepts, and 19 percent requested in-class presentations by a museum educator.

Constraints

Clearly the proximity of a museum determines the number and kind of programs teachers request. The distance that respondents reported from the art museum ranged from one mile to 700 miles. However, over half of the sample (52 percent) indicated being within 20 miles of the art museum on which they rely for resources; more than one-third (34 percent) said they were between 21 and 70 miles away; and only a small percent (13 percent) of respondents are more than 70 miles from an art museum.

Table I

Survey Results of Elementary Art Specialists

	Percent
Do you borrow resources from art museums?	
yes	32
no	68

What types of resources do you borrow?

slides	25
reproductions	14
filmstrips	5
teacher handbooks	12
films	10
originals on loan	4

How often do you borrow resources?

weekly	4
every two weeks	9
monthly	22
every six months	32
annually	34

What kinds of art museum-school programs have you requested in the last two years?

programs tailored to your curriculum	28
programs based on special exhibits	38
programs based on selected concepts	20
tours of museum collections	47
in-class presentations by a museum	19

What obstacles have you encountered when using museum resources?

Access to art museum resources is:

unavailable	17
limited	52
no obstacle	31

Information regarding resources is:

unavailable	11
limited	46
no obstacle	43

Assistance by museum educators is:

unavailable	16
limited	42
no obstacle	42

Class time to include resources is:

unavailable	16
limited	59
no obstacle	25

Are you involved in art museum activities?

yes	25
no	75

	Percent
If yes, in what capacity are you involved?	
board member	1
planning committee member	3
docent	2
evaluator of teacher-related materials	6
volunteer	3
other	18

In your opinion, is there a relationship formal/informal between your school district and an art museum?

yes	55
no	45

Characteristics of informal relationship

ongoing communication	22
regular meetings with museum educators	7
use of museum educational services	34
use of museum resources	30

Characteristics of formal relationship

participation of teacher on museum planning board	4
participation of teacher on museum advisory board	4
inclusion of district teacher on museum staff	4
participation of museum staff on school district committee	6
receipt of museum newsletter	29

If no relationship exists, to what extent is there interest on the part of your school district in developing a relationship with an art museum? *(scale 1-7)*

no interest	1	16
	2	12
	3	15
neutral	4	17
	5	11
	6	10
much interest	7	20

How far away is the art museum on which you have relied for services and resources?

1-20 miles	52
21-70 miles	34
more than 70 miles	13

Approximate number of student you teach

1-400	27
401-550	24
more than 550	49

Notes: Percentages may not add up to 100 due to rounding. Multiresponse items will not add up to 100 percent.
N=524

Assigned responsibilities of elementary art specialists may explain low level of use of art museums. According to the data, almost half (49 percent) are responsible for teaching more than 550 students; about one-quarter (24 percent) have between 401 and 550 students; and more than one-quarter (27 percent) have 1 to 400 students.

School-related constraints also affect the art specialist's ability to request programs. Unsolicited comments volunteered by some respondents indicated that field trip costs, transportation, lack of administrative support, and problems related to teaching schedules hindered their opportunity to take advantage of museum services.

A majority of elementary art specialists said that limited class time (59 percent) and access (52 percent) were constraints on their use of art museum resources. Only 31 percent of teachers said that access was no obstacle, and only 25 percent reported that class time was no problem. Assistance by art museum educators was perceived as limited by 42 percent of teachers, and an equal percent said that it was no obstacle. Information about art museum resources was available to 43 percent of teachers and limited to 46 percent of respondents. A small number of teachers (11 percent) said that no information was available. Cost prevented some teachers (5 percent) from taking advantage of art museum resources. These costs related to field trip expenses and transportation.

Museum Relationships

Twenty-five percent of elementary art specialists said they were involved in an art museum in some capacity. Of all who responded, 6 percent evaluate teacher-related materials, 3 percent serve as volunteers, and 3 percent serve on planning committees. Some other types of involvement that were indicated include museum memberships (6 percent), participation in teacher workshops (3 percent), teaching responsibilities in the museum (4 percent), and attendance at museum programs (3 percent).

More than half of elementary art specialists (55 percent) said that there was a relationship, informal or formal, between their school district and an art museum. If no relationship existed, respondents were asked whether there was interest on the part of the school district to develop one. Of those who responded, only 20 percent said there was much interest on the part of school districts, while 16 percent said there was no interest at all.

The most important characteristics of an informal relationship were the use of museum educational services (34 percent), use of museum resources (30 percent), and ongoing communication with museum educators (22 percent). Formal relationships were characterized primarily by the receipt of museum newsletters (29 percent).

Discussion

What do these numbers mean? Is the art museum an important resource to elementary art specialists? The results provide some interesting insights into these questions. From these data, one would not conclude that the art museum is an important resource for elementary art specialists. Not even half of respondents requested tours in the last two years, not quite one-third borrowed art museum resources, and only one-quarter are involved in an art museum. However, the results and the nature of the art specialists' responsibilities also suggest that other factors prevent elementary art specialists from taking advantage of art museum resources.

First, elementary art specialists' responsibilities and schedules pose major restrictions on field trip opportunities. The data indicate that teachers are responsible for a large number of students. It is not unusual for a specialist to teach six to eight classes a day. This heavy teaching load limits teachers' time to plan for using an external resource such as an art museum. In addition, elementary art specialists usually travel among several schools and provide services to different classroom teachers. Their teaching is restricted to school premises. In light of these factors, the low levels of art museum use by art specialists are understandable.

Second, cost is a serious limitation. Elementary art specialists report that their budgets are low and do not cover field trip expenses such as transportation or entrance fees. Teachers are, in effect, dependent on administrative support to provide such monies, and where it is lacking teachers sometimes cannot use museum resources.

A third limiting factor is a lack of training. The preparation of elementary art specialists usually includes coursework in studio-related subjects but little coursework in art history, art criticism, and the use of art resources in the community. These subjects would generally help teachers learn to use art museums as a resource. The National Art Education Association's 1979 guidelines for teacher preparation recommend a minimum of nine semester hours in art history, a minimum that would barely prepare teachers in this field. Recent research by E. T. Rogers and R. E. Brogdon suggests that teacher preparation programs do not generally comply with even these low requirements. Lack of training impedes elementary art specialists from recognizing the full benefit of art museums. In addition, teachers may not know how to incorporate art museum resources in the classroom and may be reluctant to try.

Fourth, lack of administrative support hampers the use of art museums by elementary art specialists. The fact that just over one-half of school districts had a relationship with an art museum is revealing. It is also telling that only 20 percent of respondents said their school districts would be very interested in developing a relationship when none existed. This lack of museum involvement most likely reflects administrative attitudes toward art museums as resources. Administrators are typically not knowledgeable about art and therefore do not fully realize the value of the art museum's resources. As a result, there appears to be little administrative support for their use.

Implications for Art Museum Educators

In light of these realities and constraints, it is possible that art museums are more important to elementary art specialists than they appear to be from teachers' actual use of them. There is certainly potential for making art museum resources more central to art education instruction. What approach can art museum educators take to promote the use of the art museum for elementary art education? What can art museum educators do to help teachers expand their selection of art museum resources for classroom use? The following suggestions might be helpful:

1. *Continue to educate teachers through workshops.* Art museum educators have presented excellent workshops that have provided teachers with invaluable experiences. Teachers need to become "museum-wise." They need information about the exciting possibilities museum resources offer and about ways to incorporate museum information into the classroom. Informed teachers may become more aggressive in their use of art museums and may become museum advocates in the school setting.

2. *Work with elementary art specialists to inform school administrators of the value of art museums to school curriculums.* Administrators are often unaware of how pertinent museum resources are to the classroom and how they can enliven students' learning experiences. Because administrators control time and money, their support is critical in establishing relationships between museums and schools.

3. *Establish communication strategies with elementary art specialists.* The results of this survey indicate that teachers could use more information about museums and that ongoing communication between art specialists and art museum educators could be improved. Additional efforts to promote museum resources will improve teachers' awareness of museums in general. Teachers who are aware of what is available may expand their choice of programming beyond the traditional museum tour.

Art museums are invaluable resources for art education. Indeed, art museum resources can be critical to the kind and quality of instruction that elementary art specialists provide students. These specialists may need some assistance in learning about and using the art museum. With proper assistance and pertinent information provided by museum educators, teachers can initi-

ate connections with museums that will allow them to enjoy fully the benefits that museums have to offer.

_____ *Journal of Museum Education* 17, no. 1 (Winter 1992): 9–11.

_____ **References** _____

Rogers, E. T., and R. E. Brogdon. "A Survey of the NAEA Curriculum Standards in Art Teacher Preparation Programs." *Studies in Art Education* 31, no. 3 (1990): 168–73.

National Art Education Association. *Standards for Art Teacher Preparation Programs.* Reston, Va.: NAEA, 1979.

The Public Dimension Assessment: Reviewing the First 10 Years

Elizabeth Merritt

In 1990, the American Association of Museums and the Institute of Museum and Library Services (then the Institute of Museum Services) introduced a new program to help museums improve their public service—the Public Dimension Assessment (PDA). It was linked to the implementation within AAM of *Excellence and Equity: Education and the Public Dimension of Museums*, a report adopted as a policy statement by the AAM board in 1991. That initiative and the Public Dimension Assessment were driven in part by the philosophy that museums should be responsive and accountable to the public they serve in order to fulfill their educational mission and in part by the realistic awareness that without such responsiveness, museums could damage their financial viability.

The Public Dimension Assessment is the third module in the AAM's Museum Assessment Program (MAP), which was started in 1981 to promote professional standards, institutional assessment, and peer review. The first two modules were the Institutional Assessment, which surveys the entire museum operation, and the Collections Management Assessment, which examines collections policies and procedures. The Institute of Museum and Library Services provides partial funding for these assessments, permitting a peer reviewer to conduct a one- or two-day site visit to a museum in the program. This site visit is the basis for the reviewer's report and recommendations that, together with the self-study conducted by the museum, are used by the museum as part of its institutional planning process.

The Public Dimension Assessment was, from the beginning, a departure from the initial modules. While it retains the basic outline of self-study, on-site visit, and final report, it requires a much greater commitment of time on the part of both the museum and the peer reviewer because it covers a broader range of issues than the Collections Management Assessment and complex areas in greater depth than the Institutional Assessment. IMLS funding for the PDA supports a two- or three-day site visit by two peer reviewers. Ten years after the initiation of the PDA, it is clear that this complexity is both its strength and its weakness.

The Public Dimension Assessment

The PDA ambitiously sets out to address the entire scope of the public's perception and experience of, and involvement with, the museum. As with other MAP assessments, museums undertaking the PDA are asked to answer self-study questions, with a focus on public relations, marketing, exhibits and educational programs, and visitor services. Some of these questions are factual (What is your attendance? How do you evaluate exhibits?), while others ask the team handling the study to analyze the museum's strengths and weaknesses and to lay out a vision of the future they want to create.

In the initial MAP modules, all the expertise and knowledge needed to answer these questions were assumed to reside inside the organization. Because the PDA is intended to turn the institution outward, it introduced a new element to the self-study—three "activities" that the museum must perform.

•The public perception activity involves role-playing by staff and board members, volunteers, and other community leaders, who "become visitors" in their community and ask for directions to the museum and for information about what it offers.

MAP continues to evolve through a process of feedback from participating museums, MAP surveyors, and assessments conducted by AAM or IMLS. Through these processes, we have identified several changes that are being integrated into the way all three MAP modules are designed.

•The public experience activity directs the museum to invite a group to visit a special exhibit or the permanent collection or to take a program or tour and answer a questionnaire provided by the AAM. This questionnaire elicits feedback before and after the visit about the visitors' expectations and their experience in the museum.

•The public involvement activity facilitates a dialogue with the community through a community meeting, focus group, or mass-mailing questionnaire.

Some PDA participants choose to complete all three of these options.

MAP self-studies are intended to increase institutional self-awareness and result in both new knowledge and increased information sharing among museum staff, but MAP staff believe that the success of these studies in the initial modules has been limited. While the self-study is rated as useful by participants (for example, of institutions undertaking the Institutional Assessment, 50 percent rate it excellent and 48 percent rate it good), it rarely results in an organization changing its self-perception or analysis of its needs. In the PDA, however, the activities seem to be among the most valued elements of the process and the most likely to help the museum learn about itself. The public perception activity, in particular, produces some real eye-openers! However, these activities are also very time consuming, and so, in 1994, the grant period for the PDA was extended to two years.

Scorecard: Assessing the Assessment

Since its inception in 1990, 344 museums have undertaken the PDA. Each museum that completes MAP is asked to fill out a satisfaction survey and return it to the AAM offices. In 1998 a review of survey results to date was conducted, and a new survey instrument was designed and sent to museums that had completed MAP in the last three years but had not yet returned an evaluation form (see sample 1 in table 1). This revised survey instrument has been used since that time, with the results compiled on SurveyPro software.

Table 1

Rankings of Overall PDA Experience

Ranking	Sample 1 ('95–'98, n = 24)	Sample 2 ('98–'99, n = 36)
Excellent	29%	31%
Very Good	25%	28%
Good	33%	33%
Fair	12%	8%
Poor	0%	0%
Unacceptable	0%	0%

Museums undertaking the PDA rate the experience highly but express lower satisfaction with it than with the older MAP modules. For the Institutional and Collections Management Assessments very good/excellent ratings (combined) constitute over 75 percent of the responses, versus approximately 57 percent very good/excellent (combined) for the PDA.

When asked to rate how well the assessment addressed the issues and concerns the museum identified in its application or previsit agreement, participants award the ratings shown in table 2.

Table 2

How Well the PDA Addresses Issues and Concerns

Ranking	Sample 1 ('95–'98, n = 24)	Sample 2 ('98–'99, n = 36)
Excellent	21%	19%
Very Good	8%	36%
Good	25%	33%
Fair	12%	8%
Poor	0%	3%
Unacceptable	0%	0%

Outcomes identified by participants as occurring as a result of the assessment are listed below.

<u>**Table 3**</u>

Outcomes Occurring as a Result of the PDA

% Respondents

>75%	clearer understanding of the museum's image in the community
>65%	insight into developing or improving marketing
>40%	improved service to the museum's current audience
	increased ability to broaden the museum's audience
	improvement in public programs
	increased community support for and involvement in public activities
>25%	improved public relations
	better communications between board and staff
	positive publicity
<25%	increased access to museum programs and services
	improvements in exhibits
	increased diversity of board and staff

As in other MAP assessments, many museums comment on the benefits of review by an "outside expert." These museums note that reviewers' reports served to validate their strategic plans or helped convince key stakeholders to move forward. Other benefits cited include encouraging the museum to listen to outside input; contributing to strategic planning; increasing the board's awareness of and involvement in the museum; and providing a "reality check" on the museum's image in the community. Deborah Staber, director of the L.C. Bates Museum in Hinkley, Maine, commented in an article for the *Maine Association of Museums Newsletter* that the PDA "revealed some surprises about our public image and has been an effective tool for promoting new audiences, setting priorities, and developing strategic plans. [The process] called our attention to underserved audiences, and ways to reach those audiences. The many recommendations of the assessment and survey results will have long-term results at our museum."

Our research shows that the peer reviewers who act as surveyors are key to the quality of the museum's experience with the MAP process. And, overall, museums give the surveyors good marks. About 33 percent of museums rate the appropriateness of surveyors as excellent, 50 percent as good, and 17 percent as fair. Curiously, they rank the surveyors themselves more highly than the "fit" (this may be because the PDA covers such a broad range of topics that surveyors are rarely experts in all these fields). Fifty percent rate the preparation and knowledge of their surveyors as excellent, and 39 percent as good, with similarly high scores for ability to listen, collegial attitude, and overall helpfulness. These rankings are, again, lower than the comparable ratings of surveyors in the Institutional and Collections Management

Assessments. We plan to refine the survey instrument to identify where the "fit" can be improved (e.g., improved surveyor recruitment or training, increasing sophistication in the matching of the surveyors' expertise with the museum's needs, better quality control on the final report).

The Surveyors' Experience

Most MAP surveyors cite "giving back to the field" and "learning from other museums" as two of the main motivations for serving as a peer reviewer. "I always pick up new ideas when studying a site, that I can take home with me," says one reviewer. "These are always very stimulating." Another comments, "It underscored in my mind the need for all museums to have a fresh perspective on their operations, and helps me to realize many situations are the same in all museums." PDA surveyors add that they greatly enjoy and learn from working with a colleague as a team in doing the assessment. Some peer reviewers in fact want to participate only in PDAs, as they value the team experience so highly. Peer reviewers do comment, however, that the PDA requires a large commitment of time and effort. The documentation submitted by the museum is more extensive than for the other assessments, and the site visit is longer. Coordinating the report writing between two people sometimes makes the process easier, and sometimes harder, depending on the people involved.

Possible Future Developments

MAP continues to evolve through a process of feedback from participating museums, MAP surveyors, and assessments conducted by AAM or IMLS. Through these processes, we have identified several changes that are being integrated into the way all three MAP modules are designed.

First, it has become clear that MAP is ineffective when its implementation and results are confined to a small group within the museum. Even now, the Institutional Assessment is sometimes initiated by the director, and the staff do not see the resulting report. The Collections Management Assessment is often started by the registrar or collections manager and may not have "buy-in" from other staff who are involved in collections care. To reach its full potential as a tool for change, the process should be managed by a team of key stakeholders in the museum. This team should include board members, volunteers, and paid employees who have the power to make decisions about change, who have knowledge about how things really work or don't work in their organization, and who will be expected to implement any changes that are made. Because of the way it is structured, the PDA has led the way in encouraging museums to form teams to manage the process, and we now urge museums engaging in the Institutional Assessment and Collections Management Assessment to manage them in the same way.

Second, it is clear that MAP is, or should be, part of an ongoing process of change in the museum rather than an end in and of itself. Again the PDA led the way in emphasizing this perception by requiring that the museum demonstrate its engagement in a planning process as a prerequisite for participation. Staff are now modifying the other MAP modules to encourage integration into strategic planning as well. While planning is not a prerequisite for these assessments, the surveyors will review with the museum's implementation team the process for incorporating the self-study and final report into planning. A number of museums and surveyors have indicated the desirability of a follow-up several months or even a year after the site visit, and we are looking into ways to accomplish this as well.

There are improvements we would like to make to the PDA specifically, based on our experience with its first 10 years. By combining public relations, marketing, exhibits and educational programs, and visitor services, we have encouraged holistic thinking and helped to break down internal barriers between "mission" and "marketing" staff in the museum. However, this target is so broad that, given the practical limitations of time and resources, we can rarely deliver an in-depth examination of all these areas. As a result, there is frustration on the part of the museum if staff feel the assessment did not yield everything anticipated, and on the part of the surveyors if they feel too much was expected of them. We hope to improve the previsit process for negotiation of expectations to achieve a clearer agreement with each museum as to what will and will not be focused on within the broad rubric of "public dimension."

Taken as a whole, the Public Dimension Assessment has been highly successful in delivering a needed service to museums, helping them to achieve their goals, and testing methods that are being used to improve the initial MAP modules. The Museum Assessment Program staff continue to study the feedback we receive from "MAPped" museums and from peer reviewers and to work on ways to make the PDA better still.

A report on the program described in Susan Graziano, "Assessing a Museum's Public Dimension," *Journal of Museum Education* **18, no. 1 (Winter 1993): 11–13.**

Further Reading

From the AAM Technical Information Service Professional Practice Series:

Taking Charge of Your Museum's Public Relations Destiny, #819

Visitor Surveys: A User's Manual, #820

Museums, Trustees, and Communities: Building a Reciprocal Relationship, #855

American Association of Museums, *Excellence and Equity: Education and the Public Dimension of Museums.* Washington, D.C.: American Association of Museums, 1992. 28 pp. This report helps museums define how well they are carrying out their educational mission and serving the public.

Kirshenblatt-Gimblett, Barbara. *Destination Culture: Tourism, Museums and Heritage.* Berkeley and Los Angeles: University of California Press, 1998. 311 pp. A commentary on museums' marketing of themselves as tourist destinations, and tourism's packaging of destinations as museums.

McLean, Fiona. *Marketing the Museum.* London and New York: Routledge, 1997. 257 pp. In this volume, the marketing of a museum is seen not in terms of a "product" but rather as the "process" by which a relationship between the public and the museum is built.

Wireman, Peggy. *Partnerships for Prosperity: Museums and Economic Development.* Washington, D.C.: American Association of Museums, 1997. 175 pp. As tourist attractions, museums have long contributed to the economic development of their communities. Yet financial planners rarely see museums as potential partners. This manual offers practical advice for institutions seeking better collaborations with business and government.

These publications, and others pertinent to this topic, are available through the American Association of Museums Bookstore Catalogue. Check the AAM Web site at www.aam-us.org, e-mail the bookstore at: bookstore@aam-us.org, or call (202) 289-9127.

UNDERSTANDING: THEORY, RESEARCH AND EVALUATION—HOW DO YOU KNOW?

Use these questions and the essays in this section to stimulate discussion. You may want to consider your own museum, or you may draw on your experience in other museums or other settings.

1/ What do visitors to your museum want? How do you find out?

2/ What steps would you take to improve or modify your museum's evaluation efforts?

3/ What theories inspire your work? Why?

4/ Most often, as in the articles in this section, theoretical discussion is applied to the visitor experience as opposed to docent training, staff development, or management. In what other ways can you apply theory to museum practice?

5/ How could your museum support and promote reflective practice more effectively?

6/ You have six months off and a large grant to study any topic in research. With all this freedom and money, what issue would you study, and how would you go about it? The only requirement is that you share your results with the field. How would you report the fruit of your six-month research effort?

Part 4

LINKAGES:
BUILDING KNOWLEDGE

TRANSFORMING PRACTICE THROUGH
CHANGE, RESPONSE, AND UNDERSTANDING

Joanne S. Hirsch and Lois H. Silverman

Transforming Practice is a record of the thinking and practice of museum professionals who are committed to documenting their thoughts and experience for the benefit of the profession. Both the breadth of content and the diversity of writing styles enrich our professional literature. Writers of the introductions to the parts of this book provide an overview suited to the content of the section. From Carol B. Stapp we have the big picture of change; Gretchen Jennings employs an integrative approach to reporting practice; and Ken Yellis, simultaneously humorous and probing, offers a personal reflection on theory, research, and evaluation.

In this final part we have assembled four case studies that exemplify the ways two or more of the elements essential to transforming practice are linked. These examples are not formulaic. Indeed, they present change, action, and reflection in varied formats with strikingly different effects. For example, the bulleted points of Jim Zien's findings alert the reader to the potential and pitfalls of establishing partnerships. The poetry of Marek Stokowski's entries convey an emotional meaning that undergirds the political implications of the article. The charted findings of Wade H. Richards and Margaret Menninger's evaluative research and the conversational tone of Kathleen McLean's presentation offer readers varied models for telling a story.

In every instance, key elements of practice intersect and lead to transformation within individuals and institutions. Behind each story is the impetus that drives the research, the change in practice, or the restructuring of space. Each author cites a motivation for work—a challenge from a director, a needed practice supported by theory and research, an effort to break down cultural and national myths and barriers, a community's desire to address issues of economic and cultural diversity. The case studies link motivation to other key elements—strategies and practice, theory, research and evaluation—to build meaningful outcomes.

In a report of evaluative research conducted at the Getty Museum, Richards and Menninger identify a gap in the museum's strategic approaches to working with adult visitors. Drawing on the work of theorists such as Howard Gardner, Malcolm Knowles, and Jerome Bruner, a team designed and installed interactive galleries for adults that would become the bedrock of future decisions regarding adult visitors at the new Getty Center.

Provoked by contemporary enmity in the political and historical environment, Stokowski describes an attempt to establish an atmosphere of mutual respect and understanding between young people in Poland and Germany. His innovative response involves role-playing an encounter at a 15th-century castle as a pathway to appreciating differing cultural values. The poetic, journal-like account becomes an ongoing assessment of the experience. In it, the reader takes the pulse of enormous societal change, its dramatic effect on individuals, and the potential impact on the commitment of a few museum people.

How do you gauge the progress of a project that exposes the warts and beauty marks? The Museums in the Life of a City project measured the ability to establish productive collaborations between museums and community-based arts and social service organizations. Zien's report of the focus group of collaborators who evaluated the projects is rich with suggestions for useful strategies, revealing an array of successful outcomes and dissatisfactions with their experience as partners. Too often, a record of such disappointments does not see the light of day and certainly is not published. Yet the lessons for museums responding to the call for inclusiveness are invaluable.

McLean accepted her director's challenge to improve the public experience at the Exploratorium while changing the physical space. Infusing the project with the theory of place memory, the staff and an on-site research team used video documentation, visitor participation, and performance in innovative ways to arrive at a new understanding of public space. The interplay of theory, research, and practice was at work.

The immediate impact of these activities may be seen in the authors' institutions or professional communities. And the results always have meaning for the individuals involved—those designing and conducting the activities, those researching interactive approaches to enhance adult understanding or adapting the use of the video camera as a research tool, those matching evaluative techniques such as focus groups to project goals or drawing on the outcomes of pilot studies to promote enhanced experiences prior to the design and installation of new spaces.

Yet without published reports of our professional activity, few benefit and the museum field loses. With these reports, we draw courage to take risks, to face challenges we witness in the broader society with bold strokes of our own making. Reports of imperfect and unanticipated results or flawed strategies become guideposts for the next effort—the bumps in a team's decision-making process, the barriers to continuity of community-based partnerships, the impossible bureaucracy, or a board's resistance. Through shared information and publication, we contribute to the body of knowledge and to transforming practice.

A Discovery Room for Adults

Wade H. Richards and Margaret Menninger

> *Most museums are not interactive at all. Sometimes it's hard to make any con-nection with the works of art. . . . You can see it in class and take notes all day about it, but this gallery just made it clear and brought it to life.*
>
> —*Visitor to the Interactive Gallery*
> *J. Paul Getty Museum, 1989*

The notion that interaction makes for effective learning is not new; Socratic questioning and hands-on activities are standard components of most mu-seum teachers' repertoires. But we generally stop using these strategies when our visitors reach the age of 18, as if graduation from high school somehow instantly transforms their cognitive processes. Educational services for adults have traditionally been characterized by a one-way flow of information and a structured format. At the J. Paul Getty Museum, however, the Interactive Gallery gives adults the chance to learn by participating.

When the gallery opened in 1989, its purpose was to help visitors learn about materials and manufacture, function and context, and conservation through hands-on activities and informal conversations with a staff or docent teacher, called a facilitator. We hoped that the Interactive Gallery, if successful, could be a model for three similar galleries planned for a new Getty Museum now under construction.

Educational Assumptions

A review of the research on learning gave us every reason to believe that an interactive gallery for adults would work (see Further Reading). According to Jerome Bruner, for example, people learn by modeling the behavior of an expert. We hoped that visitors could learn new skills by talking with facilita-tors and adopting the facilitators' behavior of looking closely, constructing a hypothesis, and testing it with further observations. Bruner also states that people develop and retain new skills by having the chance to practice them. In an interactive format, the facilitator can make visitors actually use new infor-mation by asking them to explain it to others or make a decision based on it.

Bernice McCarthy and Howard Gardner argue that different people learn in different ways (what McCarthy calls "learning styles"). Therefore, the ideal learning experience should contain something for all types of learners. We hoped that by providing a flexible format and training facilitators to respond to visitor interest, we could offer something for everyone. We also hoped to create a longer-lasting experience by including auditory and kinesthetic as well as visual elements.

Malcolm Knowles has written extensively on what he calls "andragogy" (helping adults learn), as distinct from "pedagogy" (teaching of children). He found that adults view learning as a process of active inquiry rather than as the reception of a set body of knowledge. Active inquiry—exactly what the Interactive Gallery was meant to provide—is the best way to get adults to invest emotionally in an educational experience. Equally important to adult learning, Knowles states, are self-direction and independence, so we conceived of Interactive Gallery installations that would offer a choice of what to do, what to look at, and what issues to engage in. Knowles also asserts that adult learning must be "life-centered" instead of "subject-centered." It must value and relate to an adult's existing knowledge and experiences. The Interactive Gallery format does just this by allowing visitors to contribute to the discussion from their own points of view. As a result, we expand the number of "voices" that talk about the museum's collections and acknowledge the multiple perspectives that exist.

Location and Size

The four Interactive Gallery installations have used two different spaces in the museum. Three of them—on photography, bronze casting, and decorative arts—have been located in a former curatorial office on the second level. This small carpeted room, roughly 250 square feet in area, creates an intimate feeling but also limits the size and complexity of the exhibitions. The installation on antiquities conservation was located in a larger room on the first level. This gallery is open to an area with greater visitor traffic, but it was too spacious to be conducive to the interactive experience we were seeking.

Design

Each of the exhibit and activity "stations" in the Interactive Gallery relates to one or more themes. Sometimes there is a preferred order to the stations, but sometimes the design is purposely less structured, allowing the visitor to begin viewing the stations at any point. To satisfy a wide range of learning styles, stations incorporate traditional didactic panels and object labels so that they can function as stand-alone exhibits. In recent installations we have tried to use more graphics and larger type size to improve the legibility and holding power of text panels.

Staffing and Staff Training

The role of the staff or docent teacher, or facilitator, is to engage visitors in conversation, answer questions, and point out connections among stations. Docents for Interactive Gallery service are recruited annually from the museum's 120 docents. Both staff and docent facilitators participate in 15 to 20 hours of special training, which includes art historical information, close study of works in the museum's collection, and activities to strengthen interactive teaching skills. After the installation opens, periodic facilitator updates provide occasions for continuing education.

Interactive Gallery Installations

Installations in the Interactive Gallery change annually and are limited to topics relating to the museum's permanent collection. For the inaugural installation in 1989, we focused on the materials, techniques, and esthetic issues of 19th- and early 20th-century photography. The title, *The Art of Fixing a Shadow*, was taken from William Henry Fox Talbot's description of his early experiments with the medium.

In this installation visitors had the opportunity to handle and compare photographs made with the variety of processes available during photogra-

---

A review of the research on learning gave us every reason to believe that an interactive gallery for adults would work.

---

phy's first 100 years. They could try to make a sketch using a *camera obscura* and thereby understand the first urge to capture an image. They could also manipulate 19th-century cameras and gain some understanding of artistic choices by comparing photographs of the same subject taken by different artists.

After visiting this installation, many people spoke with awe about the heavy equipment and difficult processes involved. One visitor said: "It's more enjoyable when you have more information. Before, you could look at a photograph and think, what's so great about that? But if you know . . . the difficulties they had to overcome to create it—well, I have more appreciation for it." Others mentioned an increased appreciation of the photographer's role: "I didn't realize that the artist could do so many things with it—special effects, shadowing, placement, and the proper lighting—the atmosphere."

In 1990, the second installation, *Dirty Business/Princely Bronzes*, explained Renaissance bronze casting. The centerpiece was a six-stage model illustrating various steps in the process of lost-wax casting, from preliminary model to chased and patinated statue. Facilitators answered questions and discussed with visitors actual 16th-century bronzes that showed evidence of their manufacture and use. A video showing modern bronze casters at work, slides of comparative material, x-rays of works in the museum's collection, and artists' tools and materials provided other means for exploring how bronzes have been made, used, and valued over the centuries.

In spite of the technical nature of the information in this show, visitors were willing and able to engage. One facilitator noted: "A lot of people are able to make connections to their daily lives with the material in the room—I wouldn't have thought so. But one man who was a metallurgical engineer said that the technique for bronzes is also used to cast jet engine blades. And a woman who was a nurse understood the x-rays especially well."

Even children were drawn in. Another facilitator commented: "Even though the room is for adults, people sometimes bring their kids in. Parents with children tend to interact very closely with them, explaining the process with our touchable objects and keeping a close eye on their kids. People really want to understand the technical information and are willing to go through it again and again until they get it."

Greek and Roman works of art rarely survive undamaged over the centuries. Why and how are they repaired? And what does the museum do to protect objects from future harm such as earthquakes? These are some of the questions addressed by our third Interactive Gallery installation, *Preserving the Past*, which opened in 1991. The exhibition was located on the museum's first level adjacent to the gallery of Greek vases. An introductory video showed conservators at work in the labs on a variety of projects. Visitors could compare an authentic Greek vase with a modern imitation or use a microscope to study samples of ancient materials. Text panels dealt with the conservation of bronze and stone, and a display showed the step-by-step reconstruction of ancient ceramics. The installation also illustrated how mounts and earthquake protection devices work. And at a worktable, visitors could attempt to reassemble fragments of a replica of a Greek vase.

Without question, the replica fragments were the most popular activity. One visitor said: "We noticed the video monitor which said that there would be a movie about how they take care of the things they find. But then I noticed the table with the broken pieces of vases that you could touch; and seeing that they were the only things you could touch, they naturally drew our attention." After using this station and looking at a restored vase nearby, visitors not only understood how pottery is repaired but also realized that there is a philosophy that guides conservators' work: "I was impressed by the attention to fixing the work of art but doing it in such a way that it was evident that the restorer had added modern material to the old. There was an obvious attempt to show where the restoration was. That impressed me."

The Dubois Corner Cupboard: A Closer Look, the fourth installation, which opened in 1992, takes a close look at the creation and history of one of the museum's most important and best-documented pieces of furniture: a corner cupboard made in the late 1740s by Jacques Dubois for an aristocratic Polish patron. Two broad objectives are to help visitors understand (1) the range of issues that experts consider when looking at a piece of furniture and (2) how experts learn the things they know about objects. Visitors' observations of the cabinet are enriched by prints, an inventory, and other documents that explain the cabinet's design, manufacture, patronage, and history. Objects that may be handled, such as pieces of marquetry and gilt bronze, help facilitators explain materials and techniques.

Installation and Planning: The Team Approach

Installations are planned and implemented by a team that includes educators, curatorial and conservation staff, designers, preparators, and a program evaluator. A staff member from the Department of Education and Academic Affairs serves as team leader, while other education staff oversee budget and organize the training and scheduling of gallery facilitators. The museum's collections projects administrator coordinates fabrication and installation and serves as liaison between staff in various departments. These roles may vary depending on the nature of the installation and the individuals involved.

For some installations, objectives are dictated by the nature of the object being spotlighted or the story to be told. For others, the team uses a brainstorming process, making a list of all possible objectives relating to the topic, grouping them into themes, and narrowing them down to form a coherent exhibition. Exhibit stations are then designed to meet the agreed-upon objectives.

Without question, this collaborative work has proven the most challenging aspect of Interactive Gallery installations. We have found that curators, educators, and conservators often do not speak the same language, nor do they necessarily conceive or realize ideas in the same way. And because team members come from departments that are physically dispersed throughout the museum, opportunities for communication are fewer.

Team members may also have different priorities for the installation based on their differing experiences with objects and visitors. In such cases, some front-end evaluation is often helpful. Surveys or interviews with visitors before the planning process begins help to define or clarify the areas of the public's greatest interest. Furthermore, personal statements from visitors—

especially in a focus group or similar format—have a genuine and unbiased quality that makes them particularly compelling.

Despite our best efforts, there have been occasions when we could not reach consensus. For the project to move forward, someone had to make the final decision. Although this kind of predicament does undermine the notion of a true team approach, we have found that the situation is eased by keeping two points in mind. First, the team needs to know from the outset who the decision maker is and what the scope of his or her authority is. Second, the team needs to trust that the decision maker will consider all members' concerns fairly. The perfect person for this unenviable job is often someone from outside the departments that have the strongest stakes in the outcome.

We have learned that working together can be facilitated by using the first planning team meeting to clearly identify responsibilities and discuss how difficulties will be handled. This initial discussion can help gain the commitment of every team member, not only in relation to content but to the interactive, visitor-driven format. We have also discovered that the success of a team depends on individuals developing good working relationships *as individuals*. When the discussion expanded to include people not involved in the planning team, things got more difficult, suggesting that it is beneficial to empower team members to make independent decisions.

Key Evaluation Findings

The challenges of planning and implementation notwithstanding, we have determined from evaluation that the Interactive Gallery has been quite successful. We have used a variety of methods—including observation, interview, and survey—to obtain both quantitative and qualitative data. Full reports of the evaluation studies are available from the authors. Here we will summarize key findings about the audience and their response to the gallery.

Formal Evaluation

Survey data from general visitor exit questionnaires indicate that approximately 45 percent of our visitors (500 to 600 people per day) spend some time in the Interactive Gallery. The demographic profile of Interactive Gallery visitors does not differ significantly from the museum's general visitor profile.

The amount of time visitors spend in the gallery varies with the installation and the space it occupies. For the photography and the antiquities conservation installations, time in the gallery varied widely, from just a few seconds to more than 20 minutes (table 1). For the photography installation, the median holding time (table 2) was about 1 minute greater (3:42 min:sec) than for the antiquities conservation installation (2:25 min:sec). And in the photog-

Table 1

Visitor Time in the Interactive Gallery (Min:Sec)

"Time" (Min:Sec)	Photography Installation %	Antiquities Installation %
0:00–0:59	17%	22%
1:00–4:59	43%	51%
5:00–9:59	25%	20%
10:00 +	15%	07%

Table 2

Interactive Gallery Holding Time (Min:Sec)

			Median Time	
Installation	*Range in Time*	*All Visitors*	*No Interaction with Facilitator*	*Interaction with Facilitator*
Photography	0:14–14:48	3:42	1:20	7:15
Antiquities	0:04–21:26	2:25	1:42	3:15

raphy installation, 40 percent of the visitors spent more than 5 minutes in the gallery, while in the antiquities conservation installation only 27 percent of visitors did so (table 1). The greater holding time in the photography installation can be attributed to the greater percentage of visitors who interacted with the facilitator. And the greater degree of interaction can, in turn, be attributed to the smaller space the photography installation occupied, which was more conducive to an intimate experience.

During the photography installation, we found that roughly half (53 percent) of those who visited the gallery interacted with the facilitator in some way. Visitors who interacted with the facilitator spent much more time in the gallery—a median time of 7:15 compared to 1:20 for those who did not interact with the facilitator (table 2). We also found that the facilitator's individual teaching style had a direct effect on the amount of time visitors spent in the gallery and what they did there. Some facilitators gave lecture-style presentations, while others were more comfortable with informal discussion; some immediately engaged visitors when they entered the gallery, while others waited for visitors to approach them with questions.

The antiquities conservation installation in the larger, downstairs gallery functioned more as a stand-alone didactic exhibit. Less than one-fifth (17 percent) of visitors interacted with the facilitator, and the interaction centered on fewer stations than in the upstairs gallery. Nonetheless, visitors who interacted with the facilitator spent more time in the gallery—a median time of 3:15 compared to 1:42 for those who did not interact with the facilitator (table 2). These time data highlight the importance of the facilitator's role in the Interactive Gallery and emphasize the need for the facilitator to help the visitor acquire new knowledge and skills in a relatively short time.

Another feature of the downstairs gallery—its three exits—probably had an adverse effect on the holding time of the installation. In his classic 1935 study of art museum visitors, Arthur Melton described the problem as an "exit gradient effect," in which galleries with more exits tend to have less holding power. But the larger space also had its benefits: it allowed the team to plan a larger and more complex installation than could be accommodated upstairs. Also, gallery teachers were able occasionally to bring an interested school group into the gallery to talk about conservation—something not possible in the smaller space upstairs.

In both interviews and written surveys, Interactive Gallery visitors were appreciative of the facilitators and gave them very favorable ratings. One visitor remarked: "The staff person there was very good. I liked that there was someone there who didn't just give a 'canned' speech, but instead answered questions—that was very effective." Another said: "It is very good to have a demonstrator there. . . . She draws you into the discussion, whereas I probably would not have gone up to her and asked her to explain things,. . . . so she added something to the written material."

Visitors also responded favorably to the participatory nature of the experience. Said one, "This is the first time I saw displays in an [art] museum where you could touch things and also have explanations of how things are done." Another visitor remarked, "I think the idea of having a small-scale place where you go to have some hands-on experiences is a nice addition."

Visitors rated the overall educational value of the gallery very high. Based on survey and interview data we have concluded that the Interactive Gallery has most successfully met educational objectives related to attitudes and knowledge of materials and techniques and has had less success with skill objectives. Achieving skill objectives might require more time than most visitors spend in the Interactive Gallery.

We are satisfied that visitors have a positive experience *in* the Interactive Gallery, but what happens after they leave? Probably the greatest challenge we face is finding a way to motivate our visitors to use what they have learned in the gallery when they look at works of art in the permanent collection. We found that we were able to encourage them to spend more time in part of the permanent collection by distributing a handout that led them from the

Interactive Gallery to specific objects elsewhere in the museum and invited them to practice their new knowledge, skills, and attitudes. For the photography and bronze-casting installations, the handout had a "looking game" format, with questions on the front and answers on the back. It also restated key concepts from the exhibition so that the visitors had a souvenir with some educational value. Most were very happy to receive it (23 percent picked it up), although fewer than we had expected (only 6 percent) actually used it to look at original objects immediately after their visit to the Interactive Gallery. (We believe that explicit encouragement from the facilitator could raise this percentage.)

Unfortunately, we do not know what effect visitors' experiences in the Interactive Gallery might have on subsequent visits to the Getty or to other museums. We recognize the need to evaluate the long-term impact of the interactive experience, and we hope in the future to interview visitors three to six months after they visit the gallery.

We have also used surveys to determine facilitator satisfaction with the experience. Both staff and docent facilitators agreed that the kind of teaching that takes place in the Interactive Gallery is very challenging. One said: "In the gallery, you're 'on' for two and a half hours straight—which is exhausting. And when visitors come in, you have to figure them out in just a few minutes—how much time they want to spend, who they're with, what they already know about the subject, and what's going to interest them." Even given the taxing nature of the teaching, facilitators enjoyed the opportunity to interact with visitors on a more intimate level than is possible in gallery talks or other similar formats—one of the very things that visitors most enjoyed about the room.

Informal Evaluation

During each installation, facilitators have recorded casual visitor comments in the gallery logbook. For the most part, these remarks have echoed the findings of the formal study. Visitors have greatly appreciated having a person present to answer questions about materials and techniques. Many said that learning about the difficulty involved in creating a daguerreotype or a bronze statuette or cleaning an ancient statue increased their appreciation of those objects. Visitors also liked the informality of the encounter. Most of all, they seemed to value the change of pace. One visitor remarked, "You get very tired just walking around—it's good to come to a place where you can touch something, and do something different besides just looking."

Journal of Museum Education 18, no. 1 (Winter 1993): 6–11.

Further Reading

Bruner, Jerome. *The Process of Education.* Cambridge, Mass.: Harvard University Press, 1960.

Collins, Zipporah W., ed. *Museums, Adults and the Humanities: A Guide for Educational Programming.* Washington, D.C.: American Association of Museums, 1981.

Eder, Elizabeth. "Innovations in Exhibition Interpretation: Hands-On Activity Centers in Art Museums." Paper presented at American Association of Museums annual meeting, Denver, Colorado, 1991.

Gardner, Howard. *Frames of Mind: The Theory of Multiple Intelligences.* New York: Basic Books, 1983.

Gurian, Elaine Heumann. "Noodling around with Exhibition Opportunities." In *Exhibiting Cultures: The Poetics and Politics of Museum Display,* edited by Ivan Karp and Steven D. Lavine, pp. 176–90. Washington, D.C.: Smithsonian Institution Press, 1991.

Karp, Ivan, and Steven D. Lavine. *Exhibiting Cultures: The Poetics and Politics of Museum Display.* Washington, D.C.: Smithsonian Institution Press, 1991.

Knowles, Malcolm. *The Adult Learner: A Neglected Species:* Houston: Gulf Publishing, 1973.

———. *The Modern Practice of Adult Education: Andragogy versus Pedagogy.* Chicago: Follett Publishing, 1980.

———. "Andragogy." In *Museums, Adults and the Humanities: A Guide for Educational Programming,* edited by Zipporah W. Collins, pp. 49–60. Washington, D.C.: American Association of Museums, 1981.

McCarthy, Bernice. *The 4MAT System.* Barrington, Ill.: Excel, Inc., 1986.

McDermott-Lewis, Melora. "The Denver Art Museum Interpretive Project." Unpublished report. Denver: Denver Art Museum, 1990.

Melton, Arthur W. *Problems of Installation in Museums of Art.* 1935. Reprint. Washington, D.C.: American Association of Museums, 1988.

Menninger, Margaret. "The Interactive Education Gallery: An Information Center at the J. Paul Getty Museum. Evaluation Report." Unpublished report. Malibu, Calif.: J. Paul Getty Museum, 1989.

REFLECTIONS

The interactive gallery was a laboratory for testing new ways to teach adult visitors about the Getty Museum's permanent collection. Its goal was to develop successful models that could be put into practice at the Getty Center, which opened to the public in 1997. Evaluation was a "given" for every installation, and it is gratifying to see how the evaluation results guided decisions about educational services at the Getty Museum. Each of the Getty's Center's four gallery pavilions has an Art Information Room, which provides educational resources for adult visitors. These rooms clearly incorporate the most successful elements of the interactive gallery: a focus on discovery learning, hands-on activities, and full-time staffing by docent facilitators.

Wade Richards, coauthor of this article, strongly believed that art museum education had to become more dynamic, interactive, and appealing to new audiences. As team leader of the earliest interactive gallery installations, he made groundbreaking contributions to the practice of museum education. Wade died of AIDS in 1994. Those of us who had the good fortune to work with him recognize the great loss to the museum community of an inspiring teacher and a dear friend.

—*Margaret Menninger*

Borders and Encounters

Marek Stokowski

1

I remember seeing a huge castle on the other side of the river. But I didn't even get a chance to take a closer look. They herded us back into the same boxcars they used before the war to transport beets. This time they were transporting us, the Warsaw Uprising fighters. To the crematories in Stutthof. The castle, though, was the one in Malbork. For sure.

—*from the memoirs of H.Z., a female prisoner of the concentration camp in Stutthof*

2

A mighty castle has towered over the waters of the Nogat River for more than 700 years: the castle of Malbork (German, Marienburg). Built by the Teutonic Knights, it served as the capital of the order's state for the next century and a half. The fortress became the stronghold of the Polish Crown officials, their arsenal and a temporary residence of the Polish kings beginning in the mid-1400s and throughout the next three centuries. After Poland's first partition in 1772, the castle's ownership went to the Prussian king and the leaders of the united Germany that followed him. The fall of the Third Reich put Malbork again within the boundaries of the Polish Republic.

3

I will never forget the majesty of those ramparts. You know yourself that there is nothing like it in the whole wide world. But then everything had turned into rubble, just like my youth. Now here, in Westphalia, I visit those places in my dreams. You must understand that I could never call the place Malbork; it will always be Marienburg. You must understand.

—*from a conversation with K.K., a repatriate from East Prussia*

4

Malbork has seen many encounters between the Poles and Germans. According to popular belief, they always met as rivals or enemies. But who knows on how many occasions they met as neighbors, families, fellow workers, merchants, farmers, priests, tradesmen, lovers, betrothed couples,

---

children? Those encounters are remembered less frequently, or not at all. Visions of our medieval struggles against the Teutonic Knights and of this century's tragedy of Nazism overwhelm us and what we might call our "historical imagination." Can this void of myth and painful memories between the two cultures ever be bridged? Can encounters between the Poles and the Germans ever permit hope for partnership, coexistence, and cooperation among future generations? How can a person escape the tangle of fears and prejudice—especially a young person with no direct experience of wartime suffering and with no moral authority to forgive on someone else's behalf?

5

If I had been told, as an almost 19-year-old Pole from Warsaw, shivering from cold, hunger, and fear while standing in Auschwitz's assembly square on a winter day in 1940—a nameless and faceless Schutzhäftling Pole No. 4427—that within my lifetime I would see Germany transform into a European parliamentary democracy respecting human rights and abiding by all laws, I would have probably dismissed such words as an optimistic utopian dream. . . .

When I reflect on my own experience as a so-called peace activist, I must stand by the conviction that the most important developments helping the cause are not the politicians' statements or signatures, although those should not be underestimated. The most important are the processes occurring in the feelings, consciences, and intellects of people from different nations, processes that cause us to overcome stereotypes in thinking about others, to overcome our own egotism. It is the extent to which people, for example, grow to understand that the land we inhabit today on both sides of the Elbe, the Rhein, the Oder, and the Vistula must continue to serve the generations of our grandchildren and their descendants as a living space where people, for better or worse, must learn to get along. . . . This is one great task our generation must complete—not only despite the experience of World War II but exactly because of that experience. Above all, that experience has shown us that thinking in extremist categories and in notions of superiority and one-sided advantage lead nowhere. The past can be overcome first of all through closer relations and a better understanding among the largest possible numbers of people.

—*Professor Władysław Bartoszewski, speech in Frankfurt/Main, October 5, 1986* [1]

6

Reconciliation is thus conceivable even to someone who once stood utterly degraded in Auschwitz's assembly square. And those with the moral

---

authority to forgive or let others forgive on their behalf not only allow us to open our arms, but openly urge us to do so.

During an international conference in 1986 I met two young museum educators from Hamburg, Ina Seifert and Uwe Franzen. A daring duo, indeed, they proposed we attempt a risky and difficult endeavor: organizing a first-ever among European museums, or first anywhere, international Polish-German historic role-playing experience for youth. It would be called "Encounter at the Castle, 1480."

In 1987 and 1988 we codesigned the concept of the play. Next came many months of theoretical and organizational preparations carried out independently in Malbork and in Hamburg.[2] The Castle Youth Club, which had been in existence for many years, became a natural organizational center for the young Poles in Malbork; their German peers practiced at school and at the Museum of Hamburg History. The two groups studied the political and cultural history of the European Middle Ages and learned the arts, songs, and skills of selected trades. At the same time they prepared themselves linguistically and mentally for a meeting with young people from another culture. At their respective ends, they were building a pathway converging on the castle, a place of mythical and historical importance to both nations.

7

No one . . . should ever forget the suffering that for many [Germans] began immediately after May 8, 1945, but we cannot see the war's end as a cause of all escapes, deportations, and captivity. To find a cause, we must go back to the outbreak of the war, to the dictatorship that led us to it. We cannot separate May 8, 1945, from January 30, 1933.

—Dr. Richard von Weizsäcker, president, German Federal Republic[3]

8

One August day in 1480, but also in 1988, a ship from Lübeck put in at the port of Gdansk, A group of artists, tradesmen, scholars, and merchants from Hamburg left the ship for the Polish shore. They came to establish relations with the subjects of King Casimir Jagellonian.

Guided by casually met travelers, who would leave their cart and horse at the foreigners' disposal, the Germans experienced many strange adventures along the way. They encountered lepers and the Black Death. They had to pay tolls, conquer rivers, sleep on hay, and wash in the water from wells and lakes. Wandering across fields and forests, they journeyed for several days before reaching Malbork, the towering fortress on the Nogat. They received a warm welcome from the castle's garrison under the command of Piotr Dunin, the king's steward who bore a swan on his coat of arms. Now there came a time of sharing all daily routines: chores, cooking, bread baking, handling medical procedures, record keeping, performing archery drills, garden tending, printing, and learning arts, crafts, songs, and games. Tournaments and many other activities engaged the youth of both cultures. After several days, the encounter ended with a final crowning event: a castle fair displaying the wares manufactured by the garrison members and the guests.

These few sentences conceal the drama of a profound encounter with history, with the land in the Vistula and Nogat valleys, with the castle's mystery, with the cultures of both nations, and, finally, the drama of a meeting between young individuals from two countries that are both very close and very distant. Each group and each participant had come to the encounter with something prepared ahead of time to share: a task, a story, a dish, a song, a theatrical scene, a dress, or an object. But on another level, cultural values were exchanged spontaneously. I am referring to all those human behaviors displayed in daily, often difficult situations where sensitivity, heart, fear, humor, temper, and attitudes toward others are

---

Our encounter, we must remember, is just one among many undertakings organized in Poland and Germany to foster better understanding between our youth. Its uniqueness comes from the role-play form and from the extraordinary place where it all happens.

---

revealed. This cultural exchange was immensely enriched by those members in the German group who came from immigrant families or had roots in other European countries and Asia.

The 15th century offered us a space for a symmetrical meeting without the feelings of inferiority or superiority that have infected the 20th century. We aimed at appreciating every person's humanity, at exploring every individual's nature and potential. The goal was to expose every person's unique way of absorbing and processing cultural values. We did not want to allow such things as money, the humiliations of communism, the wrongs of the last war, or the fate of immigrants to set us apart.

The "Encounter at the Castle" is by no means a form of cultural rivalry between groups or individuals. Rather, it is an attempt to cooperate and exchange feelings and experiences. It tests possibilities of coexisting in mutual respect and trust. Our encounter, we must remember, is just one among many undertakings organized in Poland and Germany to foster

---

better understanding between our youth. Its uniqueness comes from the role-play form and from the extraordinary place where it all happens.

___9___

I am particularly pleased that on the initiative of our intelligentsia's younger generation . . . some concrete efforts are made to bring people closer and to promote, in the interest of us all, the ra-tional building of a sound future for the neighboring nations.

—*Professor Władysław Bartoszewski, letter of August 28, 1991*

___10___

The year 1988 became the starting point of an entire series of encounters at the castle and in Hamburg. Since then, young Poles and Germans have taken three joint trips into the 15th century in Poland (1988, 1990, 1993) and three more in the city on the Alster (1989, 1991, 1993). By occurring about every year, the three pairs of encounters coincided with three distinct periods in Europe's modern history: 1988 marked the twilight stage of Soviet totalitarianism; 1989 and 1990 saw political breakthroughs; 1991 and the following years marked the first attempts to give Central and Eastern Europe a new shape. Our medieval travelers pushed stubbornly for the castle, trekked to Hamburg, shared their bread and joy, while the old world crumbled around them in a much-delayed conclusion to World War II. This nightmarish reality crumbled also because of journeys like ours, because of yeast and bread, because thousands of nameless people were opening up their arms.

___11___

Mister Cogito's monster
has no dimensions

. . .

and if it weren't for its stifling weight
and the death it sends
one could believe it to be
just a hallucination,
a disease of the imagination
—*Zbigniew Herbert, from "Mr. Cogito's Monster"*[4]

___12___

The first "Encounter at the Castle, 1480" took place at the end of the 1980s. Throughout that same decade the Polish communist authorities viewed West Germany as an important trading partner, a valuable source of loans, but also, in the most general sense, an unfriendly country. Any spontaneous Polish-German initiatives seemed suspicious to the authorities and required official permits. The state carefully watched and monitored such developments. Although this situation cannot be compared to the anti-Western and anti-German hysteria of the cold war era, any person from the so-called Regained Territories attempting independently some form of cooperation with the West Germans still risked facing veiled accusations of unpatriotic, shady, if not traitorous, dealings.

Despite the full legality of all preparations for the first encounter, I kept sensing an atmosphere of crime, corruption, and guilt. I do not believe that my feelings were shared by the younger participants in the event. I, however, a 30-year-old *homo Sovieticus* with a long history of exposure to intimidation, could not help acting like a conspirator. To this day I ask myself how much interest the secret Security Service had in our affairs.

Despite the risk of troubles and accusations, the management of the Castle Museum showed much support for the initiative from the moment of its conception and sponsored it with substantial amounts of money. No less than three ministries had to be convinced that our project deserved their official approval: the Ministry of Art and Culture, Ministry of Foreign Affairs, and Ministry of Education.

Our preparations for the event in Poland and for the trip to Hamburg soon became a process of endless official letters, explanations, and requests. We fought a deadly battle to obtain passports and German visas. I vividly recall the deluge of paper, the mandatory exchange of official invitations, the constant trips to various offices in Warsaw. Waiting for permits gave me the sensation of awaiting a court sentence and made me feel like Franz Kafka's protagonist in *The Trial*, Joseph K., with the pervasive suspense and uncertainty.

It should be remembered that this tremendous effort, or rather, struggle for the encounter, took place with only limited communication with the organizers on the other side. After two working sessions in Malbork, we communicated almost exclusively by mail. Each letter took two weeks to travel one way, and not all letters reached their destination. Telephones were practically useless, as no international connections were available to us. It was the intention of the Ministry of Internal Affairs to keep Polish telecommunications underdeveloped. With a bit of luck and persistence, we could occasionally use the telex. Our only remaining option was to apply unswerving discipline toward reaching the objectives outlined during our working sessions. We could only hope that the other side would do the same. Creativity and flexibility helped us cope with emergencies.

Negotiations became hardships when we had to deal with officials and civil servants eager to display the "socialist" attitude toward their duties. I was often dumbfounded by their incompetence and irresponsible actions.

Paradoxically, we were best served by volunteers who did not receive a single penny for their troubles.

And how difficult was it for us, Poles, to provide food, sanitary supplies, and other basic provisions? In a country of empty store shelves and high inflation and where special "connections" were needed for almost any purchase, the difficulty was enormous. This task must remain incomprehensible to those with no direct experiences of such tribulations.

The Polish group endured an even worse kind of humiliation through some incidents during their trip to Germany in 1989. I have already mentioned our desperate attempts to obtain passports. To communist authorities, granting a passport always seemed like a major concession. A similar battle had to be fought to receive visas from the West German consulate, where the ill will of some individuals contrasted with the big heart and goodwill of others and where a happy ending to our endeavors became a matter of a few tense seconds.

There was also the shame of a shabby bus—but, as always, jokes and laughter helped us cope. We strongly felt the discomfort of our limited financial abilities. The Polish *złoty* was not officially exchangeable at that time, and spiraling inflation drove the exchange rates to irrational heights. We shared a sadness at the vast difference in the standard of living between our two countries. To some of us, the 15th century really did seem like a better place to be. Finally, we shared another experience of great significance. At the checkpoint on the East-West German border an East German customs officer rudely ordered the Polish group out of the bus. Surrounded by barbed wire, gun turrets, concrete, and contempt, we stood for many hours in the cold wind. Yes, we were guilty. We were singing on the bus. Slaves are not supposed to sing merry tunes, especially near the border. It was provocation.

Our hosts in Hamburg made sure that the sadness disappeared quickly, replaced by the joy of sharing work and play, of meeting new people and seeing new places. On the other hand, I would not want to lose those painful memories completely. I want to remember; such memories add to our maturity and understanding. They make us watch out.

13

When the medieval travelers from Hamburg approached the port of Gdansk in August 1988, only passenger ships were allowed entry. A massive Solidarity-led strike gripped the city. We drove down the streets lined with special militia units, flags, slogans, and the arms of the striking workers reaching out through shipyard fences. It was the start of the changes spreading through all of Poland, all of Eastern Europe. The world of concrete and barbed wire was beginning to crumble.

Two years later I had nothing to fear. There was no need to beg for permits for the next encounter. The governments of both countries had signed a treaty on neighborly relations and youth exchange programs. The Security Service had ceased to exist. Our situation today is radically different, despite the many problems that remain. Money continues as the Achilles' heel of undertakings like ours, although in 1993 we received substantial support from the European Community.

Polish-German cooperation in the fields of culture and education has lost its aura of sin and is now a norm, even a necessity. Besides their involvement in our encounter, the museum educators from Hamburg participate in Malbork's educational enterprises almost every year. We also regularly join them to work in Hamburg. Curiously, German support for cultural and youth programs has declined below the level of the "difficult years," despite the official treaty. One explanation is the attention and money now directed toward solving the problems of unification.

Let's return to the Polish scene. No one, except for the continually supportive museum management, is in a position of controlling our actions through official approvals or opinions. Slowly, we acquire enough telephones and fax machines to maintain normal links with the world, although the effects of our telecommunications' underdevelopment in the last half-century can still be felt. Letters circulate faster and more accurately. The Polish service sector runs smoothly and sometimes even smoother than in some countries I got to know. These achievements, however, do not mean that we are free from any shoddy work. Providing food and any other provisions presents no problems, if, of course, we do not consider the horrendous prices of goods. The era of struggles to receive a passport has also ended: owning one today is as common as owning a student I.D. card. Visas are not needed for travel in most European countries. Strict controls over the movement of money have been removed. Also gone is the old rule that caused our guests much annoyance, whereby a set amount of a Western currency had to be exchanged for each day spent in Poland. The złoty, now exchangeable against other currencies at real rates, allows Poles to feel more self-assured on trips abroad. Although the disparity of financial resources on both sides is still shocking, the youth from Malbork no longer stop in the streets, dazzled by German shop windows; they do not have to feel ashamed of their shoes and their dreams.

When we return home, we no longer feel a great iron door closing noiselessly behind us and locking us once again in the treasure house of all misery.[5]

14

Shadows of evil begin to appear in the glow of positive changes. On two occasions we visited Hamburg in April, around the time of Hitler's birthday. Each time our hosts were concerned about our safety. In some German cities the ultraright fighting squads demonstrated in the streets. Today they go so far as to set ablaze the homes of asylum seekers. Poland also has its homegrown fighting squads assaulting foreigners, including Germans. Is the fall of communism followed by the rise of nationalism? I don't know. I know, however, that we must keep on meeting at the castle to form the drops that will merge with the drops formed by other people in many places across our two countries and penetrate the rock of our conscience.

15

Autumn 1986. I am traveling to attend my first international conference in Germany, where I will also meet my future partners, Ina and Uwe, the museum educators from Hamburg. The train crosses East Germany. It's raining. A policeman enters my compartment. He is wearing a heavy coat strikingly similar to those used in the early 1940s. *Ausweis!*: that's for me. I hand him my passport. Deadly silence. A lengthy, thorough examination of every page. Two other characters in coats are blocking the compartment's door. Silence. After a long moment I receive the document back. The men in coats leave without a word, furious, full of contempt. I catch a glance of an elderly lady sitting opposite to me. I point to the French map of Europe unfolded on the small table before me. She nods in agreement. So that was my crime: a spy map of Europe.

1988. Ina's and Uwe's first visit to Poland. They had figured that a trip to Poland would take them two days, and it did.

Today they get in the car after a late breakfast and arrive for an early supper. The distance has not changed. But an iron border vanished from the map of Europe, bringing down the borders in our minds. We live closer.

Journal of Museum Education 19, no. 2 (Spring/Summer 1994): 3–6.

Notes

1. Władysław Bartoszewski, "Nie ma pokoju bez wolności" (There Is No Peace without Freedom), in *Warto być przyzwoitym* (It Pays to Be Honest) (Poznań: W. Drodze, 1990), pp. 301–14.

2. Detailed information on preparations and the progress of the described educational events can be found in *Spotkanie w Zamkul/Begegnung im Schloss, 1480* (Hamburg: Atelier-Gemeinschaft Handwerk, 1989; Malbork: Muzeum Zamkowe w Malborku, 1991).

3. Quoted in Bartoszewski, "Nie ma pokoju bez wolności" pp. 308–9.

4. Zbigniew Herbert, *Raport z oblężonego miasta* (A Report from the Besieged City) (Wrocław: Wydawnictwo Dolnośląskie, 1992), p. 23.

5. Paraphrase from Zbigniew Herbert, "Mister Cogito: The Return," in Herbert, *Raport z oblężonego miasta*, p. 23.

REFLECTIONS

We—the curators of education in Malbork Castle Museum—still cooperate with our German colleagues from Hamburg, mainly from Kunsthalle, Museum for the History of Hamburg and Museum of Technology. We have run four "Encounters at the Castle—1480" and four "Encounters in Hamburg" so far. We have also developed a new mutual project for teenagers called "Feast at the Castle" and "Feast in Hamburg." Both parts (each 10 days long) were inaugurated this summer in Malbork and in Hamburg. Moreover, almost each year the museum educators from Hamburg participate in our projects in Malbork or run some of them themselves, especially theatrical workshops.

—*Marek Stokowski*

Opening Up the Exploratorium

Kathleen McLean

> *The phrase public realm means different things to different people. Architects and planners tend to define it as the totality of the physical elements, buildings, amenities, and landscapes that together form what we see when we are in a city. For others, the public realm is the sphere of public activities, from the simplest act, like sitting on a bench watching people go by, to the most complex public interactions like community and social events, commercial transactions and political rallies. To me the public realm implies the confluence of the two: the coming together of the form of a place with the activities that occur there. One cannot exist without the other.*
>
> —Gianni Longo, *A Guide to Great American Public Places*

Even before the Exploratorium opened its doors in 1969, its site was a major influence on the culture of the organization. The remarkable open space of Bernard Maybeck's Palace of Fine Arts, built for the 1915 Panama-Pacific International Exposition, evoked an expansive sense of possibilities. This spaciousness, combined with founder Frank Oppenheimer's commitment to self-directed learning and individual discovery, imbued the organization with a unique character and vision as a place of exploration for both staff and visitors.

From the beginning, staff activity focused on exhibit development. The exhibit curriculum was practically infinite, and artists, scientists, and exhibit developers designed and built exhibits with few physical constraints. The large doors were thrown open, and visitors to the Palace of Fine Arts gardens and lagoon could simply wander in and amble around. Wandering epitomized Oppenheimer's self-directed philosophy that became a core value of the organization:

> It is a place for sightseeing, a woods of natural phenomena through which to wander. Sightseeing is more than just pleasurable; it can build the experiences and intuitions on which other opportunities for learning rely; it can arouse curiosity and, in a broad sense, it can help people determine where they are going and where they want to make their home.[1]

More recently, and still in keeping with a sense of sightseeing and wandering, Rob Semper likened the Exploratorium to Paris,

---

a space formed by association. In its ideal design, there are centralized large and dramatic icon exhibits, which define the overall space, and a set of smaller exhibits, which form a thematic neighborhood. A series of main roads connects the major icons. The exhibits are juxtaposed at many angles to each other, creating a personally scaled neighborhood radiating out from the central space. . . . Because the design of the space does not force a single visitation path, visitors are encouraged to follow their own road map.[2]

Over time, the building filled, not only with exhibits but also with large office trailers, brought in to accommodate increasing numbers of staff. As exhibits began to crowd in on each other, visitor pathways constricted and tightened. At the same time, the number of visitors increased as the reputation of the organization grew. Most of the museum's resources continued to flow to exhibit development, with little invested in the infrastructure—lighting, heating, acoustics, rest rooms, and food services. In this metaphorical woods or streetscape, wandering took on an edge as people traipsed around the building and parking lots trying to find the entrance, backed up at the admissions desks trying to orient themselves, and stood in lines to use the exhibits and the rest rooms. Many visitors, when asked, complained of the noise, darkness, air quality, confusing layout of exhibits, and an overall lack of amenities. As one staff person described the situation, the Exploratorium had become a severely overconstrained system.

Refocusing on the Floor

In 1994, I was hired by the new executive director, Goéry Delacôte, to oversee the public aspects of the organization, from its spaces and amenities to its exhibits and programs. Goéry articulated the challenge: to take a place with sophisticated thinkers and deep values and improve the public experience without losing the organization's essence, to try to more closely align the actual physical environment with core values of the place. If the Exploratorium is like a woods, then my work would be one of conservation—cutting back some of the thicket to allow room once again for the process of succession. If it is like a small city, with streets and neighborhoods, then my work would be to oversee the downtown restoration, to upgrade the environment without losing its early character. And like similar projects, this revitalization process would come with its range of diverse participants and stakeholders, from the preservationists who balk at any change to the opportunistic developers who lobby for the bulldozer.

It seemed like an overwhelming task at first. While the Exploratorium often brought together some of the best minds in the world to work with light, color, sound, heat, and temperature in the exhibits, that same expertise was not brought to bear when considering the public space. Goéry insisted that I would have to be "a long-distance runner," starting out slowly and keeping at it a long time. As with any significant change process, we needed to be careful but also proactive, to change what needed changing and retain the essences—indeed, protect them and keep them intact. I began by giving this effort a name—"Refocusing on the Floor"—in order to create a projectlike quality that we could wrap our minds around. At the same time that new staff, like me, needed to spend time understanding the traditions of the place, this focused effort was also essential for the longtime staff who would participate in decisions about what to keep and what to change.

We began by looking at the past and identifying those essential qualities that gave the Exploratorium its singular personality. We focused on what Ed Casey calls "place memory," the "stabilizing persistence of place as a container of experiences that contributes so powerfully to its memorability."[3] We spent a year in conversation, describing early design configurations, remembering significant programs and events, retelling the stories of the "old days." We reread Maybeck's original intentions for the building, critiqued a number of early interior renovations, and reviewed the planning from more recent architectural charettes. Managers pointed to the gross inefficiencies in this ongoing conversation. But this honoring of the past was arguably the most

---

We started out with the theory informing our practice, but our research and experimentation have, in turn, informed our theory, and they will contribute significantly to our design process going forward.

---

important aspect of envisioning the future for the Exploratorium. It helped us to determine which aspects we should change and highlighted the essential qualities that made the place so exceptional—qualities we need to retain as we evolve over the next few years.

Although the project grew out of our response to the constraints of the physical space, it was really about the whole place. I gathered staff from across the organization into small groups or task forces that concentrated on three major aspects of the place—Space (the physical environment), Pedagogy (the intellectual environment), and Mediated Experiences (the social environment). All three were interconnected: we couldn't think about one aspect without considering the other two. As the Pedagogy task force discussed what we are about and how we might re-present it, the Mediated Experiences group considered how people (staff and visitors) interact, and the Space group grappled with the physical settings that could embody the values of the organization while encouraging a broad range of social interactions.

A Real Place?

Some of our board members and strategic planning consultants suggested that perhaps we should not put resources into the space, that within the next 10 years people would come to rely more on virtual places and the notion of public place would shift from the real to the virtual. But, staff argued, if museums are simultaneously a forum, a showcase, and a place of celebration, then they must have a physical presence. If public places "bring people together for the face-to-face contact that is essential to a healthy society,"[4] then the physicality of our place makes sense. If the interactions among staff and visitors are essential to our research and development efforts, then visitors and staff have to be in the same place at the same time and have to rub up against each other. As a result of these many conversations during the "Refocusing on the Floor" effort, we came to agree that the physical place of the Exploratorium was central to the culture of the organization—that the actual coming together of visitors, scientists, artists, and staff was an essential aspect of our "placeness."

Orientation and Exploration

We found ourselves always back at the same pesky question: What makes the Exploratorium a unique and vital public place? What enhances people coming together to share powerful experiences in powerful ways? We agreed that the space influenced the social relations and the social relations defined the place. But beyond that, we had a range of disagreements. While we reflected on visitors' needs for orientation, some staff were concerned that orientation would undermine the exploratory nature of the place. Are orientation and exploration really contradictory? Ed Casey, in *Getting Back into Place*, doesn't think so: "In exploration the primary issue, so far as place is concerned, is orientation. Unless we are oriented to some degree in the places through which we pass, we do not even know what we are in the process of discovering: witness Columbus's confusion as to just what he had come upon in the New World."[5] How might we provide orientation for those who want it, and at the same time encourage exploration?

Research

We began with an assessment of the current state of the place. Staff took video cameras out into the public spaces and documented a variety of physical aspects, from the scale of exhibit groupings to the patterns of light on a wall. I created a video walk-through, beginning a block from the building and looking at the way-finding clues (or lack of them) that helped guide people to our front doors. Researchers walked with visitors from the parking lot through the entrance into the building and documented their perceptions and questions.

We discovered that there were zones of experience where visitors had specific types of questions: What is this place all about? Who owns the building? Is there food inside? Where should I begin? Where's the cow's eye dissection?[6]

Research also revealed that some visitors wanted to know what they "should see" on their visit. Our biggest challenge was not to not go too far, not to make the organization of the space too controlled and predigested. Kevin Lynch's comments in *The Image of the City* had contributed to the shaping of the Exploratorium's philosophy:

> there is some value in mystification, labyrinth, or surprise in the environment. Many of us enjoy the House of Mirrors, and there is a certain charm in the crooked streets of Boston. This is so, however, only under two conditions. First, there must be no danger of losing basic form or orientation, of never coming out. The surprise must occur in an overall framework; the confusions must be small regions in a visible whole. Furthermore, the labyrinth or mystery must in itself have some form that can be explored and in time be apprehended.[7]

So while some visitors asked for a prescribed path, we described "popular exhibits" and offered as guidance the phrase "Many people enjoy . . ." .

Fifteen small research studies led to many iterations of a floor map, an associated display on "Getting Started," a scale model of the building, information about current and future programs, and exhibits that provide a variety of contexts for people as they begin their visit. We spent time envisioning the Exploratorium as an ideal public place, using William Whyte's description of the principal public needs of indoor spaces (seating, food, retailing, and toilets) and Lynch's five types of elements of city image (paths, edges, districts, nodes, and landmarks).[8] In our "Café Bench" study, researchers sat with visitors on the benches surrounding the café and discussed their feelings about the space after having navigated almost all the way through it. We asked visitors to describe what elements they would use as spontaneous landmarks—navigational references or places to meet others. We even examined the language staff used to describe areas of the building and compared these to visitor descriptions. What staff described as "the mezzanine," for example, visitors described as "upstairs." (In fact, when asked, most visitors said they did not know the meaning of "mezzanine," a finding that was troublesome since we used the word on directional signage and as a locator.)

Along with employing video documentation and visitor research in assessing the physical space of the Exploratorium, we wanted to consider its cultural qualities as well. How might we describe the place through narrative and storytelling? Inspired by Daniel Kemmis's description of the plaza as a theater, "a stage upon which the city might continue to unfold its story,"[9] we presented "Public Viewing: How Do People Really Use Museums?"—an event that employed performance as a way of examining our public space and visitors' experiences within it. Twenty performers from a variety of cultures, including dancers, actors, performance artists, and musicians, created short pieces that reflected their observations of visitors and exhibits at the Exploratorium. These pieces were crafted into an evening performance during which an invited audience of museum and theater professionals, artists, and architects moved from area to area to see each piece. The second half of the evening was spent in a facilitated discussion. Pamela Winfrey, director of performing arts programs, explained, "The event was a telescoped investigation about the visitor experience. The invited audience became visitors watching performers, who were also visitors, create performances based on their observations about our visitors."

Design

Once we had considered broad, overarching public space issues, we directed our attention to specific areas. One of our most difficult spots was the portico or lobby, a dreary entrance area with battleship gray walls and a deteriorating vinyl floor. It is a small space, much too small to welcome the hundreds of thousands of people who visit the Exploratorium each year. In the early days, it had been an exterior space used mostly by neighborhood men to play chess. It housed our only rest rooms, which also served all the people in the surrounding park. When staff enclosed the space in the 1980s, it became the admissions area, although because of its small size, on busy days visitors often had to stand in lines in the rain. Eventually, the admissions desks moved further inside, and the portico space became a free space once again. Because we had so many needs for signage, orientation, and amenities, we kept trying to cram them into the portico, but issues of traffic flow and congestion always brought us up short. Architectural consultants didn't do any better, and one of their solutions was even laughable: pathways painted on the floor accompanied by a voice on a loudspeaker telling visitors to stay in line.

Our breakthrough came when we finally began thinking about the portico as a transitional space, the connection between the outside (a beaux-arts building with elegant columns and a massive rotunda) and the inside (a multisensory learning environment full of individual exhibits on science, art, and human perception). Because the portico is the only interior space at the Exploratorium where visitors don't have to pay an admission fee, it is in some ways more connected to the outside than the inside. To emphasize its outdoor connection and history, we painted the portico walls the same color (and patina) as the exterior. The café latte cart, previously inside the main space, was moved to this transition space so that it could serve park visitors and neighbors as well as our museum visitors. Sales increased dramatically. We installed two exhibits in the space that not only serve as examples of the Exploratorium experience but that also play with the tensions between outside and inside, old and new, low- and high-tech. The female columns in the exhibit *Angel Caryatids*, a large figure-ground illusion, reference the columns and the historical character of the exterior. Juxtaposed next to the *Angel Caryatids*, closed-circuit television monitors capture some of the activities taking place inside the Exploratorium: looking down from the top of the *Tornado* exhibit, watching the images created by visitors on the screen of the *Recollections* exhibit, peering into the electric sphere of *Quiet Lightning*. The real-time images make use of new wiring throughout the building and provide a reference to the new digital technology that the Exploratorium is incorporating more and more.

Beyond the portico inside the building, we created an "entry plaza" where visitors can enter, pay their admission fees, get information at a staffed desk, use an ATM machine, and store their bags. The orientation exhibits, focused on the theme "You Are Here," play with the notion of "here" in scale as well as in place: visitors can locate themselves on a scale model of the building, in a self-directed video flyover of the surrounding environment, in Landsat photographs of San Francisco neighborhoods, and on real-time marine radar images of the San Francisco Bay. We installed a small, traditional marquee on our theater, and now, for the first time, visitors know we actually have a theater and know what to expect inside. Attendance at special theater programs has increased. We painted the theater one of the historic Palace of Fine Arts colors, again referencing the exterior of the building.

The significant change of ambience in the entry plaza is, more than anything else, the result of opening a previously covered skylight. But in opening the building to more light, we came up against another organizational tension. The first major collection of exhibits that Oppenheimer and his staff created was on light and color—exhibits that needed darkness—so most of the skylights in the roof remained covered, creating a dark, mysterious feel to the space that many staff felt was a significant aspect of the Exploratorium's character. Although we knew that some visitors had difficulty making the transition from the bright exterior to the dark interior, when we asked visitors for their preference the results were no help. Fully half of our visitors liked the darkness because it "focuses you on the exhibits," "draws you in," and "is a little bit exciting."

Our decision to open the skylight came at director Goéry Delacôte's insistence: "The brightness is welcoming to our visitors. It helps them orient themselves and is a metaphor for the need for greater clarity and less obfuscation about how science works in the world. Our museum should reflect this modern sensibility, rather than the bunker mentality evident in museums designed in the 1960s." The effect was dramatic. Not only did daylight pour into the building, making it seem much larger, but from the floor of the public space we could see outside to the tops of surrounding redwood trees and the adjacent rotunda. The daylight changed significantly the quality of the entrance experience, and people began to spend more time in the area. We also installed glass panes in the large paneled doors toward the back of the space, creating a sense of porousness in the building that connects it much more directly with its surrounding environment. This ability to see outside from the interior of the space and to see in from the exterior is essential in defining the building as a geographic place with a unique physical location. And it is an important quality of public space, providing a transparency and accessibility that encourage public interactions.

But are we truly a public place? William Whyte suggests, "A common-sense interpretation would be that the public could use the space in the same manner as it did any public space, with the same freedoms and the same constraints."[10] Some would argue that, like the "public" spaces of theme parks or shopping malls, museums control, to some extent, the freedom and activities of the people who visit. "There are no demonstrations in Disneyland," observes Michael Sorkin.[11] And because we charge an entrance fee, we are often seen as only quasi-public. Of the 60 places profiled in *A Guide to Great American Public Places*, only one is a museum—the Franklin Institute—and only its admission-free Atrium is considered "public."[12]

However the Exploratorium is defined, its informal and sometimes chaotic character makes it feel like a public place: on any afternoon you might encounter staff skateboarding from one end of the huge building to the other or breakdancing in front of the *Colored Shadows* exhibit. Dogs come and go. People sit on benches with coffee in hand. One visitor frequently presents his own bubble-making demonstration. For me, we are truly at our public best on monthly Free Days, when attendance is higher and visitors are much more diverse. Even on these crowded days the atmosphere is relaxed and friendly, since we doubled the seating throughout the building, upgraded the café and store, and installed a second set of rest rooms toward the back of the building. For our visitors, I believe the Exploratorium is, indeed, a forum, where people speak their minds, and a place of celebration, where people come together to share common interests and common experiences.

We are now entering another phase of public place research and design at the Exploratorium. Architects and engineers are working with Exploratorium staff to redesign the interior spaces, move the entrance back to its original Maybeck location, create a central public plaza, and provide a dynamic outdoor space on the "back" side of the building. The process of research and design that led us to this point will continue with the new activity. In a sense, we started out with the theory informing our practice, but our research and experimentation have, in turn, informed our theory, and they will contribute significantly to our design process going forward. Most important, our research work with visitors—the public—will continue to be essential in the development of the Exploratorium as a public place.

Journal of Museum Education 24, nos. 1 and 2 (1999): 11–15.

Notes

The epigraph is from Gianni Longo, *A Guide to Great American Public Places* (New York: Urban Initiatives, 1996), p. 5.

1. Frank Oppenheimer and the Staff of the Exploratorium, *Working Prototypes* (San Francisco: Exploratorium, 1986), p. 6.

2. Rob Semper, "The Importance of Place," *ASTC Newsletter*, September/October 1996, pp. 2–5.

3. Edward Casey, *Remembering: A Phenomenological Study* (Bloomington, Ind.: Indiana University Press, 1987), pp. 186–87, quoted in Dolores Hayden, *The Power of Place: Urban Landscapes as Public History* (Cambridge, Mass.: MIT Press, 1997), p. 46.

4. Longo, *Guide to Great American Public Places*, p. xiii.

5. Edward Casey, *Getting Back into Place: Toward a Renewed Understanding of the Place-World* (Bloomington, Ind.: Indiana University Press, 1993), p. 121.

6. Sue Allen and Veronica Garcia-Luis, Exploratorium internal research report, 1998.

7. Kevin Lynch, *The Image of the City* (Cambridge, Mass.: MIT Press, 1960), pp. 5–6.

8. William H. Whyte, *The Social Life of Small Urban Spaces* (Washington, D.C.: Conservation Foundation, 1980), pp. 50–53; Lynch, *Image of the City*, pp. 46–85.

9. Daniel Kemmis, *The Good City and the Good Life* (New York: Houghton Mifflin, 1995), pp. 66–67.

10. Whyte, *Social Life of Small Urban Spaces*, pp. 64–65.

11. Michael Sorkin, ed., *Variations on a Theme Park: The New American City and the End of Public Space* (New York: Noonday Press, 1992), p. xv.

12. Longo, *Guide to Great American Public Places*, pp. 126–27.

Further Reading

McLean, Kathleen. "Museum Exhibitions and the Dynamics of Dialogue," *Daedalus* 128, no. 3 (Summer 1999): 83–107.

Hayden, Dolores. *The Power of Place: Urban Landscapes as Public History*. Cambridge, Mass.: MIT Press, 1997.

Sardello, Robert, and Gail Thomas. *Stirrings of Culture*. Dallas: Dallas Institute Publications, 1986.

Strategies for Long-Term Community Partnerships

Jim Zien

Museums in the Life of a City evolved in response to the perception that Philadelphia's cultural institutions should and can play a larger role in fostering public appreciation of ethnic and economic diversity and thereby enhance the prospects for social harmony in the community. The premise of the initiative was that museums could most effectively pursue this goal by establishing education-oriented program partnerships with community-based arts and social service organizations. The opportunity to obtain grant funds served as the principal incentive to partnership formation.

In November 1994—two years after the pilot projects were completed—Public Placemakers convened three focus groups composed of (1) community organization representatives, (2) museum representatives, and (3) representatives of both. The focus group discussions revealed a wide range of assessments, pro and con, regarding the experience of forming partnerships, planning cooperative projects, and implementing joint programs.

The focus group participants were asked to address several key questions about the Museums in the Life of a City initiative:

1. What factors promoted strong museum-community organization partnerships and productive outcomes, and what factors caused partner dissatisfaction and program difficulties in the formative stage? in the program planning and development stage? in the implementation stage?

2. Do the present programs and services of the participants reflect the underlying goals of the initiative?

3. Considering the experience and the participants' current endeavors, what factors encourage museums and community organizations to collaborate for the purpose of serving economically and socially diverse constituencies, and what factors constrain them?

4. What strategies might AAM and the other sponsors of Museums in the Life of a City pursue in the future to foster mutually beneficial cooperation among museums and community organizations?

The first two focus groups discussed the planning, development, and implementation dynamics of their partnerships. The combined group talked about current planning, development, and programming practices that reflect the goals of the initiative. The participants represented many, but not all, of the original partners.

All things considered, a majority of the community organization and museum representatives who attended the sessions said that their participation in the initiative proved worth the investment of time and resources. A museum staff member said:

> [At first] I thought it was taking too much time and that I should have delegated more responsibility. . . . And at times I was resentful because I didn't think the return was there. But in hindsight . . . I look at the little push it has given me to . . . continue—although it's hard work—to diversify our audiences [and] diversify staff [and] board membership.

A community organization participant had a similar reaction:

> I think it's a wonderful project that should be expanded locally and nationally. . . . The primary change I would make is to [allow] . . . more time . . . [for] coming up with shared visions, goals, and understanding of the time and commitment everybody . . . has to make.

The successes and failures of Museums in the Life of a City suggest that museums and community organizations can join forces effectively to address some of the educational needs of socially and economically diverse urban constituencies.

Despite such positive views of the experience, however, lasting partnerships failed in most cases to materialize.

Influences on Partnership Formation and Success

In a few instances, an existing cooperative relationship between a museum and a community organization was the foundation for a project collaboration. More often, partnerships were forged by relative strangers introduced through the efforts of the initiative staff.

The motivations for investing time and resources in partnership development varied widely, from pecuniary to pragmatic to political to philosophical. In general, the strongest partnerships were built on objectives closely related to the central missions, core capabilities, and natural resources of the partners. The weakest alliances were those that pursued projects only tangentially associated with the partners' fundamental purposes and those that depended on imported skills and means.

Linkages: Building Knowledge

Satisfactions and Dissatisfactions

The highly diverse partnerships evoked a wide range of positive and negative assessments. On the plus side, many participants credited the initiative with bringing together organizations that would not otherwise have collaborated for the educational benefit of people who would not otherwise have gained meaningful access to geographically or psychologically remote cultural resources. The initiative also offered the partners useful insights into their respective missions, capabilities, and constraints. Some partnerships helped launch continuing professional relationships between collaboration-minded staff members.

A number of community organizations learned about program development resources and techniques from their partners. In the words of a participant in the Johnson Homes oral history video project: "A couple of the projects called for in the grant brought people from Johnson Homes into the Main Library [of the Philadelphia Free Library] . . . to do research using some of the specialized departments . . . that were not available in the neighborhood library."

Staff members of some museums gained greater understanding of the needs and interests of poorly served constituencies by visiting the neighborhoods in which their community partners operated and by implementing neighborhood-based programs for the first time. At the beginning of the Johnson Homes project, for example,

> several library staff came over and took a tour of Johnson Homes [and the community] garden, and the [residents] had prepared something special for them . . . . I know that those people had not been in a [housing] development before. . . . Maybe the concept hadn't seemed very attractive until they . . . met the [residents] . . . and walked the streets . . . [and] were given fresh tomatoes and eggplants. . . . It just felt very good.

One museum educator talked about the satisfaction of getting out into the community:

> I spend so much time in the museum that to . . . deal with . . . students [outside] the school setting, [without] a teacher . . . and to deal [directly] with parents . . . was very satisfying. I figure I learned a lot more than I ever taught in that regard.

The partners' primary dissatisfactions with their experiences appear rooted in three basic flaws in the structure of the initiative:

1. the dollar-driven constitution of more than a few of the partnerships
2. the short time frame that was allowed for partnership growth, program planning, and implementation

3. the small allotments of project funding relative to the intensity of staff effort required to achieve partnership objectives.

These underlying problems bred partnership deficiencies in some key areas of project management: communications, decision making, and organizational capacity and commitment.

Communications

Particularly for partnerships consisting of organizations with no history of cooperation, establishing and maintaining effective staff contact proved difficult. This problem was especially acute for several projects that had early changes in personnel. Predictably, communications difficulties and misunderstandings multiplied in direct proportion to the number of partners involved.

Decision Making

The terms of the project grants called for equitable sharing of authority and responsibility among the partners. In practice, some projects suffered from indirection because individual participants were reluctant to assume decision-making roles, while others struggled to resolve both real and perceived control issues.

Organizational Capacity and Commitment

Community organizations and museums expressed concern over the low level of commitment by partners. Two factors influenced these perceptions: (1) funding for the pilot projects represented proportionately a much higher contribution to the finances of small-budget community organizations than to those of their (mostly) much larger museum partners, and (2) major staffing disparities between partners resulted in project teams populated by senior leaders of community organizations on the one hand and lower-level staff of museums on the other.

Amplifying the usual demands of collaborations, these structurally different relationships to the initiative sometimes caused community organizations to conclude that certain cultural partners valued their joint ventures minimally. Museums, by contrast, sometimes concluded that certain community partners lacked the capacity to sustain their project roles.

Partnership Continuity and Pursuit of Goals Today

Very few of the partnerships represented in the focus group sessions continue to function today. The primary reasons that they do not are lack of funding, "fit," and familiarization time.

Lack of Funding

The availability of grants was the basis for many of the partnerships. Some projects achieved their objectives, while others fell short. The brief period of funding, however, placed a premium on program design, development, and implementation. Consequently, no group of partners had the luxury of time to plan strategically, even if the members had the motivation to do so.

After exhausting the grant funds (which sometimes failed to cover the actual costs of participation), most of the partnerships dissolved. The exceptions are a few relationships of previous standing, maintained through continuing staff communication. The Free Library of Philadelphia, for example, continues working with Johnson Homes. The tenants' association president and the branch library have cooperated to establish a reading center at the housing project. The director of Taller Puertorriqueño comments that

> the communication between Taller . . . and the Philadelphia Museum of Art has been consistent . . . because one of the reasons that I became involved was to make the museum aware of . . . Latin American artists here in the city. I've been working [at it] for decades . . . . Now we do an annual event at the museum through the education program.

Lack of "Fit"

Some partnerships revolved around objectives only tangentially related to the missions of the participating organizations. As a result, they faltered in the face of staff changes or competition for resources from more central organizational endeavors. One museum participant remarked that

> often, institutions have to jump through hoops to get money for a project that [finally] doesn't fit within [their] mission. . . . They sort of fit square pegs into round holes . . . because money is so hard to find. . . . I think that is what [happened] with [our] project.

A community organization participant agreed:

> We were able to map out what the museum's benefit was going to be, but we really couldn't [figure out] our benefit . . . except that we're getting a piece of this funding.

Lack of Familiarization Time

Asked to recommend refinements to the design of the initiative, community organization and museum representatives agreed unanimously on the need for partners to become familiar with one another's programs, staffs, facilities, and audiences and to engage in team- and trust-building exercises before beginning program development.

Support for Successful Partnerships

In the future, what support strategies would foster long-term, educationally oriented relationships between museums and community organizations for the purpose of advancing esteem for social diversity?

Support for Essential Groundwork

The Philadelphia experience suggests that partnerships between museums and community-based human service organizations grow best in a firm ground of mutual knowledge and understanding. The groundwork needed to support successful program collaborations includes these key elements:

Mission Matching

Partnerships should advance the fundamental missions of their partners in important ways. Participating staff should clearly articulate, openly discuss, and explicitly acknowledge the missions, program and service priorities, and partnership expectations of their organizations. The educational, social, and material objectives of partnership projects should relate closely to the capabilities of the partner organizations and to the expertise of the personnel who will carry out the work.

Leadership Commitment

The leaders of partner organizations should formally and jointly endorse their partnership and participate personally in its planning, development, and implementation in more than token ways.

Core Staff Involvement

Primary responsibility for partnership planning and management should rest with key members of each partner's core staff. Contract employees, interns, volunteers, and other nonpermanent personnel should play supporting roles.

Team Building

Before attempting to develop and conduct collaborative programs, partner staffs should enhance their capacity to work together productively by pursuing formal or informal team building. These experiences should include thorough familiarization with one another's programs, facilities, neighborhoods, and constituencies.

Low-Risk Exchanges of Learning Experience

Partners' ongoing programs represent ready resources for a series of reciprocal learning experiences. Hosted in turn by each partner for staff and audience members of the others, these experiences can reveal areas of opportunity for collaboration and indicate potential sources of difficulty.

Support for Progressive Program Development

Educational and cultural programs of real value to both audiences and sponsors most often evolve progressively, through several developmental stages—from concept and content development to program design, staff training, piloting, refinement, and full-scale implementation. For any single museum or community organization, the process requires a substantial investment of money, time, and talent. A collaborative enterprise makes even higher demands on participant resources. Consequently, program partnerships that lack a series of phased and methodical creation stages seldom succeed or endure.

The critical components of effective program planning and development include:

Clear Assignment of Partnership Management and Decision-Making Roles

The partnership as a whole and the individual partners must confer leadership responsibility and ultimate authority on capable, trusted team members. Approaches to resolving disputes among partners should be agreed upon in advance.

Creative Concept Formulation

The program concepts that a partnership pursues should represent the creative thinking of all team members. Professional facilitation of concept development discussions can prove worthwhile.

Coherent Content Determination

The content focus of a program partnership should emerge from a systematic consideration of each partner's relevant and significant resources as well as the needs and interests of prospective audiences.

Manageable Program Design

The functional and logistical requirements of partnership programs should closely match the human, material, and facility capacities of the partners. These capacities should be assessed and understood in advance by all team members.

Staff Skill Building for Cooperative Programming

The staff members who will develop and conduct the programs of a partnership must learn to work effectively across organizational (and possibly cultural) boundaries. Early in the planning phase of a collaborative relationship, the partners should seek a professional assessment of the most useful types of training for their joint purposes, in such areas as teamwork, creative planning methods, effective communication techniques, or cultural awareness. Time and funds then should be set aside to engage appropriate organizational and professional development expertise.

Program Trials, Formative Evaluation, and Revision

Programs under development require trial runs in order to realize their highest potential. Partnerships must try out their program content and delivery methods, and they must also put their cooperative operating arrangements to the test. Provision should be made for a round of pilot programs followed by an assessment of strengths and weaknesses and execution of needed refinements.

Support for Structurally Innovative Partnerships

The Philadelphia initiative offered support to museums and community organizations to undertake collaborative programs for constituents of the community-based partners. The short-term, product-driven nature of the partnerships was not destined to affect significantly the established purposes and regular activities of the participants. As an alternative, partnership projects might focus on developing permanent new structural relationships—relationships that fundamentally improve the participants' ability to serve socially diverse constituencies well in the long run.

Structurally innovative partnerships would, for example, facilitate frequent interaction among partner organization staffs; establish a visible physical or programmatic presence for each partner within the facilities of the others; regularly represent the existence and activities of the partnership in the public information disseminated by the partners; freely share administrative resources (such as mailing lists), where feasible and mutually beneficial.

Important characteristics of such partnerships include:

Accessibility

The partners would devise a variety of mechanisms for making their facilities, resources, and programs well known and fully accessible to their respective staffs and audiences—in psychological as well as physical and economic terms.

Habitual Consultation

As a matter of course, partner staff members would consult together about opportunities to incorporate one another's concerns into prospective programs and services while they are still in the planning and development phase.

Multiple Forms of Cooperation

Partners would experiment with ways to cooperate in carrying out a wide variety of activities, such as in-school and after-school programs, exhibits, performances, festivals, special events, and educational resource development and dissemination.

Museums in the Life of a City engendered diverse experiments in collaborative programming among Philadelphia community organizations and museums. The range and variety of the projects implemented by 11 partnerships offer many insights into the benefits and the hazards of such functionally mixed organizational mariages.

To the satisfaction of a majority of the participants, the projects afforded new and positive learning experiences to youngsters and adults who otherwise lack meaningful access to the educational and cultural resources involved. In addition, the planning and implementation process exposed museum staff members to the daily life, dedicated people, and diverse environments of urban neighborhoods previously known in name only. In a few instances, mutually rewarding contact has continued beyond the project period.

Less productively, more than a few of the partnerships rested on shaky foundations. Some lacked objectives central to the purposes and capabilities of the partners. Others lacked strong leadership. Several simply involved too many partners with diffuse interests. Challenged to plan and implement cooperative programs in a relatively short period with relatively small amounts of money, many such partnerships experienced difficulty maintaining effective communications and operations.

In the final analysis, the successes and failures of Museums in the Life of a City suggest that museums and community organizations can join forces effectively to address some of the educational needs of socially and economically diverse urban constituencies. To succeed, however, partnerships must evolve gradually, through successive stages of familiarization; functional relationship building; program planning, development, piloting, evaluation, and refinement; and, ideally, structural innovation. Accordingly, support for serious initiatives in museum–community organization collaboration must be well targeted, reasonably generous, and patient.

Journal of Museum Education 20, no. 2 (Spring/Summer 1995): 17–21.

Further Reading

Schneider, Beth B. *A Place for All People*. Houston: Museum of Fine Arts, 1998.

Steuert, Patricia A., Aylette Jenness, and Joanne Jones-Rizzi. *Opening the Museum: History and Strategies toward a More Inclusive Institution*. Boston: Children's Museum, 1993.

REFLECTIONS

The diversity of organizational purposes, structures, and practices encompassed by the participants in the Museums in the Life of a City initiative might lead some to conclude that their collective experiences offer no useful lessons to any singular cultural institution or community organizations. Yet the opposite applies. The methodology employed for the evaluation—a series of focus groups involving leaders of many of the Museums in the Life of a City programs—yielded widely shared perceptions of the strengths and weaknesses of very distinct collaborative enterprises. That these perceptions cross a wide range of organizational boundaries, cultural and communal, lends them a validity and durability that the observations of a more narrow cohort would lack.

—Jim Zien

CONTRIBUTORS

David Anderson is head of the Education Department at the Victoria and Albert Museum, South Kensington, London. He has also taught high school history, served as education officer at the Royal Pavilion, Art Gallery, and Museums, Brighton, and head of education at the National Maritime Museum, Greenwich. Contact: d.anderson@vam.ac.uk

Minda Borun is director of research and evaluation at the Franklin Institute Science Museum in Philadelphia. She has served as chair of the American Association of Museums Committee on Audience Research and Evaluation (CARE) and as an associate professor in the graduate program in museum education at the University of the Arts in Philadelphia. Contact: mborun@erols.com

Deirdre Brown, at the time her article was published, was head of the Education Department at the Ulster Folk and Transport Museum, Cultra, County Down, Northern Ireland, and was responsible for the development of the museum's Educational Residential Centre. She has since retired.

David Carr is associate professor in the School of Information and Library Science at the University of North Carolina at Chapel Hill. When his article was published, he was associate professor in the School of Communication, Information, and Library Studies at Rutgers, the State University of New Jersey, in New Brunswick. Contact: carr@ils.unc.edu

Roberta Cooks is senior scientist and exhibit developer at the Franklin Institute Science Museum in Philadelphia. She has developed many national traveling exhibitions, including *What about AIDS?*, *The Brain*, and *Powers of Nature*. Contact: rcooks@fi.edu

Lynn D. Dierking is associate director of the Institute for Learning Innovation, a nonprofit educational research and development company in Annapolis, Maryland, that specializes in helping museums and other community-based organizations better serve their publics. Her research has focused on family learning in museums. Contact: dierking@ilnet.org. Web site: www.ilinet.org

Zahava D. Doering is director of the Institutional Studies Office, Smithsonian Institution. She was trained as a sociologist. Before coming to the Smithsonian, she held research positions in the federal government and at the Johns Hopkins University. Contact: zdoering@iso.si.edu

Jacqueline Eyl is director of education at Discovery Creek Children's Museum in Washington, D.C. She has served as director of education at the National Museum of Dentistry in Baltimore, Maryland, and as an educator at the National Building Museum and the Smithsonian Institution, both in Washington, D.C. Contact: jeyl@erols.com

John H. Falk is executive director of the Institute for Learning Innovation, a nonprofit educational research and development company in Annapolis, Maryland, that specializes in helping museums and other community-based organizations better serve their publics. He conducts research on learning in museums and other informal settings. Contact: falk@ilnet.org. Web site: www.ilinet.org.

Larissa B. Fawkner is manager of children's education at the New York Botanical Garden, the Bronx. At the time this article was published, she was an environmental science educator and coordinator of school programs at Discovery Creek Children's Museum, Washington, D.C. Contact: lfawkner@hotmail.com.

Bran Ferren, at the time of publication of this article, was executive vice-president for creative technology, research, and development at Walt Disney Imagineering, overseeing all research and development activities for the company.

Elaine Heumann Gurian is a senior museum consultant to governments who are beginning, building, or changing their museums. Among the museums with which she has worked are the National Museum of Australia, Prisma; the Science Children's Museum of Puerto Rico; the Jewish Museum, Berlin; Te Papa, the National Museum of New Zealand; and the Canadian Museum of Civilization. She has held senior management positions at the Cranbrook Institute of Science, the United States Holocaust Memorial Museum, the National Museum of the American Indian, the Smithsonian Institution, and the Boston Children's Museum. Contact: egurian@ix.netcom.com

Signe Hanson is director of exhibitions at the Children's Museum in Boston. Contact: hanson@bostonkids.org

Joanne S. Hirsch is chair and president of Museum Education Roundtable and project director of *Transforming Practice.* She taught as adjunct assistant professor in the Museum Education Program at the George Washington University, Washington, D.C. Her research is in the use of concept maps to document visitor understanding. Contact: jshirsch@aol.com

Kodi R. Jeffery is science educator at the Centennial Museum at the University of Texas-El Paso. At the time this article was published, she was focusing on training teachers to use museums and to use activity-oriented learning. She recently completed a Ph.D. in science education with an emphasis in museum education. Contact: kodi@utep.edu

Gretchen M. Jennings is project director for development of a hands-on exhibition at the Lemelson Center for the Study of Invention and Innovation, National Museum of American History, Smithsonian Institution, Washington, D.C. She was lead developer for *Secrets of Aging,* a traveling exhibition created by the Museum of Science, Boston. From 1997 through 1999, she was editor-in-chief of the *Journal of Museum Education.* Contact: jenningsg@nmah.si.edu

Janet A. Kamien is a consultant in Philadelphia. When her article was published, she was vice president of the Science Center at the Franklin Institute. She developed *Endings: An Exhibit about Death and Loss*, which appeared at the Children's Museum, Boston, in 1983–84. Contact: 1720 Naudain St., Philadelphia, Pa. 19146

Randi Korn is director of Randi Korn & Associates, Inc., a consulting company based in Alexandria, Virginia, that specializes in museum evaluation and visitor studies. She is also a part-time instructor in the Museum Education Program at the George Washington University, Washington, D.C. Contact: Randikorn@aol.com

Paul Krapfel is a founding teacher and bard at Chrysalis Charter School in Redding, California. He was a member of the education team at Carter House Natural Science Museum in Redding when they conceived Chrysalis. He is the author *of Seeing Nature: Deliberate Encounters with the Visual World*, published in 1999 by Chelsea Green. Contact: pkrapfel@enterprise.k12.ca.us

Gaea Leinhardt is professor in the School of Education at the University of Pittsburgh and senior scientist at the university's Learning Research and Development Center. She conducts research on the nature of effective instructional explanations in a variety of settings and subject areas. Contact: gaea+@pitt.edu

Bruce V. Lewenstein is associate professor in the Departments of Communication and Science and Technology Studies at Cornell University. He is the editor of *When Science Meets the Public* (American Association for the Advancement of Science, 1992) and an associate editor of the journal *Public Understanding of Science*.

Laura Martin is a developmental psychologist who directs educational programs and research at the Arizona Science Center. She is an editor of *Sociocultural Psychology: Theory and Practice of Doing and Knowing* and *Mind and Social Practice: Selected Writings of Sylvia Scribner*, both published by Cambridge University Press.

Hooley McLaughlin is senior adviser for science and technology at the Ontario Science Center in Toronto, Canada. He is the author of *The Ends of Our Exploring* (Malcolm Lester Books, 1999), a critique of the philosophy of the West as revealed through his travels to remote parts of the world. Contact: hooley@osc.on.ca

Kathleen McLean is director of public programs and the Center for Public Exhibition at the Exploratorium in San Francisco. For 25 years she has been involved in the conception, design, and implementation of museum exhibitions and public spaces. She is principal of Independent Exhibitions. Contact: kmclean@exploratorium.edu

Margaret Menninger is a consultant in Ojai, California. At the time this article was published, she worked in the Department of Education and Academic Affairs at the J. Paul Getty Museum in Los Angeles, planning and carrying out audience research as well as evaluations of programs, services, and facilities.

Elizabeth Merritt is head of the Museum Assessment Program at the American Association of Museums. Before joining AAM, she was director of collections and research at the Cincinnati Museum Center, where she managed curation, registration, and conservation staff. Contact: bmerritt@aam-us.org

Michael Miller is manager of the Delaware Folklife Program of the state Division of Parks and Recreation. He has worked as a folklorist on the Northern Plains and in the Middle Atlantic region since the early 1990s. Contact: mimiller@state.de.us

Sally Montgomery, at the time this article was published, was science and technology officer at the National Museums and Galleries of Northern Ireland and leader of the Science Discovery Bus project, which received the Museum of the Year Award for Best Educational Initiative in 1992. She has since retired.

Kris Morrissey is curator of interpretation at the Michigan State University Museum. She teaches a museum education course for the university and is editor of *Visitor Studies Today,* the publication of the Visitor Studies Association. Contact: morriss8@pilot.msu.edu

Mary Ellen Munley is director of the Department of Education and Outreach at the Field Museum, Chicago. At the time her article was published, she was special assistant to the deputy commissioner for cultural education, New York State Education Department, Albany. She is a past chair of the American Association of Museums Education Committee. Contact: munley@fmppr.fmnh.org

Scott G. Paris is a professor of psychology and education at the University of Michigan in Ann Arbor, where he teaches courses on human development and educational psychology. He is program director for the Center for the Improvement of Early Reading Achievement. His research focuses on children's literacy, learning, and motivation. Contact: sparis@umich.edu

Andrew J. Pekarik is a museum and exhibition audience analyst in the Institutional Studies Office, Smithsonian Institution. Previously, he was curator for the Mary and Jackson Burke Collection of Japanese Art in New York City, director of the Asia Society Galleries, and assistant director of the Cooper-Hewitt, National Design Museum. Contact: apekarik@iso.si.edu

Deborah Perry is director of Selinda Research Associates in Chicago, which specializes in the creation and assessment of informal learning experiences in leisure settings such as museums, zoos, and aquariums. Her interests are in what makes learning fun and the social construction of meaning. She is vice president of the Visitor Studies Association. Contact: perryd@compuserve.com

Will Phillips is the founder and president of Qm2, a consulting firm serving the museum community. He is a frequent speaker for the American Association of Museums and regional museum associations. Contact: willphillips@qm2.org

Danielle Rice is senior curator of education at the Philadelphia Museum of Art. She has headed education departments at the Wadsworth Atheneum in Hartford, Connecticut, and the National Gallery of Art in Washington, D.C. Her academic background is in the history of art. Contact: drice@philamuseum.org

Wade H. Richards, at the time this article was published, worked in the Department of Education and Academic Affairs at the J. Paul Getty Museum in Los Angeles. He taught in the galleries with young people and adults, worked on Interactive Gallery installations, and administered the museum's docent program. He died in 1994.

Contributors

Lisa C. Roberts is director of conservatories for the Chicago Park District. She was manager of public programming at the Chicago Botanic Garden in Glencoe, Illinois, and worked on the Kellogg Project at the Field Museum.

Eric Sandweiss, an urban and architectural historian, has been director of research at the Missouri Historical Society in St. Louis since 1992. His responsibilities include exhibition and program planning and overseeing the institution's academic and public partnerships. He is a lecturer at Washington University and University of Missouri—St. Louis. Contact: sesandw@jinx.umsl.edu

Leona Schauble is a cognitive developmental psychologist who studies thinking and learning in schools, museums, and other settings. She is associate professor in the Department of Educational Psychology at the University of Wisconsin, Madison.

Stacey L. Shelnut is education and community programs manager at the Baltimore Museum of Art, Baltimore, Maryland. At the time this article was published, she was director of youth programs at the Brooklyn Children's Museum. She has also worked at the New York State Museum and the Studio Museum in Harlem. Contact: sshelnut@artbma.org

Lois H. Silverman is a professor in the Department of Recreation and Park Administration at Indiana University, Bloomington. She has been an editorial adviser to the *Journal of Museum Education* and is associate editor of the *Journal of Interpretation Research.* Her current focus is on exploring the museum's potential in meeting human needs. Contact: lsilverm@indiana.edu

Sheela Speers, at the time this article was published, was head of education services at the Ulster Museum, Belfast, Northern Ireland. She has since retired.

Carol B. Stapp is director of the George Washington University Museum Education Program. She was editor-in-chief of the *Journal of Museum Education* from 1993 through 1996 and continues as review editor. Contact: cstapp@gwis2.circ.gwu.edu

A. T. Stephens is a member at large of the board of directors of the American Association of Museums. At the time this article appeared, he was vice president for programs at the Missouri Historical Society in St. Louis. He is a longtime member of the Board of Directors of Museum Education Roundtable. Contact: atstephens7455@aol.com

Marek Stokowski is curator of education at the Malbork Castle Museum in Malbork, Poland. From 1986 to 1988, he did postgraduate work in museum education at Warsaw University. He has written and variety of articles, booklets, and screenplays about his work.

Denise Lauzier Stone is associate professor of visual art education at the University of Kansas, Lawrence. Her research specialty is art museum education with an emphasis on art museum–school relations. Contact: denise@kuhub.cc.ukans.edu

Annie V. F. Storr is director of the Arts Management Program at the American University, Washington, D.C. At the time her article was published, she held a Smithsonian Postdoctoral Fellowship at the National Museum of American Art. She is the founding coordinator of Museum Education Roundtable's Research Colloquium. Contact: avfstorr@aol.com

Sonnet Takahisa is the founding codirector of the New York City Museum School. She has more than 20 years of experience in museum education, arts education, collaborative planning, and program evaluation. Contact: sonnetmuse@aol.com

Jeanette M. Toohey is associate curator for collections at the Delaware Art Museum in Wilmington. She was on the staff of the Pennsylvania Academy of the Fine Arts, Philadelphia, where she cocurated the award-winning exhibition *Thomas Eakins Rediscovered: At Home, At School, At Work*. Contact: jtoohey@delart.mus.de.us

Stephen E. Weil is emeritus senior scholar at the Center for Museum Studies at the Smithsonian Institution in Washington, D.C. From 1974 to 1995, he was deputy director of the Smithsonian's Hirshhorn Museum and Sculpture Garden. *A Cabinet of Curiosities: Inquiries into Museums and Their Prospects* (1995) is his most recent collection of essays. Contact: sweil@si.edu

Namita Gupta Wiggers was assistant director for communications at the Asia Society/Houston at the time this article was published. She is the former coordinator for public programs at the Blaffer Gallery, University of Houston. She now lives in Portland, Oregon, where she designs and fabricates art jewelry through her company, SCALE.

Kathryn E. Wilson is public programming coordinator at the Balch Institute for Ethnic Studies in Philadelphia. She is a folklorist with a Ph.D. from the University of Pennsylvania. Contact: wilsonk@balchinstitute.org

Inez S. Wolins is director of the Samuel P. Harn Museum of Art, University of Florida, Gainesville. At the time this article appeared, she was director of the Wichita Art Museum in Wichita, Kansas. She cocurated the award-winning exhibition *Thomas Eakins Rediscovered: At Home, At School, At Work* at the Pennsylvania Academy of the Fine Arts. Contact: iwolins@ifl.edu

Kenneth Yellis has been assistant director for public programs, Yale Peabody Museum of Natural History, since 1991. He became an editor of *Roundtable Reports* in 1975, editor-in-chief of the *Journal of Museum Education* in 1980, and in 1987 review editor. He also twice chaired Museum Education Roundtable. He is a member of the editorial advisory committee of *Curator*. Contact: kenneth.yellis@yale.edu

Jim Zien is the principal of Public Placemakers, a multidisciplinary planning and project management practice in Cambridge, Massachusetts, that provides leadership for educational, cultural, and community development. Contact: jim.zien@alum.mit.edu

For more information about how to reach authors, contact Museum Education Roundtable, 621 Pennsylvania Ave., SE, Washington, D.C. 20003; 202-547-8378.

Contributors